Integrating Sustainability Principles With AI-Driven Entrepreneurial Strategies

Muhammad Abu Naser
London Metropolitan University, UK

Jagbir Singh Kadyan
Manav Rachna University, India

Liliane Cristina Segura
Universidade Presbiteriana Mackenzie, Brazil

IGI Global
Scientific Publishing
Publishing Tomorrow's Research Today

Vice President of Editorial Melissa Wagner
Director of Acquisitions Mikaela Felty
Director of Book Development Jocelynn Hessler
Production Manager Mike Brehm
Cover Design Jose Rosado

Published in the United States of America by
IGI Global Scientific Publishing
701 East Chocolate Avenue
Hershey, PA, 17033, USA
Tel: 717-533-8845
Fax: 717-533-7115
Website: https://www.igi-global.com E-mail: cust@igi-global.com

Library of Congress Cataloging-in-Publication Data
Names: Naser, Muhammad Abu, 1976- editor | Kadyan, Jagbir Singh, 1966- editor | Segura, Liliane editor
Title: Integrating sustainability principles with AI-driven entrepreneurial strategies / edited by: Muhammad Abu Naser, Jagbir Singh Kadyan, and Liliane Cristina Segura.
Other titles: Integrating sustainability principles with artificial intelligence-driven entrepreneurial strategies
Description: Hershey : IGI Global Scientific Publishing, [2026] | Includes bibliographical references and index. | Summary: "The primary objective of this book is to provide a solid understanding of sustainability in modern business, offer actionable strategies for integrating it into practices, showcase AI's role in advancing sustainability, and inspire impactful ventures"-- Provided by publisher.
Identifiers: LCCN 2025005872 (print) | LCCN 2025005873 (ebook) | ISBN 9798337311074 hardcover | ISBN 9798337311081 paperback | ISBN 9798337311098 ebook
Subjects: LCSH: Artificial intelligence--Business applications | Business--Technological innovations | Sustainable development
Classification: LCC HD45 .I5525 2025 (print) | LCC HD45 (ebook) | DDC 658.4/063--dc23/eng/20250709
LC record available at https://lccn.loc.gov/2025005872
LC ebook record available at https://lccn.loc.gov/2025005873
British Cataloguing in Publication Data
A Cataloguing in Publication record for this book is available from the British Library.

Table of Contents

Preface ix

Chapter 1
The Intersection of Sustainability and AI in Modern Business 1
Mustafa Kayyali, Maaref University of Applied Sciences, Idlib, Syria

Chapter 2
Impact of AI on Sustainable Value Creation in Business 31
Niaz Mohammad, American International University, Dhaka, Bangladesh

Chapter 3
Integrating AI into Corporate Social Responsibility (CSR) for Ethical and Sustainable Business Practices 41
Shayak Hussain, Christ University, Ghaziabad, India

Chapter 4
The Crucial Role of Environmental and Social Responsibility in Modern Entrepreneurship 71
Oindrilla Ghosh, Christ University, Bengaluru, India
Binod Kumar, Radha Govind University, Ranchi, India

Chapter 5
AI Ethics and Responsible AI Deployment in Sustainable Entrepreneurship .. 101
Laura Dragos-Radoi, University of Buckingham, Timisoara, Romania

Chapter 6
Empowering Entrepreneurial Skills for Success and Sustainability 143
Stephanie Sandland, University of East London, UK
Alina Maria Vaduva, University of East London, UK
Toyin Coker, University of East London, UK

Chapter 7
Ethical Entrepreneurship: Navigating the Path to Responsible Business 207
Mustafa Kayyali, Maaref University of Applied Sciences, Idlib, Syria

Chapter 8
Personality Traits and AI-Driven Strategies for Sustainable Growth Among Women Entrepreneurs in Bangalore 241
Jyothsna Thimmaiah B., Periyar University, Salem, India
V.R. Palanivelu, Periyar University, Salem, India

Compilation of References 269

About the Contributors 321

Index 327

Detailed Table of Contents

Preface.. ix

Chapter 1
The Intersection of Sustainability and AI in Modern Business 1
Mustafa Kayyali, Maaref University of Applied Sciences, Idlib, Syria

The convergence of sustainability and artificial intelligence (AI) in modern business is a quickly expanding field of study, with increased emphasis on how AI might assist in the attainment of sustainability goals. As organizations attempt to reconcile economic success with environmental and ethical obligations, AI has emerged as a potent tool to drive innovation, efficiency, and responsibility. The chapter also analyzes the social and ethical implications of AI in business, including concerns over privacy, prejudice, and inequality, as well as the problems companies have in deploying sustainable AI solutions. Finally, the chapter gives insights into the future possibilities of AI-driven sustainability practices, outlining upcoming trends and technologies that are likely to define the future of sustainable business. The integration of AI with sustainability principles gives an exciting opportunity for businesses to innovate, while simultaneously tackling global concerns like climate change, resource depletion, and social inequity.

Chapter 2
Impact of AI on Sustainable Value Creation in Business 31
Niaz Mohammad, American International University, Dhaka, Bangladesh

Artificial intelligence has emerged as a technological innovation that transforms the way businesses operate. In recent years, the use of AI in the financial sector has been growing and they can solve complex problems and are emerging fast in the business ecosystem. The objective of this chapter is to understand the impact of AI on customers' experience and how AI helps to create sustainable value creation in the financial sectors. It also examines how AI affects business, highlighting both the potential and difficulties it poses in banking sectors of Bangladesh. A thorough literature review, survey and case study analysis, and published annual reports from 2020 to 2023 are taken into consideration. According to the study's findings, artificial intelligence (AI) has the potential to significantly improve business operations, including decision-making, cost reductions, and productivity.

Chapter 3
Integrating AI into Corporate Social Responsibility (CSR) for Ethical and Sustainable Business Practices 41
Shayak Hussain, Christ University, Ghaziabad, India

The rapid advancement of artificial intelligence (AI) technologies has significantly transformed various facets of business operations, including corporate social responsibility (CSR). As businesses strive to align their growth strategies with ethical, social, and environmental responsibilities, AI emerges as a powerful tool to enhance the effectiveness of CSR initiatives. This research investigates the integration of AI into CSR, exploring its potential to drive more sustainable business practices, improve transparency, and foster ethical decision-making within organizations. By employing a combination of qualitative and quantitative research methods, this study examines how AI-powered analytics, automation, and decision-making frameworks can optimize CSR efforts. Key areas of exploration include AI's role in enhancing supply chain sustainability, optimizing resource allocation, detecting unethical business practices, and enabling real-time monitoring and reporting of CSR initiatives.

Chapter 4
The Crucial Role of Environmental and Social Responsibility in Modern Entrepreneurship 71
Oindrilla Ghosh, Christ University, Bengaluru, India
Binod Kumar, Radha Govind University, Ranchi, India

In today's business landscape, environmental and social responsibility (ESR) has become a fundamental aspect of modern entrepreneurship. Companies are no longer judged solely on profitability but also on their impact on society and the planet. Entrepreneurs who prioritize sustainability, ethical sourcing, and fair labor practices gain a competitive advantage by appealing to conscious consumers. Environmental responsibility involves reducing carbon footprints, minimizing waste, and adopting sustainable business practices. Entrepreneurs are increasingly investing in green technologies, renewable energy, and eco-friendly production methods to align with global sustainability goals. Similarly, social responsibility entails fair wages, diversity, community engagement, and ethical labor practices. Incorporating ESR not only benefits the planet and society but also enhances brand value, attracts investors, and secures long-term success. As consumer expectations evolve, businesses that embrace environmental and social responsibility will thrive in the modern economy.

Chapter 5
AI Ethics and Responsible AI Deployment in Sustainable Entrepreneurship .. 101
Laura Dragos-Radoi, University of Buckingham, Timisoara, Romania

In today's fast-changing business environment, artificial intelligence (AI) has become a key factor, presenting both challenges and opportunities depending on its implementation. This chapter explores how responsible AI practices can help businesses transition from a profit-centric mindset to a broader vision that embraces sustainability and long-term viability. By prioritizing ethical principles, companies—whether multinational corporations or startups—can harness AI to drive innovation, foster sustainable growth, and promote equitable progress for all stakeholders. It examines the macro-level influences of these technologies and their interconnectedness with external environments, offering a holistic perspective on how emerging technologies are reshaping the modern business ecosystem. This provides business leaders and enthusiasts with practical insights to navigate the systemic impacts of AI and leverage its potential responsibly.

Chapter 6
Empowering Entrepreneurial Skills for Success and Sustainability 143
Stephanie Sandland, University of East London, UK
Alina Maria Vaduva, University of East London, UK
Toyin Coker, University of East London, UK

Entrepreneurs play a critical role in driving sustainability, but incorporating sustainability into an enterprise adds complexity and diffusion challenges. This chapter explores key skills and tools to enhance success. Systems thinking aids in problem analysis and intervention planning, while structured idea generation techniques foster viable solutions. A positive entrepreneurial mindset is essential, alongside strategies to mitigate risks tied to radical innovation. The case of electric car adoption illustrates these challenges. Success also hinges on assembling a skilled team to navigate the launch and scaling phases. Securing finance requires aligning with funders' priorities, crafting compelling brand stories, and refining pitching techniques for various forms of funding. Finally, entrepreneurs can leverage networks, government support, and AI-driven analytical tools to manage sustainability's complexities and enhance decision-making. Throughout this chapter, the specific skills and tools to support these activities are explained.

Chapter 7
Ethical Entrepreneurship: Navigating the Path to Responsible Business 207
Mustafa Kayyali, Maaref University of Applied Sciences, Idlib, Syria

This chapter examines the developing notion of ethical entrepreneurship concerning AI-driven business strategies and sustainability ideals. As artificial intelligence transforms sectors and business models, entrepreneurs encounter substantial opportunities and considerable ethical dilemmas. The incorporation of AI into entrepreneurial operations requires a responsible strategy to guarantee that innovation does not compromise social, environmental, or economic welfare. The chapter provides insights into how entrepreneurs can establish businesses that are both profitable and socially and environmentally responsible by examining ethical dilemmas in AI decision-making, the significance of a responsible business culture, and the incorporation of sustainability principles. The chapter finishes by delineating solutions to surmount the hurdles of adopting ethical AI and the course for promoting responsible, sustainable enterprise in the AI epoch.

Chapter 8
Personality Traits and AI-Driven Strategies for Sustainable Growth Among Women Entrepreneurs in Bangalore 241
Jyothsna Thimmaiah B., Periyar University, Salem, India
V.R. Palanivelu, Periyar University, Salem, India

In this chapter, the authors explore whether strong personality traits also shape the entrepreneurial mindset of women entrepreneurs in Bangalore, as well as how AI-driven interventions create sustainability in their business growth. It's about perseverance, and it's about creativity, and it's about being bold, and it's about how those things end up affecting one's personal decision-making and business outcomes. Finally, the chapter reviews AI tools for strategic planning, market analysis, resource allocation, and environmental sustainability. A framework for the alchemical integration of entrepreneurial behaviour, AI breakthroughs, and sustainability principles is presented with prescriptive relevance to policymakers, scholars, and business practitioners. When we combine technology passion points and sustainable goals, we can afford to help women entrepreneurs fast-track stand-out growth and contribute to creating the world's best-in-class inclusive and responsible entrepreneur community.

Compilation of References 269

About the Contributors 321

Index 327

Preface

As the global business landscape evolves, the convergence of sustainability, artificial intelligence (AI), and entrepreneurship presents unprecedented opportunities to address pressing environmental, social, and economic challenges. *Integrating Sustainability Principles With AI-Driven Entrepreneurial Strategies* is a timely exploration of how these dynamic forces can be harnessed to create impactful, responsible, and innovative enterprises. As editors, we are thrilled to bring together a diverse collection of perspectives from scholars, practitioners, and thought leaders to guide business professionals, entrepreneurs, and students through this transformative intersection. Our aim is to provide a comprehensive resource that not only deepens understanding of sustainable business practices but also equips readers with actionable strategies to leverage AI for sustainability and entrepreneurial success. This book bridges theory and practice, offering insights into how businesses can thrive while contributing positively to society and the planet.

Chapter 1, "The Intersection of Sustainability and AI in Modern Business," sets the stage by exploring the synergy between sustainability and AI in contemporary business. It examines how AI can drive innovation and efficiency to achieve sustainability goals while addressing ethical challenges such as privacy, bias, and inequality. Through a forward-looking lens, the chapter highlights emerging trends and technologies shaping the future of sustainable business practices.

Chapter 2, "Impact of AI on Sustainable Value Creation in Business," delves into AI's transformative role in the financial sector, with a focus on Bangladesh's banking industry. Through a comprehensive analysis of literature, surveys, and case studies from 2020 to 2023, it illustrates how AI enhances customer experiences, streamlines operations, and fosters sustainable value creation, while also addressing implementation challenges.

Chapter 3, "Integrating AI Into Corporate Social Responsibility (CSR) for Ethical and Sustainable Business Practices," investigates how AI can amplify CSR initiatives. By combining qualitative and quantitative research, it explores AI's contributions to supply chain sustainability, resource optimization, and ethical decision-making, offering a roadmap for businesses to align growth with social and environmental responsibilities.

Chapter 4, "The Crucial Role of Environmental and Social Responsibility in Modern Entrepreneurship," underscores the importance of environmental and social responsibility (ESR) in today's entrepreneurial landscape. It highlights how entrepreneurs can gain a competitive edge by adopting sustainable practices, such as reducing carbon footprints and promoting ethical labor standards, to meet the expectations of conscious consumers and investors.

Chapter 5, "AI Ethics and Responsible AI Deployment in Sustainable Entrepreneurship," examines the ethical dimensions of AI in business. It provides a framework for responsible AI deployment, emphasizing how ethical principles can drive sustainable growth and equitable progress across startups and established enterprises.

Chapter 6, "Empowering Entrepreneurial Skills for Success and Sustainability," focuses on the skills and tools entrepreneurs need to navigate the complexities of sustainable enterprises. From systems thinking to AI-driven analytics, it provides practical insights for building resilient, impactful ventures, using the case of electric car adoption as an example.

Chapter 7, "Ethical Entrepreneurship: Navigating the Path to Responsible Business," addresses the ethical challenges of AI-driven entrepreneurship. It offers strategies for building businesses that balance profitability with social and environmental responsibility, ensuring sustainable innovation in the AI era.

Chapter 8, "Personality Traits and AI-Driven Strategies for Sustainable Growth Among Women Entrepreneurs in Bangalore," examines how personality traits shape the entrepreneurial mindset of women in Bangalore. It presents a framework for integrating AI tools with sustainability principles to foster inclusive, responsible growth in female-led enterprises.

We extend our gratitude to the contributors whose expertise and dedication have made this book a reality. We hope this volume inspires readers to embrace sustainability and AI as catalysts for innovation, resilience, and positive change in the entrepreneurial world.

Muhammad Abu Naser
London Metropolitan University, UK

Jagbir Singh Kadyan
Manav Rachna University, India

Liliane Cristina Segura
Universidade Presbiteriana Mackenzie, Brazil

Chapter 1

The Intersection of Sustainability and AI in Modern Business

Mustafa Kayyali
https://orcid.org/0000-0003-3300-262X
Maaref University of Applied Sciences, Idlib, Syria

ABSTRACT

The convergence of sustainability and artificial intelligence (AI) in modern business is a quickly expanding field of study, with increased emphasis on how AI might assist in the attainment of sustainability goals. As organizations attempt to reconcile economic success with environmental and ethical obligations, AI has emerged as a potent tool to drive innovation, efficiency, and responsibility. The chapter also analyzes the social and ethical implications of AI in business, including concerns over privacy, prejudice, and inequality, as well as the problems companies have in deploying sustainable AI solutions. Finally, the chapter gives insights into the future possibilities of AI-driven sustainability practices, outlining upcoming trends and technologies that are likely to define the future of sustainable business. The integration of AI with sustainability principles gives an exciting opportunity for businesses to innovate, while simultaneously tackling global concerns like climate change, resource depletion, and social inequity.

INTRODUCTION

As the global business environment quickly develops, one of the most crucial and disruptive innovations has been the convergence of artificial intelligence (AI) and sustainability. The fundamental issues posed by climate change, resource de-

DOI: 10.4018/979-8-3373-1107-4.ch001

pletion, and environmental degradation have reinforced the desire for corporations to adopt more sustainable operations (Dwivedi, 2022). At the same time, AI, with its extraordinary ability to analyze enormous quantities of data, make predictions, and improve processes, provides a novel way to solve these environmental concerns. The combination of these two forces—AI and sustainability—has the potential to alter businesses, boost economic development, and create a future that is both technologically sophisticated and ecologically responsible. In recent years, the increased awareness of the environmental effect of corporate operations has forced corporations to re-evaluate their plans and practices. Sustainability is no longer only a phrase or a regulatory obligation for organizations; it has become a major strategic objective (Sheehy & Farneti, 2021). Companies that traditionally placed short-term profitability above all else are increasingly understanding the long-term worth of sustainability, not only in terms of environmental effect but also in the context of customer demand, regulatory demands, and competitive advantage. Consumers nowadays are more conscious about their shopping decisions, increasingly selecting companies that demonstrate a commitment to social and environmental responsibility. Simultaneously, regulatory authorities are strengthening environmental requirements, compelling corporations to employ more sustainable operations. This transformation has forced the incorporation of sustainability into business models, and AI, with its tremendous potential to improve operations and decrease waste, has emerged as a vital enabler in this transition.

AI's promise to transform sectors and unlock new levels of efficiency and creativity makes it a strong weapon in reaching environmental goals (Dauvergne, 2021). From decreasing energy usage to simplifying supply chains, AI is being deployed across many industries to increase operational efficiency and decrease environmental impact. The development of AI-powered technologies such as machine learning, predictive analytics, and autonomous systems has offered new potential for corporations to boost their sustainability efforts. By embracing the power of AI, organizations may not only minimize resource consumption but also make better-informed decisions that match long-term environmental goals. For example, AI may be used to detect and anticipate energy usage trends, optimize industrial processes, and improve waste management systems. In agriculture, AI is helping to boost agricultural yields while lowering water usage, pesticides, and fertilizer consumption. The opportunity for AI's contribution to sustainable practices is huge, and its potential applications are fast growing across sectors (Nishant et al, 2020). As organizations increasingly look to AI as a tool for sustainability, it is crucial to acknowledge that some obstacles and limitations must be addressed. The integration of AI technology into current business frameworks may be hard and costly, requiring large expenditures in infrastructure, data management, and specialized labor. Furthermore, while AI has enormous promise in advancing sustainability, it also poses ethical problems concerning data privacy, algorithmic prejudice, and the possible displacement of employment due to automation. For AI to successfully assist sustainable business practices, these ethical considerations must be carefully managed, ensuring that AI is applied ethically and openly.

Moreover, corporations must also be conscious of the larger effects of AI on society. While AI has the potential to promote innovation and enhance efficiency, it must be incorporated in a way that benefits not only corporations but also the communities and stakeholders they serve. The relevance of AI in corporate sustainability extends beyond merely operational efficiency; it is about building a more equal and responsible future for everybody. As AI grows more prevalent, its influence on labor markets, societal structures, and ethical standards will continue to develop, forcing businesses to carefully assess how their AI-driven initiatives connect with their social and environmental objectives. This chapter explores the interaction between AI and sustainability in current business practices. It analyzes how AI is being deployed to enhance efficiency, stimulate creativity, and contribute to environmental sustainability. The chapter also addresses the obstacles and limitations to deploying sustainable AI solutions and underlines the ethical implications of AI in the context of sustainability. Additionally, it looks at the future potential of AI in sustainable business practices, presenting insights into how developing AI technologies might change sectors and contribute to a more sustainable and equitable global economy. By studying these processes, this chapter attempts to give a thorough understanding of the essential role that AI plays in determining the future of corporate sustainability and the larger social effect of these advances. As the globe continues to face serious environmental concerns, the demand for sustainable business practices has never been higher. At the same time, the tremendous speed of AI advancement gives an extraordinary chance to influence positive change. Businesses that effectively integrate AI into their sustainability strategy will not only gain a competitive edge but will also play a critical role in crafting a more sustainable future. As we move forward, the partnership between AI and sustainability will be a defining aspect of the corporate environment, delivering answers to some of the most important concerns of our day. The integration of AI into business processes is not only about boosting efficiency; it is about harnessing technology as a force for good, contributing to the global fight to combat climate change, conserve resources, and build a more equal society for future generations.

THE GROWING IMPORTANCE OF SUSTAINABILITY IN MODERN BUSINESS

The rising relevance of sustainability in modern business is not simply a passing trend but a fundamental shift in the way organizations are expected to function in the 21st century (Thiele, 2024). As worries about environmental degradation, climate change, and social inequality continue to mount, corporations are under greater pressure to operate ethically, balancing profit production with long-term ecological and social well-being. This change has redefined the expectations put on organizations and has spurred a transition in how they function, make decisions and connect with society at large. Sustainable business practices have become crucial not just to corporate social responsibility but also to the entire business strategy, competitiveness, and future viability. Historically, corporate success was judged largely by financial metrics—profit margins, return on investment, and market share (Rashid, 2021). However, in recent decades, a greater realization of the environmental and socioeconomic difficulties facing the world has driven a more holistic vision of success. Today, corporations are being held accountable not just for their financial success but also for their influence on the earth and society. This trend is driven by a mix of causes, including greater public awareness of environmental and social concerns, the emergence of conscious consumption, regulatory pressures, and the knowledge that sustainability is directly connected to long-term company resilience.

One of the primary causes of this transition is the increased realization of the environmental concerns that endanger the planet's future (Uralovich et al, 2023). Climate change, biodiversity loss, deforestation, and pollution are just a few of the crucial challenges that have attracted substantial attention in recent years. These difficulties are not only global in magnitude but also linked, meaning that solving one issue typically necessitates tackling others concurrently. The repercussions of inactivity are severe, with possible impacts on human health, food security, water resources, and general quality of life. Businesses that fail to understand these dangers and change accordingly are increasingly at risk of being left behind. Consumers, employees, and investors are demanding more sustainable practices, and organizations that fail to satisfy these expectations may find themselves facing reputational harm, regulatory fines, or a loss of market share. The emergence of conscious consumption is another key element contributing to the rising relevance of sustainability in business (Yarimoglu & Binboga, 2019). In the past, consumers were frequently primarily concerned with the price and quality of items and services. Today, however, a rising number of consumers are making purchase decisions based on a company's environmental and social performance. According to different surveys, customers, particularly younger generations, are increasingly prepared to pay a premium for products and services that match their beliefs, such as those that are environmentally friendly, ethically created, and socially responsible. This shift in customer behavior has driven companies to reassess their methods and implement more sustainable alternatives, not just as a moral duty but also as a competitive advantage. Businesses that fail to adapt to these changing tastes risk losing relevance in an increasingly competitive market.

At the same time, businesses are experiencing rising pressure from investors and stakeholders to embrace sustainable practices. The emergence of environmental, social, and governance (ESG) factors in investment choices has made sustainability a fundamental concern in the financial industry (Dmuchowski et al, 2023). Investors are increasingly judging companies not just on their financial success but also on their environmental and social effects. As a result, corporations are being driven to embrace more open and responsible corporate processes, proving their commitment to sustainability via quantifiable actions and outcomes. For many companies, adopting sustainability is no longer only an ethical option but also a strategic one, as it may directly affect their access to funding, market position, and long-term viability. Regulatory forces are also playing a crucial influence in the rising relevance of sustainability in business (Qiu et al, 2020). Governments throughout the world are establishing stronger rules aimed at limiting environmental harm and supporting sustainable activities. For example, the European Union's Green Deal and the Paris Agreement on climate change are establishing ambitious objectives for carbon reductions and sustainable development (Kokotović et al, 2019). These regulatory frameworks are pressuring corporations to adopt more sustainable practices or risk penalties, fees, or limitations. Compliance with these requirements is becoming increasingly crucial for companies that operate in several locations, since failing to conform to environmental and social norms may result in hefty penalties, legal battles, and harm to their brand.

However, sustainability in business is not simply about avoiding risks or complying with rules. It also offers considerable prospects for development, innovation, and distinctiveness. Sustainable business strategies may contribute to cost savings through resource efficiency, waste reduction, and energy optimization (Hannan et al, 2020). By implementing circular economy ideas, organizations may minimize their dependency on finite resources, cut waste, and develop new income streams through the reuse or recycling of products. Companies that invest in renewable energy, energy-efficient technology, and sustainable supply chains may lower their environmental impact while also enhancing their financial line. Additionally, sustainability-driven innovation may open up new markets and produce products that respond to the rising need for eco-friendly and socially responsible items. Integrating sustainability into business strategy may enhance a company's reputation, generate brand loyalty, and attract top personnel. Employees, especially millennials and Gen Z, are increasingly seeking jobs that agree with their beliefs and give a sense of purpose beyond just financial gain. Companies that value sustainability are more likely to recruit and keep a highly motivated and engaged staff, which may lead to increased productivity, innovation, and employee happiness. Additionally, companies that are viewed as leaders in sustainability are typically able to develop deeper connections with customers, suppliers, and other stakeholders, boosting their overall competitiveness in the marketplace.

Another key element driving the growing relevance of sustainability is the increasing realization that environmental and social difficulties are strongly connected with economic issues (Hariram et al, 2023). The notion of the "triple bottom line" - people, planet, and profit — stresses that corporations should not just focus on financial success but also examine their influence on society and the environment. This holistic approach to business understands that long-term success is contingent on a healthy and sustainable earth, flourishing communities, and equitable economic systems. By implementing sustainable practices, companies may help to tackle some of the world's most serious concerns, such as poverty, inequality, and environmental degradation, while also assuring their long-term prosperity. As the corporate landscape continues to shift, the importance of sustainability will only continue to expand. The advent of new technologies, such as artificial intelligence (AI), automation, and blockchain, has the potential to hasten the transition to more sustainable corporate practices. AI, in particular, may play a crucial role in optimizing resource consumption, eliminating waste, and enhancing decision-making across numerous industries. From supply chain management to energy usage, AI-driven solutions may help companies reach their sustainability goals more efficiently and effectively. The rising relevance of sustainability in modern business is a reflection of the changing expectations of customers, investors, regulators, and society at large. Businesses that fail to grasp the relevance of sustainability risk falling behind, while those who embrace it are positioned to prosper in a quickly changing world. Sustainability is no longer a niche factor or a "nice-to-have" but a crucial component of long-term economic success. By implementing sustainable practices, organizations may not only manage risks and comply with regulations but also open new prospects for development, innovation, and market leadership. As the globe continues to face difficult environmental and social issues, corporations have a unique opportunity to play a major role in crafting a more sustainable and equitable future.

THE ROLE OF AI IN DRIVING BUSINESS EFFICIENCY AND INNOVATION

The role of Artificial Intelligence (AI) in driving company efficiency and innovation is becoming increasingly crucial in the current business landscape (Lee et al,

2019). As organizations confront the challenges of fast technology breakthroughs, increasing customer expectations, and the need to remain competitive in a global market, AI provides a strong tool for altering operations, boosting decision-making, and providing new avenues for innovation. While the promise of AI typically conjures thoughts of futuristic technology or automation, its actual potential rests in its capacity to improve existing processes, solve complicated challenges, and unearth new possibilities that were previously imagined. At its heart, AI is about harnessing complex algorithms, machine learning models, and massive quantities of data to make smarter judgments, automate repetitive processes, and reveal hidden patterns. In a corporate setting, this implies AI may greatly enhance operational efficiency by simplifying workflows, eliminating mistakes, and speeding up procedures. Whether it's boosting supply chain management, enhancing customer service, or optimizing marketing activities, AI has the power to deliver huge cost savings while improving overall efficiency.

One of the most fundamental ways AI promotes company efficiency is through automation (Tschang & Almirall, 2021). Traditional corporate processes frequently entail a large amount of physical work, which is time-consuming, prone to human error, and often inefficient. AI, however, may automate repetitive work across multiple corporate departments, from finance and accounting to human resources and customer support. For instance, AI-powered chatbots can handle client requests 24/7, freeing up human agents to focus on more difficult issues. In manufacturing, AI systems may manage inventories, detect equipment problems, and optimize production schedules, all of which lead to decreased downtime and better efficiency. The potential of AI to take over routine activities helps people to focus on more strategic and creative parts of their work, resulting in a more effective use of human resources. Beyond automation, AI also promotes efficiency by enhancing decision-making processes. Traditional decision-making frequently depends on a combination of historical facts, intuition, and experience, which can occasionally lead to poor decisions (Julmi, 2019). AI, on the other hand, can evaluate massive volumes of data in real-time, discovering patterns and trends that may not be immediately visible to human decision-makers. For example, AI-powered analytics solutions may assist companies in forecasting client behavior, recognizing market trends, and optimizing pricing tactics. This data-driven strategy helps companies to make better-informed decisions, lower risks, and exploit opportunities more effectively. In areas such as finance, AI has already demonstrated its usefulness by giving insights into market trends, fraud detection, and investment strategies, all of which boost decision-making and efficiency.

In addition to enhancing efficiency, AI plays a crucial role in encouraging innovation. As organizations attempt to differentiate themselves in an increasingly crowded environment, AI presents new methods to innovate goods and services, enhance consumer experiences, and explore novel business models. The strength of AI rests not just in its ability to improve existing processes but also in its capacity to allow new ways to do business (Canhoto & Clear, 2020). For instance, in the field of product creation, AI may help organizations build more customized and tailored goods by studying user data and preferences. By employing machine learning algorithms, organizations may design adaptable products that change based on customer feedback and changing market conditions. In the automobile business, companies like Tesla are leveraging AI to drive innovation in autonomous driving, building vehicles that can learn from their environment and improve their performance over time. The potential for AI to drive innovation extends beyond product development to customer experience and engagement (Rane, 2023). Today's consumers want customized, frictionless, and engaging experiences with the companies they connect with. AI helps organizations to deliver on these expectations by harnessing data to build highly tailored services. For instance, AI algorithms may assess a customer's browsing history, purchasing behavior, and preferences to give tailored suggestions, whether it's on an e-commerce website, a streaming platform, or in the form of targeted adverts. Moreover, AI may be utilized to enhance customer relationships through chatbots, virtual assistants, and speech recognition systems, delivering more efficient and pleasurable experiences for customers. As consumer expectations continue to increase, AI's capacity to offer tailored and timely services will be a major determinant in corporate success. AI also contributes to innovation by enabling new business models and operational paradigms. One such approach is the subscription economy, where companies supply items or services on an ongoing basis rather than through one-time purchases (Olimjonovich, 2024). AI plays a significant role in supporting this paradigm by evaluating consumer usage habits, improving inventory management, and forecasting demand. Companies like Netflix and Spotify, for example, utilize AI to generate tailored content suggestions, ensuring that consumers are interested and pleased with the service. This degree of customization not only builds client loyalty but also generates new revenue sources for enterprises. Similarly, the sharing economy, epitomized by companies like Uber and Airbnb, depends on AI to streamline logistics, connect clients with service providers, and ease transactions, therefore generating new opportunities for both businesses and consumers.

Another key method AI is promoting innovation is through its involvement in research and development R&D (Johnson et al, 2022). In industries such as pharmaceuticals, AI is transforming the process of drug development by analyzing enormous volumes of chemical data to uncover promising molecules that might lead to novel therapies. AI-powered simulations can also forecast how different pharmaceuticals would interact with the body, drastically speeding up the testing process and cutting expenses. In the field of materials science, AI is being used to identify novel materials with specified features, such as lightweight composites for use in aircraft or high-efficiency solar cells. By speeding the pace of R&D, AI is helping companies to bring breakthrough goods to market faster and more cost-effectively. While AI's influence on corporate productivity and creativity is apparent, it also raises crucial issues about its larger consequences for the workforce, society, and economy. As AI continues to advance and take on increasingly complicated jobs, there is a rising concern about the possibility of job displacement. Automation, although boosting efficiency, may lead to the elimination of certain job categories, particularly those that entail repetitive, manual work. However, AI also has the potential to offer new job possibilities by helping companies enter new markets, develop new products, and enhance customer service. The challenge for businesses and politicians will be to guarantee that the advantages of AI-driven innovation are shared broadly and that people are prepared with the skills needed to succeed in an AI-powered economy.

Another problem is ensuring that AI is applied ethically and responsibly (Díaz-Rodríguez et al, 2023). As organizations increasingly rely on AI to make judgments, there are worries about transparency, bias, and responsibility. AI systems are only as good as the data they are trained on, and if that data is skewed or inadequate, it can lead to unjust or discriminating outputs. For example, AI-driven recruiting tools have been criticized for perpetuating gender and racial prejudices, as they generally depend on past data that reflects current inequities. To address these issues, organizations must emphasize ethical AI practices, ensuring that AI systems are created and operated in a way that promotes justice, accountability, and transparency. The role of AI in driving corporate efficiency and creativity is revolutionary, enabling companies new opportunities to streamline operations, better decision-making, and generate unique goods and services. As AI continues to advance, it will play an increasingly vital role in determining the future of business. However, organizations must approach AI deployment with prudence, ensuring that ethical issues remain at the forefront of decision-making. By doing so, they can leverage the full potential of AI while producing value for their customers, workers, and society as a whole.

INTEGRATING SUSTAINABILITY WITH AI: A STRATEGIC IMPERATIVE

Integrating sustainability with artificial intelligence (AI) is becoming not just a strategic imperative but also a need for organizations hoping to survive in an increasingly competitive, environmentally-conscious, and socially responsible market. Sustainability, which has typically been regarded through the perspective of environmental stewardship, social responsibility, and economic viability, has now found a powerful partner in AI, a technology that promises to expedite and enhance how enterprises accomplish sustainability goals (Dauvergne, 2020). The combination of these two powerful forces — sustainability and AI — provides organizations with a unique chance to generate enduring value, increase efficiency, and manage risks while contributing to the development of society and the world. As the globe grapples with the complexity of climate change, resource depletion, and social inequity, corporations are under growing pressure to show their commitment to sustainable operations. Consumers, investors, employees, and governments are all demanding that companies take action to minimize their carbon footprints, solve social concerns, and contribute to global sustainability objectives. The United Nations Sustainable Development Goals (SDGs), for instance, have created a worldwide agenda for corporations to embrace more sustainable practices in areas such as climate action, responsible consumerism, and renewable energy (Montiel et al, 2021). These goals have become standards for judging the efficacy of sustainability programs across the industry.

Yet, despite rising awareness of the significance of sustainability, organizations typically struggle to adopt effective strategies that provide substantial benefits (Journeault et al, 2021). This is when AI comes into play. AI technologies have the potential to change sustainability initiatives by offering organizations new tools to evaluate data, forecast outcomes, improve processes, and automate operations. By embracing AI, companies may uncover creative solutions that not only promote efficiency and profitability but also help the attainment of sustainability objectives. One of the most fundamental ways in which AI may contribute to sustainability is through data-driven decision-making. AI excels in processing and analyzing massive amounts of data, identifying patterns, and making predictions based on previous trends. In the context of sustainability, this skill helps companies to make better-informed decisions about how they manage resources, decrease waste, and optimize energy use. For example, AI-powered algorithms may evaluate a company's supply chain to find inefficiencies, estimate demand for products, and recommend methods to cut energy use. This data-driven strategy helps companies to decrease their environmental footprint while simultaneously enhancing operational efficiency.

In areas including manufacturing and logistics, AI is being utilized to improve production processes, reduce energy use, and eliminate waste. For instance, AI-driven systems may monitor production equipment in real-time, recognize inefficiencies or possible problems, and change operations appropriately to cut energy consumption and prevent waste. Predictive maintenance driven by AI may extend the lifespan of machinery, lowering the need for replacements and eliminating the environmental impact involved with building new equipment. Similarly, in logistics, AI algorithms may optimize delivery routes, minimize fuel usage, and enhance fleet management, all of which lead to fewer carbon emissions and more sustainable business practices. AI also plays a key role in the creation of sustainable products and services (Van

Wynsberghe, 2021). By harnessing AI's capacity to analyze massive volumes of data, organizations may build goods that are more resource-efficient, durable, and recyclable. For example, AI may be used to model the life cycle of a product, from raw material extraction to disposal, to discover possibilities to decrease environmental effects at each stage. In the fashion business, AI is being utilized to design more sustainable clothes by evaluating patterns in customer demand, optimizing material consumption, and even anticipating trends to minimize overproduction. In the food business, AI may help companies decrease food waste by forecasting customer demand and modifying production schedules appropriately.

Beyond its influence on product design, AI is also helping companies implement circular economy techniques, where things are reused, repaired, or recycled to prolong their life cycle (Ghoreishi & Happonen, 2020). AI may be used to track items throughout their full life cycle, ensuring that they are correctly disposed of or recycled at the end of their useful life. For instance, AI-powered waste management systems can recognize recyclable elements in waste streams and classify them accordingly, boosting recycling rates and minimizing the amount of garbage that ends up in landfills. Similarly, AI may be used to monitor the operation of items in the field, allowing companies to offer maintenance services, repairs, or upgrades that extend the lifespan of the product and eliminate the need for new resources. Sustainability is also directly tied to energy usage, and AI may play a crucial role in optimizing energy use across industries. AI-powered smart grids, for example, may evaluate real-time data on energy usage and modify electricity distribution to optimal efficiency. In buildings, AI-driven systems can monitor and regulate heating, ventilation, and air conditioning (HVAC) systems to cut energy use while maintaining ideal comfort levels (Ali et al, 2024). In the transportation industry, AI can assist maximize the usage of electric vehicles (EVs) by monitoring traffic patterns, weather conditions, and charging infrastructure to find the most effective routes and charging schedules.

Another area where AI is making a huge influence on sustainability is agriculture (Martos et al, 2021). As the world population continues to rise, the need for sustainable agriculture techniques grows increasingly critical. AI may help farmers maximize agricultural yields, reduce water consumption, and minimize the use of pesticides and fertilizers. For example, AI-powered drones and sensors may monitor soil conditions, identify early symptoms of insect infestations, and give real-time data on crop health, allowing farmers to take targeted decisions that lessen the environmental effect of their operations. Similarly, AI may be used to design precision irrigation systems that maximize water utilization, ensuring that crops receive the proper quantity of water at the right time. While the potential benefits of combining AI with sustainability are considerable, it is crucial to realize the obstacles and ethical issues that come with this integration. One of the primary issues is the environmental impact of AI itself. Training big AI models needs enormous processing power, which can result in excessive energy usage and carbon emissions. As AI usage develops, organizations must be cautious of the energy consumption involved with the development and implementation of AI systems.

One potential answer is to employ renewable energy sources to power AI infrastructure or to develop more energy-efficient AI algorithms that reduce the environmental effect of training and deployment (Ukoba et al, 2024). Ethical considerations can arise when AI is used to make judgments that effect sustainability results. For example, AI systems that optimize resource utilization may erroneously emphasize short-term efficiency benefits above long-term sustainability goals. To address these issues, organizations must ensure that AI systems are created with sustainability principles in mind and that they are frequently assessed for fairness, transparency, and accountability. AI should be used as a tool to supplement human decision-making, not replace it, and organizations should emphasize ethical issues in the design and deployment of AI systems. The integration of AI with environmental goals raises problems regarding equality and access (Goralski & Tan, 2020). As AI technologies become more generally accepted, there is a concern that certain people, particularly those in developing regions or disadvantaged communities, may be left behind. To guarantee that the advantages of AI-driven sustainability are shared fairly, businesses must endeavor to ensure that AI technologies are available to all and that their implementation does not worsen existing inequities. Integrating sustainability with AI is not just a strategic requirement, but also an opportunity for organizations to strengthen their competitiveness, contribute to global sustainability initiatives and drive innovation in a quickly changing environment. By using the potential of AI, organizations can improve their operations, decrease their environmental footprint, and create goods and services that satisfy the rising need for sustainability. However, businesses must approach the integration of AI with sustainability cautiously, ensuring that ethical concerns are at the forefront of their decision-making and that AI is used in a way that benefits all stakeholders. With the correct approach, AI may become a strong force for good, helping to build a more sustainable and affluent future for everybody.

CHALLENGES AND BARRIERS TO IMPLEMENTING SUSTAINABLE AI SOLUTIONS

Implementing sustainable AI solutions is an ambitious and vital aim for enterprises, governments, and society at large (Yigitcanlar & Cugurullo, 2020). AI can alter various sectors, making operations more efficient, lowering environmental consequences, and driving forward innovation. However, the route toward combining AI with sustainability principles is plagued with hurdles and barriers. From technological impediments to budgetary limits, legal difficulties, and societal issues, the route to fulfilling the full promise of sustainable AI is not easy. In this conversation, we address the numerous obstacles and constraints that businesses encounter when seeking to adopt AI solutions that are both successful and sustainable. One of the major hurdles in deploying sustainable AI is the technological complexity required. AI systems, particularly those that rely on machine learning, deep learning, and neural networks, require massive quantities of data, computer power, and energy. The training of AI models generally entails processing enormous datasets and conducting computations that might be energy-intensive. While AI has the potential to optimize resource consumption, the sheer magnitude of processing power necessary for many sophisticated AI approaches raises concerns about the environmental effect of these systems. The energy consumption associated with training large-scale AI models can be enormous, leading to worries regarding the sustainability of AI solutions themselves.

In addition to the technological constraints, there are major financial challenges connected with deploying sustainable AI solutions (Nishant et al, 2020). The initial investment required for AI systems, particularly in terms of infrastructure, technology, and professional personnel, can be enormous. AI models frequently require specialized hardware such as Graphics Processing Units (GPUs) or Tensor Processing Units (TPUs), which are intended to handle the large computing demands of AI training (Shahid & Mushtaq, 2020). These physical components can be costly, yet their purchase represents just a small fraction of the entire cost. In addition to technology, companies must also spend on software, data storage, and individuals with the requisite experience to build, operate, and maintain AI systems. The financial burden of adopting sustainable AI can be particularly onerous for small and medium-sized companies (SMEs), who may lack the means to invest in cutting-edge technology (Costa, 2024). For SMEs, the cost of adopting AI systems for sustainability might appear unreasonably costly, especially when compared to the possible return on investment (ROI) that may not be immediately visible. Without a clear grasp of the long-term advantages, such as cost savings through resource efficiency or greater customer loyalty through sustainable practices, organizations may be hesitant to engage in AI solutions that offer just incremental gains. The upfront expenditures associated with implementing AI, along with the uncertainties around its ROI, might make it difficult for enterprises to justify the investment in sustaining AI programs. Regulatory concerns also offer a substantial impediment to the broad application of sustainable AI systems. As AI technology continues to grow at a rapid rate, the regulatory framework struggles to keep up. Governments around the globe are wrestling with how to govern AI in a way that stimulates innovation while safeguarding against possible hazards. In many jurisdictions, there is a lack of defined standards or laws regulating the ethical use of AI, particularly in the context of sustainability. This legislative ambiguity can generate confusion and hesitancy among organizations trying to deploy AI for sustainability goals.

In certain circumstances, restrictions may even inhibit the adoption of AI (Cubric, 2020). For example, privacy rules such as the General Data Protection Regulation (GDPR) in the European Union set severe limitations on the collecting, storage, and processing of personal data. While these restrictions are meant to safeguard individuals' privacy, they can also present difficulties for AI systems that require enormous volumes of data to perform properly. In areas where AI may be used to promote sustainability—such as energy management, waste reduction, or water conservation—these legal frameworks may place constraints on data gathering and exchange, making it tougher for enterprises to exploit AI to its full potential. The lack of a clear worldwide framework for regulating AI also means that enterprises operating in several areas must pass over a complicated patchwork of rules. For instance, AI systems that are consistent with European regulations may not fulfill the criteria in other locations, such as Asia or North America. This lack of regulatory uniformity may generate difficulties for companies, particularly those with a global presence. Additionally, companies may be reluctant to employ AI for sustainability if they are concerned about the possible legal issues involved with its implementation. Beyond technological and financial constraints, there are also substantial social and ethical challenges to applying AI solutions for sustainability. The societal effect of AI is a topic of rising concern, particularly as AI systems become more pervasive in our daily lives (Hagerty & Rubinov, 2019). One of the key ethical problems is the potential for AI to aggravate current socioeconomic disparities. AI systems are only as good as the data they are trained on, and if this data is biased or inadequate, the resulting models might perpetuate or even aggravate existing imbalances. In the context of sustainability, AI solutions that are biased or unfair might disproportionately benefit certain groups while leaving others behind.

For example, if AI is employed to improve resource allocation in sectors like electricity distribution or trash management, there is a risk that these systems might favor wealthy places with greater resources while neglecting underprivileged neighborhoods. In many circumstances, the advantages of AI-driven sustainability might be unevenly distributed, worsening societal inequality (Montgomery, 2024). Ensuring that AI systems are created and implemented in a way that promotes diversity and inclusion is a significant problem for corporations, governments, and researchers alike. Another important ethical worry is the potential for AI to damage human occupations. While AI might enhance efficiency and reduce resource consumption, it can also contribute to job displacement, particularly in areas where automation is replacing human labor. This is an especially delicate topic in areas such as manufacturing, agriculture, and transportation, where AI-powered robots and autonomous systems are rapidly being employed to simplify processes. As AI continues to advance, organizations must carefully evaluate the impact of automation on their workforce, ensuring that the transition to AI-driven systems is done in a way that benefits people rather than leaving them behind. There are worries regarding the openness and accountability of AI systems. As AI algorithms get increasingly complicated and opaque, it can be challenging for businesses, consumers, and regulators to comprehend how choices are being made (De Marcellis-Warin et al, 2022). This lack of transparency is particularly disturbing in the context of sustainability, where AI systems are supposed to influence decisions that have substantial environmental and societal effects. Without a comprehensive knowledge of how AI systems function, it can be tough to guarantee that these systems are being utilized ethically and in keeping with sustainability goals.

Another societal issue is the potential for AI to perpetuate current power disparities (Zajko, 2021). Large companies and governments that have access to powerful AI technology may have an even larger edge over smaller organizations or emerging countries. This might result in a situation where the advantages of AI-driven sustainability are concentrated in the hands of a few, rather than being dispersed equally across society. Addressing this challenge demands not just technological innovation but also the adoption of rules and regulations that assure the appropriate and fair deployment of AI technology. There is the problem of promoting cooperation and knowledge-sharing in the AI and sustainability arena. Many of the most serious sustainability challenges—such as climate change, resource depletion, and biodiversity loss—require global cooperation and collaborative action. While AI can address these difficulties, it cannot do so in isolation. Businesses, governments, academic institutions, and non-governmental organizations (NGOs) must work together to ensure that AI solutions are created and deployed in ways that are both successful and equitable. However, developing such a partnership is no easy feat. Different stakeholders typically have opposing interests, and there may be a lack of trust or understanding between them. Bridging these gaps and increasing cooperation will be key to overcoming the hurdles involved with adopting sustainable AI solutions. While the potential for AI to advance sustainability is tremendous, the challenges to its application are equally important. From technological problems such as energy consumption and data integration to budgetary limits, legal impediments, and societal issues, the road to sustainable AI is hard and diverse. Overcoming these issues will need concerted efforts from all sectors of society, including governments, corporations, scholars, and the public. By addressing these limitations head-on, we can unlock the full potential of AI in driving sustainability and build a future where technology works in harmony with the world and its people.

FUTURE PROSPECTS: EVOLVING AI TECHNOLOGIES FOR SUSTAINABLE BUSINESS PRACTICES

The future of AI technology holds considerable promise for altering business processes across a wide range of sectors (Wamba-Taguimdje et al, 2020). As the globe grapples with serious concerns like climate change, resource depletion, and the need for more sustainable growth, businesses are turning to AI to drive innovation and build more sustainable practices. The convergence of AI and sustainability is becoming an increasingly important topic, and as AI technologies continue to improve, their significance in supporting sustainable business practices will increase. One of the primary ways in which AI will have a dramatic influence on corporate sustainability is by enhancing operational efficiency. As organizations face increasing pressure to decrease their carbon footprints and optimize resource utilization, AI technologies are perfectly positioned to deliver solutions that help cut waste, slash energy consumption, and streamline operations. For example, AI-driven systems may monitor manufacturing processes in real-time to discover inefficiencies and recommend changes, helping organizations to employ resources more effectively. This can result in considerable cost savings, decreased environmental impact, and enhanced competitiveness in the market. The capacity to monitor and manage energy use in real-time, for instance, may help organizations dramatically cut their electricity use, contributing to a reduced carbon footprint and more sustainable operations overall (Farghali et al, 2023). The emergence of AI-powered predictive analytics is another interesting path for enhancing sustainability in a company. Predictive analytics, which employs AI algorithms to estimate future patterns and behaviors based on previous data, is already being utilized in areas such as supply chain management, logistics, and inventory control. As these technologies grow more refined, companies will be able to estimate demand with more accuracy, allowing for more efficient production schedules, decreased waste, and a lower environmental effect. In the energy industry, predictive models are already being used to enhance grid management and decrease energy waste by forecasting changes in supply and demand. In the future, these AI-powered prediction tools will become more complex, allowing organizations more insights into their operations and enabling more accurate decision-making.

AI's significance in the creation of circular economies is another interesting field that offers tremendous potential for sustainable business practices (Bag & Pretorius, 2022). A circular economy is one in which resources are used for as long as feasible, then recovered and regenerated at the end of their service life. The transition toward a circular economy implies a major change in the way organizations function, and AI will play a vital role in aiding this transformation. For instance, AI-powered systems may track the lifespan of items, enabling companies to better understand how to recover and reuse resources. Machine learning algorithms may be used to detect which materials can be reused and anticipate the possible environmental effect of recycling or reusing specific resources. Additionally, AI can assist in streamlining logistics in the collection and redistribution of used items, ensuring that resources are regularly cycled back into the market rather than being discarded. The application of AI in circular business models is still in its infancy, but as technologies continue to improve, we should expect to see more organizations embracing circular practices powered by AI-driven insights. One of the most intriguing opportunities for AI in sustainable business practices is its ability to facilitate the creation of green technology (Nishant et al, 2020). Green technologies, which focus on lowering the environmental effect of industrial operations, are becoming increasingly vital as the globe faces escalating environmental concerns. AI can speed the development of green technology by giving researchers and engineers the capabilities to build more efficient, environmentally friendly goods and solutions. In industries like renewable energy, AI can maximize the efficiency of wind turbines and solar panels by forecasting weather patterns and modifying energy output depending on real-time circumstances (Ukoba et al, 2024). Additionally, AI may be employed in energy storage systems, helping to enhance battery efficiency and expand the capacity for storing renewable energy. As AI technologies grow, their capacity to help the development of green technology will become ever more sophisticated, bringing up new options for organizations to embrace sustainable practices.

Beyond energy, AI will play a crucial role in maximizing other resources, such as water and raw materials (Jose et al, 2020). Water shortage is one of the most important concerns confronting businesses and communities throughout the world, and AI can help companies manage their water consumption more efficiently. For example, AI-driven systems may monitor water use in real time and identify places where water is being wasted, enabling businesses to implement more efficient water conservation programs. In industries such as agriculture, AI-powered irrigation systems can optimize water consumption by taking into account parameters like soil moisture, weather forecasts, and crop varieties. This will not only assist cut water usage but also boost crop yields, contributing to more sustainable food production systems. AI may also promote more sustainable raw material extraction and processing by streamlining supply chains and discovering alternative, more sustainable resources.

In addition to its applications in resource management, AI technologies are also positioned to play a significant role in promoting sustainable mobility. The transportation industry is one of the greatest contributors to greenhouse gas emissions, and lowering its carbon footprint is a crucial focus for organizations trying to embrace sustainable practices (Onukwulu et al, 2023). AI can assist minimize the environmental effect of transportation by enabling more efficient routing, reducing fuel usage, and optimizing vehicle performance. In the logistics industry, AI-powered systems may evaluate traffic patterns, weather conditions, and delivery schedules to advise the most effective routes for delivery vehicles, lowering fuel usage and emissions. In the automotive sector, AI is driving the development of electric vehicles (EVs) and autonomous cars, which have the potential to alter the way we think about transportation (Vermesan et al, 2021). As the technology continues to improve, AI will be essential in driving the adoption of electric and autonomous cars, leading to a more sustainable future for transportation. The continuing advancement of AI technology also gives new potential for companies to engage in more sustainable product creation. As consumers increasingly demand environmentally friendly products, companies are under pressure to innovate and provide more sustainable offers (Demirel & Kesidou, 2019). AI can complement this process by helping companies create goods with little environmental effect. For example, AI-powered design tools may examine the lifetime of a product and offer improvements that would lower its carbon footprint, such as utilizing more sustainable materials or optimizing manufacturing procedures. Additionally, AI may be used to optimize package design, helping companies avoid waste and limit the environmental effects of their products. By incorporating AI into the product design process, organizations may build offers that correspond with the rising need for sustainability while simultaneously decreasing their operating expenses.

The integration of AI into company sustainability initiatives is not without its obstacles, but the future possibilities are certainly exciting (Sanders et al, 2019). As AI technologies continue to improve, we can expect to see discoveries that enable organizations to run more sustainably across all facets of their operations. For instance, developments in deep learning and natural language processing could enable AI systems to evaluate unstructured data from sources like social media, customer feedback, and environmental sensors, giving businesses better insights into consumer preferences and environmental trends. These data may be utilized to influence sustainability initiatives, find new possibilities for innovation, and produce more sustainable goods and services. As AI becomes more available and inexpensive, small and medium-sized companies (SMEs) will have increased chances to employ sustainable business practices. The democratization of AI technology will empower organizations of all sizes to adopt AI-driven solutions to better their sustainability efforts. Open-source AI tools and cloud-based platforms are making it simpler for SMEs to access advanced AI technologies without the requirement for considerable upfront investment in hardware or specialist knowledge. This will help level the playing field and guarantee that the advantages of AI-driven sustainability are available to a larger variety of organizations.

Despite the immense promise, the use of AI in sustainable business practices will also demand careful evaluation of the ethical aspects (Nishant et al, 2020). As

AI systems become increasingly integrated into company processes, there will be increased worries regarding the social and ethical effects of these technologies. Businesses must ensure that AI is applied in a way that fosters justice, transparency, and accountability. Additionally, as AI plays a bigger part in sustainability initiatives, companies will need to address challenges relating to data privacy, security, and prejudice. Ensuring that AI is utilized properly and ethically will be crucial to preserving confidence with consumers, employees, and other stakeholders (Shneiderman, 2020). The prospects for AI technology in sustainable business practices are intriguing and full of possibilities. As AI continues to advance, it will empower organizations to maximize resources, eliminate waste, develop green technologies, and produce more sustainable goods and services. The incorporation of AI into sustainability initiatives will not only help organizations decrease their environmental impact but also stimulate innovation, increase efficiency, and enhance competitiveness in the marketplace. While difficulties exist, the emergence of AI technology presents an extraordinary potential for businesses to contribute to a more sustainable future while simultaneously reaping the fruits of innovation and advancement.

TOWARD INCLUSIVE, PRACTICAL, AND HIGH-IMPACT SUSTAINABLE AI: REFRAMING FOR EMERGING REALITIES

As we consider the transformative potential of artificial intelligence in promoting sustainable business practices, it becomes increasingly clear that a deeper, more inclusive, and strategically grounded perspective is essential. The current literature offers rich conceptual frameworks and visionary insights, but the reality on the ground—particularly in emerging economies, small to medium-sized enterprises (SMEs), and sector-specific applications—demands more than ideals. It calls for pragmatic tools, sharper clarity, and a broader canvas that includes the often-overlooked voices and challenges at the global periphery. This section aims to bridge these gaps by tightening the analytical focus, reducing thematic redundancy, and expanding the global relevance of the discussion.

One of the most pressing critiques of current discourse on AI and sustainability is the overrepresentation of narratives from developed economies (Robertson & Maccarone, 2023). While countries in the Global North undoubtedly play a central role in shaping AI development, many of the world's most urgent sustainability battles are being fought in the Global South—where infrastructure is often fragile, resources are scarce, and climate vulnerability is most acute. For example, in India, AI-powered irrigation systems have been piloted in rural areas to monitor soil health and reduce water consumption—a critical intervention in regions facing increasing drought. Similarly, in Kenya, smallholder farmers are using AI-based apps to predict crop disease and optimize yields, creating a tangible link between digital innovation and food security. These cases highlight how emerging economies are not passive recipients of technology but active experimenters—adapting AI under constraints that demand frugality, resilience, and inclusiveness. Yet these innovations rarely surface in mainstream sustainability discourse. To address this imbalance, academic literature must integrate more case-based evidence from diverse regions. Doing so will not only enhance inclusivity but also enrich the theoretical toolkit by exposing it to alternative models of innovation—ones that are improvisational, community-driven, and often more sustainable than their high-tech counterparts. For example, AI's role in Indonesia's smart fishing systems, which use satellite data to guide traditional fishermen, illustrates how technology can support informal economies while respecting indigenous knowledge systems. These are not just footnotes; they are central to building a truly global, sustainable AI framework.

Another underexplored frontier is the role of SMEs. Too often, sustainability and AI are discussed in the context of large multinational corporations with the capital and infrastructure to experiment, scale, and pivot. But SMEs constitute over 90% of businesses globally and are vital to employment and economic dynamism (Pulka & Gawuna, 2022). For these entities, the integration of AI into sustainability strategy is not merely about innovation—it's about survival. However, their pathways into AI adoption are riddled with roadblocks: lack of access to talent, limited capital, and an overwhelming array of vendor options with unclear value propositions. Practical support must go beyond policy rhetoric. Toolkits, open-source platforms, regional incubators, and low-cost AI-as-a-service models could lower the barrier to entry. Partnerships with universities and local governments could further facilitate knowledge transfer and trust. There is a critical need to provide clearer structuring within such discussions without fragmenting the narrative into artificial silos. Many texts repeat similar arguments—such as AI's power to reduce waste or optimize energy—without adding fresh insight. Instead of revisiting those claims, we can enhance the impact of this conversation by linking them to sector-specific case studies. In logistics, for instance, AI is optimizing delivery routes in densely populated cities like Lagos and Dhaka, cutting emissions while tackling urban chaos. In textiles, AI is enabling zero-waste pattern generation in Bangladesh's garment industry—a sector that often receives criticism for its environmental footprint but rarely gets recognition for innovation at the margins. These examples provide more than evidence; they serve as a mirror to rethink where progress is truly taking shape.

Ethical concerns must also be expanded with more precision. While bias and transparency are vital pillars, they are not the full story. One area requiring urgent development is the intersection of AI, gender, and labor ethics. Automated hiring systems have already shown tendencies to sideline women and non-binary individuals, particularly in STEM sectors (Zou, 2022). Additionally, in some regions,

AI systems used for performance monitoring have intensified labor surveillance—creating new forms of exploitation under the guise of efficiency. Responsible AI must include redress mechanisms, algorithmic literacy programs for workers, and democratic oversight boards that involve affected communities. It is time to move from abstract ethical principles to institutional mechanisms that protect the most vulnerable. Beyond critique, chapters like this must close the loop with actionable outcomes. Practical recommendations could include a modular AI-for-sustainability assessment tool tailored for SMEs; a set of policy guidelines for ethical AI procurement; and a checklist for evaluating gender and labor impacts during algorithm design. Equally important is the use of visual tools—flow diagrams, sectoral maps, and decision trees—that translate theory into navigable strategy. These are not just pedagogical enhancements; they are instruments of change that allow practitioners, not just academics, to act on the insights offered.

To maintain academic credibility and reflect contemporary dynamics, a refreshed and diversified reference base is needed (Musendekwa, 2025). This includes not only recent journal articles but also reports from the Global Partnership on AI, regional think tanks, and grassroots case repositories. Labor-focused research, particularly from interdisciplinary perspectives such as feminist economics, development studies, and environmental justice, would give the chapter a more balanced and globally grounded scholarly posture. Summarizing key insights clearly and concisely is not just a stylistic choice—it is a responsibility. At a time when decision-makers are inundated with white papers, briefings, and frameworks, what lingers are not the volume of pages but the clarity of takeaways. In this context, the integration of AI and sustainability is not a one-size-fits-all solution but a diverse, evolving ecosystem of approaches. A strong closing section should not merely recap but synthesize—distilling practical wisdom that readers can carry into their own contexts.

By incorporating these revisions—cutting duplication, amplifying underrepresented voices, offering implementable tools, and tightening narrative cohesion—this chapter can move from informative to indispensable. It can serve not only as a scholarly contribution but as a pragmatic guide for those working to align technology with the planet's most pressing needs.

CONCLUSION

In conclusion, the integration of artificial intelligence (AI) into business operations presents great potential to advance sustainability while simultaneously boosting efficiency, creativity, and competitiveness. As global concerns such as climate change, resource scarcity, and environmental degradation continue to grow, businesses across industries must re-evaluate their operations and strategy to fit with sustainability goals. AI, with its sophisticated analytical skills, prediction algorithms, and optimization approaches, provides a mechanism to attack these difficulties head-on, giving answers that were previously inconceivable. From eliminating waste in manufacturing processes to optimizing energy consumption in buildings, AI has shown to be a significant tool for attaining sustainable results, enabling companies to not only meet environmental norms but even surpass them in some circumstances.

AI's capacity to process huge volumes of data and generate meaningful insights has the potential to transform how organizations manage their resources, engage with consumers, and organize their operations. In areas such as agriculture, energy, transportation, and manufacturing, AI technologies are already playing a crucial role in advancing sustainability. In agriculture, AI-driven solutions assist optimize water consumption, anticipating crop yields, and minimizing the need for pesticides and fertilizers, supporting more sustainable agricultural methods. In the energy industry, AI allows smart grid systems that optimize the distribution of electricity, resulting in more efficient energy consumption and less carbon emissions. Similarly, AI in logistics and transportation helps cut fuel consumption and emissions through optimal routing and predictive maintenance, contributing to greener transportation solutions. Across all of these sectors, the importance of AI in helping organizations decrease their environmental effect is evident. While AI brings enormous prospects for boosting sustainability, it also creates issues that must be addressed. The initial investment necessary for integrating AI technology can be large, and small organizations in particular may find it difficult to get the resources needed to incorporate AI into their operations. Data management is another difficulty, as AI relies largely on vast amounts of accurate, high-quality data. Without effective data governance and infrastructure, AI systems may not produce the anticipated outputs, and organizations may risk making decisions based on erroneous or insufficient information. Furthermore, the fast evolution of AI technology provides a challenge in terms of staying ahead of the curve and ensuring that organizations can exploit the latest advancements successfully.

Another major aspect is the ethical consequences of AI. As businesses utilize AI to optimize their operations and increase sustainability, it is crucial to guarantee that the deployment of AI systems is transparent, fair, and aligned with larger social and environmental ideals. AI-driven solutions must be designed and deployed with consideration to challenges such as data privacy, algorithmic fairness, and the potential for bias in decision-making processes. Additionally, the rising use of automation in numerous areas raises worries about job displacement and the need for workers to adapt to new roles in an AI-driven economy. Ensuring that AI technologies are implemented in a way that benefits society as a whole requires enterprises to adopt a proactive approach to ethical issues, from the design phase through to implementation. The future potential of AI in sustainable business practices is both exciting and uncertain. As AI technologies continue to grow, new applications and opportunities will emerge that might further change the corporate environment. The combination of AI with other cutting-edge technologies, such as blockchain, IoT, and quantum computing, might lead to new advances in resource efficiency and environmental management. For instance, the coupling of AI with blockchain might establish transparent and verifiable supply chains, enabling companies to track the environmental effect of their products from raw material procurement through to customer delivery. Similarly, AI-powered systems, in combination with IoT sensors, may enable real-time monitoring of environmental conditions, enabling businesses to alter their operations instantaneously and effectively in reaction to changes in resource availability or demand.

To fully exploit the promise of AI in sustainable business operations, there has to be a coordinated effort to overcome the hurdles and constraints that now limit mainstream use. Collaboration among corporations, governments, researchers, and other stakeholders will be vital to ensuring that AI technologies are developed and applied in ways that are both successful and ethical. Governments have a crucial role to play in setting rules and regulations that assist the development of sustainable AI solutions while also safeguarding the interests of workers and society. Businesses, for their part, must continue to invest in AI research and development, ensuring that they are not merely embracing the latest technology but also applying it in ways that promote long-term, good change. The integration of AI into corporate processes must be examined through a holistic lens, one that examines not only environmental and economic concerns but also social and ethical consequences. AI should not be considered as a solution for all sustainability concerns, but rather as a tool that, when used appropriately, may help organizations make better-informed decisions, lower their environmental impact, and stimulate innovation. Sustainability is not merely a commercial fad; it is a need for the survival of both the earth and future generations. AI, as a transformational technology, may contribute considerably to this cause, but it must be employed in a way that is conscious of the greater social consequences.

As corporations continue to wrestle with the difficulties of sustainability, AI will surely play an increasingly significant role in determining the future of corporate responsibility. The road toward a more sustainable and fair society demands teamwork, creativity, and a commitment to continual improvement. AI is not an end in itself but rather a means to an end—a technology that, when used successfully, can help organizations accomplish their sustainability targets and create value for all stakeholders. As we look to the future, the potential for AI to promote sustainable business practices is great, but it will need careful planning, intelligent decision-making, and a commitment to responsible innovation. The integration of AI with sustainability principles is not only about making corporate operations more effective; it is about building a future in which both people and the earth flourish. The convergence of

AI and sustainability brings both important potential and concerns. By embracing AI technology, organizations may make steps toward lowering their environmental footprint, maximizing resources, and building a more sustainable future. However, companies must overcome the difficulties of AI deployment, resolve ethical issues, and overcome hurdles to acceptance. The future of sustainable business practices will surely be affected by the continued development of AI technology, but this evolution must be treated with care, accountability, and a commitment to social and environmental equality. Through deliberate cooperation and strategic planning, AI may become a strong driver for good change in the corporate sector, pushing development toward a more sustainable, fair, and affluent future.

REFERENCES

Ali, D. M. T. E., Motuzienė, V., & Džiugaitė-Tumėnienė, R. (2024). Ai-driven innovations in building energy management systems: A review of potential applications and energy savings. *Energies*, *17*(17), 4277.

Bag, S., & Pretorius, J. H. C. (2022). Relationships between industry 4.0, sustainable manufacturing and circular economy: Proposal of a research framework. *The International Journal of Organizational Analysis*, *30*(4), 864–898.

Canhoto, A. I., & Clear, F. (2020). Artificial intelligence and machine learning as business tools: A framework for diagnosing value destruction potential. *Business Horizons*, *63*(2), 183–193.

Costa, A. (2024). *Navigating the twin transition: digital transformation and sustainability in low-tech industries: a small and medium-sized companies' perspective*. Academic Press.

Cubric, M. (2020). Drivers, barriers and social considerations for AI adoption in business and management: A tertiary study. *Technology in Society*, *62*, 101257.

Dauvergne, P. (2020). *AI in the Wild: Sustainability in the Age of Artificial Intelligence*. MIT Press.

De Marcellis-Warin, N., Marty, F., Thelisson, E., & Warin, T. (2022). Artificial intelligence and consumer manipulations: From consumer's counter algorithms to firm's self-regulation tools. *AI and Ethics*, *2*(2), 259–268.

Demirel, P., & Kesidou, E. (2019). Sustainability-oriented capabilities for eco-innovation: Meeting the regulatory, technology, and market demands. *Business Strategy and the Environment*, *28*(5), 847–857.

Díaz-Rodríguez, N., Del Ser, J., Coeckelbergh, M., de Prado, M. L., Herrera-Viedma, E., & Herrera, F. (2023). Connecting the dots in trustworthy Artificial Intelligence: From AI principles, ethics, and key requirements to responsible AI systems and regulation. *Information Fusion*, *99*, 101896.

Dmuchowski, P., Dmuchowski, W., Baczewska-Dąbrowska, A. H., & Gworek, B. (2023). Environmental, social, and governance (ESG) model; impacts and sustainable investment–Global trends and Poland's perspective. *Journal of Environmental Management*, *329*, 117023. PMID: 36571952

Dwivedi, Y. K., Hughes, L., Kar, A. K., Baabdullah, A. M., Grover, P., Abbas, R., & Wade, M. (2022). Climate change and COP26: Are digital technologies and information management part of the problem or the solution? An editorial reflection and call to action. *International Journal of Information Management*, *63*, 102456.

Farghali, M., Osman, A. I., Mohamed, I. M., Chen, Z., Chen, L., Ihara, I., & Rooney, D. W. (2023). Strategies to save energy in the context of the energy crisis: A review. *Environmental Chemistry Letters*, *21*(4), 2003–2039. PMID: 37362011

Ghoreishi, M., & Happonen, A. (2020, May). Key enablers for deploying artificial intelligence for circular economy embracing sustainable product design: Three case studies. In *AIP conference proceedings* (Vol. 2233, No. 1). AIP Publishing.

Goralski, M. A., & Tan, T. K. (2020). Artificial intelligence and sustainable development. *International Journal of Management Education*, *18*(1), 100330.

Hagerty, A., & Rubinov, I. (2019). Global AI ethics: a review of the social impacts and ethical implications of artificial intelligence. arXiv preprint arXiv:1907.07892.

Hannan, M. A., Begum, R. A., Al-Shetwi, A. Q., Ker, P. J., Al Mamun, M. A., Hussain, A., & Mahlia, T. M. I. (2020). Waste collection route optimisation model for linking cost saving and emission reduction to achieve sustainable development goals. *Sustainable Cities and Society*, *62*, 102393.

Hariram, N. P., Mekha, K. B., Suganthan, V., & Sudhakar, K. (2023). Sustainalism: An integrated socio-economic-environmental model to address sustainable development and sustainability. *Sustainability*, *15*(13), 10682.

Johnson, P. C., Laurell, C., Ots, M., & Sandström, C. (2022). Digital innovation and the effects of artificial intelligence on firms' research and development–Automation or augmentation, exploration or exploitation? *Technological Forecasting and Social Change*, *179*, 121636.

Jose, R., Panigrahi, S. K., Patil, R. A., Fernando, Y., & Ramakrishna, S. (2020). Artificial intelligence-driven circular economy as a key enabler for sustainable energy management. *Materials Circular Economy*, *2*, 1–7.

Journeault, M., Perron, A., & Vallières, L. (2021). The collaborative roles of stakeholders in supporting the adoption of sustainability in SMEs. *Journal of Environmental Management*, *287*, 112349. PMID: 33735683

Julmi, C. (2019). When rational decision-making becomes irrational: A critical assessment and re-conceptualization of intuition effectiveness. *Business Research*, *12*(1), 291–314.

Kokotović, F., Kurečić, P., & Mjeda, T. (2019). Accomplishing the sustainable development goal 13–climate action and the role of the European Union. *Interdisciplinary Description of Complex Systems: INDECS, 17*(1-B), 132–145.

Lee, J., Suh, T., Roy, D., & Baucus, M. (2019). Emerging technology and business model innovation: The case of artificial intelligence. *Journal of Open Innovation, 5*(3), 44.

Martos, V., Ahmad, A., Cartujo, P., & Ordoñez, J. (2021). Ensuring agricultural sustainability through remote sensing in the era of agriculture 5.0. *Applied Sciences (Basel, Switzerland), 11*(13), 5911.

Montgomery, R. M. (2024). The Rise of Inequality and Artificial Intelligence: Impacts, Challenges, and Opportunities in a Globalized Economy. *Challenges, and Opportunities in a Globalized Economy.*

Montiel, I., Cuervo-Cazurra, A., Park, J., Antolín-López, R., & Husted, B. W. (2021). Implementing the United Nations' sustainable development goals in international business. *Journal of International Business Studies, 52*(5), 999. PMID: 34054154

Musendekwa, M. (2025). Unveiling the Foundations of Quality Research in Higher Education: A Contemporary Perspective. In *Higher Education and Quality Assurance Practices* (pp. 421-454). IGI Global Scientific Publishing.

Nishant, R., Kennedy, M., & Corbett, J. (2020). Artificial intelligence for sustainability: Challenges, opportunities, and a research agenda. *International Journal of Information Management, 53*, 102104.

Olimjonovich, D. B. (2024). The subscription economy: Transforming business models. Web of Discoveries. *Journal of Analysis and Inventions, 2*(3), 71–76.

Onukwulu, E. C., Agho, M. O., & Eyo-Udo, N. L. (2023). Sustainable supply chain practices to reduce carbon footprint in oil and gas. *Global Journal of Research in Multidisciplinary Studies, 1*(2), 24–43.

Pulka, B. M., & Gawuna, M. S. (2022). Contributions of SMEs to employment, gross domestic product, economic growth and development. *Jalingo Journal of Social and Management Sciences, 4*(1), 1–18.

Qiu, L., Hu, D., & Wang, Y. (2020). How do firms achieve sustainability through green innovation under external pressures of environmental regulation and market turbulence? *Business Strategy and the Environment, 29*(6), 2695–2714.

Rane, N. (2023). Enhancing customer loyalty through Artificial Intelligence (AI), Internet of Things (IoT), and Big Data technologies: improving customer satisfaction, engagement, relationship, and experience. *Internet of Things (IoT), and Big Data Technologies: Improving Customer Satisfaction, Engagement, Relationship, and Experience.*

Rashid, C. A. (2021). The efficiency of financial ratios analysis to evaluate company's profitability. *Journal of Global Economics and Business, 2*(4), 119–132.

Robertson, A., & Maccarone, M. (2023). AI narratives and unequal conditions. Analyzing the discourse of liminal expert voices in discursive communicative spaces. *Telecommunications Policy, 47*(5), 102462.

Sanders, N. R., Boone, T., Ganeshan, R., & Wood, J. D. (2019). Sustainable supply chains in the age of AI and digitization: Research challenges and opportunities. *Journal of Business Logistics, 40*(3), 229–240.

Shahid, A., & Mushtaq, M. (2020, November). A survey comparing specialized hardware and evolution in TPUs for neural networks. In *2020 IEEE 23rd International Multitopic Conference (INMIC)* (pp. 1-6). IEEE.

Shechy, B., & Farneti, F. (2021). Corporate social responsibility, sustainability, sustainable development and corporate sustainability: What is the difference, and does it matter? *Sustainability, 13*(11), 5965.

Shneiderman, B. (2020). Bridging the gap between ethics and practice: Guidelines for reliable, safe, and trustworthy human-centered AI systems. *ACM Transactions on Interactive Intelligent Systems, 10*(4), 1–31.

Thiele, L. P. (2024). *Sustainability*. John Wiley & Sons.

Tschang, F. T., & Almirall, E. (2021). Artificial intelligence as augmenting automation: Implications for employment. *The Academy of Management Perspectives, 35*(4), 642–659.

Ukoba, K., Olatunji, K. O., Adeoye, E., Jen, T. C., & Madyira, D. M. (2024). Optimizing renewable energy systems through artificial intelligence: Review and future prospects. *Energy & Environment, 35*(7), 3833–3879.

Uralovich, K. S., Toshmamatovich, T. U., Kubayevich, K. F., Sapaev, I. B., Saylaubaevna, S. S., Beknazarova, Z. F., & Khurramov, A. (2023). A primary factor in sustainable development and environmental sustainability is environmental education. *Caspian Journal of Environmental Sciences, 21*(4), 965–975.

Van Wynsberghe, A. (2021). Sustainable AI: AI for sustainability and the sustainability of AI. *AI and Ethics*, *1*(3), 213–218.

Vermesan, O., John, R., Pype, P., Daalderop, G., Kriegel, K., Mitic, G., & Waldhör, S. (2021). Automotive intelligence embedded in electric connected autonomous and shared vehicles technology for sustainable green mobility. *Frontiers in Future Transportation*, *2*, 688482.

Wamba-Taguimdje, S. L., Wamba, S. F., Kamdjoug, J. R. K., & Wanko, C. E. T. (2020). Influence of artificial intelligence (AI) on firm performance: The business value of AI-based transformation projects. *Business Process Management Journal*, *26*(7), 1893–1924.

Yarimoglu, E., & Binboga, G. (2019). Understanding sustainable consumption in an emerging country: The antecedents and consequences of the ecologically conscious consumer behavior model. *Business Strategy and the Environment*, *28*(4), 642–651.

Yigitcanlar, T., & Cugurullo, F. (2020). The sustainability of artificial intelligence: An urbanistic viewpoint from the lens of smart and sustainable cities. *Sustainability*, *12*(20), 8548.

Zajko, M. (2021). Conservative AI and social inequality: Conceptualizing alternatives to bias through social theory. *AI & Society*, *36*(3), 1047–1056.

Zou, X. (2022). *Perspectives and experiences of gender inclusion for STEM programs through an intersectional lens* (Doctoral dissertation, University of Oxford).

KEY TERMS AND DEFINITIONS

Artificial Intelligence (AI): The simulation of human intelligence in machines, allowing them to learn, analyze data, and make decisions to optimize processes and improve efficiency.

Carbon Footprint Reduction: The use of AI-driven technologies to monitor, measure, and minimize greenhouse gas emissions in business operations.

Circular Economy: A system that minimizes waste by designing products for reuse, recycling, and regeneration, ensuring resources are used efficiently and sustainably.

Ethical AI: The responsible development and application of artificial intelligence, ensuring transparency, fairness, and the avoidance of bias or harm to society.

Green AI: The development and deployment of AI models that prioritize energy efficiency and sustainability to reduce the environmental impact of artificial intelligence systems.

Resource Optimization: The strategic use of AI and data analytics to maximize efficiency in energy, water, and material consumption while reducing waste.

Smart Grids: AI-enhanced energy distribution networks that optimize electricity supply and demand in real-time, reducing waste and integrating renewable energy sources.

Sustainability: The practice of meeting present needs without compromising the ability of future generations to meet theirs, often focusing on environmental, social, and economic responsibility.

Chapter 2
Impact of AI on Sustainable Value Creation in Business

Niaz Mohammad
https://orcid.org/0000-0001-9233-2800
American International University, Dhaka, Bangladesh

ABSTRACT

Artificial intelligence has emerged as a technological innovation that transforms the way businesses operate. In recent years, the use of AI in the financial sector has been growing and they can solve complex problems and are emerging fast in the business ecosystem. The objective of this chapter is to understand the impact of AI on customers' experience and how AI helps to create sustainable value creation in the financial sectors. It also examines how AI affects business, highlighting both the potential and difficulties it poses in banking sectors of Bangladesh. A thorough literature review, survey and case study analysis, and published annual reports from 2020 to 2023 are taken into consideration. According to the study's findings, artificial intelligence (AI) has the potential to significantly improve business operations, including decision-making, cost reductions, and productivity.

INTRODUCTION

Our economy, society, and culture urgently need to shift to practices and policies that support ecological sustainability. Such a dramatic change necessitates an equally drastic shift in how resources are used, and decisions are made. Artificial intelligence has emerged as a transformative weapon in the global economy and the cornerstone of the fourth industrial revolution. The impact of AI on sustainable value

DOI: 10.4018/979-8-3373-1107-4.ch002

creation in Bangladesh is significant and offering opportunities for economic growth, environmental sustainability and social development especially in the finance and banking sectors. This chapter explores how customers recognize and banks utilized artificial intelligence devices in the realm of sustainable value creation. Bangladesh is actively incorporating Artificial Intelligence (AI) into its digitization efforts, which began a decade ago with the adoption of future technologies like cybersecurity, data science, big data, blockchain and cloud computing. Data were collected from the annual reports of twenty banks listed in DSE in Bangladesh, determined through convenience sampling. Findings of the study suggest that customers were willing to get online services for account opening, making payment through online banking and focused on real time transactions through e-banking. The study emphasizes the importance of acquiring comprehensive knowledge about AI technologies and their potential value generation processes. It will also provide a better understanding of how AI can transform sustainable business practices and thus global operations.

RATIONALE OF THIS STUDY

In order to sustain stability and confidence, the financial sector must manage risks and maintain compliance in a complicated and constantly changing regulatory environment. Conventional approaches to risk management and compliance frequently depend on rule-based systems and manual procedures, which are not only laborious but also prone to inefficiencies and human mistakes (Arner, Zetzsche, & Buckley, 2019). These traditional methods find it difficult to keep up with the quick changes in financial services and products as well as the growing number and complexity of regulatory regulations. As a result, financial institutions have a difficult time continuously fulfilling compliance requirements and successfully reducing risks (FSB, 2020). In addition to raising operating expenses, this fragmented strategy makes it more difficult to obtain an organization-wide perspective of compliance. Additionally, the enormous volumes of data produced by contemporary financial operations cannot be handled by manual procedures, which leads to insufficient risk assessment and delayed identification of compliance violations (Veale & Edwards, 2018).

LITERATURE REVIEW

According to Smith and Gupta (2022) the banking sector is crucial to the quickly changing modern economic environment because it acts as a stimulant for financial transactions, investment, and economic expansion. However, this industry is not the only one facing difficulties and market shifts. According to Jones (2020), financial organizations have faced both possibilities and challenges as a result of the enormous developments brought about by the development of artificial intelligence. Extant literature provides evidence that AI has a positive impact on the financial industry. Goodell et al. (2021) use co-citation and bibliometric-coupling analyses to identify differnt groups of research in finance related to AI and Machine Learning, which are (1) portfolio construction, valuation, and investor behavior (Braun et al., 2023; Boehmer et al., 2007); (2) financial fraud and distress (West and Bhattacharya, 2016; Liang et al., 2015).

By automating repetitive jobs, streamlining processes, and generating insights through data analysis, artificial intelligence (AI) holds promise for greatly enhancing enterprises in Bangladesh (Babu, 2021a,2021b). AI, for instance, can be used to increase productivity in the manufacturing industry by forecasting maintenance requirements, detecting flaws, and managing and monitoring production processes. Additionally, chatbots with AI capabilities can be utilized to assist customers, and AI-based systems can be employed in the retail sector to forecast client demand and optimize inventory management. AI can be applied in the banking sector to assess credit risks and identify fraud (Komal Singh, Hasan, & Rajendran, 2023). Furthermore, by evaluating medical images, identifying illnesses, and forecasting patient outcomes, AI can be utilized to enhance healthcare in Bangladesh (Uzir, Al Halbusi, Jerin, Hamid, Ramayah, & Haque, 2021). In finance, in particular AI has the potential to cut costs significantly and to reduce the large processing times in the industry.

For the effective implementation of AI, several specific sectors have been identified here where we see extensive use of AI technologies. For implementing AI technology, Bangladesh government should have to undertake huge preparation. The main technological innovation in financial transactions is electronic banking. Commercial banks are divided into two groups by Bangladesh Bank: Data centers (DCs) are used to administer centralized ICT activities in Category 1, while branch offices or DCs host dispersed ICT operations in Category 2. Critical connectivity and service continuity are given top priority in both categories. By utilizing technology, NLP Bot-driven RSD bridges the gap between technology and education while saving money and time. AI-powered credit management improves the economy, lowers fraud, and increases loan availability. Robotic Process Automation (RPA) removes redundancy in trade and e-government, while centralized KYC automation enhances service quality. Additionally, G2B single point service delivery is being streamlined by AI-driven solutions, increasing efficacy and efficiency.

AI-driven automation has significantly increased operational process efficiency by automating routine tasks like data entry and document processing. As a result, operating costs have been reduced by an average of 30% across all of the evaluated institutions, and human errors have been reduced. Chatbots and AI-powered virtual assistants have completely changed consumer interactions. Real-time customer service is provided by chatbots, and personalized product recommendations produced by AI algorithms have increased cross-selling and upselling by 25%. (Svoboda, 2023)

In order to improve customer service, the client only needs to visit the website; the pre-programmed chatbot will begin to gather the necessary information. Following the collection of primary data from customers, the chatbot begins to inquire about the issues in order to determine whether they satisfy the edibility requirements and whether to keep communicating or to cease. The Chatbot will proceed and direct the customer in accordance with the written instructions if the problem statement is covered by the Chatbot algorithm. However, in another instance, the chatbot will direct the client to physically visit the local branch in order to resolve the issue.

The maturity of generative AI (GenAI) use cases is still developing, despite the fact that many wealth and asset management companies have already integrated AI into their fundamental business processes. Financial institutions must proceed with an integrated enterprise-wide approach if they are to deploy GenAI at scale, even though some use cases have shown early indications of potential.

This chapter emphasizes the necessity of taking a balanced approach to utilizing AI's potential in banking, taking into account both the ethical and legal issues as well as the revolutionary advantages of the technology. By doing this, banks may use AI to improve their operations while maintaining regulatory compliance, fairness, and openness.

IMPACT OF BANKING AND AI

The incorporation of this technology into the banking sector has enhanced operational procedures in relation to customer satisfaction, virtual assistance, and risk reduction. This generative AI is employed to streamline activities and improve how decisions are made in this sector. Because of its inherent versatility, artificial intelligence—particularly generative AI—can be used in a number of contexts within the finance sector. They can be utilized to improve client satisfaction, raise the caliber of services offered in the sector, and more effectively streamline the supply of said services (McKinsey Digital 2023). To put it another way, AI might improve the financial industry's front, middle, and back offices. AI can be used in the front office to improve client profiles and user interfaces. AI can readily identify payment fraud in the middle office, offer guidance on loan selection, and help with credit rating. AI streamlines backend processes in the back office and offers insights into company and strategy. Different applications of AI such as machine learning, automation and robotics, and machine visions have the capability of collecting, analyzing, and storing digital data of customers (Ghoreishi et al., 2023). Also, banks are using AI-based solutions for regulatory compliance and reporting purposes. Although the use of AI is not sufficiently high in the banking sector of Bangladesh, there is huge scope of using AI-based solutions. The following tables shows the functional areas where banks can use AI.

Table 1. Functional areas of using AI in banks

Name of functional areas	Name of products
Business operation	NID and Face Verification for A/C Opening, Cloud Vision API from Google
ADCs Operations/Services	ADC Apps, ATM Switching Software
AML and CFT issues	Transaction monitoring software
Financial risk analysis	Risk analysis
Cyber/IT risk analysis	SIEM, Check Point Next Generation Firewall, Securex
Cyber Fraud Detection and Prevention	McAfee – FIM (file integrity Monitoring), NGFW, IBM Qradar SIEM, Securex
Regulatory Compliance/Reporting	Selenium, goAML and CIB, Transaction Monitoring Software

BENEFITS OF USING AI IN BANKING

It improves customer experience and interaction in consumer banking, streamline research and financial modeling in investment banking, and improves business lending and risk management in corporate and SME banking. GenAI is transforming trading, risk management, and compliance in the financial markets.

AI now allows banks to tackle challenges of scale in a way banks have not been able to achieve without adding staff. If a particular function in a bank could be done better or faster by adding one hundred extra trained staff, it's likely that AI can be transformative for that function. AI offers vast additional operational capacity, at low marginal cost compared to hiring the equivalent processing capacity as staff. Artificial intelligence is used to spare time that would take a human to process information that is high in volume and it provides results that are lower in cost and more accurate (Ris et al, 2020)

More than that, though, the game that players are playing will probably change. AI is about to undergo a paradigm change. Our experience with banks worldwide reveals that top innovators are already moving from using AI as a "instrument of strategy," which speeds up the delivery of today's business plan, to using it as a "determinant of strategy," where future business is planned around new AI capabilities.

Automation driven by AI can expedite procedures like fraud detection, loan processing, and customer support. According to EY (2023), artificial intelligence (AI) has the potential to revolutionize wealth management by democratizing services, improving operational effectiveness, and offering deeper insights into customer behavior—all of which could save banks millions of dollars in operating expenses.

AI algorithms can analyze vast amounts of data to identify patterns and assess creditworthiness more accurately. This can lead to fewer loan defaults, reduced risk provisions, and improved profit margins.

Financial products and services can be tailored for specific clients using AI-powered technologies, increasing client loyalty and satisfaction. AI can also optimize marketing campaigns and find new company prospects, which could increase revenue streams. Bank of America, for example, uses AI to suggest customized investment plans, which might boost client interaction and product uptake.

These developments mark a new frontier where AI converges with fundamental financial functions, launching the industry into a period of never-before-seen efficiency and creativity.

USE OF AI IN BANKING SECTORS OF BANGLADESH

Investments into digital technologies and businesses have risen and are rewarded by the public markets (PWC Editorial, 2016). AI is one of the parts of this development, and the banking sector is hereby deemed to see a major impact (Accenture, 2016). The following table shows how banks introduced AI and automation in their products and services:

Table 2. Implication of AI in banks

Name of functional areas	Name of AI products
Central Bank Reporting: Monthly return	Selenium
Top Management Report Generation for the quick and right decision making	Selenium
Business Operation	CellFin
Vault Security	Intruder Alert System
e-Govt. Procurement (e-GP)	Selenium
DC Environment Monitoring System (EMS)	EMS (Auto Notification for DC environment control)

continued on following page

Table 2. Continued

Name of functional areas	Name of AI products
Cash Counting	Cash Counting Machine with AI Intelligence
Data Center Humidity Control	Precision Air Cooler
Data Center Tape Library Management System of Storage	IBM Tivoli Storage Manager
A/C Verification	Artificially Intelligent Workforce (AIW) (FernTech Solution Ltd.)
NID Verification	
e-KYC	ERA eKYC

Implementing AI technology presents numerous obstacles for banks. The largest obstacles are the high cost of AI solutions and the dearth of affordable, locally available AI solutions of putting latest technologies into practice in banks. However, most of the banks and financial institutions pointed out that inadequate funding and a shortage of skilled workers also make it difficult for banks to implement AI. Other difficulties include human behavior, a secure cloud computing platform, dependable high-speed network channels, and a lack of local support and changes in regulations.

CONCLUSION

The rapid integration of Artificial Intelligence (AI) in the banking sector is modernizing operations, with significant implications for risk management and fraud detection. Banks generate a lot of paperwork and profit, two things that artificial intelligence promises to help with. Rapid technological advancements should assist in increasing the first and decrease the second. However, despite being such a powerful and seemingly ubiquitous force for financial services, there is currently little concrete evidence that investors believe in the industry's potential for value growth. But in addition to these technological developments, artificial intelligence (AI) presents significant obstacles that need to be overcome before utilizing the technology. The possible abuse of AI has been sparked by worries about data privacy, algorithmic bias, accountability, dependability, fairness, and confidential banking information. AI is a two-edged sword that can cut through the banking industry's mundane activities and excessive volumes of data, but businesses must exercise caution to avoid hurting themselves with this new advancement in artificial, or rather human, inventiveness. Government and Bangladesh Bank should encourage and give preference to local software companies to be able to build robust and cost-effective AI based solutions for the banks and financial institutions in Bangladesh.

REFERENCES

Accenture. (2016). The Promise of Artificial Intelligence: Redefining Management in the Workforce of the Future. https://www.accenture.com/us-en/insight-promise-artificial-intelligence

Arner, D. W., Zetzsche, D. A., & Buckley, R. P. (2019). The Identity Challenge in Finance: From Analogue Identity to Digitized Identification to Digital KYC Utilities. *European Business Organization Law Review*, *20*, 55–80. DOI: 10.1007/s40804-019-00135-1

Babu, K. E. K. (2021a). Artificial intelligence in Bangladesh, its applications in different sectors and relevant challenges for the government: An analysis. *International Journal of Public Law and Policy*, *7*(4), 319–333.

Babu, K. E. K. (2021b). Artificial intelligence, its applications in different sectors and challenges: Bangladesh context. In *Artificial intelligence in cyber security: Impact and implications: Security challenges, technical and ethical issues, forensic investigative challenges* (pp. 103–119).

Boehmer, E., Grammig, J., & Theissen, E. (2007). Estimating the probability of informed trading—Does trade misclassification matter? *Journal of Financial Markets*, *10*(1), 26–47.

Braun, D., Han, Y., & Wang, H. E. (2023). The application of feed forward neural networks to merger arbitrage: A return-based analysis. *Finance Research Letters*, *58*, 104391.

Editorial, P. W. C. (2016). https://www.pwc.com/gx/en/industries/industries-4.0/landing-page/industry-4.0-building-your-digital-enterprise-april-2016.pdf

Ghoreishi, M., Treves, L., Teplov, R., & Pynnönen, M. (2023). The Impact of Artificial Intelligence on Circular Value Creation for Sustainable Development Goals. In Mazzi, F., & Floridi, L. (Eds.), *The Ethics of Artificial Intelligence for the Sustainable Development Goals. Philosophical Studies Series* (Vol. 152). Springer.

Goodell, J. W., Kumar, S., Lim, W. M., & Pattanaik, D. (2023). Artificial intelligence and machine learning in finance: Identifying foundations, themes, and research clusters from bibliometric analysis. *Journal of Behavioral and Experimental Finance*, *32*, 100577.

Jones, R. (2020). The role of Artificial Intelligence in regulatory compliance. *Journal of Compliance and Regulation, 12*(2), 87-104.

Komal Singh, K., Hasan, M., & Rajendran, R. P. (2023). Opportunities and challenges of AI/ML in finance. In Irfan, M., Elmogy, M., Majid, M. S. A., & El-Sappagh, S. (Eds.), *The impact of AI innovation on financial sectors in the era of industry 5.0* (pp. 238–260). IGI Global. DOI: 10.4018/979-8-3693-0082-4.ch014

Liang, D., Tsai, C. F., & Wu, H. T. (2015). The effect of feature selection on financial distress prediction. *Knowledge-Based Systems*, *73*, 289–297.

McKinsey Technology Council and McKinsey Digital. (2023). What Every CEO Should Know about Generative AI. https://www.mckinsey.com/capabilities/mckinsey-digital/ourinsights/what-every-ceo-should-know-about-generative-ai

Ris, K., Stankovic, Z., & Avramovic, Z. (2020). Implications of Implementation of Artificial Intelligence in the Banking Business with Correlation to the Human Factor. *Journal of Computer and Communications*, *8*, 130–144.

Smith, A. & Gupta, A. (2022). Adapting to regulatory changes with AI: Strategies for financial institutions. *Regulatory Compliance Journal, 28*(1), 22-39.

Svoboda, A. (2023). The impact of artificial intelligence on the banking industry. *Journal of Banking and Finance Management*, *4*(1), 7–13.

Uzir, M. U. H., Al Halbusi, H., Lim, R., Jerin, I., Abdul Hamid, A. B., Ramayah, T., & Haque, A. (2021). Applied Artificial Intelligence and user satisfaction: Smartwatch usage for healthcare in Bangladesh during COVID-19. *Technology in Society*, *67*, 101780. PMID: 34697510

Veale, M., Binns, R., & Edwards, L. (2018). Algorithms that remember: Model inversion attacks and Data Protection Law. *Philosophical Transactions. Series A, Mathematical, Physical, and Engineering Sciences*, *376*(2133), 20180083. DOI: 10.1098/rsta.2018.0083 PMID: 30322998

West, J., & Bhattacharya, M. (2016). Intelligent financial fraud detection: A comprehensive review. *Computers & Security*, *57*, 47–66.

APPENDIX

Table 3. List of banks

Sl	Name of banks
1	AB Bank PLC
2	Bank Asia PLC
3	Dutch Bangla Bank PLC
4	Agrani Bank PLC
5	IFIC Bank PLC
6	Islami Bank Bangladesh PLC
7	EXIM Bank PLC
8	Mercantile Bank PLC
9	BRAC Bank PLC
10	NCC Bank PLC
11	One Bank PLC
12	Pubali Bank PLC
13	Rupali Bank PLC
14	Sonali Bank PLC
15	Shahajalal Islami Bank PLC
16	Prime Bank PLC
17	Eastern Bank PLC
18	Standard Bank PLC
19	Trust Bank PLC
20	United Commercial Bank PLC

Chapter 3
Integrating AI into Corporate Social Responsibility (CSR) for Ethical and Sustainable Business Practices

Shayak Hussain
https://orcid.org/0009-0005-0798-5994
Christ University, Ghaziabad, India

ABSTRACT

The rapid advancement of artificial intelligence (AI) technologies has significantly transformed various facets of business operations, including corporate social responsibility (CSR). As businesses strive to align their growth strategies with ethical, social, and environmental responsibilities, AI emerges as a powerful tool to enhance the effectiveness of CSR initiatives. This research investigates the integration of AI into CSR, exploring its potential to drive more sustainable business practices, improve transparency, and foster ethical decision-making within organizations. By employing a combination of qualitative and quantitative research methods, this study examines how AI-powered analytics, automation, and decision-making frameworks can optimize CSR efforts. Key areas of exploration include AI's role in enhancing supply chain sustainability, optimizing resource allocation, detecting unethical business practices, and enabling real-time monitoring and reporting of CSR initiatives.

DOI: 10.4018/979-8-3373-1107-4.ch003

1. INTRODUCTION

Corporate Social Responsibility (CSR) has evolved from a voluntary business initiative to a fundamental business strategy (Carroll, 1991). Initially, CSR was largely philanthropic, with corporations engaging in charitable donations and community service. However, as environmental, social, and governance (ESG) concerns gained traction, CSR became an integrated component of business operations (Elkington, 1997).

With the rise of Artificial Intelligence (AI), businesses are transforming their CSR initiatives through automated sustainability reporting, ethical AI frameworks, and AI-driven stakeholder engagement (Renieris, Kiron, & Mills, 2022). Companies like Tesla, IBM, and Unilever have leveraged AI to optimize energy efficiency, monitor ethical supply chains, and drive sustainable product innovations (World Economic Forum, 2023).

1.1 Background of CSR in Business

Corporate Social Responsibility (CSR) has transformed into a crucial element of business strategy, shifting from a discretionary effort to a core requirement for companies globally. Historically, companies prioritized profit maximization, with minimal responsibility for their social and environmental consequences. In recent decades, however, stakeholders—such as employees, consumers, investors, and regulators—have progressively sought increased corporate responsibility. Consequently, CSR has evolved from a marginal issue to an essential business activity, with companies actively engaging in social welfare, environmental sustainability, and ethical governance.

CSR includes various activities such as environmental sustainability initiatives, ethical workforce practices, community involvement, philanthropy, and accountable supply chain management. Businesses that successfully implement CSR not only meet legal and ethical requirements but also improve their brand image, build customer loyalty, and achieve a competitive edge. Moreover, governments and international bodies have implemented numerous regulations and guidelines to guarantee that businesses align their activities with wider societal objectives. In the digital age, technology is essential in influencing CSR strategies. Businesses are progressively utilizing digital tools, from blockchain for transparency in supply chains to big data analytics for measuring impact, to improve their CSR initiatives. Among these technologies, Artificial Intelligence (AI) has surfaced as a notably impactful force, providing fresh opportunities for automation, predictive analysis, and decision-making that can promote sustainable and ethical business practices.

1.2 Evolution of AI in Business Practices

AI has shifted from a specialized field of theoretical study to a widespread business instrument that transforms processes across various sectors. At first, AI was limited to universities and research laboratories, concentrating on theoretical approaches to machine learning and neural networks. Nonetheless, due to progress in computing power, data accessibility, and algorithm enhancements, AI has emerged as a viable option for companies aiming to boost efficiency, creativity, and decision-making.

AI applications currently cover multiple areas, such as customer relationship management, supply chain enhancement, fraud detection, predictive analysis, and automation of processes. Companies utilize AI-powered chatbots for customer support, machine learning techniques for demand prediction, and natural language processing (NLP) for emotion assessment. Moreover, AI is essential in financial services, healthcare, manufacturing, and marketing, enhancing efficiency and precision in intricate decision-making processes. Although it has advantages, AI also induces worries regarding job loss, ethical issues, algorithmic prejudices, and data confidentiality. As companies embed AI into their fundamental operations, the necessity for responsible AI governance becomes crucial. It is vital to ensure that decisions made by AI are consistent with ethical standards and societal values to uphold public trust and adhere to regulations.

1.3 Intersection of AI and CSR

The intersection of AI and CSR presents a notable chance for companies to improve their social and environmental influence via technological advancements. AI can significantly impact CSR by allowing companies to process extensive data, recognize trends, and streamline processes that support ethical and sustainable business operations. Several important domains where AI and CSR overlap encompass:

- Eco-friendly Supply Chains: Analytics powered by AI can assist businesses in tracking their supply chains for responsible sourcing, ecological effects, and working conditions. Machine learning algorithms can identify potential threats, including human rights abuses or carbon emissions, enabling firms to implement preventative actions.
- Environmental Sustainability: AI-driven solutions can enhance energy use, minimize waste, and increase resource effectiveness. For instance, AI technologies can forecast climate hazards, improve renewable energy networks, and augment environmental impact evaluations.

- Ethical Decision-Making: AI can help businesses pinpoint ethical risks in their practices by examining consumer opinions, social media attitudes, and compliance information.
- Corporate Governance and Transparency: Automation powered by AI can enhance financial and operational clarity by identifying fraudulent actions, guaranteeing adherence to regulatory requirements, and minimizing human bias in decision processes.
- Social Impact Programs: AI can improve CSR initiatives by pinpointing sectors where companies can make a meaningful impact, including poverty reduction, education, healthcare, and disaster assistance. AI-driven tools can examine social data to suggest focused actions that enhance effectiveness.

While these opportunities exist, incorporating AI into CSR introduces challenges, including ethical issues, algorithmic biases, and worries regarding the unintended effects of automation. Consequently, companies need to create plans that guarantee AI applications coincide with CSR goals while preserving human supervision and responsibility.

1.4 Research Objectives and Questions

This research aims to investigate the role of AI in enhancing CSR practices, focusing on ethical considerations and sustainable outcomes. The primary objective is to explore how businesses can leverage AI to drive CSR initiatives while addressing potential risks and ethical challenges. To achieve this goal, the study will address the following key research questions:

1. **How can AI improve CSR initiatives?**
    - What specific AI technologies are currently being used in CSR?
    - How do businesses integrate AI into their CSR strategies?
    - What are the measurable benefits of AI-driven CSR initiatives?
2. **What are the ethical implications of using AI in CSR?**
    - How does AI influence corporate decision-making related to ethical and sustainable practices?
    - What are the risk of data privacy violations, and automation-driven job displacement in CSR?
    - How can businesses ensure responsible AI implementation in CSR?
3. **How can businesses balance AI innovation with CSR commitments?**
    - What strategies can businesses adopt to align AI advancements with social and environmental responsibilities?

- How can businesses develop ethical AI frameworks that prioritize CSR objectives?
- What role do stakeholders, including consumers, investors, and regulators, play in shaping AI-driven CSR policies?

By answering these research questions, this study will provide a comprehensive understanding of the intersection between AI and CSR, highlighting both opportunities and challenges.

1.5 Research Contributions

This study contributes to the academic and business discourse on AI and CSR by providing empirical evidence and practical insights on integrating AI into CSR frameworks. The research offers several key contributions:

1. Theoretical Contribution: This study expands existing literature on CSR and AI by providing a structured analysis of how AI technologies influence CSR initiatives. It introduces a conceptual framework that explains the mechanisms through which AI enhances CSR effectiveness.
2. Practical Contribution: Businesses can use the findings to develop AI-driven CSR strategies that improve transparency, efficiency, and sustainability. The study provides recommendations for integrating AI into CSR policies while ensuring ethical compliance and stakeholder engagement.
3. Policy Implications: The research offers valuable insights for policymakers and regulatory bodies on developing guidelines for responsible AI implementation in CSR. It highlights the importance of balancing AI innovation with ethical considerations and social responsibility.
4. Stakeholder Perspective: By analysing the perspectives of businesses, consumers, and regulators, the study provides a holistic view of AI's impact on CSR. It examines how businesses can build trust and credibility through AI-driven CSR initiatives.
5. Future Research Directions: This study identifies gaps in current research and suggests areas for further exploration, such as AI's role in social entrepreneurship, the long-term impact of AI-driven CSR, and the development of ethical AI governance frameworks.

The incorporation of AI into CSR signifies a notable change in how companies tackle ethical and sustainable methods. AI can potentially boost CSR efforts through increased transparency, efficiency, and better decision-making. Nonetheless, its execution also presents ethical dilemmas that need to be thoughtfully addressed. This study seeks to deliver an objective viewpoint on the advantages and challenges of AI-enabled CSR, supplying useful information for companies, policymakers, and scholars. As AI advances, its influence on defining corporate responsibility will grow in significance. Companies that effectively incorporate AI into their CSR strategies can attain both operational efficiency and long-lasting sustainability along with social impact. This research adds to the expanding understanding of responsible AI implementation, highlighting the necessity for ethical guidelines that harmonize technological progress with corporate accountability objectives.

2. LITERATURE REVIEW

2.1 Overview of Corporate Social Responsibility

CSR is broadly categorized into four dimensions—economic, legal, ethical, and philanthropic responsibilities (Carroll, 1991). The Triple Bottom Line (TBL) framework further expands this concept, emphasizing People (social responsibility), Planet (environmental sustainability), and Profit (economic performance) (Elkington, 1997).

The growing reliance on AI in CSR raises new ethical challenges. Algorithmic biases have been reported in AI-powered hiring platforms and loan approvals, where discriminatory patterns have resulted in unfair decision-making (O'Neil, 2016). Similarly, data privacy violations have been a major concern, with companies like Facebook and Google facing regulatory scrutiny over their AI-driven data collection methods (Zuboff, 2019).

The literature on Corporate Social Responsibility (CSR) and Artificial Intelligence (AI) highlights the evolving role of businesses in addressing social, environmental, and ethical concerns. CSR has transitioned from a voluntary initiative to a strategic necessity, while AI is revolutionizing corporate decision-making, efficiency, and transparency. As companies adopt AI in their CSR strategies, new opportunities and challenges emerge, requiring a deeper exploration of ethical considerations, governance frameworks, and stakeholder impacts. This section provides a comprehensive review of the existing literature on CSR, ethical business practices, AI technologies in business, AI's role in CSR, and research gaps in the field.

2.1.1 The Evolution of CSR

Corporate Social Responsibility (CSR) has evolved from a voluntary business initiative to a critical component of corporate strategy, emphasizing companies' obligations to contribute positively to society and the environment. CSR encompasses various practices, including environmental stewardship, ethical labour practices, community engagement, and philanthropy, aiming to assess and take responsibility for a company's effects on environmental and social well-being beyond legal compliance. This evolution reflects a shift in corporate philosophy, recognizing that businesses are integral parts of society and, therefore, bear responsibility for their impact on stakeholders and the environment.

2.1.2 Dimensions of CSR

CSR encompasses multiple dimensions, including economic, legal, ethical, and philanthropic responsibilities (Carroll, 1991). These dimensions require businesses to balance profitability with social and environmental impact. The Triple Bottom Line (TBL) framework further expands on this concept, emphasizing that companies must focus on People (social responsibility), Planet (environmental sustainability), and Profit (economic performance) (Elkington, 1997).

2.1.3 CSR in the Digital Age

With the advent of digital transformation, corporate accountability and transparency have become crucial components of CSR. Businesses now leverage technology, including AI, blockchain, and big data analytics, to track and report their social and environmental performance. This technological shift allows companies to move beyond traditional CSR reporting and adopt data-driven, impact-oriented CSR initiatives (Deloitte Insights, 2023).

2.2 Ethical Considerations in Business Practices

2.2.1 Ethics and Corporate Governance

Ethics in business involves adhering to moral principles and standards that guide behaviour in the corporate world. It encompasses issues such as fairness, transparency, integrity, and respect for stakeholders, including employees, customers, suppliers, and the broader community. Incorporating ethics into business decision-making requires companies to go beyond profit maximization and consider the broader impact of their actions. This includes implementing fair labour practices, ensuring product safety, engaging in honest marketing, and taking responsibility for environmental sustainability. By fostering an ethical corporate culture, businesses can enhance stakeholder relationships, reduce legal risks, and contribute to societal well-being.

2.2.2 Ethical Dilemmas in AI-Driven Businesses

As AI technologies become more integrated into corporate strategies, businesses face complex ethical dilemmas. Key concerns include:

- Algorithmic Bias: AI systems, if not properly designed, can reinforce societal biases, leading to discrimination in hiring, lending, and customer service (O'Neil, 2016).
- Data Privacy and Security: Companies must handle customer and employee data responsibly, ensuring compliance with privacy regulations like GDPR and CCPA.
- AI's Impact on Employment: Automation and AI-driven processes replace traditional jobs, raising concerns about job displacement and economic inequality (Brynjolfsson & McAfee, 2014).

2.2.3 The Role of Ethical AI in CSR

To address these challenges, businesses must develop AI ethics frameworks that emphasize fairness, accountability, transparency, and explainability (FATE). Ethical AI principles should align with CSR values to ensure that AI applications benefit society rather than contribute to inequality or ethical misconduct (Jobin, Ienca, & Vayena, 2019).

2.3 AI Technologies in Business

Artificial Intelligence (AI) encompasses a range of technologies, including machine learning, natural language processing, and predictive analytics, that enable machines to perform tasks typically requiring human intelligence. In the business context, AI is transforming models and operations by enhancing efficiency, accuracy, and decision-making capabilities. Machine learning algorithms analyse vast datasets to identify patterns and make predictions, aiding in areas such as customer behaviour analysis, demand forecasting, and risk assessment. Natural language processing allows for the interpretation and generation of human language, facilitating improved customer interactions through chatbots and virtual assistants. Predictive analytics leverages historical data to forecast future trends, enabling proactive strategy formulation. The integration of AI into business processes not only streamlines operations but also fosters innovation and competitive advantage.

2.4 AI's Role in Enhancing CSR

The integration of AI into CSR strategies offers transformative potential for enhancing corporate social responsibility initiatives. AI can improve resource efficiency, enable better stakeholder engagement, and provide data-driven insights for strategic decision-making. In terms of resource efficiency, AI-driven analytics can optimize energy consumption and reduce waste, contributing to environmental sustainability. For instance, AI models can predict equipment maintenance needs, preventing breakdowns and minimizing resource use. In stakeholder engagement, AI-powered tools can analyse social media and customer feedback, allowing companies to address concerns promptly and effectively. Moreover, AI facilitates real-time monitoring and reporting of CSR activities, enhancing transparency and accountability. By automating routine tasks, AI enables employees to focus on strategic initiatives, fostering a culture of innovation and ethical responsibility.

However, the deployment of AI in CSR also raises ethical considerations. Concerns about data privacy, algorithmic bias, and the potential for job displacement must be addressed to ensure that AI applications align with the ethical standards and social responsibilities of the organization. Developing robust governance frameworks and engaging stakeholders in the AI integration process are critical steps toward responsible AI adoption in CSR.

2.5 Gaps in Current Research

While the potential of AI in business operations is widely recognized, its specific applications within CSR remain underexplored. Existing literature primarily focuses on the technological and economic aspects of AI, with limited attention to its role in promoting ethical and sustainable business practices. There is a need for empirical studies that examine how AI can be effectively integrated into CSR strategies, the challenges involved, and the impact on various stakeholders.

Furthermore, research on the ethical implications of AI in CSR is scarce. Understanding how to mitigate risks such as algorithmic bias, ensure data privacy, and balance automation with human oversight is crucial for responsible AI deployment. Addressing these gaps requires interdisciplinary approaches that combine insights from technology, ethics, and business management to develop comprehensive frameworks for AI-enhanced CSR.

The literature review highlights that AI presents both opportunities and challenges in CSR. While AI can enhance sustainability reporting, stakeholder engagement, and ethical business practices, its deployment must be carefully managed to mitigate risks such as bias, data privacy concerns, and ethical dilemmas. Future research should focus on developing practical AI-CSR integration frameworks, ensuring that

AI-driven corporate strategies contribute to a more ethical, sustainable, and socially responsible business environment.

In conclusion, the integration of AI into CSR presents both opportunities and challenges. While AI can significantly enhance the effectiveness of CSR initiatives, careful consideration of ethical implications and stakeholder engagement is essential to ensure that technological advancements align with corporate social responsibilities. Future research should focus on developing practical guidelines and governance structures to navigate the complex interplay between AI and CSR, fostering sustainable and ethical business practices in the digital age.

3. METHODOLOGY

3.1 Research Design

This study employs a mixed-method strategy, combining qualitative and quantitative techniques to offer a thorough insight into how AI improves Corporate Social Responsibility (CSR) efforts. A mixed-method approach provides a comprehensive analysis, incorporating contextual insights from qualitative case studies and measurable outcomes from quantitative surveys. The research utilizes an exploratory and descriptive methodology to investigate different aspects of AI incorporation into CSR, emphasizing its ethical consequences, sustainability results, and operational effectiveness. The qualitative part includes case studies examining businesses that have effectively incorporated AI into their CSR strategies, offering practical insights into difficulties, optimal practices, and effects. In the meantime, the quantitative element encompasses organized surveys and statistical evaluations to measure AI's impact on CSR performance indicators like transparency, stakeholder involvement, and environmental sustainability.

3.1.1 Why Mixed-Methods Is Appropriate

Capturing Quantitative Trends: AI’s integration into CSR involves measurable changes in sustainability metrics, corporate transparency scores, and stakeholder satisfaction levels. A quantitative approach allows for statistical analysis of trends, correlations, and performance outcomes.

Understanding Ethical and Social Context: AI’s role in CSR extends beyond numbers—it also involves ethical considerations, stakeholder perceptions, and policy implications. A qualitative approach provides deeper insights into how businesses navigate ethical dilemmas, regulatory concerns, and consumer trust issues.

Validation and Triangulation: By combining survey data, case studies, and computational analysis (machine learning & sentiment analysis), the research findings are cross-validated to ensure reliability and reduce biases.

3.2 Data Collection Methods

Data is gathered using both primary and secondary sources to guarantee the precision and dependability of the results.

Main Data Gathering:

- Interviews: Comprehensive semi-structured interviews are carried out with industry professionals, CSR directors, AI experts, and corporate leaders engaged in AI-powered CSR projects. These interviews contribute to comprehending the strategic execution, ethical issues, and practical difficulties of AI in CSR.
- Surveys: Organized surveys are sent to professionals in the CSR, technology, and sustainability fields to collect quantitative information on how AI improves CSR initiatives. The survey consists of Likert-scale items, multiple-choice queries, and open-ended answers to guarantee a comprehensive dataset.

Gathering Secondary Data:

- Corporate Reports & CSR Disclosures: Sustainability reports, AI ethics frameworks, and CSR strategy documents that are publicly accessible from multinational corporations, startups, and governmental organizations are analyzed.
- Scholarly Articles & Policy Documents: Peer-reviewed journals, conference proceedings, industry white papers, and government reports offer theoretical frameworks, case studies, and empirical data that underpin the research.

3.3 Sampling Design

A purposive sampling method is used to choose companies and individuals pertinent to the goals of the study. This method guarantees that only those organizations that are actively incorporating AI into their CSR efforts are taken into account, thereby enhancing the relevance and depth of the research outcomes. The research chooses companies from various sectors, such as technology, manufacturing, finance, and retail, to investigate AI applications in CSR that are particular to each industry.

For qualitative interviews, 10–15 CSR managers and AI specialists from top companies employing AI-based CSR strategies are chosen. For quantitative surveys, the target is a minimum sample size of 200 respondents, including CSR professionals, sustainability analysts, AI researchers, and business executives.

3.4 Data Analysis Techniques

Qualitative Data Analysis:

- Thematic Analysis is used to identify recurring themes and patterns in interview transcripts and case study narratives.
- A coding framework is developed to categorize insights related to AI applications, ethical concerns, sustainability outcomes, and stakeholder perceptions.
- NVivo or MAXQDA software is employed to organize and analyze qualitative data systematically.

Quantitative Data Analysis:

- Descriptive Statistics (mean, median, frequency distributions) are applied to summarize survey responses.
- Inferential Statistics, such as correlation and regression analysis, are conducted to examine the relationships between AI implementation and CSR effectiveness.
- SPSS, R, or Python is used for quantitative analysis, ensuring statistical accuracy and validity of findings.

A triangulation approach is applied to compare insights from qualitative and quantitative data, ensuring a well-rounded and validated conclusion.

3.5 Ethical Considerations in Research

This study follows strict ethical research guidelines to ensure participant rights, data confidentiality, and research integrity.

- **Ethical Approval & Compliance:** The research follows institutional and academic ethical approval processes, ensuring adherence to established research guidelines.
- **Informed Consent:** All participants in interviews and surveys are provided with detailed information about the study's purpose, voluntary participation, and their right to withdraw at any time. Written consent is obtained before conducting interviews.
- **Confidentiality & Anonymity:** To protect the privacy of participants and organizations, all collected data is anonymized, and company names are only disclosed if permission is granted.

- **Data Security & Protection:** Data is stored in encrypted, password-protected systems, ensuring compliance with GDPR (General Data Protection Regulation) and other applicable data protection laws.

By employing a mixed-method research design, utilizing rigorous data collection and analysis techniques, and adhering to ethical research principles, this study aims to provide empirical evidence and practical insights into the role of AI in enhancing CSR. The methodology ensures validity, reliability, and applicability of findings, contributing to both academic literature and industry best practices.

4. THEORIES USED IN THE RESEARCH

The incorporation of Artificial Intelligence (AI) into Corporate Social Responsibility (CSR) is an active and developing area that necessitates a strong theoretical basis. Different theories offer a systematic perspective for comprehending, evaluating, and executing AI-driven CSR initiatives. This segment examines four important theoretical frameworks—Triple Bottom Line (TBL) Theory, Stakeholder Theory, Ethical Frameworks in AI, and AI in Corporate Governance Models—to demonstrate how AI can improve ethical and sustainable business practices. These theories together offer an all-encompassing view of the ethical, social, environmental, and economic aspects of AI-driven CSR efforts.

4.1 The Triple Bottom Line (TBL) Theory

Theory This theory emphasizes the importance of balancing economic, social, and The Triple Bottom Line (TBL) Theory, proposed by John Elkington in 1994, broadens the conventional financial performance model by including three aspects of corporate responsibility—economic, social, and environmental performance. The central concept of TBL is that companies should not concentrate only on profits but also take into account their effects on society and the environment. This theory holds particular significance in the realm of AI-driven CSR, since AI can greatly impact all three pillars.

From an economic viewpoint, AI-driven analytics can boost operational efficiency, streamline resource distribution, and strengthen financial sustainability. Machine learning algorithms can enhance supply chain management, minimize waste, and predict market trends more precisely, resulting in cost reductions and higher profitability. Additionally, automation powered by AI can enhance productivity, but issues related to job displacement must be tackled through ethical labour management and upskilling programs.

In terms of social aspects, AI technologies can promote workplace diversity, improve working conditions, and boost employee well-being. For instance, AI-powered HR tools can detect and reduce biases in recruitment, promoting a more diverse workforce. Sentiment analysis driven by AI can assist companies in grasping how consumers view their CSR activities, enabling them to customize initiatives that align with stakeholder interests. Moreover, AI can aid social impact initiatives by enhancing access to education and healthcare in disadvantaged areas via AI-based e-learning and telemedicine services. Regarding environmental sustainability, AI is essential for combating climate change, enhancing energy efficiency, and minimizing waste. Smart grids powered by AI enhance energy usage, lowering carbon emissions, while predictive analytics in production assist in decreasing material waste. Firms such as Google have effectively deployed AI to lower energy use in data centres by as much as 40%, showcasing AI's capability in reaching sustainability objectives.

4.2 Stakeholder Theory

Stakeholder theory highlights the importance of considering the interests of all stakeholders, Stakeholder Theory, introduced by Edward Freeman in 1984, asserts that companies ought to take into account the interests of every stakeholder instead of prioritizing only shareholders. Stakeholders of a company encompass employees, customers, investors, suppliers, communities, governments, and the environment as well. The incorporation of AI in CSR initiatives should, thus, align with stakeholder expectations, ethical values, and wider societal principles.

AI improves stakeholder engagement by increasing transparency, facilitating communication, and enabling data-driven decision-making. For instance, AI-driven real-time sustainability reporting tools enable companies to monitor and reveal their environmental effects more precisely, enhancing trust and accountability with investors and regulatory agencies. AI-powered social listening tools assist companies in grasping public sentiment and community issues, allowing them to create CSR initiatives that more effectively meet stakeholder demands.

For employees, AI-powered HR analytics can track workplace health, pinpoint skill deficiencies, and recommend tailored training initiatives, ensuring that companies invest in the growth of their workforce. AI additionally boosts customer engagement by offering personalized suggestions, ensuring transparency in ethical sourcing, and utilizing AI-powered customer service bots that enhance user experiences and encourage sustainable options.

Nonetheless, there are obstacles to the adoption of AI in the stakeholder framework. Bias in AI algorithms can negatively impact specific stakeholder groups, prompting ethical issues regarding discrimination and fairness. Moreover, concerns over data privacy persist significantly, since AI-driven tools for stakeholder engagement typically need access to sensitive personal information. Companies need to focus on AI governance and compliance with regulations to guarantee that AI-powered CSR stays ethical, inclusive, and advantageous for all stakeholders.

4.3 Ethical Frameworks in AI

Stakeholder Theory, introduced by Edward Freeman in 1984, contends that companies should take into account the interests of all stakeholders instead of concentrating only on shareholders. A company's stakeholders encompass employees, customers, investors, suppliers, communities, governments, and also the environment. Consequently, the incorporation of AI into CSR programs must align with the expectations of stakeholders, ethical factors, and wider societal principles.

AI boosts stakeholder involvement by enhancing transparency, communication, and decisions based on data analysis. For instance, real-time sustainability reporting systems driven by AI enable businesses to monitor and reveal their environmental effects with greater precision, enhancing trust and accountability with investors and regulatory agencies. AI-powered social listening tools assist companies in grasping public sentiment and community issues, allowing them to create CSR initiatives that more effectively meet stakeholder demands.

The application of AI in CSR brings up important ethical issues about fairness, transparency, accountability, and data privacy. Different ethical frameworks offer direction for the responsible development and implementation of AI, ensuring that AI applications are in harmony with societal values and corporate accountability.

A frequently utilized ethical framework is Utilitarianism, which assesses the ethical impacts of AI by its potential to enhance overall societal benefits and reduce harm. AI-powered CSR initiatives, like predictive analytics for disaster management or AI-enhanced healthcare solutions, resonate with utilitarian ethics by maximizing resource efficiency and enhancing social well-being. Nevertheless, utilitarian AI systems may occasionally emphasize efficiency at the expense of personal rights, resulting in ethical challenges related to privacy, fairness, and algorithmic choices.

A significant ethical view is Deontological Ethics, grounded in the principles of duty and moral obligation as proposed by Immanuel Kant. This framework suggests that AI-based CSR initiatives must follow ethical guidelines, irrespective of their outcomes. For example, AI algorithms need to guarantee equitable hiring methods, safeguard data privacy, and maintain clear decision-making, even if these actions hinder operational efficiency. Companies implementing deontological AI ethics should emphasize moral accountability and fairness.

Moreover, the “AI for Good” movement, supported by organizations like UNESCO, the European Commission, and the World Economic Forum, advocates for AI-driven solutions that promote social well-being and sustainability. This framework encourages businesses to adopt AI in ways that reduce inequality, enhance accessibility, and protect the environment. Companies that align their AI-powered CSR strategies with these ethical principles can strengthen their brand reputation and gain public trust.

4.4 AI and Corporate Governance Models

Corporate governance involves the regulations, procedures, and practices that steer corporate decision-making, promoting accountability and ethical business behaviour. As AI plays a greater role in strategic decision-making, risk management, and compliance, integrating AI governance frameworks within corporate structures becomes essential for ensuring transparency, fairness, and accountability.

AI improves corporate governance through enhancing decision-making precision, identifying financial fraud, and ensuring compliance with regulations. For example, AI-driven fraud detection technologies assist businesses in recognizing dishonest financial behaviours, minimizing risks of corporate misconduct. Models for risk assessment powered by AI allow companies to foresee possible compliance challenges and modify their policies as needed.

Nevertheless, incorporating AI into corporate governance presents obstacles, including AI accountability and transparency. Numerous AI models function as "black boxes," which complicates the understanding of their decision-making processes. When an AI system results in an unethical or biased decision, it is frequently uncertain who is responsible—should it be the AI developers, the corporate executives, or the regulators? To tackle these issues, companies need to establish ethical AI governance frameworks, guaranteeing that AI is transparent, understandable, and in accordance with corporate responsibility criteria.

The intersection of AI and CSR necessitates a strong theoretical foundation to guide ethical, sustainable, and responsible AI implementation. The Triple Bottom Line (TBL) Theory emphasizes balancing economic, social, and environmental responsibilities, while Stakeholder Theory highlights the importance of considering all stakeholder interests in AI-driven CSR strategies.

5. RESULTS

The results of this study emphasize the significant influence of Artificial Intelligence (AI) on Corporate Social Responsibility (CSR) efforts. The findings suggest that adopting AI greatly improves CSR effectiveness, ethical adherence, and sustainability results. Firms utilizing AI in their CSR initiatives achieve enhanced transparency, better decision-making, and quantifiable positive effects on social and environmental challenges. This segment outlines significant discoveries regarding AI integration in CSR, its impact on ethical behaviours, practical case studies, and a numerical assessment of its influence on CSR metrics.

5.1 AI Adoption in CSR Initiatives

The research shows that companies that incorporate AI into their CSR strategies see significant enhancements in operational efficiency, resource management, and reductions in environmental impact. AI technologies like machine learning, big data analysis, and blockchain allow businesses to automate intricate CSR processes, improve sustainability initiatives, and refine resource distribution.

A major area of AI implementation in CSR is the monitoring of the environment and the management of sustainability. Predictive analytics powered by AI and IoT sensors enable businesses to monitor carbon emissions, enhance energy efficiency, and pinpoint opportunities for sustainability advancements. For example, AI-driven environmental risk assessment tools assist firms in predicting possible ecological threats, allowing for proactive actions to mitigate adverse environmental effects.

Moreover, AI improves supply chain visibility, guaranteeing ethical sourcing and responsible manufacturing methods. By utilizing AI systems based on blockchain technology, businesses can track the origins of products, confirm fair trade practices, and avert exploitative labor conditions. This adoption greatly enhances CSR by synchronizing business practices with worldwide sustainability objectives.

AI is changing corporate giving and social impact programs as well. Data analytics driven by AI assist companies in recognizing underserved communities, guaranteeing that CSR funds and resources are directed to the areas that require them the most. Chatbots and virtual assistants powered by AI improve community engagement by delivering immediate answers to social issues, gathering feedback, and tailoring CSR initiatives.

Even with these advantages, the study highlights obstacles in adopting AI for CSR, such as significant implementation expenses, insufficient technical skills, and possible biases in AI-driven decisions. Numerous companies encounter challenges in incorporating AI into conventional CSR frameworks because of data privacy issues, regulatory obstacles, and ethical quandaries in AI-led decision-making. Tackling these issues necessitates strong AI governance policies, ethical AI frameworks, and continuous collaboration among stakeholders.

5.2 Impacts of AI on Ethical Practices

AI significantly contributes to bolstering corporate ethical standards by increasing transparency, minimizing human biases, and enhancing regulatory adherence. The research indicates that AI-powered CSR efforts assist companies in establishing trust with stakeholders by providing precise reporting, impartial decision-making, and ethical business practices.

A major ethical benefit of AI is its capacity to minimize human biases in decision-making. AI-driven HR analytics tools, for example, detect and remove biases in hiring, performance assessments, and promotions, promoting equitable recruitment methods and workplace diversity. This aids a company's CSR goals by enhancing equal opportunities and lessening discrimination in the workplace.

AI further improves corporate transparency by streamlining CSR reporting procedures. AI-driven Natural Language Processing (NLP) algorithms can examine extensive datasets from corporate documents, news outlets, and social media to identify unethical business behaviours and reveal inconsistencies in CSR pledges. This ability stops greenwashing, making sure that companies are responsible for their CSR assertions.

Additionally, systems for detecting fraud powered by AI are essential in corporate governance and ethics. Businesses that adopt AI-driven financial monitoring solutions encounter reduced instances of fraud, corruption, and unethical financial behaviour. AI is capable of identifying irregularities in financial transactions, guaranteeing adherence to ethical financial reporting standards.

Nevertheless, although AI improves ethical standards, it also brings ethical challenges. AI systems may occasionally reinforce biases when trained on skewed datasets, resulting in unintentional discrimination in their decision-making processes. Furthermore, AI's capacity to gather and examine extensive personal data triggers privacy issues, necessitating that companies implement stringent data protection policies and ethical guidelines for AI.

5.3 Case Studies of AI-Driven CSR Success

The study examines several real-world case studies from different industries where AI-driven CSR initiatives have led to significant positive outcomes in sustainability, ethical business practices, and stakeholder engagement.

Case Study 1: Google's Sustainability Initiatives Enhanced by AI

Google has effectively adopted AI-based energy management solutions to decrease the carbon emissions of its data centers. Employing DeepMind's AI solutions, Google enhanced cooling systems, cutting energy use by 40% and greatly diminishing greenhouse gas emissions. This effort emphasizes how AI can promote environmental sustainability within business practices.

Case Analysis 2: Unilever's Supply Chain Transparency Boosted by AI

Unilever utilizes AI-powered blockchain and machine learning technologies to monitor raw material sourcing, guaranteeing ethical practices within the supply chain. By utilizing AI-driven analysis, the company guarantees that its palm oil suppliers adhere to environmental regulations, thereby decreasing deforestation and supporting equitable labor practices. AI aids Unilever in upholding CSR commitments by stopping unethical sourcing and exploitation within the supply chain.

Case Study 3: Microsoft's AI for Positive Impact Initiative

Microsoft's AI for Good initiative utilizes AI to tackle worldwide social issues, including climate change, accessibility, and humanitarian assistance. By utilizing AI-driven climate modelling, Microsoft aids governments and organizations in forecasting and alleviating climate-related crises, showcasing AI's contribution to improving worldwide sustainability initiatives.

Case Study 4: IBM Watson and Ethical Artificial Intelligence in Recruitment

Corporations utilize IBM Watson to remove biases from their recruitment and hiring procedures. Through the examination of extensive hiring data, Watson guarantees equitable assessments of candidates, assisting organizations in fostering diversity and inclusion. The use of AI in CSR improves ethical workforce management and fair employment prospects.

These case studies illustrate how AI-powered CSR initiatives aid in achieving corporate sustainability objectives, promoting ethical business conduct, and improving stakeholder involvement.

5.4 Quantitative Analysis of AI's Impact on CSR Metrics

The study conducted a quantitative analysis to measure the impact of AI adoption on CSR performance metrics. The analysis focused on sustainability scores, stakeholder satisfaction levels, and environmental impact data across AI-driven CSR initiatives.

5.4.1 Correlation Between AI Adoption and Sustainability Scores

Statistical analysis reveals a strong positive correlation between AI adoption and corporate sustainability scores. Companies that actively integrate AI into their CSR strategies achieve higher ESG (Environmental, Social, and Governance) ratings, indicating that AI contributes to better sustainability outcomes.

5.4.2 Stakeholder Satisfaction and AI Implementation

Survey results from CSR managers, employees, and consumers indicate that businesses leveraging AI for CSR initiatives experience greater stakeholder trust and satisfaction. AI-powered real-time reporting systems enable greater transparency and engagement, improving stakeholder confidence in corporate sustainability commitments.

5.4.3 Environmental Impact Reduction Through AI

Data analysis shows that AI-powered energy management, waste reduction, and carbon footprint monitoring systems lead to measurable reductions in environmental impact. Companies utilizing AI for energy efficiency report an average reduction of 25-40% in energy consumption, directly contributing to climate change mitigation efforts.

5.4.4 Ethical Business Practices and AI-Driven Compliance

Businesses that implement AI-powered compliance monitoring tools report fewer regulatory violations and ethical misconduct cases. AI-driven fraud detection systems help businesses maintain higher levels of corporate integrity and ethical governance.

The findings of this study demonstrate that AI adoption significantly enhances CSR effectiveness by improving efficiency, ethical compliance, and sustainability performance. AI-driven CSR initiatives lead to greater transparency, reduced environmental impact, improved stakeholder engagement, and better governance practices.

However, AI implementation also presents challenges, including ethical dilemmas, potential biases, and data privacy concerns. Businesses must ensure that AI is ethically designed, regulated, and continuously monitored to align with CSR commitments and societal expectations.

These results provide valuable insights for organizations seeking to integrate AI into their CSR frameworks, emphasizing the need for responsible AI practices to maximize positive social and environmental impact.

6. DISCUSSION

The integration of Artificial Intelligence (AI) in Corporate Social Responsibility (CSR) represents a transformative shift in how businesses approach sustainability, ethics, and corporate governance. This study has provided insights into the role of AI in enhancing CSR initiatives, improving transparency, and fostering ethical decision-making. While AI offers unprecedented opportunities for businesses to strengthen their social and environmental commitments, it also presents significant challenges that must be addressed. This section discusses the interpretation of key findings, business implications, challenges and limitations, and directions for future research.

6.1 Interpretation of Key Findings

The findings of this study highlight that AI adoption in CSR has substantial benefits, particularly in enhancing operational efficiency, increasing transparency, and strengthening ethical business practices. AI-driven technologies, such as machine learning, predictive analytics, blockchain, and natural language processing, enable companies to monitor sustainability goals, optimize resource usage, and improve corporate governance structures.

One of the most notable findings is that AI significantly enhances CSR reporting and transparency. Many corporations face challenges in tracking and measuring their social and environmental impact, often leading to greenwashing or insufficient accountability. However, AI-powered data analytics platforms and blockchain verification systems improve accuracy in sustainability reporting, ensuring that businesses remain accountable for their CSR commitments.

Moreover, AI-driven ethical compliance monitoring helps businesses detect and prevent unethical practices, such as supply chain exploitation, unfair labor conditions, and financial fraud. The ability of AI to eliminate human biases in decision-making is a crucial factor in ensuring that CSR strategies are genuinely ethical and inclusive.

Another significant finding is that AI contributes to environmental sustainability by enabling real-time monitoring of carbon emissions, optimizing energy consumption, and improving waste management practices. AI-powered predictive models help companies identify potential environmental risks, allowing for proactive intervention to minimize harm.

However, despite these benefits, this research also highlights challenges in AI-driven CSR initiatives. Issues related to AI biases, data privacy concerns, and the absence of clear regulatory frameworks remain key obstacles. While AI enhances decision-making, it is only as ethical as the data it is trained on, raising concerns about algorithmic biases that may reinforce societal inequalities.

Overall, the study confirms that AI can be a powerful tool for advancing CSR objectives, but businesses must adopt ethical AI frameworks and governance models to maximize its positive impact while mitigating risks.

6.2 Implications for Businesses

Businesses can leverage AI-powered tools to align their technological advancements with social and environmental responsibilities. The implications of AI in CSR extend to various areas, including supply chain management, ethical workforce practices, sustainable product development, and corporate governance.

6.2.1 AI-Driven Sustainable Business Models

AI allows businesses to develop innovative, sustainable business models by optimizing resource efficiency and minimizing waste. For example, AI-powered smart grids and energy optimization tools help companies reduce energy consumption and transition to renewable energy sources. In industries like manufacturing, AI-driven circular economy models enable waste reduction and material recycling, enhancing overall sustainability.

6.2.2 Ethical AI in Workforce Management

AI can improve workforce diversity, fairness, and inclusion by eliminating biases in hiring, promotions, and performance evaluations. AI-driven HR analytics ensure that recruitment processes are transparent, merit-based, and free from unconscious bias, fostering a more equitable corporate environment. Businesses integrating AI in HR and CSR initiatives must ensure that their AI systems are regularly audited for fairness and ethical compliance.

6.2.3 AI for Supply Chain Transparency

AI-powered blockchain technology and real-time monitoring systems enable companies to track their supply chains with greater transparency. Businesses can verify the ethical sourcing of raw materials, prevent labour exploitation, and ensure compliance with environmental regulations. This has significant implications for global supply chains, particularly in industries such as fashion, electronics, and food production, where ethical sourcing and sustainability concerns are prominent.

6.2.4 AI for Stakeholder Engagement

AI-driven chatbots, sentiment analysis tools, and social media monitoring platforms provide businesses with valuable insights into consumer perceptions of their CSR initiatives. By analysing consumer feedback in real-time, companies can adapt their CSR strategies to better align with public expectations and societal needs.

6.2.5 Corporate Governance and AI Ethics

The implementation of AI in CSR requires strong corporate governance frameworks to ensure ethical AI use, compliance with legal standards, and protection of stakeholder interests. Companies must establish AI ethics committees and governance policies to regulate the use of AI in CSR decision-making.

These implications highlight that while AI presents numerous opportunities for businesses to enhance their CSR strategies, its responsible implementation is critical for long-term success and related to AI biases, data privacy concerns, and the need for regulatory frameworks to govern AI applications in CSR.

6.3 Challenges and Limitations

Despite the positive impact of AI on CSR, this research identifies several challenges and limitations that businesses must address to ensure ethical and sustainable AI implementation.

6.3.1 AI Bias and Ethical Dilemmas

One of the primary challenges in AI-driven CSR is algorithmic bias. If AI systems are trained on biased datasets, they can reinforce discriminatory practices, leading to unethical business decisions. For example, biased AI hiring algorithms may unintentionally Favor certain demographics over others, contradicting CSR goals related to diversity and inclusion.

6.3.2 Data Privacy and Security Concerns

AI-driven CSR initiatives often require large-scale data collection, raising concerns about data privacy, security, and consumer trust. Businesses using AI for stakeholder engagement and CSR impact assessments must ensure that personal data is collected ethically and used transparently. Compliance with global data protection regulations, such as GDPR and CCPA, is essential to prevent misuse of sensitive information.

6.3.3 High Implementation Costs and Technical Barriers

Implementing AI in CSR requires significant financial investment and technical expertise. Many businesses, particularly small and medium-sized enterprises (SMEs), may struggle with the high costs of AI adoption. Additionally, the lack of AI-skilled professionals in CSR departments poses a barrier to effective AI integration.

6.3.4 Regulatory and Legal Uncertainty

AI applications in CSR operate within an uncertain regulatory landscape, as governments and international organizations are still developing policies to govern AI ethics and sustainability. The lack of clear legal frameworks creates challenges for businesses in ensuring compliance with emerging AI governance standards.

Addressing these challenges requires businesses to invest in ethical AI research, develop responsible AI governance policies, and collaborate with regulators to establish standardized guidelines for AI in CSR.

6.4 Future Research Directions

While this study provides valuable insights into the role of AI in CSR, there are several areas that require further exploration to enhance the understanding and effectiveness of AI-driven CSR strategies.

6.4.1 Long-Term Impacts of AI on CSR

Future research should explore the long-term effects of AI integration in CSR, particularly in areas such as sustainability reporting, workforce diversity, and corporate governance. Studies should analyse whether AI-driven CSR initiatives lead to sustained positive impacts or introduce new challenges over time.

6.4.2 AI in CSR Across Different Industry Contexts

AI adoption in CSR may vary across different industries, and future research should examine industry-specific challenges and opportunities. For example, AI's role in reducing carbon emissions in the energy sector may differ from its role in ensuring ethical labour practices in the manufacturing sector.

6.4.3 Development of Ethical AI Guidelines for CSR

There is a growing need for standardized ethical AI frameworks to guide businesses in responsible AI adoption for CSR initiatives. Future studies should focus on developing global ethical AI standards that businesses can adopt to ensure fairness, accountability, and transparency in AI-driven CSR strategies.

6.4.4 Human-AI Collaboration in CSR Decision-Making

Future research should investigate how businesses can effectively combine human expertise with AI-driven decision-making to enhance CSR effectiveness while mitigating AI risks.

The integration of AI in CSR represents a pivotal shift in corporate responsibility practices, offering businesses new opportunities to enhance sustainability, ethics, and transparency. However, ethical challenges, biases, data privacy concerns, and regulatory uncertainties must be addressed to ensure responsible AI adoption. Businesses must prioritize ethical AI governance, stakeholder collaboration, and continuous evaluation of AI-driven CSR initiatives.

As AI continues to evolve, it holds immense potential to reshape CSR strategies, drive sustainable innovation, and create a more responsible corporate ecosystem. However, its success depends on how businesses navigate the ethical and regulatory landscape, ensuring that AI remains a force for social good and sustainable development.

7. CONCLUSION

The integration of Artificial Intelligence (AI) in Corporate Social Responsibility (CSR) has profound implications for businesses, policymakers, stakeholders, and the broader field of CSR and AI research. As businesses increasingly adopt AI-driven CSR initiatives, they must navigate practical challenges, regulatory requirements, stakeholder expectations, and ethical considerations. This section explores the key implications of AI-driven CSR in four major areas: practical applications for businesses, policy recommendations, stakeholder engagement, and contributions to academic and industry knowledge.

7.1 Practical Implications for Businesses

The findings of this research offer valuable, actionable insights for businesses looking to integrate AI into their CSR strategies. AI has the potential to enhance operational efficiency, improve transparency, optimize resource utilization, and drive sustainable innovation. However, to fully realize these benefits, businesses must develop strategic frameworks that align AI adoption with CSR objectives.

7.1.1 AI-Driven Sustainability Strategies

AI enables businesses to enhance their sustainability efforts by using predictive analytics, IoT-based monitoring systems, and blockchain technology to track and reduce their environmental footprint. For example, AI-powered smart grids optimize energy consumption, while machine learning algorithms analyze waste patterns to enhance recycling efforts. Companies must invest in AI-based sustainability solutions to meet regulatory requirements and consumer expectations.

7.1.2 Ethical AI Governance

To ensure the responsible adoption of AI in CSR, businesses must establish AI ethics committees and integrate AI governance frameworks within their corporate structures. Ethical AI governance ensures that AI-driven decisions align with human rights, social justice, and corporate responsibility standards. Regular AI audits and bias detection mechanisms should be implemented to prevent unethical practices.

7.1.3 Enhancing Employee Well-being and Diversity

AI can be used to improve workplace diversity and inclusion by ensuring fair recruitment, performance assessment, and talent management. AI-driven HR analytics can help businesses eliminate unconscious bias in hiring decisions, contributing to inclusive workforce policies. Additionally, AI-driven mental health monitoring tools can enhance employee well-being, allowing companies to implement personalized well-being programs.

7.1.4 Transparency and Consumer Trust

AI can strengthen consumer trust by improving CSR reporting and real-time stakeholder engagement. Businesses must use AI-driven data transparency tools to ensure their CSR claims are backed by verifiable, real-time data. AI-powered chatbots, sentiment analysis tools, and automated sustainability reporting platforms allow businesses to engage with customers proactively, improving corporate credibility.

In summary, businesses that strategically integrate AI into their CSR frameworks can achieve higher efficiency, greater stakeholder trust, and enhanced sustainability impact. However, they must also address ethical, regulatory, and operational challenges to ensure AI adoption aligns with CSR values and societal well-being.

7.2 Policy Recommendations

Given the ethical and regulatory challenges associated with AI in CSR, policymakers must play a proactive role in establishing clear guidelines for AI-driven corporate responsibility practices. AI's growing influence in supply chain transparency, environmental sustainability, and corporate governance calls for robust legal frameworks to regulate its use.

7.2.1 Development of AI Ethics and Compliance Standards

Governments and international organizations should establish global AI ethics standards to ensure that businesses use AI responsibly and transparently. Policymakers must develop comprehensive compliance frameworks that regulate AI applications in areas such as sustainability reporting, labour rights, and consumer protection.

7.2.2 Data Privacy and AI Governance Regulations

With AI-powered CSR initiatives relying heavily on big data analytics, policymakers must enforce strong data privacy laws to prevent misuse of personal and corporate data. Governments should strengthen regulations like the General Data Protection Regulation (GDPR) and the California Consumer Privacy Act (CCPA) to ensure AI-driven CSR strategies respect consumer rights and data protection norms.

7.2.3 AI-Based Carbon Footprint Monitoring Policies

AI plays a significant role in monitoring carbon footprints and optimizing environmental sustainability efforts. Policymakers should incentivize businesses to adopt AI-driven carbon tracking systems by providing tax incentives, grants, and policy support. Additionally, governments can mandate AI-based real-time environmental reporting to hold corporations accountable for their sustainability commitments.

7.2.4 Public-Private Collaboration for AI-Driven CSR

Governments, corporations, and non-profit organizations must collaborate on AI-driven CSR projects to maximize social and environmental impact. Public-private partnerships (PPPs) can drive innovative AI solutions for social development, including poverty reduction, climate action, and ethical labour practices. Governments should facilitate these partnerships by providing funding, technological support, and policy frameworks.

In conclusion, policymakers must ensure that AI applications in CSR align with ethical, legal, and societal standards, protecting public interest while fostering corporate responsibility and sustainable innovation.

7.3 Implications for Stakeholders

The integration of AI in CSR has wide-ranging implications for multiple stakeholders, including investors, customers, employees, and communities. AI-powered corporate responsibility initiatives can enhance transparency, accountability, and ethical business practices, benefiting both internal and external stakeholders.

7.3.1 Investors and Shareholders

AI-powered CSR initiatives provide investors with data-driven insights on corporate sustainability performance, helping them make informed investment decisions. Sustainability-focused investors increasingly demand real-time ESG (Environmental, Social, and Governance) metrics, which AI-driven reporting tools can provide. Businesses with strong AI-driven CSR strategies attract higher investment and shareholder trust.

7.3.2 Customers and Consumer Expectations

Customers are increasingly conscious of corporate ethics and sustainability. AI-driven CSR allows businesses to provide greater transparency in their environmental impact, labor practices, and ethical sourcing. AI-powered blockchain solutions enable consumers to verify the authenticity of sustainability claims, reducing concerns over greenwashing.

7.3.3 Employees and Workplace Ethics

AI has the potential to revolutionize employee well-being programs by providing personalized career development, mental health support, and diversity analytics. However, businesses must ensure ethical AI-driven workforce monitoring to prevent excessive surveillance or workplace discrimination.

7.3.4 Communities and Social Development

AI-powered CSR strategies can enhance community welfare programs, environmental conservation, and social development projects. For instance, AI-driven climate modeling tools help communities prepare for environmental risks, while AI-powered education platforms provide learning opportunities for underprivileged populations.

By aligning AI-driven CSR with stakeholder needs, businesses can create inclusive, ethical, and sustainable corporate ecosystems.7.4 Contribution to the Field of CSR and AI

This research contributes to the growing academic discourse on AI and CSR, bridging the gap between technological advancements and corporate responsibility theories.

7.3.5 Advancing AI-Driven CSR Research

This study highlights the emerging role of AI in CSR, providing empirical insights into how AI enhances sustainability reporting, ethical governance, and corporate transparency. By integrating theoretical frameworks like the Triple Bottom Line and Stakeholder Theory, this research enriches academic discussions on ethical AI adoption in business.

7.3.6 Practical Implications for Business Strategy

The findings provide business leaders with a roadmap for integrating AI into CSR initiatives, offering practical guidance on AI-driven sustainability strategies, stakeholder engagement, and corporate governance models.

7.3.6 Future Research Directions

This study encourages future researchers to explore AI-driven CSR frameworks in different industry contexts, examining how AI adoption varies across finance, healthcare, manufacturing, and retail. Additionally, future studies should assess the long-term impact of AI in CSR, particularly in terms of regulatory challenges and ethical risks.

REFERENCES

Brynjolfsson, E., & McAfee, A. (2014). *The second machine age: Work, progress, and prosperity in a time of brilliant technologies*. W.W. Norton & Company.

Carroll, A. B. (1991). The pyramid of corporate social responsibility: Toward the moral management of organizational stakeholders. *Business Horizons*, *34*(4), 39–48. DOI: 10.1016/0007-6813(91)90005-G

Deloitte Insights. (2023). *The rise of AI in corporate sustainability: Leveraging AI for transparent and impactful CSR initiatives*. Deloitte LLP.

Elkington, J. (1997). *Cannibals with forks: The triple bottom line of 21st-century business*. Capstone Publishing.

Jobin, A., Ienca, M., & Vayena, E. (2019). The global landscape of AI ethics guidelines. *Nature Machine Intelligence*, *1*(9), 389–399. DOI: 10.1038/s42256-019-0088-2

Liu, Y., Dai, W., Liao, M., & Wei, J. (2021). AI-driven CSR initiatives: A review of sustainability, transparency, and ethical challenges. *Sustainability*, *13*(6), 3450. DOI: 10.3390/su13063450

O'Neil, C. (2016). *Weapons of math destruction: How big data increases inequality and threatens democracy*. Crown Publishing.

Renieris, E. M., Kiron, D., & Mills, S. (2022). The responsible AI imperative: Aligning CSR with technological innovation. *MIT Sloan Management Review*, *64*(1), 45–59.

World Economic Forum. (2023). *AI governance: The role of corporations in ethical AI deployment*. WEF Annual Report.

Zuboff, S. (2019). *The age of surveillance capitalism: The fight for a human future at the new frontier of power*. PublicAffairs.

Chapter 4
The Crucial Role of Environmental and Social Responsibility in Modern Entrepreneurship

Oindrilla Ghosh
https://orcid.org/0000-0001-9609-0781
Christ University, Bengaluru, India

Binod Kumar
https://orcid.org/0009-0002-9721-1367
Radha Govind University, Ranchi, India

ABSTRACT

In today's business landscape, environmental and social responsibility (ESR) has become a fundamental aspect of modern entrepreneurship. Companies are no longer judged solely on profitability but also on their impact on society and the planet. Entrepreneurs who prioritize sustainability, ethical sourcing, and fair labor practices gain a competitive advantage by appealing to conscious consumers. Environmental responsibility involves reducing carbon footprints, minimizing waste, and adopting sustainable business practices. Entrepreneurs are increasingly investing in green technologies, renewable energy, and eco-friendly production methods to align with global sustainability goals. Similarly, social responsibility entails fair wages, diversity, community engagement, and ethical labor practices. Incorporating ESR not only benefits the planet and society but also enhances brand value, attracts investors, and secures long-term success. As consumer expectations evolve, businesses that embrace environmental and social responsibility will thrive in the modern economy.

DOI: 10.4018/979-8-3373-1107-4.ch004

INTRODUCTION

In an era marked by rapid globalization, technological innovation, and heightened awareness of environmental and social issues, the landscape of entrepreneurship has fundamentally transformed (Felicetti et al., 2024). Entrepreneurs are no longer seen merely as profit-seeking individuals; they are increasingly viewed as pivotal players in addressing pressing global challenges (Ndagi & Salihu, 2019). The convergence of business with social and environmental responsibilities has prompted a new wave of entrepreneurial thinking that emphasizes sustainable practices and ethical considerations (Wujarso, 2023). This shift reflects a growing recognition that businesses can successfully integrate profitability with environmental sustainability and social equity to create value for all stakeholders (Codini et al., 2023).

Modern consumers, investors, and employees are increasingly demanding a commitment to environmental and social responsibility from businesses. Millennial and Gen Z consumers, in particular, prioritize brands that align with their values (Kiyabo & Isaga, 2020), seeking products and services that contribute positively to society while minimizing ecological impact. This trend has led companies to rethink their core values and operational strategies, emphasizing corporate social responsibility (CSR) and environmental, social, and governance (ESG) criteria (Mariotti & Marzano, 2021). As a result, entrepreneurs are not only motivated by profit; they are also driven by a desire to make a meaningful impact on the world around them.

The concept of sustainable entrepreneurship goes beyond compliance; it encompasses the idea of creating value that lasts over time (Pinto Borges et al., 2021). Entrepreneurs who prioritize environmental and social responsibility are more likely to foster trust with their stakeholders be it customers, employees, or investors thus achieving a competitive advantage (Si et al., 2023). Furthermore, a commitment to ESG principles often attracts investment from ESG-focused funds and socially responsible investors, which can provide essential capital for growth (Guerrero et al., 2021).

Ultimately, modern entrepreneurship encompasses a broader mission: to contribute to societal well-being and environmental preservation while achieving business success (Cammack, 2022). By embedding environmental and social responsibility into their business models, entrepreneurs are transforming the way we perceive economic success and leadership (Neumann, 2021). The journey toward responsible entrepreneurship is challenging and requires a rethinking of traditional business paradigms. However, the benefits ranging from enhanced brand loyalty to increased operational efficiency illustrate that fostering a responsible business culture is not just an ethical imperative (Matalamäki & Joensuu-Salo, 2022) but a strategic advantage in an increasingly competitive marketplace.

BACKGROUND

The evolution of environmental and social responsibility in entrepreneurship has deep roots that reflect changing societal values, scientific discoveries, and economic pressures (Ammar et al., 2021). Historically, capitalism has placed a strong emphasis on profit maximization, often at the expense of social and environmental considerations. The industrial revolution epitomized this approach, leading to significant economic growth but also resulting in environmental degradation (Parviainen et al., 2017), worker exploitation, and stark social inequalities. As these negative consequences became apparent, calls for greater corporate accountability began to echo in society.

The mid-20th century marked a significant turning point as activists and scholars began to highlight the importance of corporate social responsibility (Batool et al., 2021). The publication of seminal works, such as "The Social Responsibility of Business is to Increase its Profits" by Milton Friedman in 1970, sparked debate on the role of businesses in society (Usman et al., 2024). While Friedman argued that businesses exist primarily to generate profit, opposing voices emerged to underscore the necessity of integrating ethical considerations into business decisions (Koivusalo, 2023). The rise of the environmental movement in the 1960s and 1970s prompted a more profound awareness of the interconnectedness of business operations and environmental impacts, leading to the establishment of regulations like the Clean Air Act and the National Environmental Policy Act in the United States (Tekin & Küsbeci, 2021).

Towards the end of the 20th century, globalization intensified the pressures on businesses to take social and environmental responsibility seriously due to increasing public awareness facilitated by technology and communication (Bharadwaj et al., 2013). As information became more accessible, businesses could no longer operate in silos, shielded from scrutiny. The rise of the internet and social media allowed consumers and activists to voice concerns about ethical practices, pushing companies to adapt or face public backlash (Li et al., 2022).

The 21st century has witnessed the emergence of sustainability as a defining characteristic of successful business strategies. The United Nations' Sustainable Development Goals (SDGs), established in 2015, provided a concrete framework for businesses to align their practices with global priorities (Todaro & Smith, 2020) related to poverty alleviation, environmental sustainability, and social justice. Consequently, many entrepreneurs have recognized that addressing these issues can be well-aligned with their business objectives (Thorpe, 2016).

In corporate boardrooms and among entrepreneurs, the understanding of stakeholder theory a concept advocating for the consideration of all parties impacted by a business has gained momentum (Kadwa & Barnard, 2019). This has ushered in a new era of entrepreneurship focused on creating shared value, where economic and social benefits can coexist. Entrepreneurs today are tasked not only with overcoming economic challenges but also with leveraging their businesses as platforms for driving positive change (Johnson et al., 2020).

METHODOLOGY

The methodology for examining the crucial role of environmental and social responsibility in modern entrepreneurship will adopt a qualitative approach, focusing on case studies, interviews, and thematic analysis. This multifaceted method allows for a holistic understanding of how entrepreneurial ventures integrate sustainability and social responsibility into their core business strategies (Karantza, 2017).

Case Studies: The research will include an examination of various entrepreneurial ventures that have successfully integrated environmental and social responsibility into their business models. Case studies will be chosen from diverse industries such as renewable energy, sustainable fashion, and community-driven enterprises. Each case study will detail the company's mission, the specific environmental and social practices it employs, and the effects of these practices on its business performance and community impact (Amaghouss & Ibourk, 2013). By analyzing both successful and less successful cases, we can identify best practices and common challenges that entrepreneurs face when trying to incorporate responsibility into their operations.

Interviews: To gain deeper insights into the motivations, challenges, and strategies of entrepreneurs engaged in responsible business practices, semi-structured interviews will be conducted with founders, business leaders, and key stakeholders. The interview questions will be designed to elicit responses about their experiences in prioritizing sustainability, the benefits they have observed, and any difficulties they encounter. This qualitative data will be invaluable in understanding the individual perspectives and experiences of entrepreneurs, providing rich context to quantitative findings.

Thematic Analysis: Following the collection of qualitative data, a thematic analysis will be employed to identify patterns and themes that emerge from both the case studies and interviews. This will involve coding the data for key themes (Shane, 2007) related to environmental and social responsibility, such as innovation, stakeholder engagement, regulatory frameworks, and financial performance. The themes will be analyzed in relation to each case and interview response and synthesized to draw broader conclusions about the role of responsibility in modern entrepreneurship.

Surveys: Complementing qualitative methods, quantitative data collection through surveys may also be employed. Surveys can help understand broader trends and attitudes among a larger population of entrepreneurs and consumers regarding environmental and social responsibility. For example, questions may target the perceived importance of sustainability in purchasing decisions, the challenges entrepreneurs face in implementing responsible practices, and the criteria they follow when making business decisions (Dutz et al., 2000). Analysis of this data will facilitate a comparative understanding of different entrepreneurial sectors and highlight areas of best practice.

Triangulation: Finally, this methodology will use a triangulated approach, combining qualitative and quantitative data sources for a comprehensive understanding of the subject matter. This will help in validating findings and ensuring a balanced perspective is provided on the complexities involved in integrating environmental and social responsibility within entrepreneurial practices.

THEORETICAL FRAMEWORKS

The study of environmental and social responsibility in modern entrepreneurship can be grounded in several theoretical frameworks, which help elucidate the complexities and dynamics of sustainable business practices (Van Praag & Versloot, 2007). These frameworks include Stakeholder Theory, Triple Bottom Line (TBL) Theory, Institutional Theory, and Social Capital Theory.

Stakeholder Theory: Proposed by R. Edward Freeman, Stakeholder Theory posits that businesses must consider various stakeholders, including employees, customers, suppliers, the environment, and local communities, in their decision-making processes (Acs & Varga, 2005). This theory supports the notion that responsible entrepreneurship requires balancing the needs and interests of these stakeholders. Entrepreneurs who adopt this perspective recognize that their actions have repercussions beyond profit generation (O'Kane et al., 2023). By actively engaging stakeholders and incorporating their feedback, businesses can foster trust, enhance reputation, and create long-term value.

Triple Bottom Line (TBL): The TBL framework emphasizes the importance of measuring business performance not only in financial terms but also through social and environmental lenses (Mintzberg, 1973). Coined by John Elkington, the TBL advocates for a balance between economic prosperity, social equity, and environmental health, often succinctly referred to as "people, planet, and profit." Entrepreneurs who apply the TBL framework are more likely (Covin & Wales, 2012) to innovate sustainable practices that benefit all three dimensions, ultimately positioning themselves favorably in a competitive market increasingly driven by consumer preferences for socially responsible products and services (Miller, 1983).

Institutional Theory: This framework explores how institutional pressures influence businesses' adoption of socially and environmentally responsible practices.

Institutional Theory suggests that entrepreneurs face pressures from regulatory bodies, industry norms, and cultural expectations that can shape their behavior (Covin and Slevin, 1989). By understanding these pressures, entrepreneurs can navigate the complex landscape of sustainability more effectively. This theory also emphasizes the importance of legitimacy and reputation in modern entrepreneurship, as businesses that align with societal values are more likely to gain public support and foster partnerships (Miller and Friesen, 1982).

Social Capital Theory: The concept of social capital focuses on the value created through relationships, networks, and social interactions. Entrepreneurs who cultivate social capital are better positioned to understand community needs, garner support for their initiatives (Lumpkin and Dess, 1996), and create collaborative solutions to social and environmental challenges. By leveraging social capital, these entrepreneurs can enhance their understanding of local issues, foster community engagement, and ultimately drive social and environmental change within their business models (Covin & Lumpkin, 2011).

Ethical Theory and Corporate Social Responsibility (CSR): Finally, the integration of ethical theories, such as deontology or consequentialism, provides a moral framework for understanding the responsibilities of entrepreneurs in society (Chota, 2020). CSR frameworks extend beyond compliance with regulations, urging businesses to proactively contribute to social and environmental wellbeing. Entrepreneurs who incorporate ethical considerations into their decision-making processes are more likely to transition toward sustainable business practices that reflect their values and societal expectations (Van Doorn et al., 2015).

USE OF AI AND ML

One significant application of AI and ML is in the area of resource optimization. Companies are increasingly utilizing AI algorithms to analyze data on resource consumption, supply chains, and production processes (Karami et al., 2023). This allows businesses to reduce inefficiencies and waste, ultimately leading to lower carbon footprints and resource utilization. For instance, companies like Google use AI to manage energy consumption in their data centers, achieving significant reductions in energy use and emissions (Hassan et al., 2021). By predicting energy needs based on historical data, these systems help in shifting demand to off-peak times when renewable energy sources, like solar or wind, are more available.

AI and ML also play a crucial role in supply chain transparency, enhancing ethical sourcing and production practices (Rauch et al., 2009). Businesses can leverage these technologies to analyze and track their supply chains, identifying points of ethical concern such as labor practices or environmental impacts (Bernoster et al.,

2020). By using blockchain technology in conjunction with AI, entrepreneurs can ensure greater accountability and traceability in sourcing materials. Consumers are increasingly demanding transparency and ethical practices, and those businesses that adopt these technologies stand to build stronger trust with their clientele (Ferreras-Méndez et al., 2021).

Furthermore, AI-driven analytics can facilitate corporate social responsibility (CSR) initiatives by measuring the impact of social programs. Companies can analyze data on community engagement, environmental impact, and stakeholder feedback to refine their CSR strategies (Corrêa et al., 2022). Sophisticated algorithms can also assess the effectiveness of different initiatives in real-time, helping businesses adapt and optimize their social and environmental contributions (Zahra, 1991).

The rise of AI and ML also fosters innovative approaches to marketing and customer engagement centered around sustainability. Brands that utilize AI-driven insights can tailor their messaging to highlight their environmental efforts, resonating with the growing demographic of eco-conscious consumers (Wu et al., 2021). This symbiotic relationship between technology and consumer psychology not only boosts sales but also reinforces a culture of responsibility and sustainability in the marketplace (Favaretto et al., 2020).

THE ROLE OF AR, VR, AND MR

In today's dynamic business environment, Augmented Reality (AR), Virtual Reality (VR), and Mixed Reality (MR) technologies have the potential to transform how companies approach environmental and social responsibility (Naqvi et al., 2021). These immersive technologies offer innovative ways to engage consumers, enhance training and educational programs, and foster sustainable practices, all while promoting a deeper understanding of social issues (Cui et al., 2020).

One of the most prominent applications of AR, VR, and MR is in consumer engagement. Businesses can create immersive experiences that educate consumers about their environmental practices, products, and services in a way that traditional marketing cannot (Riahi & Riahi, 2018). For example, AR can allow customers to visualize the environmental impact of a product by overlaying data in their physical environment, thus enabling them to make informed purchasing decisions (Ruzgas et al., 2016). Similarly, VR can transport users to virtual environments depicting the consequences of climate change, enhancing awareness and fostering a sense of responsibility among consumers (Sedkaoui, 2018). By creating personalized and engaging experiences, businesses can evoke emotional responses that align consumer behavior with sustainable practices, furthering their social impact (Mohammed & Isa, 2021).

In the context of corporate training, AR and VR are being utilized to simulate real-world scenarios that emphasize ethical and sustainable practices. Companies can train employees in virtual environments to deal with social challenges and environmental responsibilities (Kaggwa et al., 2024). For instance, a retail company might use VR simulations to teach staff about the importance of ethical sourcing and responsible social practices (Aydemir 2018). This hands-on approach to learning ensures that employees internalize these values, thereby cultivating a culture of responsibility within the organization (Chen et al., 2023).

Furthermore, AR and VR can play a crucial role in enhancing corporate communication regarding social responsibility initiatives, immersive storytelling allows businesses to present their efforts in a more engaging manner, resonating with audiences on a deeper level (Labanauskaitė et al., 2021). Virtual tours that demonstrate a company's sustainability initiatives or social impact projects effectively communicate these efforts, building credibility and trust with consumers and stakeholders (Aydemir, 2018). This transparency is increasingly important in an age where consumers demand accountability from corporations (He et al., 2021).

ADVANTAGES

In today's rapidly evolving business landscape, environmental and social responsibility has emerged as a pivotal factor shaping the success and sustainability of modern entrepreneurship (Modayil & Kuipers, 2008). Companies that adopt a commitment to responsible practices not only enhance their reputations but also experience a variety of tangible advantages (Arucu, 2021). Firstly, one of the most significant benefits of embracing environmental and social responsibility is improved brand image and customer loyalty (Misaros et al., 2023). Consumers are becoming increasingly aware of the ecological footprint of their purchases, with a growing number prioritizing brands that demonstrate commitment to sustainable practices (Liu, 2023). A company perceived as environmentally friendly and socially responsible can create a loyal customer base, thereby increasing retention rates and sales (Hua et al., 2023). Studies reveal that millennials and Generation Z consumers are particularly inclined to support brands with strong sustainability values, sometimes even willing to pay a premium for ethically sourced products (Liberatore & Wagner, 2021).

Secondly, environmental and social responsibility can lead to substantial cost savings (Floridi, 2019). By implementing energy-efficient processes, reducing waste, and opting for sustainable materials, businesses can cut operational costs significantly over time (Zhao, 2009). For example, companies that focus on reducing energy consumption often find themselves benefiting from lower utility bills, facilitating a better allocation of resources (El Miedany, 2019). Additionally, supply chain optimization through sustainable practices can result in reduced material costs and less waste, thus contributing directly to the bottom line (Turner, 2022).

Another important advantage relates to innovation and competitive advantage. The growing emphasis on sustainability has propelled companies to think creatively about their product offerings and operational models (Schumpeter, 1934). Businesses are increasingly exploring eco-friendly innovations, from biodegradable packaging to renewable energy solutions, establishing themselves as pioneers in their respective industries (Drucker, 1998). This not only differentiates them in a crowded market but also positions them as leaders in sustainability, attracting investment opportunities and partnerships (Turienzo et al., 2023).

Lastly, companies that actively engage in environmental and social responsibility are often favored by investors (Bessant & Tidd, 2007). With the rise of Environmental, Social, and Governance (ESG) investing, many investors are evaluating potential investments not only on financial returns but also on the company's ethical practices (Davidsson, 2015). Firms that exhibit a strong commitment to sustainability are more likely to attract funding, as investors increasingly seek out responsible investments aligned with their personal or institutional values (Makhloufi et al., 2021).

CHALLENGES

One of the foremost challenges is the initial financial investment required for sustainable practices (Wiklund & Shepherd, 2005). Transitioning to environmentally friendly processes, sourcing sustainable materials, and implementing ethical labor practices can require substantial upfront investments (Drucker, 1985). For startups and small businesses, these costs may pose insurmountable obstacles, potentially limiting their competitiveness against larger firms that can absorb these expenses more easily (Hult et al., 2004). Even established companies may struggle to balance short-term financial performance with long-term sustainability investments, leading to a hesitance to implement necessary changes (Lumpkin & Dess, 2001).

Moreover, achieving genuine social and environmental responsibility requires a thorough examination of the entire supply chain, which can be complex and opaque (Corrêa et al., 2022). Many businesses find it challenging to verify the sustainability claims of their suppliers, particularly in global supply chains where sub-suppliers might not share the same commitment to ethical practices (Kreiser & Davis, 2010). This lack of transparency can hinder a business's ability to ensure that every aspect of its operations aligns with its sustainability goals (Okoli et al., 2021).

Another challenge lies in employee engagement and culture. While socially responsible practices can enhance workplace morale, there is often resistance within organizations when it comes to changing established processes (Alegre & Chiva, 2013). Convincing employees to embrace new sustainable practices may involve overcoming entrenched mindsets, a task that requires strong leadership and effective communication (Otero-Neira et al., 2013).

Lastly, the rapid pace of change in societal expectations concerning social issues can lead to uncertainty (Rajest et al., 2023). Social responsibility is not a static concept; it evolves according to cultural norms and crises, such as racial equality movements or labor rights advocacy (Tornatzky & Fleischer, 1990). As public expectations shift, businesses must be agile and willing to adapt their strategies, which can be both challenging and resource-intensive (Putniņš & Sauka, 2020).

ETHICAL CONSIDERATIONS

A primary ethical consideration is the principle of stewardship, which posits that businesses have a responsibility to manage resources sustainably (Al-Jabri & Sohail, 2012). Entrepreneurs must consider the long-term impacts of their activities on the environment, not merely as a compliance measure but as a moral obligation (Siddiqui & Goyal, 2023). For examplc, a company that prioritizes profit over environmental conservation may contribute to pollution and climate change, ultimately harming future generations (Alsheibani et al., 2018). Adopting ethical practices necessitates a shift from short-term gain to long-term value creation, wherein businesses recognize their role as custodians of natural and social resources (Al Hadwer et al., 2021).

Transparency is another crucial ethical consideration. Modern consumers demand accountability and clarity about the products they purchase and the practices behind them (Malik et al., 2021). Entrepreneurs should cultivate a culture of openness, providing stakeholders with information about sourcing, production practices, and community involvement (Awa et al., 2017). Ethical dilemmas can ensue when companies choose to obscure their practices to enhance profitability (Raisch & Krakowski, 2021). However, transparency fosters trust and loyalty among consumers, enhancing brand reputation (Pertusa-Ortega et al., 2010). Ethical entrepreneurship calls for leaders who prioritize honesty and integrity and apply these values to every facet of their operations (Lichtenthaler, 2020).

The balance between profit and ethics raises questions about fairness and equity, particularly in supply chain management (Zhang & Lu, 2021). Many entrepreneurs partner with suppliers and subcontractors whose labor practices may differ significantly from national or international standards (Merhi & Harfouche, 2024). Ethical considerations compel entrepreneurs to ensure fair labor practices throughout their supply chains, combating exploitative practices such as child labor or unfair wages (Miikkulainen et al., 2018). Companies that prioritize social responsibility not only comply with regulations but actively seek partnerships that enhance the overall well-being of workers, even beyond their immediate operations (Arrieta et al., 2020).

Finally, the environmental and social responsibilities of entrepreneurs are inherently tied to the ethical frameworks guiding their actions (Keding, 2021). Ethics serve as the foundation for defining what it means to operate responsibly, compelling entrepreneurs to align their strategies with broader concepts of justice and human dignity (Ahmed et al., 2021). This alignment not only enhances their moral compass but also shapes the public perception of their brands (Daugherty & Wilson, 2018). Engaging with ESR in an ethical manner transforms businesses into agents of positive change, encouraging others to adopt similar practices (Torrado et al., 2018).

IMPLEMENTATIONS OF REGULATORY FRAMEWORKS

The growing importance of environmental and social responsibility (ESR) in entrepreneurship has prompted the development of regulatory frameworks designed to guide and enforce responsible practices across industries (Jöhnk et al., 2021). One of the primary implementations of regulatory frameworks is through environmental legislation, which sets standards for businesses to reduce their ecological footprints (Pillai & Sivathanu, 2020). Regulations such as the Clean Air Act, the Clean Water Act, and the European Union's REACH regulation aim to minimize pollution and promote sustainability (Wamba-Taguimdje et al., 2020). Entrepreneurs must navigate these regulations and integrate compliance measures into their operations, which often leads to innovations in resource efficiency and waste reduction (Ramachandran et al., 2022). For instance, companies may invest in developing eco-friendly products or adopting cleaner technologies as part of their compliance strategies (Soni et al., 2020). By viewing regulations not just as constraints but as opportunities for improvement, entrepreneurs can align their systems with environmentally responsible practices (Pallathadka et al., 2023).

Social responsibility regulations, such as labor standards and consumer protection laws, also play a crucial role in guiding entrepreneurs toward ethical practices (Vaio et al., 2020). The implementation of frameworks that ensure fair labor conditions, such as the Fair Labor Standards Act in the United States, compels entrepreneurs to address issues like wage disparity, working hours, and occupational safety (Votto, 2021). Compliance with these standards is not merely about avoiding penalties; it also elevates the overall ethical framework of a business (Yeomans et al., 2019). Companies that actively engage in fair labor practices often enjoy better employee retention and consumer loyalty, translating into long-term benefits (Hughes et al., 2019).

Another critical aspect of regulatory frameworks lies in the concept of corporate social responsibility (CSR) reporting (Tong et al., 2021). Many countries and regions mandate companies to disclose their social and environmental impacts (Ensmenger, 2012). For instance, the European Union's Non-Financial Reporting Directive requires large entities to produce annual reports on their environmental, social, and governance (ESG) activities (Pournader, 2021). This form of regulation pushes entrepreneurs to meticulously track their impact and engage in self-assessment, thereby fostering a culture of accountability (Haefner, 2021). Reporting also serves as a tool for stakeholders to scrutinize a company's commitment to ESR, incentivizing businesses to enhance their practices to maintain a positive public image (Syed et al., 2020).

Partnerships between the public and private sectors are also instrumental in the effective implementation of ESR frameworks. Governments can collaborate with entrepreneurs to promote best practices while providing resources for compliance (Jarrahi, 2018). For instance, initiatives like the United Nations Global Compact encourage businesses to adopt sustainable and socially responsible policies aligned with international standards (Bharadiya, 2023). By creating platforms for collaboration, these partnerships facilitate knowledge sharing and innovation, enabling businesses to adopt comprehensive ESR approaches that can lead to systemic change (Alblushi, 2021).

FOSTERING COLLABORATION

One of the foremost ways to foster collaboration is through stakeholder engagement (Davenport and Ronanki, 2018). Entrepreneurs must actively seek to involve a diverse array of stakeholders, including employees, suppliers, customers, and local communities, in the decision-making process (Humble & Altun, 2020). By listening to the perspectives, needs, and concerns of these stakeholders, businesses can better understand the social and environmental implications of their operations (Haenlein & Kaplan, 2021). This could take the shape of advisory panels, community forums, or customer feedback programs (Agrawal et al., 2017). For instance, Patagonia, the outdoor apparel company known for its environmental activism, has successfully engaged its customer base in various sustainability initiatives by integrating their feedback and promoting environmental awareness (Tien, 2017).

Partnerships between businesses and non-profits or governmental organizations can also serve as a powerful tool for fostering collaboration in ESR (Perifanis & Kitsios, 2023). Through strategic alliances, companies can gain access to expertise, resources, and networks that enhance their sustainability efforts (Robinson, 2019). A notable example is the collaboration between Unilever and the World Wildlife Fund (WWF) on sustainable sourcing methods for agricultural raw materials (Fleck,

2018). Such partnerships not only contribute to environmental conservation but also help brands burnish their image, yielding long-term economic benefits and bolstering customer loyalty (Keding, 2019).

Integrating technology can significantly enhance the capacity for collaboration in ESR initiatives (Adoli & Kilika, 2020). Digital platforms can facilitate greater transparency and communication, allowing businesses to share data regarding their sustainability practices and impact (Dwivedi et al., 2021). For example, blockchain technology can ensure traceability in supply chains, holding companies accountable for their environmental actions (Nissen & Sengupta, 2006). Such innovations not only build trust among stakeholders but also create a collaborative ecosystem where businesses can collectively forge a path toward improved environmental practices (Truong & Papagiannidis, 2022).

CONCLUSION

The integration of ESR into business operations fosters a holistic view of value creation. It brings about a paradigm shift, where companies prioritize not only profit but also their impact on society and the environment (Carlsson & Walden, 1997). This shift is reflected in the rise of ethical consumerism, with customers actively seeking brands that align with their values (Davenport & Ronanki, 2018). Companies such as Tesla have demonstrated how environmentally responsible practices can drive brand loyalty and consumer engagement (Wilson & Daugherty, 2018). The company's commitment to sustainable energy solutions has not only transformed the automotive industry but also positioned Tesla as a leader in innovation (Reeves and Ueda, 2016).

Moreover, socially responsible practices can enhance workforce motivation and retention. Organizations that prioritize inclusion, community engagement, and ethical labor practices create a more engaged and satisfied workforce (Robinson et al., 2021). Employees, especially millennials and Generation Z, are increasingly inclined to choose employers based on their values and commitment to corporate social responsibility (CSR) (Ferràs-Hernández et al., 2017). This trend indicates that companies that embrace ESR can foster a culture of loyalty and dedication among their workforce, driving productivity and innovation (Gangwani and Zhu, 2024).

However, the journey toward embedding ESR in entrepreneurship is not without challenges. Businesses must navigate complex and often conflicting stakeholder interests, regulatory requirements, and market demands (Ireland et al., 2003). This necessitates a robust framework for accountability and transparency to build trust and maintain credibility (Zafarani et al., 2014). Companies that take a proactive approach to communicating their ESR initiatives can combat skepticism and demonstrate their commitment to genuine, impactful change (Zuloaga-Rotta et al., 2024).

SUGGESTIONS

Develop a Comprehensive ESG Framework: Entrepreneurs should establish an Environmental, Social, and Governance (ESG) framework tailored to their business models and sectors. This framework should include clear metrics for sustainability, community engagement, and ethical governance (Yousfi-Monod et al., 2010). By adopting such structures, businesses can effectively track their progress and drive accountability.

Invest in Sustainable Practices: Entrepreneurs should invest significantly in sustainable practices, such as renewable energy sources, waste reduction techniques, and environmentally friendly materials. This commitment not only helps minimize environmental impact but also attracts eco-conscious consumers (Krogh et al., 2021). For instance, businesses can explore biodegradable packaging or energy-efficient production processes that reduce their carbon footprint and operational costs.

Educate and Train Employees: Employee engagement is crucial to fostering a culture of ESR within organizations. Entrepreneurs should implement training programs to educate employees about the importance of social responsibility and environmental stewardship (Cielen et al., 2004). By facilitating workshops and seminars, businesses can empower their workforce to contribute positively to the company's sustainability goals of developing leaders who prioritize ESR.

Transparent Communication: Building trust with consumers hinges on transparent communication regarding a company's ESR initiatives. Entrepreneurs should regularly report on their environmental and social impact, using clear metrics and success stories to showcase progress (Jean et al., 2016). This transparency not only cultivates consumer loyalty but also holds businesses accountable for their commitments.

Leverage Technology: Technology can serve as a powerful ally in advancing ESR initiatives. Entrepreneurs can utilize data analytics to identify areas for improvement in sustainability and social responsibility (Bail, 2014). Additionally, blockchain can enhance supply chain transparency, ensuring ethical sourcing and labor practices. Embracing innovation will allow companies to enhance efficiency and credibility in their efforts.

Incorporate Circular Economy Principles: Emphasizing circular economy principles such as reusing, recycling, and reducing waste can significantly bolster a business's sustainability credentials (Doyle et al., 2017). Entrepreneurs should seek ways to create products and services that minimize waste, such as designing for recyclability or adopting take-back programs that encourage consumers to return old products for reuse.

Advocate for Policy Changes: Beyond their operations, entrepreneurs can play a vital role in advocating for stricter environmental and social regulations. By participating in public discourse and lobbying for beneficial policies, business leaders can help shape a more sustainable and equitable marketplace (Cioffi et al., 2020). This approach not only enhances their corporate image but also contributes to broader societal change.

FUTURE RESEARCH DIRECTIONS

While many entrepreneurs implement ESR initiatives, comprehensive methods for measuring their impacts on business performance and societal outcomes remain underdeveloped (Suominen et al., 2017). Future research could focus on creating standardized frameworks and metrics to evaluate the effectiveness of various ESR practices, linking them to key performance indicators in diverse sectors.

Analyzing consumer attitudes and behaviors towards environmentally and socially responsible companies is crucial (Strohmeier & Piazza, 2013). Research could explore the factors that influence consumer trust and loyalty in relation to ESR initiatives. Understanding demographic variations in consumer responses to these practices can also provide insights for targeted marketing strategies.

While much of the existing research focuses on established economies, there is a significant gap in understanding how ESR practices are adopted and adapted in emerging markets (Kar et al., 2021). Examining local socio-economic conditions, cultural factors, and regulatory environments can shed light on the unique challenges and opportunities faced by entrepreneurs in these regions.

The intersection of technology and ESR presents numerous opportunities for research. Future studies could investigate how emerging technologies, such as artificial intelligence, machine learning, and blockchain, can enhance sustainability and social equity in business practices (Metawa et al., 2022). Analyzing case studies of tech-driven firms that prioritize ESR can also provide practical insights. Long-term studies tracking the evolution of ESR practices within entrepreneurial ventures can provide insight into the challenges and successes faced over time.

REFERENCES

Acs, Z. J., & Varga, A. (2005). Entrepreneurship, agglomeration and technological change. *Small Business Economics, 24*, 323–334.

Adoli, H. L., & Kilika, J. M. (2020). Conceptualizing the role of leadership strategy in the context of strategic management process: A review of literature. *Journal of Economics and Business, 3*(4), 1598–1623.

Agrawal, S., Chatterjee, K., & Novotný, P. (2017). Lexicographic ranking supermartingales: an efficient approach to termination of probabilistic programs. *Proceedings of the ACM on Programming Languages, 2*(POPL), 1-32.

Ahmed, N., Abbasi, M. S., Zuberi, F., Qamar, W., Halim, M. S. B., Maqsood, A., & Alam, M. K. (2021). Artificial intelligence techniques: Analysis, application, and outcome in dentistry—a systematic review. *BioMed Research International, 2021*(1), 1–15. PMID: 34258283

Al Hadwer, A., Tavana, M., Gillis, D., & Rezania, D. (2021). A systematic review of organizational factors impacting cloud-based technology adoption using technology-organization-environment framework. *Internet of Things : Engineering Cyber Physical Human Systems, 15*, 1–10.

Al-Jabri, I., & Sohail, M. S. (2012). Mobile banking adoption: Application of diffusion of innovation theory. *Journal of Electronic Commerce Research, 13*(4), 379–391.

Alblushi, A. (2021). Face recognition based on artificial neural network: A review. *Artificial Intelligence & Robotics Development Journal, 1*(2), 116–131.

Alegre, J., & Chiva, R. (2013). Linking entrepreneurial orientation and firm performance: The role of organizational learning capability and innovation performance. *Journal of Small Business Management, 51*(4), 491–507.

Alsheibani, S., Cheung, Y., & Messom, C. (2018). Artificial intelligence adoption: AI-readiness at firm-level. *Twenty-Second Pacific Asia Conference on Information Systems,* Japan 2018 (pp. 1-8). Association for Information Systems.

Amaghouss, J., & Ibourk, A. (2013). Entrepreneurial activities, innovation and economic growth: The role of cyclical factors evidence from OECD countries for the period 2001-2009. *International Business Research, 6*(1), 153–162.

Ammar, M., Haleem, A., Javaid, M., Walia, R., & Bahl, S. (2021). Improving material quality management and manufacturing organizations system through Industry 4.0 technologies. *Materials Today: Proceedings, 45*, 5089–5096.

Arrieta, A. B., Díaz-Rodríguez, N., Del Ser, J., Bennetot, A., Tabik, S., Barbado, A., & Herrera, F. (2020). Explainable Artificial Intelligence (XAI): Concepts, taxonomies, opportunities and challenges toward responsible AI. *Information Fusion*, *58*, 82–115.

Arucu, M. (2021). Industry 4.0–holistic perspective: Modeling and simulation implementations in manufacturing systems. *Journal of Innovative Science and Engineering*, *5*(1), 50–63.

Awa, H. O., Ojiabo, O. U., & Orokor, L. E. (2017). Integrated technology-organization-environment (TOE) taxonomies for technology adoption. *Journal of Enterprise Information Management*, *30*(6), 893–921.

Aydemir, E. (2018). Weka ile yapay zeka. *Seçkin Yayınevi.*

Bail, C. A. (2014). The cultural environment: Measuring culture with big data. *Theory and Society*, *43*, 465–482.

Batool, S., Gill, S. A., Javaid, S., & Khan, A. J. (2021). Good governance via E-Governance: moving towards digitalization for a digital economy. *Review of Applied Management and Social Sciences, 4*(4), 823-836.

Bernoster, I., Mukerjee, J., & Thurik, R. (2020). The role of affect in entrepreneurial orientation. *Small Business Economics*, *54*(1), 235–256.

Bessant, J., & Tidd, J. (2007). *Innovation and entrepreneurship*. John Wiley & Sons.

Bharadiya, J. P. (2023). A comparative study of business intelligence and artificial intelligence with big data analytics. *American Journal of Artificial Intelligence*, *7*(1), 24–30.

Bharadwaj, A., El Sawy, O. A., Pavlou, P. A., & Venkatraman, N. V. (2013). Digital business strategy: Toward a next generation of insights. *Management Information Systems Quarterly*, 471–482.

Cammack, P. (2022). *The politics of global competitiveness*. Oxford University Press.

Carlsson, C., & Walden, P. (1997). More effective strategic management with hyperknowledge: The Woodstrat case. *Journal of Decision Systems*, *6*(1), 23–44.

Chen, W., He, W., Shen, J., Tian, X., & Wang, X. (2023). Systematic analysis of artificial intelligence in the era of industry 4.0. *Journal of Management Analytics*, *10*(1), 89–108.

Chota, M. C. (2020). *Entrepreneurial orientation and it's effects on micro, small and medium enterprises (MSME's) business performance in Lusaka district* (Doctoral dissertation, The University of Zambia).

Cielen, A., Peeters, L., & Vanhoof, K. (2004). Bankruptcy prediction using a data envelopment analysis. *European Journal of Operational Research, 154*(2), 526–532.

Cioffi, R., Travaglioni, M., Piscitelli, G., Petrillo, A., & De Felice, F. (2020). Artificial intelligence and machine learning applications in smart production: Progress, trends, and directions. *Sustainability, 12*(2), 1–26.

Codini, A. P., Abbate, T., & Petruzzelli, A. M. (2023). Business Model Innovation and exaptation: A new way of innovating in SMEs. *Technovation, 119*, 1–16.

Corrêa, V. S., Queiroz, M. M., Cruz, M. A., & Shigaki, H. B. (2022). Entrepreneurial orientation far beyond opportunity: The influence of the necessity for innovativeness, proactiveness and risk-taking. *International Journal of Entrepreneurial Behaviour & Research, 28*(4), 952–979.

Covin, J. G., & Lumpkin, G. T. (2011). Entrepreneurial orientation theory and research: Reflections on a needed construct. *Entrepreneurship Theory and Practice, 35*(5), 855–872.

Covin, J. G., & Slevin, D. P. (1989). Strategic management of small firms in hostile and benign environments. *Strategic Management Journal, 10*(1), 75–87.

Covin, J. G., & Wales, W. J. (2012). The measurement of entrepreneurial orientation. *Entrepreneurship Theory and Practice, 36*(4), 677–702.

Cui, Y., Kara, S., & Chan, K. C. (2020). Manufacturing big data ecosystem: A systematic literature review. *Robotics and Computer-integrated Manufacturing, 62*, 1–20.

Daugherty, P. R., & Wilson, H. J. (2018). *Human+ machine: Reimagining work in the age of AI.* Harvard Business Press.

Davenport, T. H., & Ronanki, R. (2018). Artificial intelligence for the real world. *Harvard Business Review, 96*(1), 108–116.

Davidsson, P. (2015). Entrepreneurial opportunities and the entrepreneurship nexus: A re-conceptualization. *Journal of Business Venturing, 30*(5), 674–695.

Doyle, G., Srivastava, S. B., Goldberg, A., & Frank, M. C. (2017). Alignment at Work: Using Language to Distinguish the Internalization and Self-Regulation Components of Cultural Fit in Organizations. *IRLE Working Paper*, pp. 102-110. https://irle.berkeley.edu/files/2017/Alignment-At-Work.pdf

Drucker, P. F. (1985). Entrepreneurial strategies. *California Management Review, 27*(2), 9–25.

Drucker, P. F. (1998). The discipline of innovation. *Harvard Business Review, 76*(6), 149–157. PMID: 10187245

Dutz, M. A., Ordover, J. A., & Willig, R. D. (2000). Entrepreneurship, access policy and economic development: Lessons from industrial organization. *European Economic Review, 44*(4-6), 739–747.

Dwivedi, Y. K., Hughes, L., Ismagilova, E., Aarts, G., Coombs, C., Crick, T., & Williams, M. D. (2021). Artificial Intelligence (AI): Multidisciplinary perspectives on emerging challenges, opportunities, and agenda for research, practice and policy. *International Journal of Information Management, 57*, 1–47.

El Miedany, Y. (2019). Virtual reality and augmented reality. *Rheumatology teaching: the art and science of medical education*, 403-427.

Ensmenger, N. (2012). Is chess the drosophila of artificial intelligence? A social history of an algorithm. *Social Studies of Science, 42*(1), 5–30. PMID: 22530382

Favaretto, M., De Clercq, E., Schneble, C. O., & Elger, B. S. (2020). What is your definition of Big Data? Researchers' understanding of the phenomenon of the decade. *PLoS One, 15*(2), 1–20. PMID: 32097430

Felicetti, A. M., Corvello, V., & Ammirato, S. (2024). Digital innovation in entrepreneurial firms: A systematic literature review. *Review of Managerial Science, 18*(2), 315–362.

Ferràs-Hernández, X., Tarrats-Pons, E., & Arimany-Serrat, N. (2017). Disruption in the automotive industry: A Cambrian moment. *Business Horizons, 60*(6), 855–863.

Ferreras-Méndez, J. L., Olmos-Penuela, J., Salas-Vallina, A., & Alegre, J. (2021). Entrepreneurial orientation and new product development performance in SMEs: The mediating role of business model innovation. *Technovation, 108*, 1–13.

Fleck, J. (2018). Development and establishment in artificial intelligence. In *The Question of Artificial Intelligence* (pp. 106–164). Routledge.

Floridi, L. (2019). What the near future of artificial intelligence could be. *Philosophy & Technology, 32*, 1–15.

Gangwani, D., & Zhu, X. (2024). Modeling and prediction of business success: A survey. *Artificial Intelligence Review, 57*(2), 1–51.

Guerrero, M., Liñán, F., & Cáceres-Carrasco, F. R. (2021). The influence of ecosystems on the entrepreneurship process: A comparison across developed and developing economies. *Small Business Economics*, *57*(4), 1733–1759.

Haefner, N., Wincent, J., Parida, V., & Gassmann, O. (2021). Artificial intelligence and innovation management: A review, framework, and research agenda . *Technological Forecasting and Social Change*, *162*, 1–10.

Haenlein, M., & Kaplan, A. (2021). Artificial intelligence and robotics: Shaking up the business world and society at large. *Journal of Business Research*, *124*(C), 405–407.

Hassan, A., Anwar, I., Saleem, I., Islam, K. B., & Hussain, S. A. (2021). Individual entrepreneurial orientation, entrepreneurship education and entrepreneurial intention: The mediating role of entrepreneurial motivations. *Industry and Higher Education*, *35*(4), 403–418.

He, H., Gray, J., Cangelosi, A., Meng, Q., McGinnity, T. M., & Mehnen, J. (2021). The challenges and opportunities of human-centered AI for trustworthy robots and autonomous systems. *IEEE Transactions on Cognitive and Developmental Systems*, *14*(4), 1398–1412.

Hua, H., Li, Y., Wang, T., Dong, N., Li, W., & Cao, J. (2023). Edge computing with artificial intelligence: A machine learning perspective. *ACM Computing Surveys*, *55*(9), 1–35.

Hughes, C., Robert, L., Frady, K., & Arroyos, A. (2019). Artificial intelligence, employee engagement, fairness, and job outcomes. In *Managing technology and middle-and low-skilled employees* (pp. 61–68). Emerald Publishing Limited.

Hult, G. T. M., Hurley, R. F., & Knight, G. A. (2004). Innovativeness: Its antecedents and impact on business performance. *Industrial Marketing Management*, *33*(5), 429–438.

Humble, K. P., & Altun, D. (2020). Artificial Intelligence and the threat to human rights. *Journal of Internet Law*, *24*(3), 1–19.

Ireland, R. D., Hitt, M. A., & Sirmon, D. G. (2003). A model of strategic entrepreneurship: The construct and its dimensions. *Journal of Management*, *29*(6), 963–989.

Jarrahi, M. H. (2018). Artificial intelligence and the future of work: Human-AI symbiosis in organizational decision making. *Business Horizons*, *61*(4), 577–586.

Jean, N., Burke, M., Xie, M., Davis, W. M., Lobell, D. B., & Ermon, S. (2016). Combining satellite imagery and machine learning to predict poverty. *Science, 353*(6301), 790–794. PMID: 27540167

Jöhnk, J., Weißert, M., & Wyrtki, K. (2021). Ready or not, AI comes—An interview study of organizational AI readiness factors. *Business & Information Systems Engineering*, *63*(1), 5–20.

Johnson, J., Whittington, R., Regnér, P., Angwin, D., Johnson, G., & Scholes, K. (2020). Exploring strategy. Academic Press.

Kadwa, I., & Barnard, B. (2019). The impact of leadership on entrepreneurship and innovation: Perceptions of entrepreneurs. *IUP Journal of Entrepreneurship Development*, *16*(4), 7–43.

Kaggwa, S., Eleogu, T. F., Okonkwo, F., Farayola, O. A., Uwaoma, P. U., & Akinoso, A. (2024). AI in decision making: Transforming business strategies. *International Journal of Research and Scientific Innovation*, *10*(12), 423–444.

Kar, S., Kar, A. K., & Gupta, M. P. (2021). Modeling drivers and barriers of artificial intelligence adoption: Insights from a strategic management perspective. *Intelligent Systems in Accounting, Finance & Management*, *28*(4), 217–238.

Karami, M., Ojala, A., & Saarenketo, S. (2023). Entrepreneurial orientation and international opportunity development by SMEs: The mediating role of decision-making logic. *Journal of Small Business Management*, *61*(2), 994–1022.

Karantza, P. (2017). *The impact of economic crises on the development of innovation and entrepreneurship* (Doctoral dissertation, Business Administration Programm, School of Economic Sciences and Business, Neapolis University Pafos).

Keding, C. (2021). Understanding the interplay of artificial intelligence and strategic management: Four decades of research in review. *Management Review Quarterly*, *71*(1), 91–134.

Kiyabo, K., & Isaga, N. (2020). Entrepreneurial orientation, competitive advantage, and SMEs' performance: Application of firm growth and personal wealth measures. *Journal of Innovation and Entrepreneurship*, *9*(1), 1–15.

Koivusalo, S. (2023). *Digital entrepreneurship: challenges faced by Finnish professional service business owners during venture launch in online business environments*. Master's Thesis, School of Business and Economics, Jyväskylä University.

Kreiser, P. M., & Davis, J. (2010). Entrepreneurial orientation and firm performance: The unique impact of innovativeness, proactiveness, and risk-taking. *Journal of Small Business and Entrepreneurship*, *23*(1), 39–51.

Labanauskaitė, D., Župerkienė, E., Kumpf, A., Šimanskienė, L., & Koller, S. M. (2021). Development of digital and entrepreneurial competences for the future labour market needs. *Entrepreneurship and Sustainability Issues, 8*(3), 565-581.

Li, X., Li, J., Yuan, C., Guo, S., & Wang, Z. (2022). Digital infrastructure. In *Development practice of digital business environment in China* (pp. 39–55). Springer Nature Singapore.

Liberatore, M. J., & Wagner, W. P. (2021). Virtual, mixed, and augmented reality: A systematic review for immersive systems research. *Virtual Reality (Waltham Cross)*, *25*(3), 773–799.

Lichtenthaler, U. (2020). Extremes of acceptance: Employee attitudes toward artificial intelligence. *The Journal of Business Strategy*, *41*(5), 39–45.

Liu, R. (2023). Innovative research on synergistic development of digital integrated media and visual design based on kruskal algorithm. *Applied Mathematics and Nonlinear Sciences*, *9*(1), 1–13.

Lumpkin, G. T., & Dess, G. G. (1996). Clarifying the entrepreneurial orientation construct and linking it to performance. *Academy of Management Review*, *21*(1), 135–172.

Lumpkin, G. T., & Dess, G. G. (2001). Linking two dimensions of entrepreneurial orientation to firm performance: The moderating role of environment and industry life cycle. *Journal of Business Venturing*, *16*(5), 429–451.

Makhloufi, L., Laghouag, A. A., Ali Sahli, A., & Belaid, F. (2021). Impact of entrepreneurial orientation on innovation capability: The mediating role of absorptive capability and organizational learning capabilities. *Sustainability*, *13*(10), 1–20.

Malik, S., Chadhar, M., Vatanasakdakul, S., & Chetty, M. (2021). Factors affecting the organizational adoption of blockchain technology: Extending the technology–organization–environment (TOE) framework in the Australian context. *Sustainability*, *13*(16), 1–31.

Mariotti, S., & Marzano, R. (2021). The effects of competition policy, regulatory quality and trust on inward FDI in host countries. *International Business Review*, *30*(6), 1–16.

Matalamäki, M. J., & Joensuu-Salo, S. (2022). Digitalization and strategic flexibility–a recipe for business growth. *Journal of Small Business and Enterprise Development, 29*(3), 380–401.

Merhi, M. I., & Harfouche, A. (2024). Enablers of artificial intelligence adoption and implementation in production systems. *International Journal of Production Research, 62*(15), 5457–5471.

Metawa, N., Hassan, M. K., & Metawa, S. (2022). *Artificial Intelligence and Big Data for Financial Risk Management*. Routledge.

Miikkulainen, R., Iscoe, N., Shagrin, A., Rapp, R., Nazari, S., McGrath, P., & Lamba, G. (2018, April). Sentient ascend: AI-based massively multivariate conversion rate optimization. In *Proceedings of the AAAI Conference on Artificial Intelligence* (Vol. 32, No. 1), 7696-7703.

Miller, D. (1983). The correlates of entrepreneurship in three types of firms. *Management Science, 29*(7), 770–791.

Miller, D., & Friesen, P. H. (1982). Innovation in conservative and entrepreneurial firms: Two models of strategic momentum. *Strategic Management Journal, 3*(1), 1–25.

Mintzberg, H. (1973). Strategy-making in three modes. *California Management Review, 16*(2), 44–53.

Misaros, M., Stan, O. P., Donca, I. C., & Miclea, L. C. (2023). Autonomous Robots for Services—State of the Art, Challenges, and Research Areas. *Sensors (Basel), 23*(10), 1–31. PMID: 37430875

Modayil, J., & Kuipers, B. (2008). The initial development of object knowledge by a learning robot. *Robotics and Autonomous Systems, 56*(11), 879–890. PMID: 19953188

Mohammed, I. B., & Isa, S. M. (2021). The role of internet of things (IoT) in the containment and spread of the novel COVID-19 pandemic. *Computational intelligence methods in COVID-19: surveillance, prevention, prediction and diagnosis*, 109-119.

Mostafiz, M. I., Hughes, M., & Sambasivan, M. (2022). Entrepreneurial orientation, competitive advantage and strategic knowledge management capability in Malaysian family firms. *Journal of Knowledge Management, 26*(2), 423–458.

Naqvi, R., Soomro, T. R., Alzoubi, H. M., Ghazal, T. M., & Alshurideh, M. T. (2021). The nexus between big data and decision-making: A study of big data techniques and technologies. In *The international conference on artificial intelligence and computer vision* (pp. 838–853). Springer International Publishing.

Ndagi, A., & Salihu, A. A. (2019). Technology Entrepreneurship and Fourth Industrial Revolution Era. *LAPAI International Journal of Management and Social Sciences*, *11*(1), 142–153.

Neumann, T. (2021). The impact of entrepreneurship on economic, social and environmental welfare and its determinants: A systematic review. *Management Review Quarterly*, *71*(3), 553–584.

Nissen, M. E., & Sengupta, K. (2006). Incorporating software agents into supply chains: Experimental investigation with a procurement task. *Management Information Systems Quarterly*, *30*(1), 145–166.

O'Kane, C., Zhang, J. A., Haar, J., & Cunningham, J. A. (2023). How scientists interpret and address funding criteria: Value creation and undesirable side effects. *Small Business Economics*, *61*(2), 799–826. PMID: 38625286

Okoli, I. E. N., Nwosu, K. C., & Okechukwu, M. E. (2021). Entrepreneurial orientation and performance of selected SMEs in Southeast, Nigeria. *European Journal of Business and Management Research*, *6*(4), 108–115.

Otero-Neira, C., Arias, M. J. F., & Lindman, M. T. (2013). Market orientation and entrepreneurial proclivity: Antecedents of innovation. *Global Business Review*, *14*(3), 385–395.

Pallathadka, H., Ramirez-Asis, E. H., Loli-Poma, T. P., Kaliyaperumal, K., Ventayen, R. J. M., & Naved, M. (2023). Applications of artificial intelligence in business management, e-commerce and finance. *Materials Today: Proceedings*, *80*, 1–4.

Parviainen, P., Tihinen, M., Kääriäinen, J., & Teppola, S. (2017). Tackling the digitalization challenge: how to benefit from digitalization in practice. *International Journal of Information Systems and Project Management, 5*(1), 63-77.

Perifanis, N. A., & Kitsios, F. (2023). Investigating the influence of artificial intelligence on business value in the digital era of strategy: A literature review. *Information (Basel)*, *14*(2), 1–42.

Pertusa-Ortega, E. M., Zaragoza-Sáez, P., & Claver-Cortés, E. (2010). Can formalization, complexity, and centralization influence knowledge performance? *Journal of Business Research*, *63*(3), 310–320.

Pillai, R., & Sivathanu, B. (2020). Adoption of artificial intelligence (AI) for talent acquisition in IT/ITeS organizations. *Benchmarking*, *27*(9), 2599–2629.

Pinto Borges, A., Lopes, J. M., Carvalho, C., Vieira, B. M., & Lopes, J. (2021). Education as a key to provide the growth of entrepreneurial intentions. *Education + Training*, *63*(6), 809–832.

Pournader, M., Ghaderi, H., Hassanzadegan, A., & Fahimnia, B. (2021). Artificial intelligence applications in supply chain management. *International Journal of Production Economics*, *241*, 1–16.

Putniņš, T. J., & Sauka, A. (2020). Why does entrepreneurial orientation affect company performance? *Strategic Entrepreneurship Journal*, *14*(4), 711–735.

Raisch, S., & Krakowski, S. (2021). Artificial intelligence and management: The automation–augmentation paradox. *Academy of Management Review*, *46*(1), 192–210.

Rajest, S. S., Singh, B., Obaid, A. J., Regin, R., & Chinnusamy, K. (Eds.). (2023). *Advances in artificial and human intelligence in the modern era*. IGI Global.

Ramachandran, K. K., Mary, A. A. S., Hawladar, S., Asokk, D., Bhaskar, B., & Pitroda, J. R. (2022). Machine learning and role of artificial intelligence in optimizing work performance and employee behavior. *Materials Today: Proceedings*, *51*, 2327–2331.

Rauch, A., Wiklund, J., Lumpkin, G. T., & Frese, M. (2009). Entrepreneurial orientation and business performance: An assessment of past research and suggestions for the future. *Entrepreneurship Theory and Practice*, *33*(3), 761–787.

Reeves, M., & Ueda, D. (2016). Designing the machines that will design strategy. *Harvard Business Review Digital Articles*, 2–6. https://hbr.org/2016/04/welcoming-the-chief-strategy-robot

Riahi, Y., & Riahi, S. (2018). Big data and big data analytics: Concepts, types and technologies. *International Journal of Research and Engineering*, *5*(9), 524–528.

Robinson, C. V., Ahmad, F., & Simmons, J. E. (2021). Consolidation and fragmentation in environmental scanning: A review and research agenda. *Long Range Planning*, *54*(3), 1–18.

Robinson, M. F. (2019). *Artificial intelligence in hiring: Understanding attitudes and perspectives of HR practitioners*. A dissertation submitted to the faculty of Wilmington University in partial fulfillment of the requirements for the degree of Doctor of Business Administration, Wilmington University (Delaware).

Ruzgas, T., Jakubeliene, K., & Buivyte, A. (2016). Big Data Mining and Knowledge Discovery. *Journal of Communications Technology. Electronics and Computer Science*, *9*, 5–9.

Schumpeter, J. A. (1934). *The theory of economic development. An inquiry into profits, capital, credit, interest, and the business cycle*. Harvard University Press.

Sedkaoui, S. (Ed.). (2018). *Big data analytics for entrepreneurial success*. IGI Global.

Shane, S. A. (Ed.). (2007). *Economic development through entrepreneurship: Government, university and business linkages*. Edward Elgar Publishing.

Si, S., Hall, J., Suddaby, R., Ahlstrom, D., & Wei, J. (2023). Technology, entrepreneurship, innovation and social change in digital economics. *Technovation, 119*, 102484.

Siddiqui, M. K., & Goyal, K. K. (2023). A Study the Use of E-Payment Systems Based on Artifical Intelligence. *Computing & Intellegent Systems (SCTS)*, 1063-1076.

Soni, N., Sharma, E. K., Singh, N., & Kapoor, A. (2020). Artificial intelligence in business: From research and innovation to market deployment. *Procedia Computer Science, 167*, 2200–2210.

Strohmeier, S., & Piazza, F. (2013). Domain driven data mining in human resource management: A review of current research. *Expert Systems with Applications, 40*(7), 2410–2420.

Suominen, A., Toivanen, H., & Seppänen, M. (2017). Firms' knowledge profiles: Mapping patent data with unsupervised learning. *Technological Forecasting and Social Change, 115*, 131–142.

Syed, R., Suriadi, S., Adams, M., Bandara, W., Leemans, S. J., Ouyang, C., & Reijers, H. A. (2020). Robotic process automation: Contemporary themes and challenges. *Computers in Industry, 115*, 1–15.

Tekin, İ. Ç., & Küsbeci, P. (2021). Dijital dönüşüm sürecinde yükselen bir değer: Dijital girişimcilik. *Stratejik Yönetim Araştırmaları Dergisi, 4*(1), 81–102.

Thorpe, R. (2016). *Gower handbook of leadership and management development*. CRC Press.

Tien, J. M. (2017). Internet of things, real-time decision making, and artificial intelligence. *Annals of Data Science, 4*, 149–178.

Todaro, M. P., & Smith, S. C. (2020). *Economic development*.

Tong, S., Jia, N., Luo, X., & Fang, Z. (2021). The Janus face of artificial intelligence feedback: Deployment versus disclosure effects on employee performance. *Strategic Management Journal, 42*(9), 1600–1631.

Tornatzky, L. G., & Fleischer, M. (1990). *The processes of technological innovation*. Lexington Books.

Torrado, R. R., Bontrager, P., Togelius, J., Liu, J., & Perez-Liebana, D. (2018, August). Deep reinforcement learning for general video game ai. In *2018 IEEE Conference on Computational Intelligence and Games (CIG)* (pp. 1-8). IEEE.

Truong, Y., & Papagiannidis, S. (2022). Artificial intelligence as an enabler for innovation: A review and future research agenda. *Technological Forecasting and Social Change*, *183*, 1–6.

Turienzo, J., Cabanelas, P., & Lampón, J. F. (2023). Business models in times of disruption: The connected and autonomous vehicles (uncertain) domino effect. *Journal of Business Research*, *156*, 1–12.

Turner, C. (2022). Augmented reality, augmented epistemology, and the real-world web. *Philosophy & Technology*, *35*(1), 19.

Usman, F. O., Kess-Momoh, A. J., Ibeh, C. V., Elufioye, A. E., Ilojianya, V. I., & Oyeyemi, O. P. (2024). Entrepreneurial innovations and trends: A global review: Examining emerging trends, challenges, and opportunities in the field of entrepreneurship, with a focus on how technology and globalization are shaping new business ventures. *International Journal of Science and Research Archive*, *11*(1), 552–569.

Van Doorn, S., Heyden, M., Tröster, C., & Volberda, H. (2015). Entrepreneurial orientation and performance: Investigating local requirements for entrepreneurial decision-making. In *Cognition and strategy* (Vol. 32, pp. 211–239). Emerald Group Publishing Limited.

Van Praag, C. M., & Versloot, P. H. (2007). What is the value of entrepreneurship? A review of recent research. *Small Business Economics*, *29*(4), 351–382.

Von Krogh, G., Ben-Menahem, S. M., & Shrestha, Y. R. (2021). Artificial intelligence in strategizing: Prospects and challenges. *Future of Strategic Management*, 625-646.

Votto, A. M., Valecha, R., Najafirad, P., & Rao, H. R. (2021). Artificial intelligence in tactical human resource management: A systematic literature review. *International Journal of Information Management Data Insights*, *1*(2), 1–15.

Wamba-Taguimdje, S. L., Wamba, S. F., Kamdjoug, J. R. K., & Wanko, C. E. T. (2020). Influence of artificial intelligence (AI) on firm performance: The business value of AI-based transformation projects. *Business Process Management Journal*, *26*(7), 1893–1924.

Wiklund, J., & Shepherd, D. (2005). Entrepreneurial orientation and small business performance: A configurational approach. *Journal of Business Venturing*, *20*(1), 71–91.

Wilson, H. J., & Daugherty, P. R. (2018). Collaborative intelligence: Humans and AI are joining forces. *Harvard Business Review*, *96*(4), 114–123.

Wu, W. T., Li, Y. J., Feng, A. Z., Li, L., Huang, T., Xu, A. D., & Lyu, J. (2021). Data mining in clinical big data: The frequently used databases, steps, and methodological models. *Military Medical Research*, *8*, 1–12. PMID: 34380547

Wujarso, R. (2023). *Effect of digital transformation on company operational efficiency*. Asadel Publisher.

Yeomans, M., Shah, A., Mullainathan, S., & Kleinberg, J. (2019). Making sense of recommendations. *Journal of Behavioral Decision Making*, *32*(4), 403–414.

Yousfi-Monod, M., Farzindar, A., & Lapalme, G. (2010). Supervised machine learning for summarizing legal documents. *Advances in Artificial Intelligence: 23rd Canadian Conference on Artificial Intelligence, Canadian AI 2010, Ottawa, Canada, May 31–June 2, 2010 Proceedings*, *23*, 51–62.

Zafarani, R. (2014). *Social Media Mining: An Introduction*. Cambridge University Press.

Zahra, S. A. (1991). Predictors and financial outcomes of corporate entrepreneurship: An exploratory study. *Journal of Business Venturing*, *6*(4), 259–285.

Zhang, C., & Lu, Y. (2021). Study on artificial intelligence: The state of the art and future prospects. *Journal of Industrial Information Integration*, *23*, 1–9.

Zhao, Q. (2009). A survey on virtual reality. *Science in China Series F: Information Sciences*, *52*(3), 348–400.

Zuloaga-Rotta, L., Borja-Rosales, R., Rodríguez Mallma, M. J., Mauricio, D., & Maculan, N. (2024). Method to Forecast the Presidential Election Results Based on Simulation and Machine Learning. *Computation (Basel, Switzerland)*, *12*(3), 1–16.

ADDITIONAL READING

Adekunle, O. J., & Israel, O. B. (2022). Impact of resource-based theory on entrepreneurship in Nigeria. *International Journal of Management Science and Business Analysis*, *24*(7), 159–174.

Brynjolfsson, E., & Mitchell, T. (2017). What can machine learning do? Workforce implications. *Science*, *358*(6370), 1530–1534. PMID: 29269459

Harahap, M. A. K., Wurarah, R. N., Fathurohman, A., Suroso, A., & Iskandar, Y. (2023). Globalization substance and industrial revolution 4.0 and the role of technological innovation for economic development towards entrepreneurship. *Jurnal Bisnisman: Riset Bisnis Dan Manajemen*, *4*(3), 37–51.

Khithika, M. A. (2020). *Assessing the influence of entrepreneurial orientation on the performance of South African construction business* (Doctoral dissertation, North-West University (South Africa)).

Liu, C. H. (2021). Creating competitive advantage through network ties, entrepreneurial orientation and intellectual capital. *Management Decision*, *59*(9), 2238–2263.

Makarius, E. E., Mukherjee, D., Fox, J. D., & Fox, A. K. (2020). Rising with the machines: A sociotechnical framework for bringing artificial intelligence into the organization. *Journal of Business Research*, *120*, 262–273.

Weerawardena, J., Salunke, S., Haigh, N., & Mort, G. S. (2021). Business model innovation in social purpose organizations: Conceptualizing dual social-economic value creation. *Journal of Business Research*, *125*, 762–771.

KEY TERMS AND DEFINITIONS

Artificial Intelligence (AI): It is a branch of science aimed at developing computer systems that exhibit human-like intelligence. These systems can perform tasks such as learning, problem solving, speech recognition and can work without human intervention.

Augmented Reality (AR): A technology that combines the real world with digital data, allowing the user to experience the real world in an enhanced way. AR adds virtual objects or information to the real world on the screen through glasses or smartphones.

Digitalization: The process of converting information and data into digital format. Digitalization means developing and managing business processes, services and products with the help of digital technologies. Companies become faster, more efficient and more data-oriented with digitalization.

Entrepreneurship: It is defined as the process of developing innovative products or services by discovering new business opportunities. Entrepreneurship involves taking risks and organizing resources to start a new business or project.

Strategy: Refers to the planning and guidance processes that an institution follows to achieve set goals. Strategy determines which steps will be taken and which resources will be used and how to ensure long-term success.

Virtual Reality (VR): A technology that transports users to a completely digital world. Through special glasses and devices, users can interact in a virtual environment as if it were real and have a completely integrated experience with this virtual world.

Chapter 5
AI Ethics and Responsible AI Deployment in Sustainable Entrepreneurship

Laura Dragos-Radoi
https://orcid.org/0009-0006-4161-6022
University of Buckingham, Timisoara, Romania

ABSTRACT

In today's fast-changing business environment, artificial intelligence (AI) has become a key factor, presenting both challenges and opportunities depending on its implementation. This chapter explores how responsible AI practices can help businesses transition from a profit-centric mindset to a broader vision that embraces sustainability and long-term viability. By prioritizing ethical principles, companies—whether multinational corporations or startups—can harness AI to drive innovation, foster sustainable growth, and promote equitable progress for all stakeholders. It examines the macro-level influences of these technologies and their interconnectedness with external environments, offering a holistic perspective on how emerging technologies are reshaping the modern business ecosystem. This provides business leaders and enthusiasts with practical insights to navigate the systemic impacts of AI and leverage its potential responsibly.

INTRODUCTION

When thinking about Sustainability the business leaders automatically think about the present and how they can leverage their business in a more sustainable

DOI: 10.4018/979-8-3373-1107-4.ch005

way. Some are doing it for the care of all stakeholders implicated, others interest is to mark a higher sustainability score on a quarterly or annual report.

But what exactly does the term sustainability stand for? Should we look, as business leaders in the past, the present or in the future?

The definition of sustainability refers to the capacity of meeting the needs of the present generation without compromising the ability of future generations to meet their own needs. It covers environmental, economic, and social dimensions, aiming for a balance between growth, resource conservation, and fair distribution. This is the quintessence extracted from the World Commission on Environment and Development (WCED). (1987). Our Common Future. Oxford University Press.

In order to understand sustainable development, the leaders have to understand that sustainability is no longer only a buzzword; it represents a transformative business model that integrates environmental, social, and economic considerations into decision-making processes.

But how come sustainability becomes such a struggle and such crucial nowadays? Was it also a primary concern since the beginning of the corporation's era?

To fully understand the large spectrum of what this concept involves, leaders need to understand a little bit about the past as well.

Reflecting on earlier decades, such as the 1990s, we question whether sustainability was a central focus during that period and examine the factors that have led to its increased importance in recent years. In the 1990s, the concept of sustainability, while present in academic and environmental circles, was not as deeply integrated into conventional business strategies or public consciousness. Businesses largely prioritized profitability and shareholder value, often overlooking the long-term environmental and social impacts of their operations. Sustainability was perceived more as a niche concern, associated with corporate social responsibility, also known as CSR (Carroll, 1991) and environmental advocacy, rather than a fundamental pillar of business strategy.

Today, sustainability has moved to the frontline, becoming a vital agenda item in boardrooms and a key metric of organizational success. This shift is driven by several factors, including the growing awareness of climate change (IPCC, 2021), the reduction of natural resources (Meadows et al., 1972), and increased scrutiny from stakeholders, including consumers, investors, and regulators (Freeman et al., 2010). Entrepreneurs now face mounting pressure to redefine success by incorporating environmental, social, and governance (ESG) principles into their core operations (Eccles et al., 2012). This transformation reflects a broader societal expectation that businesses must not only generate profits but also actively contribute to addressing global challenges, such as inequality, environmental degradation, and climate resilience.

What was once a marginal consideration has now become an essential aspect of strategic planning. Companies are no longer judged purely on their financial performance; their commitment to sustainability and their ability to align with the Sustainable Development Goals (SDGs) are equally significant (United Nations, 2015). This approach underscores the evolving role of businesses in shaping a sustainable future, as they are increasingly seen as critical partners in achieving systemic change (Bansal & DesJardine, 2014). By embedding sustainability into their values and operations, organizations can create a lasting impact, demonstrating that economic success and environmental conservation are not mutually exclusive but deeply interconnected.

What are the essential components of business sustainability? The primary components of business sustainability include the following key elements:

1. Triple Bottom Line (TBL): This framework encourages businesses to balance economic viability, environmental care, and social responsibility, reflecting the idea that sustainable success requires consideration of "people, planet, and profit" (Elkington, 1997). The TBL approach has reshaped how organizations evaluate their performance by incorporating non-financial metrics into their core strategies.
2. Sustainable Innovation: Sustainable innovation emphasizes the development of eco-friendly products, services, and practices that support a circular economy and reduce environmental impact (Bocken et al., 2014). This includes designing waste-minimizing systems, renewable energy solutions, and sustainable production methods, which align with both environmental goals and consumer expectations. The author truly values re-plantable packaging, for instance.
3. Corporate Social Responsibility (CSR): CSR initiatives enhance brand reputation by promoting ethical labor practices and environmentally responsible actions (Carroll & Shabana, 2010). Companies that integrate CSR into their operations often experience increased consumer trust and loyalty, demonstrating the financial and social benefits of ethical practices.
4. Regulatory Compliance: International frameworks, such as ISO 14001 for environmental management, require businesses to adopt rigorous sustainability protocols (Boiral & Henri, 2012). These standards not only ensure regulatory compliance but also encourage organizations to proactively manage their environmental impacts, fostering long-term resilience.
5. Consumer Demand: A growing base of environmentally and socially conscious consumers is reshaping industry standards by rewarding businesses that adopt sustainable practices (White et al., 2019). This shift in consumer behavior pressures companies to innovate and align with sustainability expectations, reinforcing the importance of transparency and accountability.

Introducing the Entrepreneurial Role in Sustainable Business Environments

The rise of sustainable entrepreneurship represents a transformative shift from traditional business models to ventures that prioritize economic prosperity while aligning with environmental stewardship and social equity. Sustainable entrepreneurs innovate by addressing critical societal challenges, aiming not only to generate profit but also to foster meaningful, long-lasting change (Cohen & Winn, 2007; Shepherd & Patzelt, 2011). These ventures often serve as catalysts for rethinking conventional approaches to business by embedding sustainability at the core of their operations.

While large corporations, with their substantial financial resources, are increasingly integrating sustainability into their strategies, they often face structural resistance and slower adaptability due to their size (Hart & Dowell, 2011). In contrast, the entrepreneurial landscape offers an enormous opportunity for agile, technology-driven startups to drive innovation in areas such as green energy, water purification, and waste management (Hall et al., 2010). Investment trends reflect this shift, with venture capital and government funding being directed toward sustainable business solutions that align with the growing demand for environmental and social responsibility.

A key enabler of this transformation is the integration of emerging technologies, such as Artificial Intelligence (AI), into sustainable business models. AI-powered systems are accelerating the efficiency of renewable energy management, enabling smart water usage, and optimizing supply chains for waste reduction (Makridakis, 2017). These technologies not only drive operational improvements but also contribute to systemic innovation by creating interconnected ecosystems where sustainable practices can flourish.

However, this boom in technology raises an essential question: how can we build AI and other technologies responsibly to ensure they serve the broader goals of sustainability without introducing new ethical dilemmas or unintended consequences? By fostering responsible innovation at a macro level, we can shape an ecosystem where emerging technologies and entrepreneurial ventures work synergistically to redefine the future of sustainability.

However, as AI and other technologies become central to sustainable business, a crucial challenge emerges: how do we ensure these innovations are developed and deployed responsibly, in service of both people and planet? The following section addresses this challenge by exploring the ethical foundations and practical imperatives of Responsible AI.

UNDERSTANDING RESPONSIBLE AI

Against this backdrop of rapid technological change and rising sustainability expectations, Artificial Intelligence (AI) stands out as both a transformative force and a source of new ethical dilemmas.

The Urgency of Ethical AI

The convergence of artificial intelligence (AI) and sustainable entrepreneurship presents both immense opportunities and profound ethical challenges. As AI technologies become increasingly embedded in entrepreneurial ecosystems—especially those targeting social and environmental impact—issues of transparency, accountability, fairness, and data governance become central (European Commission, 2024). Recent years have seen a surge in AI-related incidents, including algorithmic bias, privacy breaches, and security vulnerabilities, particularly within generative AI applications (OECD, 2023). This has prompted a global acceleration in regulatory responses, such as the European Union's AI Act, and a growing consensus that innovation without ethical oversight risks reinforcing inequalities or causing unintended harm. Ethical AI is thus not merely a technical concern but a foundational pillar for sustainable value creation in entrepreneurship.

AI in the Business Context

The concept of Artificial Intelligence (AI) must be understood within the broader context of technological evolution, which has developed in parallel with the transformation of businesses over time. Technology has become an inseparable element of modern enterprises, with its absence transforming businesses increasingly obsolete in a competitive global market (Brynjolfsson & McAfee, 2014). Today, technological pillars such as AI, Large Language Models (LLMs), Big Data, and the Internet of Things (IoT) are not only reshaping industries but also permanently shifting market trends and economic landscapes.

AI and its associated technologies are revolutionizing how businesses operate, enabling unimaginable levels of efficiency and innovation (Makridakis, 2017). Big Data, for example, provides businesses with actionable insights from vast datasets, while IoT devices connect systems and optimize processes in real-time (Porter & Heppelmann, 2014). AI-powered solutions such as predictive analytics, natural language processing, and automation further enhance decision-making and operational workflows, allowing businesses to stay agile and competitive.

These technological advancements are not just tools but transformative forces that redefine business ecosystems. AI and related technologies enable companies to identify opportunities, predict consumer behavior, and improve supply chain efficiency, ultimately leveraging data to achieve strategic goals (Russell & Norvig, 2020). This integration of technology has led to a paradigm shift where businesses no longer merely adopt technology but rely on it as a foundation for sustained growth and innovation.

Yet, as these technologies become deeply embedded in business strategy, the question of responsibility becomes paramount

But what do we truly mean when we refer to Responsible Innovation and Responsible AI? How can we create technology that embodies responsibility? Is it even possible for technology to be responsible, and if so, in what way?

The Ethical Foundations of Responsible AI (RAI)

As AI becomes increasingly integrated into business operations and societal functions, understanding its ethical implications is not just an academic concern but a practical necessity. Responsible AI (RAI) ensures that the development and deployment of AI technologies align with ethical principles, mitigating risks while maximizing benefits. This section explores the foundational principles of AI ethics and highlights their role in enhancing business operations, maintaining trust, and preventing potential ethical pitfalls.

WHAT ARE THE CORE PRINCIPLES OF RESPONSIBLE AI?

To address these challenges, Responsible AI is guided by several foundational principles, each designed to mitigate risk and maximize societal benefit.

Dimensions of Responsible AI (RAI)

Responsible AI (RAI) represents a framework of ethical principles and practices that ensure AI technologies are developed and deployed in ways that uphold fairness, transparency, accountability, safety, and privacy. These dimensions are critical for mitigating risks, fostering trust among stakeholders, and ensuring that AI technologies contribute positively to society. The following explores these dimensions in depth, with practical examples illustrating both their necessity and potential obstacles.

Fairness is one of the cornerstones of Responsible AI, ensuring that systems treat all individuals and groups justly, avoiding biases that can lead to discrimination. Bias in AI can arise from non-representative datasets, flawed model designs, or biased implementation practices. For instance, Amazon's now-retired AI recruiting tool serves as a cautionary tale of how biased historical data led the system to systematically favor male candidates over equally qualified women, extending ongoing imbalances (Dastin, 2018). Addressing fairness in AI requires the use of balanced datasets, rigorous audits, and bias mitigation techniques to ensure equitable outcomes for all users and stakeholders.

Closely linked to fairness is the need for transparency, ensuring that systems are not only just but also understandable to those they affect.

Transparency is equally vital in building trust and fostering understanding between AI developers, users, and affected individuals. Transparent AI systems involve clear documentation of data sources, model logic, and decision-making processes. This includes informing users about what data is being collected, how it is processed, and how the system operates. A lack of transparency can lead to misuse, as illustrated by facial recognition technologies deployed in public spaces without public awareness or consent, resulting in privacy violations and potential misuse by authoritarian regimes. Transparency demands that AI developers disclose their methods, provide explanations for key decisions, and align with regulatory frameworks like GDPR, which emphasizes the "right to explanation."

Transparency alone, however, is not enough. Accountability must be established so that responsibility for outcomes is clear and actionable.

Accountability ensures that clear lines of responsibility are established for the design, deployment, and outcomes of AI systems. Without accountability, AI systems can lead to harmful consequences without any remedy for addressing these issues. For example, imagine an autonomous vehicle programmed to prioritize cost-saving measures over public safety in accident scenarios, potentially causing avoidable tragedies. Such outcomes underscore the importance of accountability frameworks that define roles and responsibilities for system failures while implementing robust monitoring and auditing mechanisms.

Privacy and data protection are critical dimensions of Responsible AI, particularly as AI systems often rely on large volumes of personal data. Adhering to global legal standards, such as GDPR, AI systems must prioritize secure data handling, anonymization, and informed consent. The Cambridge Analytica scandal, where AI algorithms were used to extract and manipulate personal data for political campaigns, exemplifies the risks of failing to defend these principles (Cadwalladr & Graham-Harrison, 2018). Responsible AI mitigates these risks by limiting data collection to what is strictly necessary and ensuring users' rights and privacy are respected.

Safety and security complete the core dimensions of RAI by emphasizing the importance of robust and secure AI systems. This includes safeguarding against cybersecurity risks, cyber threats, and unintended consequences. Malicious uses of AI, such as chatbots spreading disinformation or deepfake technologies used for blackmail or political manipulation, highlight the potential dangers of poorly managed systems. Ensuring safety involves rigorous testing, adversarial training, and secure deployment environments to minimize these risks.

AI's potential for harm lies in its ability to scale malicious actions rapidly and efficiently. For instance, deepfake technologies have been used to create hyper-realistic videos to mislead the public, while AI-driven hacking tools exploit vulnerabilities in systems with unprecedented speed and precision. Manipulative recommendation algorithms, designed to exploit user behavior, can push harmful content or foster addictive tendencies, further illustrating the need for robust safeguards. A new instance of disinformation, alongside Cambridge Analytica-style methods, impacted the 2024 elections in Romania, leading the election process to be canceled and repeated in 2025, leaving the Romanian population with their democracy severely compromised.

These dimensions of Responsible AI are deeply embedded in globally recognized frameworks such as the OECD AI Principles (2019) and the NIST AI Risk Management Framework (2021). These frameworks provide actionable guidelines for managing AI-related risks, emphasizing inclusivity, transparency, and accountability. They are instrumental in bridging the gap between theoretical ethical principles and real-world applications. For instance, Mikalef et al. (2020) demonstrate how ethical AI practices can align with organizational goals, showcasing the practical benefits of embedding these principles in business contexts.

Moving forward, the challenge lies in consistently applying these dimensions across diverse industries and technological landscapes. The question remains: "*How can AI systems be designed and governed to prevent malicious use while fostering innovation for societal benefit?*" By embedding ethical safeguards into the core of AI development, promoting interdisciplinary collaboration, and educating stakeholders, businesses can ensure that AI contributes to a sustainable and responsible global ecosystem. Such efforts not only enhance operational efficiency and stakeholder trust but also align with international standards, ensuring AI's positive impact on society as a whole.

Contrasting Views on Responsible AI

While "Responsible AI" is often invoked as a unifying ethical imperative, its practical implementation varies significantly among stakeholders. Developers may prioritize technical robustness, explainability, and bias mitigation; business leaders often focus on brand trust, reputational risk, and regulatory compliance; policymakers emphasize public safety and societal outcomes. These divergent perspectives can generate tensions between rapid deployment, ethical scrutiny, and economic efficiency. Notably, over 80% of executives believe Responsible AI provides a competitive edge, driving proactive investment in ethical frameworks beyond compliance (Accenture

& MIT Sloan Management Review, 2022). To bridge these differing priorities, it is essential to develop governance models that accommodate multiple interpretations of responsibility while reinforcing ethical common ground.

Industry-Specific Dimensions of Responsible AI

Ethical requirements for AI are highly sector-dependent, shaped by varying risk exposures, stakeholder impacts, and regulatory landscapes. In healthcare, transparency and auditability are paramount due to life-and-death implications. Retail prioritizes privacy and consent, especially in customer profiling. Manufacturing raises concerns about automation, labor displacement, and environmental impact. According to Boston Consulting Group (2024), 78% of companies use AI in at least one function, but only 26% have matured beyond pilot projects to realize tangible value. Kubanek and Szymoniak (2022) further highlight that ethical challenges—such as data bias and privacy violations—are especially acute in healthcare and similarly sensitive sectors.

Table 1. Example uses in different industries

Industry	Key Ethical Focus Areas	Example Use Case
Healthcare	Explainability, non-maleficence	AI diagnostics for disease detection
Retail	Consent, privacy, surveillance	Personalized marketing algorithms
Manufacturing	Automation, job ethics, carbon impact	AI-driven smart factories

Understanding these distinctions is essential for a credible, contextualized approach to Responsible AI.

WHAT IS THE SIGNIFICANCE FOR ENTREPRENEURS?

Responsible AI (RAI) holds significant implications for entrepreneurs, shaping how businesses interact with stakeholders, comply with regulations, and drive innovation. By embedding ethical AI principles into their operations, entrepreneurs can create competitive advantages, foster trust, and contribute to long-term sustainability. Below, we explore the key areas where RAI impacts entrepreneurship, supported by academic insights and real-world examples.

Building Trust

Ethical AI fosters trust among customers, investors, and employees, forming the foundation for customer loyalty and a resilient business reputation. Trust in AI-driven systems depends on transparency, fairness, and accountability, as these elements ensure stakeholders feel confident in the decisions made by AI technologies (Mikalef et al., 2020). For entrepreneurs, establishing trust is crucial, particularly in competitive industries where consumer confidence can make or break a business. For example, Tesla's success in deploying AI-powered autonomous vehicles is partly attributed to its emphasis on safety and transparency, which have strengthened public confidence in its innovations (Makridakis, 2017). The most important thing for an entrepreneur, especially in the early stages of their journey, is to recognize that trust is a fundamental pillar of a successful go-to-market strategy. Trust doesn't begin at launch or post-deployment—it must be built from the moment a product or service is being conceptualized. This means engaging with potential customers early to understand their needs, concerns, and fears, and addressing them with intention and empathy. Trust is not just essential for initial adoption—it's the foundation for building long-term relationships that lead to sustainable monthly recurring revenue. This principle is deeply valued in the Silicon Valley startup ecosystem and is a key consideration for early-stage venture capital investment.

Mitigating Risks

The rapid evolution of AI regulations, such as the European Union's AI Act, poses challenges and opportunities for entrepreneurs. Compliance with these regulations helps mitigate risks related to reputational damage, financial penalties, and legal ramifications (OECD, 2019). For instance, non-compliance with GDPR regulations has led to significant fines for major companies, demonstrating the importance of adhering to legal standards in data-driven industries. Entrepreneurs who proactively address ethical and legal considerations not only avoid risks but also position themselves as responsible leaders in their markets.

Driving Innovation

Entrepreneurs who prioritize RAI innovation can distinguish themselves in competitive markets by delivering trustworthy, cutting-edge solutions. Responsible AI enhances innovation by fostering consumer and investor confidence, enabling businesses to explore bold ideas without the fear of backlash (Floridi et al., 2018). For example, startups in the health-tech sector leverage AI to revolutionize diagnostics and patient care while adhering to ethical standards to ensure patient data protection and equal access to care (Raji & Buolamwini, 2019). Such approaches demonstrate how ethical AI can become a foundation for entrepreneurial success.

Fostering Social Impact

Ethically deployed AI has the potential to address critical societal challenges, from fighting climate change to improving public health. Entrepreneurs who use AI responsibly can contribute positively to social change, fulfilling corporate social responsibilities and enhancing their reputations as socially conscious innovators (Carroll & Shabana, 2010). For instance, AI-powered systems for optimizing energy consumption and reducing carbon footprints align with global sustainability goals while creating business opportunities in the green tech sector.

Promoting Long-Term Sustainability

Responsible AI aligns with sustainable business practices by improving resource efficiency, reducing waste, and fostering innovation. Entrepreneurs can leverage AI technologies to streamline supply chains, optimize resource allocation, and design circular business models (Bocken et al., 2014). For example, AI-driven waste management solutions are increasingly being adopted by startups to enhance recycling processes, reduce landfill usage, and contribute to a circular economy. These efforts not only support environmental sustainability but also enhance long-term business resilience.

In the concluding of this section the author wants to highlight that the opportunities for entrepreneurs to leverage sustainable technology are immense, offering the potential to address global challenges while creating value for businesses and society. From green energy innovations to AI-driven solutions that optimize resource efficiency, the possibilities are as diverse as they are impactful. However, the key lies in ensuring that these technologies are built responsibly from the very beginning of the business idea. By embedding ethical considerations and sustainability into the ideation process, entrepreneurs can contribute to a world where technology not only drives progress but does so in a way that benefits all stakeholders, aligning innovation with responsibility for the greater good.

The following section will present a broader perspective on the business landscape, emphasizing its interdependence and exploring a more systemic approach through the lens of the Viable System Model (VSM). This framework will provide insights into how businesses can adapt and thrive within complex, interdependent environments.

INTEGRATING VSM IN BUSINESS PRACTICES

We now have a foundational understanding of sustainability and Responsible AI in emerging tech markets, but how can we interconnect these concepts to fully understand their interactions within the business ecosystem? Is simply understanding each side separately sufficient, or do we risk overlooking the deeper connections needed for meaningful integration?

This section aims to provide readers with a systemic perspective on the business context, introducing the Viable System Model (VSM) as a comprehensive and complex framework for achieving business viability and sustainability.

Running a business is never a simple mission, whether it involves massive corporations or Small and Medium Enterprises (SMEs), including startups. In response to the challenges brought forward by the complex and disruptive digital era we are currently navigating, the author highlights the Viable System Model (VSM) as a powerful tool for managing and leveraging complexity effectively.

When it comes to Embedding AI into the Viable System Model (VSM), the Viable System Model (VSM) offers a robust framework for integrating AI into sustainable enterprises. Each VSM subsystem can be augmented with AI:

- **System 1 (Operations):** AI-driven automation, demand forecasting, decision support.
- **System 2 (Coordination):** Scheduling, workflow optimization, conflict detection.
- **System 3 (Control):** Business intelligence, performance dashboards, anomaly detection.
- **System 4 (Planning):** Predictive modeling, scenario analysis, strategic foresight.
- **System 5 (Policy):** Ethical governance, SDG alignment, compliance monitoring.

Kubanek and Szymoniak (2022) argue that system-wide ethical governance is critical, advocating for ethical oversight to be embedded in organizational architecture, supporting the application of VSM as a guiding model.

Linking theoretical frameworks like VSM with actionable strategies enhances both internal coherence and external accountability in AI-driven ventures.

The Viable System Model (VSM) represents a transformative framework for understanding and managing organizations in the face of modern business complexities. First conceptualized by Stafford Beer in *Brain of the Firm* (1972), the VSM has become a foundational element of organizational cybernetics. It provides a structured approach to designing and governing systems capable of sustaining themselves over time, even as they navigate constant changes in their Internal and External environments. Rooted in the principles of cybernetics—the science of communication and control in both biological and artificial systems—the VSM offers a lens through which organizations can balance immediate operational needs with long-term strategic objectives.

At the heart of the VSM lies the concept of viability, which Beer defined as an organization's ability to survive, adapt, and thrive within dynamic contexts. This model does not view businesses as isolated entities; rather, it positions them as interconnected systems in continuous interaction with their internal components and External environments. Through its feedback loops and communication pathways, the VSM fosters systemic coordination, adaptability, and resilience, enabling businesses to diagnose challenges and develop strategies that ensure coherence and long-term sustainability.

Angela Espinosa's recent work, *Sustainable Self-Governance in Businesses and Society: The Viable System Model in Action* (2023), builds upon Beer's foundational ideas by demonstrating the VSM's relevance to contemporary organizational challenges. Espinosa emphasizes its critical role in addressing sustainability, aligning internal operations with societal and environmental demands. By advocating for systemic thinking, adaptive structures, and interconnectivity, Espinosa highlights how the VSM enables organizations to respond effectively to issues such as climate change, resource scarcity, and social inequities while maintaining their operational efficiency and resilience.

A significant strength of the VSM lies in its ability to conceptualize an organization as a dynamic and integrated system. The model identifies three primary components: the Metahead, which provides strategic oversight; the Operational body, responsible for day-to-day activities; and the External environment, which encompasses market forces, societal influences, and other external factors. Each of these components interacts dynamically, ensuring that the organization can adapt to changes while maintaining its viability. The Metahead, acting as the organization's brain, oversees coordination and strategic direction, while the Operational body executes core functions. The External environment, meanwhile, serves as the ecosystem in which the organization operates, shaping and being shaped by the organization's actions.

The diagrams below, starting from Figure 1 to 4, illustrate a conceptualization of the Viable System Model (VSM) as interpreted by Angela Espinosa in her work, along with examples from Systemic Governance and Mark Lambertz:

Figure 1. Illustration of a simple Viable System Model designed by Angela Espinosa, illustrating the two main components (the operation (O) and the management (M)), as well as the environment (E)

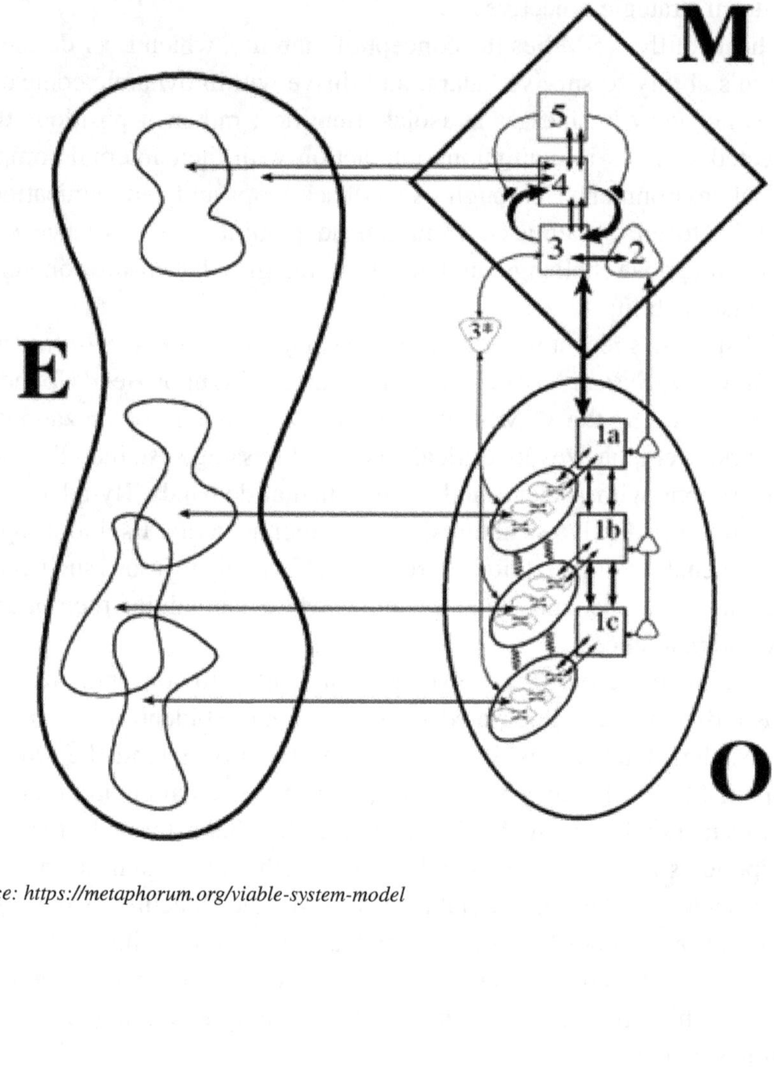

Source: https://metaphorum.org/viable-system-model

Figure 2. "An exemplary model of a corporation as a viable system. Assumption: There is one System 1 purchasing external resources and one System 1 which produces the value, delivered to the customers. The VSM applies for all kinds of organizations"

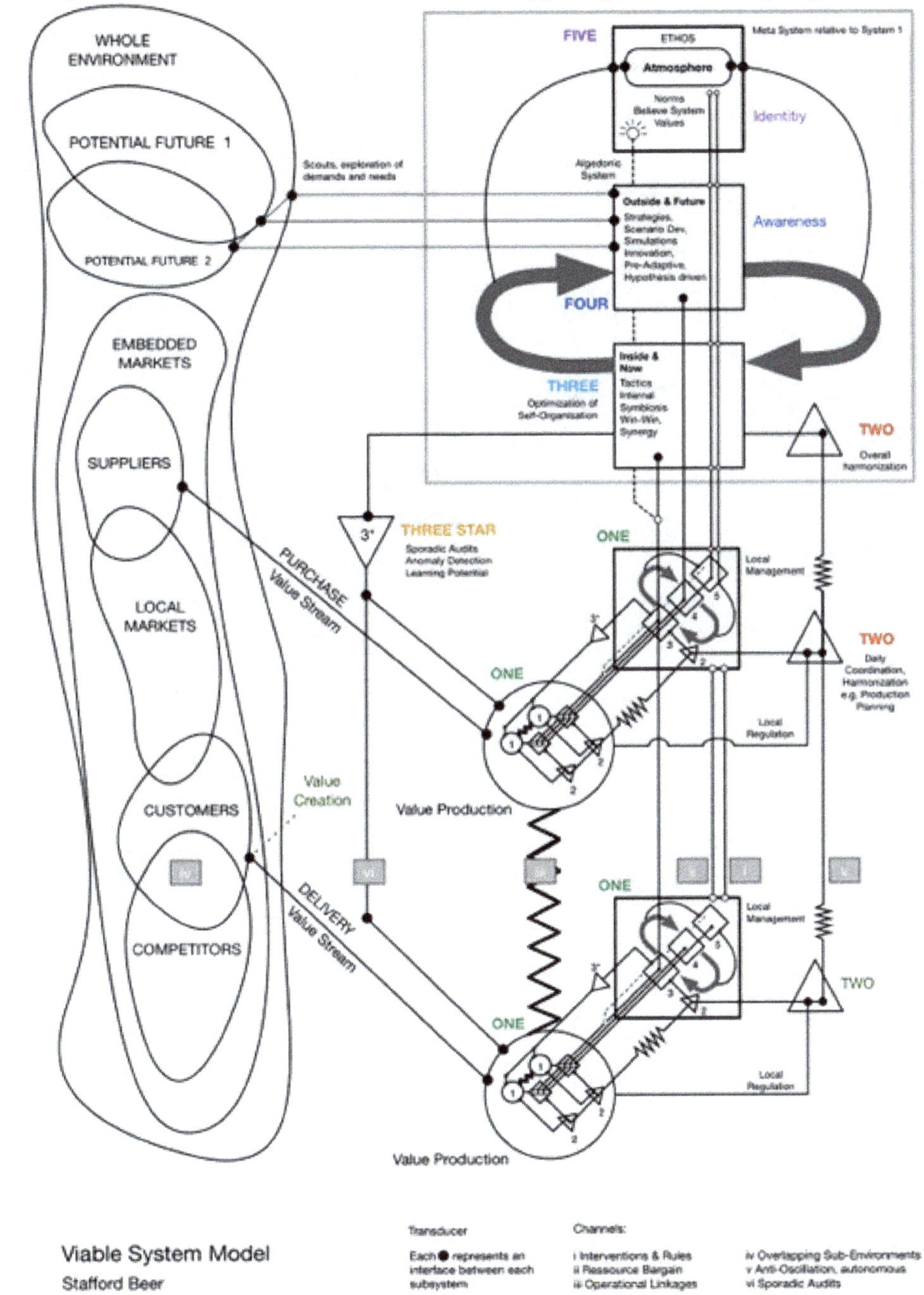

Source: Mark Lambertz's own work

Figure 3. The Viable System Model for an Agile Software Development

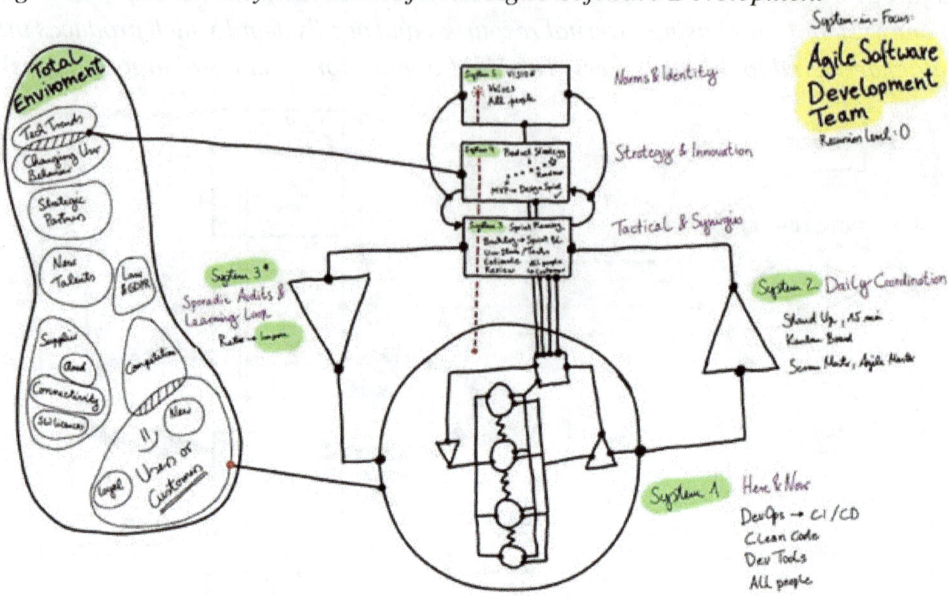

Source: Mark Lambertz's own work on Intelligente Organisationen https://intelligente-organisationen.de/viable-system-model-example

Figure 4. The Viable System Model Framework in accordance with Systemic Steering and Governance

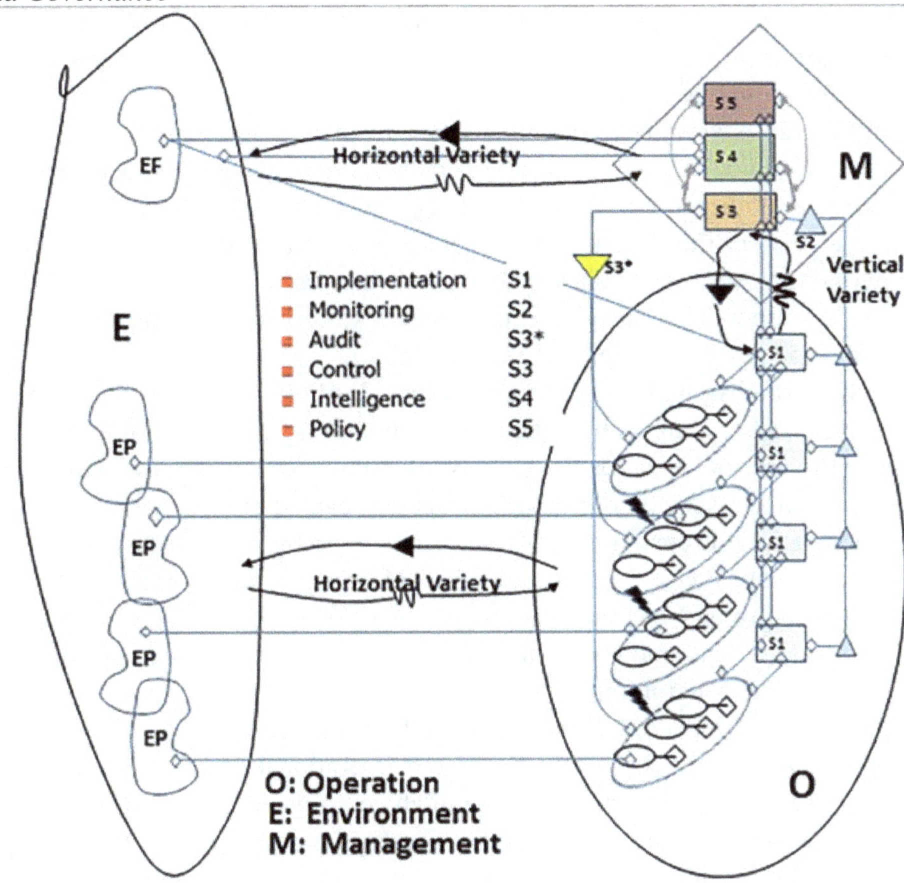

Source: https://systemic2016.wordpress.com/viable-system-model-vsm/

To simplify the complexity of the VSM, Beer drew a compelling analogy to the human body. The Metahead mirrors the brain, sending neural impulses to guide the body's functions while receiving feedback to refine its actions. Within the VSM, the Metahead is composed of Systems 5, 4, and 3. System 5 defines the organization's purpose and policies, providing a cohesive identity and ensuring alignment among all components. System 4 acts as the radar, scanning the External environment for opportunities and risks while facilitating strategic vision. System 3 focuses on internal optimization, harmonizing the operations of various subsystems and ensuring resource efficiency.

The Operational body, represented by System 1, carries out the organization's essential activities. Each operational unit functions semi-autonomously, contributing to the organization's objectives while remaining interconnected through feedback mechanisms. System 2 ensures effective coordination between these units, much like the nervous system prevents conflicts and maintains balance within the body. This systemic approach ensures that the organization operates efficiently, even when faced with disruptions.

The External environment, emphasized heavily in the VSM, reflects the complex ecosystem within which organizations operate. Survival and success depend on an organization's ability to interact with and adapt to external forces, including competitors, regulatory frameworks, and societal expectations. Systems 4 and 1 bridge the internal and external domains, enabling the organization to sense environmental changes and respond dynamically. This adaptability is crucial for navigating today's globalized and rapidly changing market conditions.

Angela Espinosa builds on these principles by linking the VSM to sustainability. Her work highlights how the model provides a framework for embedding sustainability into organizational design. By aligning internal processes with global environmental and societal objectives, businesses can contribute positively to the world while achieving operational efficiency. Espinosa emphasizes that sustainability is not a secondary concern but a core aspect of organizational viability. Through systemic thinking and interconnectivity, the VSM allows businesses to address environmental, social, and economic dimensions cohesively, fostering long-term resilience and meaningful impact.

The analogy of the VSM to the human body further reinforces its accessibility. The Metahead, akin to the brain, guides the Operational body—represented by vital organs like the heart and lungs—through coordinated actions. The External environment serves as the stimuli that the body reacts to, whether positively or negatively. For example, if System 2, analogous to the inner ear, fails to maintain balance, the body might struggle and face injuries caused by outside elements, such as a rock. Similarly, in organizations, poor coordination can lead to inefficiencies or vulnerabilities, compromising the entire system's viability. This visualization helps leaders recognize their organizations as holistic entities where all components must function in harmony to ensure success.

By framing organizations as integrated systems, the VSM enables leaders to address challenges and seize opportunities with a clearer understanding of internal and external dynamics. Just as a malfunctioning organ can weaken a human body, a lack of alignment among organizational components can affect overall performance. Strategic foresight, effective coordination, and adaptability are essential for navigating complexity, and the VSM provides a blueprint for achieving these goals.

The VSM's cybernetic foundation strengthens its practical relevance. Feedback loops facilitate seamless communication between the strategic and operational levels of an organization. Descending feedback from the Metahead provides guidance and coherence to operational units, while upward feedback ensures that ground-level insights inform higher-level decision-making. Espinosa's integration of sustainability into the VSM demonstrates its capacity to address modern organizational challenges. By focusing on both adaptation and contribution, the model aligns with contemporary priorities of corporate sustainability, encouraging businesses to balance profitability with positive societal impact.

Incorporating the VSM into business strategies redefines how organizations approach complexity, equipping them with the tools to navigate uncertainty and align operations with broader goals. As Stafford Beer and Angela Espinosa demonstrate, the VSM transcends its theoretical origins, offering a practical framework for reimagining organizations as dynamic, self-governing entities capable of thriving in an interconnected and rapidly evolving world.

The relevance of the Viable System Model (VSM) extends far beyond its utility as a framework for organizational viability—it is particularly impactful in addressing the multidimensional challenges of sustainability. In today's complex business landscape, where global environmental, social, and economic pressures converge, the VSM provides a structured approach to embedding sustainability into the core of organizational operations and strategy. Its systemic nature enables businesses to not only survive but thrive by fostering resilience, adaptability, strategic foresight, and effective governance.

One of the most critical contributions of the VSM to sustainability is its capacity to enhance resilience and adaptability. Organizations today operate in highly volatile environments marked by rapid technological advances, shifting consumer expectations, and pressing global challenges such as climate change and resource scarcity. The VSM equips enterprises with the tools to monitor external conditions through feedback loops, enabling them to sense changes and adapt swiftly without losing operational coherence. This dynamic adaptability ensures that organizations remain relevant and resilient, even in the face of unforeseen disruptions.

The VSM also promotes holistic integration, which is essential for addressing the interconnected dimensions of sustainability. Businesses often face the challenge of balancing environmental stewardship, social responsibility, and economic performance—dimensions that are traditionally treated in silos. The VSM's systemic design ensures that these elements are managed harmoniously, fostering alignment across all levels of the organization. For instance, environmental initiatives such as reducing carbon emissions can be synchronized with social goals like equitable labor practices and economic objectives like cost efficiency. This interconnectedness minimizes the risk of fragmented efforts and promotes a unified approach to sustainability that is both practical and impactful.

Strategic agility, another key aspect of the VSM, plays a vital role in sustainability efforts. The intelligence components of the model, particularly System 4, enable organizations to anticipate and respond proactively to emerging sustainability challenges. By scanning the External environment for opportunities and risks, businesses can align their strategies with long-term global priorities such as the United Nations Sustainable Development Goals (SDGs). For example, an organization leveraging the VSM may identify a growing market demand for renewable energy solutions and move its operations to capitalize on this trend while contributing positively to environmental sustainability. This forward-looking agility ensures that businesses are not only reactive but also proactive in addressing the evolving landscape of sustainability.

Effective governance is another pillar of the VSM's relevance to sustainability. Transparency and accountability are critical for ensuring that organizations remain credible and trustworthy in their sustainability initiatives. The VSM's emphasis on clear communication pathways and well-defined responsibilities supports governance structures that uphold ethical standards and stakeholder confidence. Systems 3, 4, and 5 work in concert to integrate operational oversight with strategic vision, ensuring that sustainability efforts are both effective and credible. This governance framework enables businesses to manage stakeholder expectations, report on environmental and social impacts, and comply with evolving regulatory requirements.

The systemic design of the VSM inherently aligns with contemporary sustainability frameworks, offering a practical means for businesses to operationalize their commitments to environmental and social well-being. By emphasizing resilience, integration, agility, and governance, the VSM provides a pathway for organizations to navigate the complexities of sustainable transformation. However, sustainability is not a static goal but an ongoing journey of adaptation and learning. The VSM, with its embedded feedback mechanisms and systemic alignment, ensures that organizations remain agile and responsive to the changing demands of the modern world.

Incorporating the principles of the VSM into sustainability strategies not only enhances organizational effectiveness but also reinforces a broader commitment to societal progress. Businesses that adopt this model are better equipped to balance short-term operational goals with long-term resilience, ensuring their viability in a world that increasingly demands ethical and sustainable practices. The challenge, then, is for organizations to fully embrace the systemic thinking offered by the VSM and apply it consistently to achieve sustainability outcomes that benefit both their stakeholders and the planet.

Although criticisms about the viability of the VSM exist, its effectiveness is firmly rooted only in empirical evidence. Research has consistently validated the theoretical claims of the VSM, underscoring its practical utility. Schwaninger and Scheef (2016) conducted an extensive empirical study, demonstrating the VSM's ability to diagnose organizational challenges and improve systemic alignment in complex environments. Their findings provide compelling evidence that the model's principles are not only theoretically robust but also broadly applicable across diverse organizational settings.

The following section will explore the interconnection between Sustainability, AI, and the VSM in a more practical and comprehensive way, introducing the Sustainable Development Goals (SDGs) as a central framework.

ALIGNING AI DEPLOYMENT WITH SDGS

The question now is: how can the reader synthesize all the above information to construct a framework of correlation?

First, we establish a clear understanding of sustainability, explore the foundations of Responsible AI, and examine how the Viable System Model (VSM) empowers business leaders, managers, and entrepreneurs to navigate the complexities of today's business landscape. Yet, the challenge lies in integrating these concepts—can the reader connect them effectively? Furthermore, how can we measure sustainability in a meaningful way?

In today's rapidly evolving global landscape, sustainable development has become an essential priority for governments, businesses, and individuals. At the heart of these efforts are the United Nations Sustainable Development Goals (SDGs), a set of 17 interconnected objectives aimed at eradicating poverty, protecting the planet, and ensuring prosperity for all by 2030. The list can be found on the United Nations website, along with other valuable publications. Unlike other sustainability frameworks, such as Environmental, Social, and Governance (ESG) metrics or Corporate Social Responsibility (CSR) initiatives, the SDGs provide a universal roadmap, emphasizing a comprehensive, systemic approach to addressing global challenges.

Understanding the SDGs and Their Relationship with ESG and CSR

The SDGs represent a globally endorsed framework designed to guide efforts across all sectors toward sustainable outcomes. Each goal is supported by specific targets and indicators, offering a clear structure for measuring progress. For example, SDG 7 emphasizes access to affordable and clean energy, while SDG 13 addresses climate action. These goals demand a systemic perspective, requiring collaboration across industries, geographies, and societal levels to achieve meaningful impact (Le Blanc, 2015).

In contrast, ESG metrics focus primarily on how companies manage risks and opportunities related to environmental, social, and governance factors. While ESG frameworks are crucial for corporate accountability and transparency, they are often criticized for their narrow focus on financial performance rather than broader societal impact (PWC, 2021). ESG, while aligned with SDGs in certain areas, tends to prioritize investor-centric outcomes rather than holistic, global objectives.

Corporate Social Responsibility (CSR), on the other hand, represents a company's voluntary commitment to ethical practices, environmental responsibility, and social equity. While CSR initiatives can contribute to achieving SDG-aligned outcomes, they are often project-specific, lacking the systemic, long-term focus fundamental in the SDGs. CSR tends to operate sometimes separately from a company's core strategy, which limits its transformative potential.

To fully align with the SDGs, organizations must move beyond traditional CSR and ESG metrics to embrace a more systemic and integrative approach. Here, the Viable System Model (VSM), combined with Artificial Intelligence (AI), offers a powerful framework for navigating this complexity, enabling organizations to effectively align their internal operations with external sustainability goals.

The Viable System Model and Its Parallel with the SDGs

The VSM, conceptualized by Stafford Beer (1972), provides a systemic perspective on how organizations function and adapt to dynamic environments. Within the VSM, businesses are conceptualized as living systems comprising interconnected components: the Metahead (responsible for governance, intelligence, and policy), the Operational body (which executes day-to-day activities), and the External environment (comprising stakeholders, market forces, and societal factors). The interaction between these elements mirrors the interplay between businesses and the external world, including the SDGs.

The Metahead in the VSM, affiliated to the strategic brain of an organization, provides direction and ensures alignment with overarching objectives. In the context of the SDGs, this could mean prioritizing innovation to achieve clean energy access (SDG 7) or fostering partnerships for sustainable development (SDG 17). The Operational body translates these strategic requirements into action, ensuring that business processes align with sustainability goals while maintaining internal coherence and efficiency.

The External environment—representing customers, regulators, competitors, and broader societal dynamics—provides the context within which organizations operate. Here, the SDGs act as a guiding framework, influencing organizational priorities and demanding systemic integration. Just as the External environment in the VSM provides feedback that shapes internal operations, the SDGs offer benchmarks for businesses to adapt and innovate.

The Role of Artificial Intelligence in Enhancing the VSM and SDG Alignment

Artificial Intelligence introduces unprecedented capabilities for enhancing the VSM's systemic functions and aligning businesses with the SDGs. Through advanced data processing, predictive analytics, and automation, AI strengthens the intelligence and control functions of the VSM, empowering businesses to make informed decisions and optimize processes.

In the quest to navigate the complexities of sustainable development, the blend of AI and the Viable System Model (VSM) offers businesses an unique edge. Together, they enhance decision-making processes, streamline operations, and bring groundbreaking vision, and adaptability to achieving the Sustainable Development Goals (SDGs).

At the heart of this synergy lies AI's ability to augment the intelligence functions of the VSM, particularly within System 4, which focuses on environmental scanning and future planning. By processing vast volumes of data, AI uncovers emerging trends, risks, and opportunities that might otherwise go unnoticed. Imagine a company using predictive models to forecast resource shortages or anticipate energy demands, enabling strategic decisions that directly support climate action (SDG 13). These insights help businesses proactively align their actions with a sustainable and resilient future.

AI also revolutionizes operational efficiency, a key principle of the VSM. Through automation of repetitive tasks and waste reduction, organizations can optimize their processes while advancing SDG goals such as responsible consumption and production (SDG 12). The integration of AI ensures that businesses operate not only more efficiently but also more sustainably, turning small changes into significant, scalable impacts.

Predictive analytics further deepen this advantage. With AI-driven tools, organizations gain insight into the potential consequences of their actions. For instance, AI can simulate the long-term effects of policy decisions on biodiversity (SDG 15), empowering companies to develop strategies that protect ecosystems while pursuing their goals. This forward-looking capability transforms decision-making into a powerful tool for sustainable innovation.

Perhaps most transformative is AI's capacity for real-time monitoring and reporting. Organizations can track their progress toward SDG targets with precision, gaining actionable insights that ensure accountability and foster continuous improvement. AI's real-time feedback aligns perfectly with the VSM's principles of resilience and responsiveness, enabling businesses to dynamically adapt their strategies to changing circumstances and maintain alignment with long-term goals.

Through the integration of AI and the VSM, businesses are equipped to navigate the complexities of sustainable development with intelligence, efficiency, and adaptability. This powerful combination not only addresses immediate challenges but also builds a foundation for a sustainable future, where progress is both measurable and meaningful.

Integrating SDGs, VSM, and AI for Scalable Sustainability Solutions

The integration of SDGs, the VSM, and AI creates a synergistic framework for pursuing sustainable development at scale. Together, they offer tools to enhance organizational strategy, improve decision-making, and align business practices with global sustainability objectives.

In the rapidly evolving landscape of sustainable development, the fusion of AI and the Viable System Model (VSM) emerges as a powerful catalyst for transformative change. This dynamic duo empowers businesses to pursue innovation that aligns seamlessly with the United Nations Sustainable Development Goals (SDGs). Imagine companies harnessing cutting-edge technologies to develop renewable energy solutions, bridging gaps in education, and fostering equal opportunities for all—true examples of goal-oriented innovation.

The beauty of the VSM lies in its holistic perspective, perfectly complementing the interconnected nature of the SDGs. By adopting systems thinking, businesses can tackle multiple challenges in alignment. Consider, for instance, how advancements in clean energy (SDG 7) can spread through society, simultaneously reducing inequalities (SDG 10) and shaping sustainable cities (SDG 11). This integrative approach transforms isolated efforts into a unified strategy, addressing the complexities of modern sustainability challenges.

Yet, ambition alone is not enough; scalability is the key to meaningful impact. This is where AI steps in, bringing its exceptional capacity for automation and analytics to the table. When combined with the VSM's structured, systemic framework, organizations can scale their sustainability initiatives without losing sight of their long-term vision. The result? Efforts that are both expansive and deeply coherent, reaching more people and addressing more issues than ever before.

Resilience is another cornerstone of this powerful synergy. The VSM, with its feedback loops and adaptive mechanisms, ensures that businesses remain agile and responsive to an ever-changing world. Augmented by AI, these capabilities help organizations not just survive but thrive in the face of uncertainty. By continuously adjusting their strategies, they can maintain alignment with the SDGs and secure their viability for generations to come.

Together, AI and the VSM offer businesses a pathway to a more sustainable, equitable future—one where innovation is not only impactful but also deeply rooted in the principles of interdependence and resilience. Through this union, the dream of achieving the SDGs transforms into a tangible, actionable reality.

Case Study: GreenRoutes – Open-Source AI for Sustainable Mobility

GreenRoutes is an open-source web application that uses AI to optimize eco-friendly commuting by analyzing route efficiency and environmental impact (GreenRoutes, 2024). While not a logistics startup, GreenRoutes exemplifies how open access to AI tools can democratize sustainable innovation. Although the platform does not report specific emissions statistics, it demonstrates the potential of algorithmic optimization to support responsible urban mobility. This aligns with broader industry trends where AI-driven logistics tools aim to reduce carbon emissions and promote energy efficiency, though results depend on context and implementation (McKinsey & Company, 2023).

This case underscores the growing influence of open-source initiatives in making responsible AI accessible to diverse entrepreneurial actors.

Methodological Framework for Responsible AI Impact Assessment

Evaluating Responsible AI in entrepreneurial settings requires a structured, mixed-method approach:

- **Quantitative indicators:** Carbon footprint reduction, model bias scores, ESG-aligned KPIs - It is recommended that this be driven from the business side and integrated into the early-stage strategy, as it helps clarify the true purpose of the venture and the specific problems it aims to solve. This approach leads to designing more meaningful and impactful solutions for humanity and society.
- **Qualitative assessments:** Stakeholder interviews, community feedback, employee engagement - could drive to High Expectations Customer (HEC), popularized by First Round Capital, a prominent early-stage venture capital firm in Silicon Valley. Startups like Shopify, Airbnb, and Dropbox have implicitly followed this model: building for power users or visionary customers first, and then expanding to broader markets. Entrepreneurs can think in terms of sustainability.

- **Process audits:** Regular reviews of model updates, fairness thresholds, and data provenance.

While a specific Saudi SME study could not be validated, research from Saudi Arabia's AI startup ecosystem underscores the value of combining diverse metrics for comprehensive ethical impact assessment (Alghamdi & Alharbi, 2025).

Such triangulated methodologies ensure that ethical evaluations are as robust and dynamic as the technologies they aim to govern.

The Path Forward: Achieving Sustainable Impact Through Systemic Integration

The SDGs, AI, and the VSM collectively represent a modern framework model for sustainable development. By integrating these elements, businesses can move beyond fragmented sustainability efforts to embrace a systemic approach that delivers meaningful, scalable impact.

Nonetheless, achieving this requires more than technological adoption or strategic alignment. Organizations must foster a culture of systemic thinking, prioritize cross-sector collaboration, and remain accountable to stakeholders. The cooperation between the Metahead, Operational body, and External environment in the VSM provides a powerful analogy for this alignment, with AI serving as the connective tissue that enables real-time adaptation and strategic foresight, as shown in the image 5 below:

Figure 5. Collaboration between the Viable System Model, emergent technologies and Sustainable Development Goals displayed by SDG Knowledge Hub

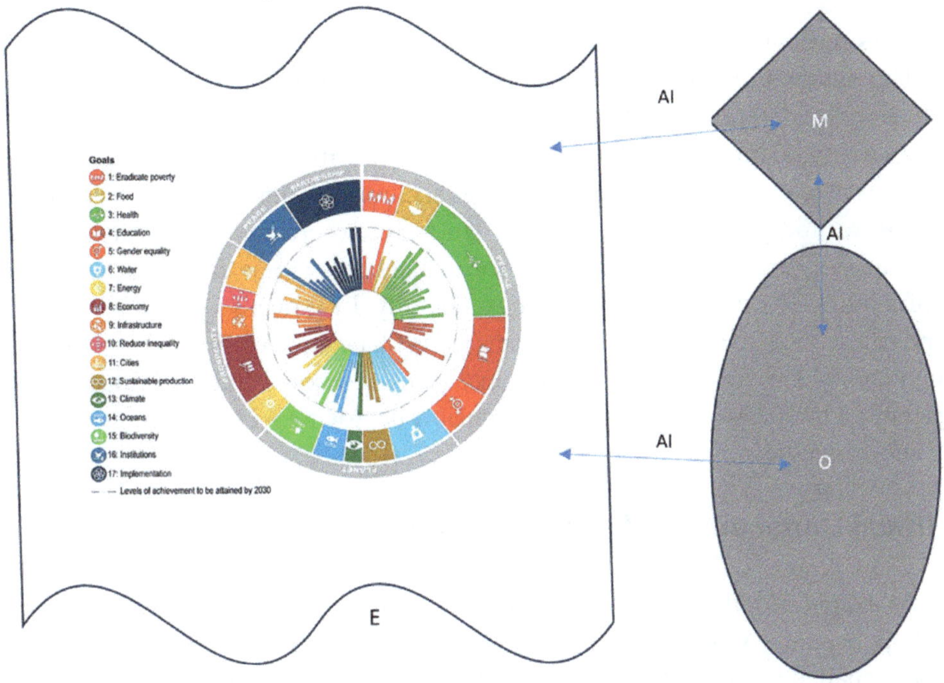

Source: Author's contribution.

As the world struggles with urgent global challenges, this integrated framework offers a pathway for businesses to contribute to sustainable development while securing their long-term viability. The question now is not whether businesses should adopt this approach but how they can implement it effectively to ensure a sustainable and equitable future for all.

The author underscores the importance of business leaders committing to achieving the SDGs, fostering responsible technology, and understanding how these concepts integrate into the entire business structure. When the organization—from its Metahead to the operational teams—is collectively dedicated to developing responsible technology that positively influences the SDGs, it creates a balance that ensures businesses are not only viable but also sustainable and profitable, ultimately contributing to a better common future.

Strategies for Responsible AI Deployment in Sustainable Businesses

Does responsibility match to ethical considerations?

The author introduces Responsible AI within Sustainable Business Models: Ethical Considerations and Strategic Approaches.

As Artificial Intelligence (AI) reshapes industries, its integration into sustainable business models presents vast opportunities and equally significant responsibilities. Businesses today operate in a complex landscape where addressing environmental concerns, social equity, and governance standards are as critical as achieving profitability. The deployment of AI must not only drive operational efficiency and innovation but also adhere to ethical standards that ensure equity, privacy, and accountability. This section explores the ethical considerations, strategic initiatives, and systemic frameworks necessary for responsibly deploying AI to achieve sustainable development goals.

Ethical Dimensions of AI Deployment

AI's rapid adoption has underscored the importance of ethics in its development and application. As powerful as AI is in transforming businesses and addressing global challenges, its potential misuse or unintended consequences necessitate a rigorous ethical framework.

The following factors are crucial for the development and deployment of AI:

1. *Consent and Transparency*: Transparency is a fundamental pillar of ethical AI practices. It requires organizations to provide clear and accessible information about how AI systems operate, the data they use, and the decisions they make. Transparency also ensures that users understand how their data is collected, processed, and stored, empowering them to make informed decisions about their interactions with AI.

For example, AI-driven recommendation systems on social media platforms often rely on user behavior data. Without clear communication, users may unwittingly contribute to data collection practices that infringe on their privacy or manipulate their preferences (Zuboff, 2019). Implementing frameworks like the *General Data Protection Regulation (GDPR)* ensures informed consent and user empowerment (Voigt & Von dem Bussche, 2017).

2. *Bias and Fairness*: AI systems are not by default neutral; they reflect the biases present in the data they are trained on. When datasets are unrepresentative

or biased, AI can carry forward and even amplify systemic inequalities. Bias in AI can have significant consequences, particularly in areas such as hiring, healthcare, and criminal justice.

For instance, studies have highlighted how facial recognition systems misidentify people of color at disproportionately higher rates than white individuals, leading to discriminatory outcomes in law enforcement applications (Buolamwini & Gebru, 2018). Addressing such biases requires rigorous data auditing, the inclusion of diverse datasets, and bias mitigation techniques.

3. *Accountability*: Clear accountability frameworks are essential to managing the risks associated with AI deployment. Without accountability, businesses risk losing public trust and facing legal or reputational consequences for AI's unintended harms. Accountability involves not only defining responsibility but also creating mechanisms for remedy when AI systems fail or cause harm.

For example, the European Union's proposed *Artificial Intelligence Act* emphasizes accountability by mandating risk assessments and transparency measures for high-risk AI systems (European Commission, 2021). Businesses can also establish internal AI ethics committees to oversee compliance and address ethical dilemmas proactively.

4. *Privacy Safeguards*: As AI relies heavily on data, privacy concerns are vital. Robust privacy safeguards ensure that personal data is protected and used responsibly. Techniques such as differential privacy, federated learning, and anonymization can help secure sensitive information while enabling AI to perform its functions effectively (Shokri & Shmatikov, 2015).

A notable example is Apple's implementation of differential privacy to analyze user behavior trends without compromising individual privacy. Such measures align with global data protection regulations and build trust with users, fostering long-term engagement.

AI as a Catalyst for Sustainability

AI's potential extends beyond ethical compliance; it can actively contribute to achieving sustainability goals by optimizing resource use, enhancing efficiency, and addressing social challenges. The following applications highlight AI's transformative role in promoting sustainability:

1. *Resource Efficiency*: AI-driven systems can optimize energy consumption, reduce waste, and improve resource allocation. In manufacturing, predictive maintenance powered by AI minimizes machine downtime and reduces material wastage by identifying potential failures before they occur (Wuest et al., 2016). In agriculture, AI-enabled precision farming ensures that water, fertilizers, and pesticides are applied efficiently, reducing environmental impact while maximizing outputs.
2. *Social Good Initiatives*: Ethical AI supports initiatives that address societal challenges, such as healthcare accessibility and education equality. For example, AI applications like IBM Watson assist in early disease detection, while adaptive learning platforms like Khan Academy provide personalized education to underserved communities (Topol, 2019). These solutions demonstrate how AI can drive social progress while aligning with sustainability goals.
3. *Circular Economy Models*: AI can facilitate the transition to a circular economy by promoting recycling, resource reuse, and waste reduction. Machine learning algorithms identify recyclable materials in waste streams, while AI-powered logistics optimize reverse supply chains for products at the end of their lifecycle (Ellen MacArthur Foundation, 2019). Such innovations contribute to reduced environmental impact and foster economic value creation.

The Intersection of AI, VSM, and SDGs

The integration of AI, the Viable System Model (VSM), and the Sustainable Development Goals (SDGs) represents a useful tool for sustainable development. These elements, when combined, create a systemic approach to addressing global challenges and driving meaningful impact.

The author will explain exactly how this is happening in the section below:

1. *AI Enhancing VSM*: AI strengthens the intelligence and control functions of the VSM by enabling data-driven decision-making, predictive analytics, and real-time monitoring. For instance:
   - *System 4 (Intelligence)* - AI enhances environmental scanning by analyzing trends, identifying risks, and forecasting future scenarios, enabling organizations to align with SDG targets such as climate action (SDG 13).
   - *System 1 (Operations)* - AI-powered automation ensures operational efficiency and sustainability, reducing resource consumption and emissions.
2. *VSM Aligning with SDGs*: The VSM provides in this case a framework for aligning an organization's internal operations with external sustainability goals.

It fosters systemic thinking, resilience, and adaptability, ensuring that businesses remain viable while contributing to the SDGs. For example, aligning with SDG 12 (Responsible Consumption and Production) requires organizations to integrate sustainable practices across all levels, which the VSM's systemic approach facilitates.

3. *AI Supporting SDG Implementation*: AI technologies play an important role in achieving specific SDGs. From using AI-driven models to monitor climate change (SDG 13) to leveraging AI for sustainable urban development (SDG 11), these technologies provide actionable insights and scalable solutions. AI-powered dashboards, for instance, enable real-time tracking of SDG progress, ensuring accountability and informed decision-making.

A Small Case Study for Readers 'To Take Home': AI, VSM, and SDGs in Action

A global logistics company seeking to align its operations with the SDGs looks to implement an AI-driven VSM approach. By leveraging AI for supply chain optimization, the company can reduce its carbon footprint (SDG 13) and enhance transparency through blockchain-powered tracking systems (SDG 12). The VSM's framework can be used to ensure that these initiatives will be integrated across all levels of the organization, from strategic oversight (Metahead) to Operational execution (System 1). The result will lead to a resilient, sustainable, and efficient business model that delivers measurable environmental and social benefits.

Toward a Sustainable Future

The intersection of AI, VSM, and SDGs provides a root for businesses to achieve systemic sustainability while addressing ethical considerations. By embedding ethical principles, leveraging AI for innovation, and aligning with systemic frameworks like the VSM, organizations can navigate the complexities of the modern business landscape and contribute positively to global development.

As the world faces pressing challenges such as climate change, inequality, and resource scarcity, the question is no longer whether businesses should adopt responsible practices but how they can implement them effectively. The integration of these frameworks offers not only a solution but a paradigm shift, demonstrating that sustainability and profitability can coexist in a rapidly evolving world.

The author highlights that maintaining a balance between the business and its External environment requires a holistic understanding of how technology is utilized and how the organization responds and adapts to external influences, including those impacting the SDGs. This perspective aligns with the principles of the Viable

System Model (VSM), which serves as a framework for systemic responsiveness. Engaging the entire organization in this process fosters the development of responsible technologies while encouraging innovation, ultimately contributing to a more sustainable and equitable future.

The next section explores deeper into the nuances of technology ethics, exploring how business leaders can strike a balance between ethical considerations and innovation to achieve greater sustainability.

BALANCING INNOVATION AND ETHICS

Balancing innovation and ethics is one of the most pressing challenges for sustainable enterprises in today's rapidly evolving technological landscape. Artificial Intelligence (AI), a key driver of innovation, holds immense potential to revolutionize industries and address global challenges, but its responsible deployment requires a careful balance between creativity and accountability. The integration of ethics into AI development is not just a matter of regulatory compliance but a strategic necessity for businesses aiming to align with sustainability goals and societal expectations.

AI's capacity for transformative innovation is undeniable. Its ability to optimize processes, enhance decision-making, and uncover new opportunities provides businesses with a competitive edge while promoting sustainable practices. For instance, AI-driven systems in agriculture enable precision farming, where resources like water and fertilizers are applied judiciously, minimizing waste and environmental impact (Wuest et al., 2016). Similarly, AI-powered tools in manufacturing reduce energy consumption and material waste through predictive maintenance, fostering ecological balance. These examples illustrate how innovation, when guided by ethical principles, can contribute to sustainability.

However, innovation without an ethical foundation can lead to unintended consequences, including bias, inequality, and mistrust. Ethical frameworks provide the necessary guardrails to navigate these risks. Transparency is an important pillar of ethical AI, ensuring that users understand how their data is used and decisions are made. This is particularly relevant in a world where data privacy concerns are predominant. Frameworks like the General Data Protection Regulation (GDPR) emphasize informed consent and accountability, empowering users while holding organizations responsible for their practices (Voigt & Von dem Bussche, 2017). Transparency also extends to AI systems' decision-making processes, enabling stakeholders to trust and verify their outcomes.

Bias is another critical ethical challenge in AI deployment. Algorithms trained on flawed or unrepresentative datasets can perpetuate systemic inequalities, as seen in hiring tools that inadvertently discriminate against certain demographics

(Dastin, 2018). Addressing bias requires a proactive approach, including the use of diverse datasets, routine audits, and bias-mitigation techniques. These measures ensure fairness and inclusivity, which are essential for building trust in AI systems.

Accountability plays a pivotal role in fostering responsible AI innovation. Establishing clear lines of responsibility for AI's outcomes ensures that organizations can address potential harms effectively. For instance, the European Union's proposed Artificial Intelligence Act emphasizes accountability by requiring risk assessments and transparency measures for high-risk AI systems (European Commission, 2021). Businesses can further strengthen accountability through ethics committees that oversee AI projects and ensure compliance with ethical standards.

Privacy safeguards are equally critical in ethical AI deployment. Techniques such as federated learning and differential privacy enable organizations to process data securely without compromising individual confidentiality (Shokri & Shmatikov, 2015). These privacy-preserving methods not only comply with regulatory standards but also build user trust, fostering long-term engagement.

While ethics form the foundation of responsible AI, its potential to drive sustainability cannot be overlooked. AI's ability to optimize resource use and reduce environmental impact is transforming industries. In energy management, AI-powered systems monitor and optimize consumption, reducing waste and carbon footprints. In healthcare, AI enhances patient outcomes by supporting early diagnosis and personalized treatment plans (Topol, 2019). Such applications demonstrate how AI can contribute to sustainability goals while delivering tangible societal benefits.

Sustainability also requires systemic thinking, where organizations align their operations with broader environmental and societal goals. The Viable System Model (VSM), developed by Stafford Beer and later Angela Esponisa, provides a systemic framework for achieving this alignment. By conceptualizing organizations as dynamic systems composed of interconnected components, the VSM emphasizes the importance of balancing internal operations with external demands. The Metahead, representing governance and strategy, interacts with the Operational body and External environment, ensuring that businesses remain adaptable and resilient.

AI strengthens the VSM's functions by enhancing decision-making, operational efficiency, and real-time monitoring. For example, AI-driven analytics can support the intelligence function (System 4) by scanning the External environment for risks and opportunities, enabling organizations to align their strategies with sustainability goals. Similarly, AI-powered automation can improve the efficiency of operational systems (System 1), ensuring that businesses can meet their objectives sustainably.

The Sustainable Development Goals (SDGs) provide a global framework for addressing environmental, social, and economic challenges, and AI offers powerful tools for achieving these targets. From reducing carbon emissions (SDG 13) to promoting sustainable urban development (SDG 11), AI enables businesses to make informed decisions and monitor progress. The integration of AI and the VSM creates a synergistic approach, where technology supports systemic alignment with the SDGs.

Real-world examples highlight the potential of AI to drive sustainable innovation. IBM Watson's deployment in healthcare demonstrates how AI can enhance access to quality care while addressing ethical considerations such as data privacy (Topol, 2019). Microsoft's AI for Earth initiative exemplifies how technology can tackle environmental challenges by providing tools for monitoring climate change, deforestation, and water scarcity. These case studies underscore the importance of integrating ethics into AI development to maximize its impact.

Even so, achieving sustainable innovation requires more than isolated success stories. It demands a cultural shift within organizations, where ethical considerations are embedded into every stage of AI development. This involves fostering a culture of accountability, engaging stakeholders, and promoting transparency. Google's AI Principles, which prioritize social benefit and fairness, set a benchmark for responsible innovation. Such commitments ensure that businesses not only meet regulatory requirements but also align with societal values.

The intersection of AI, the VSM, and the SDGs offers a pathway for businesses to balance innovation and ethics effectively. By leveraging AI's capabilities, aligning with systemic frameworks like the VSM, and addressing global challenges through the SDGs, organizations can achieve sustainable impact. This approach demonstrates that innovation and ethics are not opposing forces but complementary dimensions of a forward-thinking business strategy.

As businesses navigate the complexities of the modern world, they must embrace AI not only as a tool for efficiency but as a catalyst for meaningful change. By addressing ethical concerns, fostering systemic alignment, and leveraging technology for sustainability, organizations can create value that extends beyond profit. This integration of ethics, innovation, and systemic thinking is not just a vision for the future but a strategic essential for achieving long-term success in an interconnected and rapidly evolving world.

What Could Be a Responsible AI Toolkit for Entrepreneurs

Entrepreneurs can operationalize Responsible AI by:

1. Conducting baseline ethical audits of AI tools and practices.
2. Using model cards and datasheets to document assumptions and performance.
3. Involving stakeholders in co-design workshops to surface concerns and priorities.
4. Implementing monitoring tools to track bias, drift, and data misuse.
5. Aligning AI initiatives with at least one Sustainable Development Goal (SDG).

IBM (2024) reports that 35% of businesses now actively use AI, up from 22% in 2021, with many adopting Responsible AI toolkits to meet stakeholder and regulatory expectations.

These toolkits offer a practical roadmap for transforming abstract principles into measurable action.

As Challenges and Opportunities for SMEs

Large firms often have resources for custom AI governance, but SMEs face tighter constraints. Nevertheless, SMEs can leverage open-source ethical AI tools, lightweight checklists, and partnerships with incubators focused on responsible innovation. The Conference Board of Canada (2024) outlines SME maturity models for sustainability, which can inform ethical AI oversight. Public policy plays a catalytic role by providing SMEs with access to AI sandboxes, grants, and advisory networks, enabling even early-stage ventures to embed responsibility at the core of their digital strategies.

This points to a critical need for public-private partnerships that lower the barriers to ethical innovation.

A strong starting point is leveraging platforms like Credo AI, which align with the National Institute of Standards and Technology (2023) - NIST AI Risk Management Framework (AI RMF 1.0)—a U.S. government standard that provides principles and methodologies for designing trustworthy, transparent, and accountable AI systems. In parallel, participating in accelerators—such as those supported by EIT in Europe, particularly in sectors like Urban Mobility or clean tech (e.g., inVest – the Urban Mobility Accelerator for West Romania)—can offer entrepreneurs valuable guidance, resources, and early-stage support. These programs help validate ideas, refine business models, and scale impactful solutions effectively.

CONCLUSION

This last section underscores the critical role of ethical considerations in the integration of Artificial Intelligence (AI) within sustainable entrepreneurship. By aligning AI development with ethical principles, businesses not only enhance their operational efficacy but also contribute positively to societal and environmental goals. This integration is vital for navigating the complex interplay of innovation, regulation, and sustainability in today's rapidly evolving business landscape.

Summary of Key Points

The central theme of this chapter revolves around embedding ethics in AI development as a means to elevate business practices. Ethical AI ensures fairness, transparency, accountability, privacy, and safety, which are foundational to fostering trust among stakeholders. These principles are not only essential for risk mitigation but also serve as catalysts for innovation. Businesses that adopt robust ethical frameworks can achieve a competitive edge while aligning their strategies with broader societal objectives, such as the Sustainable Development Goals (SDGs).

Through systemic frameworks like the Viable System Model (VSM), organizations are empowered to harmonize internal operations with external sustainability goals. By leveraging AI's potential for predictive analytics, resource efficiency, and real-time monitoring, businesses can ensure a balance between operational needs and sustainable impact. Case studies, including Microsoft's AI for Earth initiative and IBM Watson's deployment in healthcare, exemplify how ethical AI innovations contribute to global challenges while enhancing business viability.

Future Outlook

As AI technologies continue to evolve, their role in shaping sustainable development will only grow in significance. Emerging innovations in AI-driven analytics, automation, and machine learning will provide unprecedented opportunities for addressing global challenges such as climate change, poverty, and inequality. However, this progress will be accompanied by increased scrutiny from regulators, stakeholders, and the public.

The evolving regulatory landscape—exemplified by initiatives like the European Union's Artificial Intelligence Act—requires businesses to stay proactive in their ethical commitments. Navigating these regulatory frameworks will not only ensure compliance but also position organizations as leaders in responsible innovation. The future of AI-driven sustainability lies in creating adaptive systems that align technological advancements with ethical requirements and societal expectations.

Call to Action

The chapter emphasizes the urgent need for businesses to lead in the ethical deployment of AI. By aligning strategies with the SDGs and adopting frameworks like the VSM, organizations can create systemic solutions that ensure sustainable impact. This requires embedding ethical considerations into the foundation of technological development, from the ideation stage to implementation and monitoring.

Cultivating a culture of ethical integrity and innovation is more than vital. Businesses must invest in educating stakeholders, forming cross-disciplinary ethics committees, and promoting transparency in their AI operations. By doing so, they not only mitigate risks but also contribute to a future where technological progress is both unprejudiced and sustainable.

Collaboration and Innovation

To fully harness AI's potential for sustainable growth, collaboration across sectors and disciplines is essential. Governments, private enterprises, academic institutions, and non-governmental organizations must work together to establish best practices, share knowledge, and drive innovation. Collaborative efforts can ensure that AI's transformative power is directed toward addressing global challenges rather than aggravating existing inequalities.

Enterprises that proactively embrace ethical AI principles can become pioneers in responsible technological advancements. By integrating systemic thinking, such as the principles of the VSM, businesses can maintain adaptability, ensure resilience, and foster holistic growth. These organizations will not only meet the demands of the present but also shape a sustainable future for generations to come.

Entrepreneurs must consider key limitations related to global variability and cultural context when developing and deploying AI solutions.

AI deployment is deeply influenced by cultural and regulatory context. Western markets emphasize data protection and transparency (e.g., GDPR), while collectivist cultures in Asia or Africa may prioritize communal well-being and localized trust models. A 2025 Finnish study found that regional norms and regulatory complexity significantly shape SME AI adoption (Laaksonen et al., 2025). OECD (2024) data reveal a proliferation of national AI strategies, reinforcing the influence of culture and governance on Responsible AI implementation.

These variations underscore the importance of culturally adaptive AI frameworks that remain ethically sound across jurisdictions.

The author has primarily operated within the European sector and maintained partial collaboration with the U.S. ecosystem. However, this focus implies certain limitations in addressing the Asian market, which is both highly dynamic and uniquely challenging.

Final Thoughts

The integration of ethics, innovation, and sustainability in AI development is not just a strategic advantage—it is a necessity for ensuring long-term viability in an interconnected world. Businesses that prioritize ethical AI deployment demonstrate leadership in addressing the challenges of the 21st century while creating a legacy of positive impact. As this chapter concludes, the overarching message is clear: ethical AI is not merely a regulatory requirement or a societal expectation; it is a transformative force that has the potential to redefine the future of entrepreneurship and sustainable development.

The future of entrepreneurship lies not in AI innovation alone but in responsible AI innovation. Entrepreneurs who integrate ethical foresight and stakeholder inclusion into their AI strategies are more likely to build enduring, equitable, and environmentally aligned ventures. OECD and BCG findings confirm that transparency, stakeholder engagement, and long-term equity are central to sustainable AI ecosystems (OECD, 2023; Boston Consulting Group, 2024). By embracing Responsible AI, business leaders help create a regenerative economic model that serves people, planet, and profit in harmony.

The Viable System Model (VSM) may not be easy to grasp—nor has it ever been—but its true value lies in encouraging young and emerging entrepreneurs to think systemically. By adopting this perspective, they can better anticipate challenges, develop strategic responses, and design solutions that contribute to a sustainable future for society as a whole. This approach inherently demands collaboration across systems and at all organizational levels. The author advocates for this mindset as a foundation for building truly viable business models.

The authors pose the following question to inspire reflection among readers: *Are you prepared to be the responsible leader who shapes and innovates the future?*

REFERENCES

Accenture & MIT Sloan Management Review. (2022). Responsible AI: Driving business value and trust. https://www.accenture.com

Alghamdi, A., & Alharbi, F. (2025). Strategic oversight of AI adoption in Saudi Arabian SMEs: A mixed-method study. *Journal of AI and Entrepreneurship*, *3*(1), 45–62.

Bansal, P., & DesJardine, M. R. (2014). Business sustainability: It is about time. *Strategic Organization*, *12*(1), 70–78.

Beer, S. (1972). *Brain of the firm*. John Wiley & Sons.

Bocken, N. M. P., Short, S. W., Rana, P., & Evans, S. (2014). A literature and practice review to develop sustainable business model archetypes. *Journal of Cleaner Production*, *65*, 42–56.

Boiral, O., & Henri, J. F. (2012). Modelling the impact of ISO 14001 on environmental performance: A comparative approach. *Journal of Environmental Management*, *99*, 84–97. PMID: 22326757

Boston Consulting Group. (2024). *Global AI adoption and value realization report*. https://www.bcg.com

Brynjolfsson, E., & McAfee, A. (2014). *The second machine age: Work, progress, and prosperity in a time of brilliant technologies*. W. W. Norton & Company.

Buolamwini, J., & Gebru, T. (2018). Gender shades: Intersectional accuracy disparities in commercial gender classification. *Proceedings of Machine Learning Research*, *81*, 77–91.

Carroll, A. B. (1991). The pyramid of corporate social responsibility: Toward the moral management of organizational stakeholders. *Business Horizons*, *34*(4), 39–48.

Carroll, A. B., & Shabana, K. M. (2010). The business case for corporate social responsibility: A review of concepts, research, and practice. *International Journal of Management Reviews*, *12*(1), 85–105.

Cohen, B., & Winn, M. I. (2007). Market imperfections, opportunity and sustainable entrepreneurship. *Journal of Business Venturing*, *22*(1), 29–49.

Dastin, J. (2018). *Amazon scraps secret AI recruiting tool that showed bias against women*. Reuters.

Eccles, R. G., Ioannou, I., & Serafeim, G. (2012). The impact of a corporate culture of sustainability on corporate behavior and performance. *Management Science, 60*(11), 2835–2857.

Elkington, J. (1997). *Cannibals with forks: The triple bottom line of 21st century business.* Capstone.

Ellen MacArthur Foundation. (2019). *Artificial intelligence and the circular economy.*

European Commission. (2021). *Proposal for a regulation laying down harmonized rules on Artificial Intelligence.* Artificial Intelligence Act.

European Commission. (2024). The AI Act: Regulation of artificial intelligence. https://digital-strategy.ec.europa.eu/en/policies/european-approach-artificial-intelligence

Freeman, R. E., Harrison, J. S., Wicks, A. C., Parmar, B. L., & De Colle, S. (2010). *Stakeholder theory: The state of the art.* Cambridge University Press.

GreenRoutes. (2024). GreenRoutes: Open-source sustainable route planning. https://github.com/GreenRoutes

Hall, J. K., Daneke, G. A., & Lenox, M. J. (2010). Sustainable development and entrepreneurship: Past contributions and future directions. *Journal of Business Venturing, 25*(5), 439–448.

Hart, S. L., & Dowell, G. (2011). A natural-resource-based view of the firm: Fifteen years after. *Journal of Management, 37*(5), 1464–1479.

IBM. (2024). AI adoption trends in business: 2024 report. https://www.ibm.com

IPCC. (2021). *Climate change 2021: The physical science basis. Contribution of Working Group I to the Sixth Assessment Report.* Cambridge University Press.

Kubanek, A., & Szymoniak, M. (2022). Ethical governance in AI integration: A system-wide approach. *AI Ethics Journal, 1*(2), 101–115.

Laaksonen, S., Virtanen, T., & Hämäläinen, M. (2025). Regional and cultural influences on AI adoption in Finnish SMEs. *Nordic Journal of Innovation, 12*(1), 78–95.

Le Blanc, D. (2015). Towards integration at last? The Sustainable Development Goals as a network of targets. *Sustainable Development, 23*(3), 176–187.

Makridakis, S. (2017). The forthcoming Artificial Intelligence (AI) revolution: Its impact on society and firms. *Futures, 90*, 46–60.

McKinsey & Company. (2023). AI and sustainability: Opportunities in logistics. https://www.mckinsey.com

Meadows, D. H., Meadows, D. L., Randers, J., & Behrens, W. W. (1972). *The limits to growth*. Potomac Associates.

Mikalef, P., Boura, M., Lekakos, G., & Krogstie, J. (2020). Big data analytics capabilities and innovation: The mediating role of dynamic capabilities and moderating effect of the environment. *British Journal of Management*, *31*(2), 356–382.

National Institute of Standards and Technology. (2023). *AI risk management framework (AI RMF 1.0)*. U.S. Department of Commerce. https://www.nist.gov/itl/ai-risk-management-framework

OECD. (2019). *OECD principles on artificial intelligence*. Organisation for Economic Co-operation and Development.

OECD. (2023). AI incident trends and governance challenges. https://www.oecd.org

OECD. (2024). National AI strategies and governance principles. https://www.oecd.org

Porter, M. E., & Heppelmann, J. E. (2014). How smart, connected products are transforming competition. *Harvard Business Review*, *92*(11), 64–88.

Raji, I. D., & Buolamwini, J. (2019). Actionable auditing: Investigating the impact of publicly naming biased performance results of commercial AI products. *Proceedings of the 2019 AAAI/ACM Conference on AI Ethics and Society,* 429–435.

Russell, S., & Norvig, P. (2020). *Artificial intelligence: A modern approach* (4th ed.). Pearson.

Shepherd, D. A., & Patzelt, H. (2011). The new field of sustainable entrepreneurship: Studying entrepreneurial action linking "what is to be sustained" with "what is to be developed.". *Entrepreneurship Theory and Practice*, *35*(1), 137–163.

Shokri, R., & Shmatikov, V. (2015). Privacy-preserving machine learning. *Proceedings on Privacy Enhancing Technologies. Privacy Enhancing Technologies Symposium*, *2015*(2), 35–50.

Topol, E. (2019). *Deep medicine: How artificial intelligence can make healthcare human again*. Basic Books.

United Nations. (2015). *Transforming our world: The 2030 Agenda for Sustainable Development.*

Voigt, P., & Von dem Bussche, A. (2017). *The EU General Data Protection Regulation (GDPR): A practical guide*. Springer.

White, K., Hardisty, D. J., & Habib, R. (2019). The elusive green consumer. *Harvard Business Review*, *97*(4), 124–133.

Wuest, T., Weimer, D., Irgens, C., & Thoben, K. D. (2016). Machine learning in manufacturing. *Production & Manufacturing Research*, *4*(1), 23–45.

Zuboff, S. (2019). *The age of surveillance capitalism: The fight for a human future at the new frontier of power*. PublicAffairs.

Chapter 6
Empowering Entrepreneurial Skills for Success and Sustainability

Stephanie Sandland
https://orcid.org/0000-0002-5183-7201
University of East London, UK

Alina Maria Vaduva
https://orcid.org/0009-0004-7886-595X
University of East London, UK

Toyin Coker
University of East London, UK

ABSTRACT

Entrepreneurs play a critical role in driving sustainability, but incorporating sustainability into an enterprise adds complexity and diffusion challenges. This chapter explores key skills and tools to enhance success. Systems thinking aids in problem analysis and intervention planning, while structured idea generation techniques foster viable solutions. A positive entrepreneurial mindset is essential, alongside strategies to mitigate risks tied to radical innovation. The case of electric car adoption illustrates these challenges. Success also hinges on assembling a skilled team to navigate the launch and scaling phases. Securing finance requires aligning with funders' priorities, crafting compelling brand stories, and refining pitching techniques for various forms of funding. Finally, entrepreneurs can leverage networks,

DOI: 10.4018/979-8-3373-1107-4.ch006

government support, and AI-driven analytical tools to manage sustainability's complexities and enhance decision-making. Throughout this chapter, the specific skills and tools to support these activities are explained.

INTRODUCTION

This chapter explores the skills, tools, and support systems entrepreneurs need to drive sustainable innovation, whether within start-ups or established firms. It focuses on three key areas: entrepreneurial mindset and core competencies, financial and operational execution, and external resources, including the use of emerging technologies like AI.

As global sustainability challenges intensify, business has become central to the solution. However, the transition cannot depend solely on policy change or regulation. Many large corporations only respond when forced to comply. By contrast, social enterprises and SMEs are showing greater agility and commitment to values-driven, sustainable action. These ventures often lead not through scale, but through purpose, innovation, and the ability to disrupt established systems from the ground up.

The urgency is clear. Over three decades after Ruckelshaus (cited in Meadows et al., 2004) warned that achieving sustainability would require a conscious societal shift, global consumption now exceeds Earth's regenerative capacity by 1.75 times (Global Footprint Network, 2022). The limits of "business as usual" have been extensively documented (Meadows et al., 2004), and despite growing rhetoric about net-zero goals (IEA, 2022), action remains limited (European Environment Agency, 2024).

The I=PAT formula (Impact = Population × Affluence × Technology), even with updates adding efficiency (da Silva et al., 2021), underscores a fundamental conflict between GDP growth and environmental limits (Groner & Moradi, 2024). Sustainable outcomes require more than policy nudges—they need business models that prioritize purpose, adapt quickly, and embed sustainability from the outset.

This is where entrepreneurs matter. Social enterprises like B Corporations, established with frameworks like Team B's SDG-focused standards, have shown how ventures can be both mission-led and accountable (B Lab, 2025). Yet of 360 million businesses globally, fewer than 0.002% are certified B Corps (Daniels, 2024). This shows the scale of the challenge—and the opportunity for responsible entrepreneurship to lead.

While SMEs and start-ups are well-placed to innovate, many fail. Two-thirds do not turn a profit (Eisenmann, 2021), and three-quarters of those launched for sale never become viable (Pollman, 2023). Entrepreneurs must navigate complex and often overlapping challenges: finance, staffing, stakeholder management, and strategic risk. Those within large organisations face additional barriers, including lack of executive buy-in and resource constraints (Onetti, 2021).

The first section of this chapter explores the traits and capabilities needed to overcome such challenges, beginning with mindset and core competencies. It then examines the practical demands of launching and scaling sustainable ventures, focusing on financing, procurement, and strategic growth. Finally, the chapter evaluates external support—from AI-driven tools to the roles of government, NGOs, and the broader ecosystem.

In a world where incremental change is not enough, sustainable entrepreneurship requires a new kind of leadership: socially responsible, technologically capable, and systems-literate. This chapter equips future entrepreneurs to meet that challenge.

CHARACTERISTICS OF THE SUCCESSFUL ENTREPRENEUR

Having established that entrepreneurship is core to societal change, this section examines the qualities of successful entrepreneurs, focusing on mindset, core competencies, and their development, while distinguishing between those in large organisations and start-ups facing scaling challenges, as well as where the competency relates specifically to the challenge of launching a venture that is specific to sustainability. Case studies illustrate key points, such as timing launches, building robust infrastructure, and ensuring market acceptability.

Understanding Entrepreneurial Activity

The activities of an entrepreneur can range from simply offering a well-established product to a new market, such as opening an independent gym in a town that has not got one, to offering something that has never been seen in the market before. It is evident that any move towards sustainability is going to require the introduction of new products, demanding creative thinking and innovative change. Innovation, both incremental and radical, can occur in four fields, referred to as the 4Ps of innovation (product, process, position and paradigm) (Tennekoon, 2023). It is important that the entrepreneur understands where the change being introduced lies if its launch and acceptance on the market is to be successful. As with the continuum between incremental and radical change, the 4Ps are not discrete, but can involve a mix of two or more. However, it is likely that one is dominant (Tidd & Bessant, 2020).

Product

When thinking of innovation, people frequently relate it to the product itself, because this is the element of greatest interest to the potential user. The market might be unaware of its utility or could be sceptical about its performance and hence needs to be educated about the product itself. Despite facing scepticism and discouragement, Matee founded Gjenge Makers, a company that transforms discarded plastic into durable building materials. Inspired by the rampant plastic pollution in Nairobi, Matee invented a machine that compresses plastic and sand into lightweight, affordable bricks. These innovative pavers have improved infrastructure in low-income communities, replacing dirt paths with safer walkways for homes and schools. Gjenge Makers now produces 1,500 pavers daily, demonstrating the feasibility of a circular economy where waste is minimized, and resources are maximized (UNEP, 2021). Clearly innovation was supported by a new process, but the focus was clearly on the product itself.

Process

When any product becomes mature, the producer tends to review the production process in order to economise and maintain profitability. It can however be a source of innovation that benefits more than the financial bottom line. Rose Marcario, former Patagonia CEO, was a driving force behind the company's commitment to environmental sustainability and social responsibility. Her leadership fostered initiatives that minimized environmental impact, supported fair labour, and advocated for environmental conservation. Marcario's tenure at Patagonia was marked by a strong focus on sustainability. She spearheaded initiatives to reduce the company's environmental footprint, promote fair labour practices, and actively advocate for environmental protection (Burbano, 2020). The impact of the change was one that potentially raised costs, and to be successful, Patagonia had to appeal to the social conscience of their potential market.

Position

When developing an innovation based on position, a familiar product is marketed with a different attribute. For instance, in Egypt, Naglaa Mohamed witnessed the damaging effects of environmental degradation on her community, including water scarcity and declining agriculture (Generation Unlimited, 2024). Determined to create change, she developed a business model for vegan, natural fertilizers for agriculture based on waste using local resources and sustainable practices to tackle environmental challenges while improving livelihoods and driving socio-economic growth (Kapoor, 2024). The users were expected to change their perception of the position of fertiliser. Instead of simply being something to add to the fields to improve their yields, it became part of a wider system supporting more elements of sustainability within the community.

Paradigm

In that the developed world is living in an unsustainable fashion, a truly sustainable way of life is a different paradigm, and it is clear that innovation is going to have to involve some that lead to a paradigm shift. This is illustrated later in this chapter when the introduction of the electric vehicle is discussed. It has involved a significant change in the product, but also in the entire infrastructure that supports refuelling, increasing the complexity involved in launching the product. In that a new paradigm is incompatible with the old, it is high risk because it involves unknown parameters (McLeod, 2023).

Innovation Ecosystem

The case of the electric car also illustrates that innovators and entrepreneurs are frequently dependent upon other entities in the environment. 7 key components have been identified and are summarised in table 1 (Granstrand & Holgersson, 2020).

Table 1. The 7 key components of the innovation ecosystem

Actors:	**These are the various participants involved in the ecosystem, such as firms, universities, research institutions, government agencies, and individuals.**
Activities:	The processes and actions undertaken by the actors, including research and development, commercialisation, collaboration, and competition.
Artifacts:	The tangible and intangible outputs of the ecosystem, such as technologies, products, services, patents, and publications.
Institutions:	The formal and informal rules, norms, and regulations that guide and constrain the interactions within the ecosystem.
Relations:	The connections and linkages between actors, which can be collaborative or competitive, and include both complementary and substitute relationships.
Complementary Relations:	Interactions where different actors or activities enhance each other's performance or value.
Substitute Relations:	Interactions where different actors or activities can replace or compete with each other.

Data adapted from Granstrand & Holgersson (2020)

Skills and Processes Supporting Innovation

Theorist and philosopher Henri Poincaré identified patterns in the process of creative thinking in 1913. He explained that hard work needed to be interspersed with periods of inactivity to allow the subconscious to work (Josić, 2024). At some point, the best solution will occur. Other philosophers have concurred with this but also identified approaches that are more disciplined. Regardless of whether the innovator adopts an intuitive or disciplined approach, it is vital that a full understanding of the problem is established, together with the environment in which the problem resides. The environment is a delicate balance between a wide range of issues, and an intervention in one area could cause an imbalance elsewhere. Systems thinking is a powerful approach to developing and communicating this complexity.

System Thinking

System Thinking is an approach that helps develop understanding and visually map complexity including the elements within the innovation ecosystem. It has been defined as "a framework for seeing interrelationships rather than things, for seeing patterns rather than static snapshots. It is a set of general principles spanning fields as diverse as physical and social sciences, engineering, and management" (Senge, 2006 as cited in Association for Project Management, 2024).

In sustainable entrepreneurship, system thinking enables entrepreneurs to comprehend the complexities of environmental issues, markets, and stakeholders, allowing them to find relevant opportunities and design solutions that address root causes rather than symptoms. By integrating systems thinking, entrepreneurs can: identify patterns and relations; foresee long-term impact; recognize opportunities, and drive sustainability (Voulvoulis et al., 2022). The entrepreneur can also get a clearer idea of the innovation ecosystem and the nature of the innovation that is required. Using various mapping techniques as described in table 2, these relationships can be clearly visualised and communicated.

Table 2. Systems Thinking Mapping Techniques

<table>
<tr><th>Tool</th><th>Description</th><th>Benefit</th></tr>
<tr><td>Mind map
(Kienapple, 2020)</td><td>A core topic that branches out with related topics, subtopics, and details, resembling a tree structure.</td><td>Reflects and organizes the haphazard and complex nature of reality</td></tr>
<tr><td></td><td>
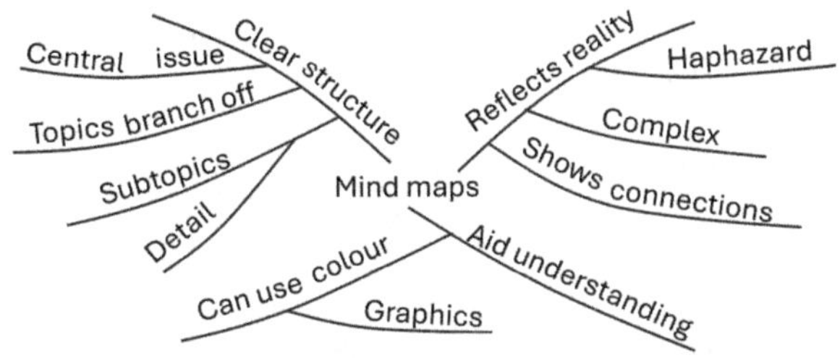

</td><td></td></tr>
<tr><td>Cluster maps / spray diagrams
(NPC, 2024)</td><td>The result of a rapid investigation into an issue. All associated factors are placed around it, which are treated in a similar fashion, resulting in nodes surrounded by details, radiating outwards. Further connections from one node to another can be added as desired.</td><td>Reflects the chaos found in life. Can be developed quickly as mini brainstorming identifies the factors related to each node in succession.</td></tr>
<tr><td></td><td>
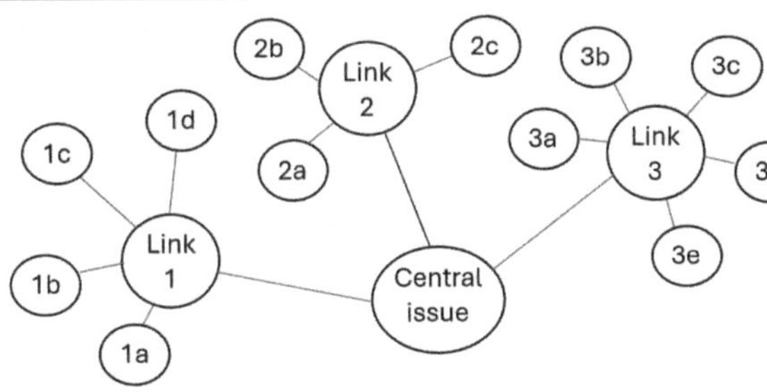

</td><td></td></tr>
<tr><td>Multiple cause diagram
(Open University, 2024)</td><td>A central Issue that branches out to its immediate cause(s), repeating until the underlying root cause is identified. It resembles a mind map, but the relationships between the elements are purely cause and effect.</td><td>Enables the complex range of issues underpinning a problem to be explored so that the "owner" of the root cause can be identified</td></tr>
<tr><td>This is not a complete diagram. There are a lot more causes of fatigue and the causes identified here.</td><td>
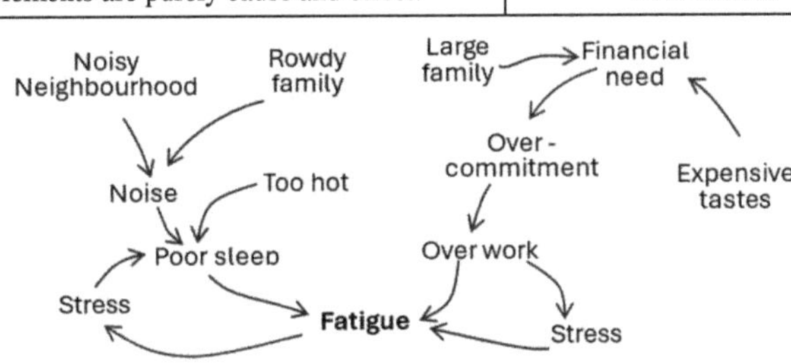

</td><td></td></tr>
</table>

continued on following page

Table 2. Continued

<table>
<tr><th>Tool</th><th>Description</th><th>Benefit</th></tr>
<tr><td>Sign graph
(Future Learn, n.d.)</td><td>Building on a multiple cause diagram, the sign graph indicates the relationship between adjacent elements indicating whether the effect is positive or negative. To be effective, the elements themselves should have a neutral value.</td><td>Helps in understanding the polarity of relationships within a system and can aid understanding of the impact of intervention.</td></tr>
<tr><td>+ positive correlation between the two ends of the arrow

- negative correlation E.g. the lower the stress levels, the better the sleep quality</td><td colspan="2">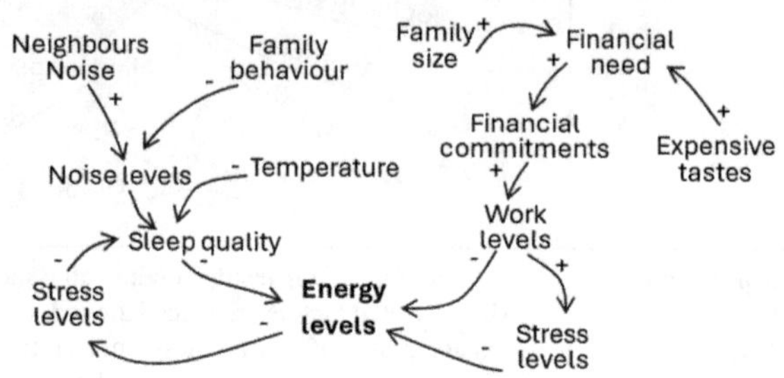
</td></tr>
<tr><td>Multi flow map
(Carpineanu, 2022)</td><td>Concentrating on just one issue, the causes are listed on the left with arrows leading into it and the effects of the issue radiate out on the right.</td><td>Clearly demonstrates the control factors for the issue and the impact of controlling it.</td></tr>
<tr><td></td><td colspan="2">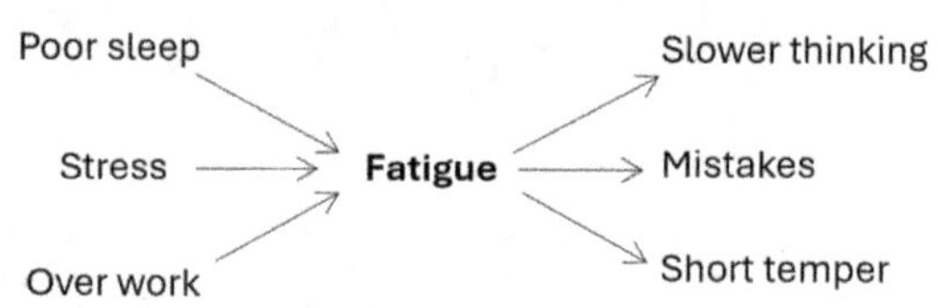
</td></tr>
<tr><td>Influence diagram
(Mulder, 2015)</td><td>Similar in concept to the mind map or cluster map relating to people or stakeholders. The power of the influence between entities is represented by the size of the elements or thickness of lines.</td><td>Helps in the identification of the most effective stakeholders to be involved in an intervention.</td></tr>
<tr><td></td><td colspan="2">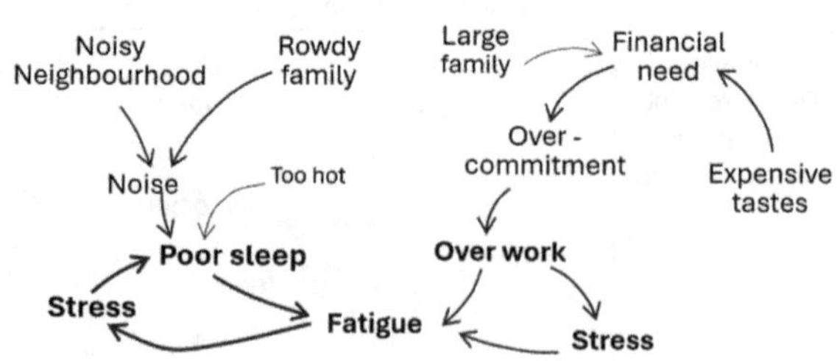
</td></tr>
</table>

Idea Generation Techniques

In working from a position of deep understanding, the innovator is more likely to develop a solution that is effective. There are a range of approaches that can then be used to help generate the innovation. Boyles (2022) offer a few simple and easy principles to use: alternate divergent and convergent thinking; reframe issues as questions and brainstorming.

Alternate Divergent and Convergent Thinking

Divergence generates ideas as a response to an issue, while *convergence* priorities them into a concise list. By balancing these two practices, ideas become concrete solutions.

Reframe Issues as Question

When rephrasing issues and challenges as questions, for example "how to questions," the mind shifts from obstacles to solutions. This offers good grounds for brainstorming ideas and opens the way to a more radical, but well focused solution (Gregersen, 2018).

Brainstorming

Ideas are kept flowing when basic rules are observed. Once ideas stop coming, it is time to evaluate them and retain and develop, combine or discard ideas.

- *Start with a clear question or problem statement to focus on.*
- *Postpone the judgement of ideas:* When brainstorming there is a natural tendency to critique or reject ideas as they are made, but this is a block to further ideas and should be deferred.
- *Welcome the crazy:* Outstanding innovations came from ideas that were considered impossible, so welcome all ideas at the outset.
- *Build on ideas:* Allow the ideas of one person to trigger others.
- *Aim at quantity rather than quality.*
- *Record ideas:* Anything can be used from post-it notes to whiteboards, using text or diagrams.
- *Stay focused:* Listen to the ideas of others rather than concentrate on your own individual ideas

(Dam & Teo Yu Siang, 2016)

SCAMPER

It is never wise to just generate one solution. It is better to develop a range and evaluate them to ensure the best solution is used. There are a range of ideation techniques, one of the most popular, being summarised by the acronym SCAMPER, a range of approaches that can be used in any order (Dam & Teo Yu Siang, 2016) and summarised in table 3. Each letter stands for a perspective from which to question or brainstorm all aspects of the existing product and its application.

Table 3. SCAMPER

Technique	Approach	Example: Fairphone (Fairphone, 2024; 2025; Miquel, 2023)
Substitute	What can be substituted without compromising performance?	Fairphone changed their sourcing policy to ensure their products were ethically sustainable.
Combine	Can any product, process or ideas be merged?	Fairphone started by avoiding conflict minerals and combined this approach with sourcing the remainder of their products using recycled materials. They do not stop adding new concepts to improve their performance.
Adapt	In what ways can we change the product?	Fairphone now make their phones more robust and facilitate upgrades so that phones do not need to be replaced.
Modify	In what ways can we change the entire process?	Fairphone started to produce spare parts to lengthen the useful life of their products
Put to another use	Can this product be more effective if it was used differently or for a different purpose?	Phones in general are an illustration of how they are given additional purposes. One product, multiple functions.
Eliminate	Can we achieve a similar output but remove elements of the process or product?	Fairphone eliminated the constant process of producing new versions of their phones. Their latest phone was developed in 2023, and they offer support for 8 years including five major upgrades.
Reverse	Can we re-arrange the elements of the product or process?	Fairphone started to obtain and recycle e-waste to the same or weight as the phones they produce so that they are "e-waste neutral". They source it from countries that do not have recycling facilities.

Launching a new venture is fraught with challenges, with 90% eventually failing, (Bryant, 2024), and 20% failing within their first year (May, 2019). It follows that the entrepreneur requires resilience and adaptability underpinned by a growth mindset. These characteristics will be explored together with practical strategies for their development highlighting entrepreneurs who, despite limited resources, created impactful and innovative businesses.

The Entrepreneurial Mindset

In contrast to a fixed mindset, based on the assumption that success is determined by innate talent that cannot change, individuals with a growth mindset view challenges and difficulties as opportunities for development and learning (Dweck, 2017). It is in itself an empowering attitude that enables the individual to recognise the value in investing the effort that entrepreneurial ventures demand, and to value and learn from both feedback and failures. It has been found that those with a strong growth mindset tend to be more passionate and enjoy a higher level of success than those with a fixed mindset, and it is the source of determination and underpins the desire to master new skills as their need emerges (Sigmundsson & Haga, 2024).

Howard Schultz, the person behind Starbucks succeeded despite setbacks because of his sheer passion for the concept. His story underscores the importance of resilience and a positive mindset in entrepreneurial success. He once remarked, "You have to passionately believe in yourself and in your ideas. Too many people with great ideas give up on them too early. You have to persevere and refuse to give up." It was this determination and optimism that enabled Schultz to overcome initial resistance and financial hurdles and build Starbucks into one of the world's most recognized and respected businesses (Horatio Alger Association, 2007; Schultz, 1997/2014).

Purdue Global (2024) offers tips on how the growth mindset can be cultivated which are summarised below. They focus largely on developing a realistic understanding of the process of growth.

- *Develop self-awareness.* Note thoughts and reactions when faced with challenges and identify your current mindset.
- *Actively undertake self-affirmation.*
    - Reject negative reactions to challenges and frequently remind yourself that success is within reach, recognising that challenges provide valuable learning and growth opportunities.
    - Focus on what is achieved rather than perceived characteristics and weaknesses. Celebrate your successes.
- *Practice self-acceptance.* Be realistic about the learning process
    - Change takes time and can involve failures. However, it is necessary to recognise that this is to be expected, and overall growth is occurring.
    - Learn that failure is a learning opportunity. At the very least it is possible to learn what does not work. Edison demonstrated this when he said, "I have not failed, I have found 10,000 ways that won't work" (Ratcliffe, 2016).

    - Accept that there are still things to be learned. If there is a temptation to state something is not possible, add the word "yet" in order to keep the facility to grow in mind.
- *Involve others.*
    - Ask for advice and feedback.
    - Congratulate other people when they enjoy success and ask how they did it.
- *Articulate goals.* Write them down and share them with someone close. Research shows that this raises the incentive to achieve them.

Changing a mindset can be very difficult. Those finding it too much of a challenge should address what is stopping them. Tony Robbins's five strategies to address mental blockers is a useful tool (Phelon, 2021):

- *Take control of your state of mind.* This could be achieved by deep breaths, pauses, moments of relaxation.
- *Focus on the present* – recent research shows that firm innovation capability is positively influenced by goal orientation and mindfulness (Muanfhun Ratanavanich & Peerayuth Charoensukmongkol, 2024). A key difference between "wantrepreneurs" and "entrepreneurs" lies in their focus on execution rather than just the idea (Nemko, 2016).
- *Ask yourself what is holding you back so that you can achieve a breakthrough.*

Barriers to entrepreneurship can be cognitive-psychological influencing opportunity recognition and pursuit (Khanin et al., 2021).

- *Reprogramme your mind.* NLP (neuro linguistic programming) tools and techniques help individuals reprogram their minds by removing limiting beliefs and encouraging positive thinking, thereby enhancing personal cognitive maps, and fostering self-development to achieve business success (Zamfir, 2018).
- *Create an atmosphere of positivism and calm in your environment.* Recent research conducted during COVID-10 showed that positive psychology effectively reduces psychological anxiety in innovative entrepreneurs during the pandemic, boosting their enthusiasm for work and enhancing their resilience (Sha, 2023).

It has been established that a positive mindset leads to better health, and a wide range of competencies that benefit the working environment. In addition to those discussed above, positive thinkers demonstrate a higher level of pride in their work, leading to improved efficiencies and the associated output. Positivity is also infectious, and those with a positive mindset influence their colleagues and the workplace environment. This can result in an improved company reputation (Smith, 2024). It is the basis of independence, determination, commitment and self-belief, all of which being characteristics of the successful entrepreneur. However, these competences need to be accompanied by a range of skills that will further empower the entrepreneur.

The Core Skillsets and Tools for Developing the Venture

Sir Clive Sinclair transformed consumer electronics with his innovations, but he was also known for some dramatic avoidable failures because he lacked basic business acumen (Williamson, 2021). Given the high failure rate of new ventures, it is useful to understand the causes of failure to identify the skillsets needed for success that are commonly lacking.

The most commonly cited cause of start-up failure, reported to account for 42% of new venture failure is that of misreading market demand. Following, this, 29% fail because they run out of finance, 23% due to weaknesses within the founding team and 19% being unable to stand up to competition. Other causes relate to choice of business and pricing models, poor marketing and timing, and the product itself being inadequate (Embroker, 2020).

Successful enterprises are found to have the following qualities: Developing a good product or service, ensuring market fit, timing the launch appropriately, developing a supportive environment and having the right character. This final point is more than just a positive mindset, but includes people skills, criticality, being open minded and having integrity (Riani, 2023). Finally, the constitution of the founding team is also recognised as being a critical factor (Hagberg, 2020).

Intrapreneurs face different challenges. The principal cause of failure of such ventures is lack of management buy-in. BOXLAB was the first corporate spin-off of BASF, the world's largest chemical producer, and became an independent startup while BASF retained minority ownership. BOXLAB offered a sustainable solution for replacing damaged packaging and labels in the chemical industry, simplifying supply chain processes while reducing waste, costs, and complexity, but there were tensions balancing the startup mindset of the BOXLAB team with that of BASF's corporate structure. BOXLAB eventually achieved success, and BASF management changed their attitude to the startup mentality, subsequently spawning more enterprises. (Studio Zao, 2024).

Failure of intrapreneurial endeavours also results from over-assessment of the potential success of the product, and when the innovation does not align with the goals of the organisation (Seshadri, 2007). A robust offer together with the empowering attributes resulting from the positive mindset are the strongest characteristics to encourage management buy-in together with a realistic approach to recognise when the potential venture is a poor fit for the organisation.

Understanding of Market and Market Demand

Achieving a product market fit requires the ability for the entrepreneur to critique their concept. This can prove challenging when they also believe in its potential benefit, and to a certain extent was one of the causes of failure for Sinclair's C5. He did not recognise the vulnerability of the target market and was blinded by the technology itself (Marks, 1989). The product had not been developed to its optimum standard and was criticised for elements of poor performance, as well as potentially not being right for society at that time (Open Now, 2023).

In that sustainability demands the more radical change, it involves greater complexity involving more stakeholders. The difficulties in achieving market acceptance of an innovation were expounded by Everet Rogers in his Theory of diffusion of innovation (2003) Rogers identified five characteristics of the new product that would aid diffusion. These have been developed further, recognising the need for the characteristics explained in Table 4 (Outcault *et al.*, 2022):

Table 4. Characteristics influencing the diffusion of novel products

Category	Technology Characteristics	Notes
Economic	Initial investment Operating costs Return on investment Market availability	User costs including installation and availability of rebates / grants, fuel costs, supplies, replacements and maintenance, energy cost savings, payback period. Path to market, necessary intermediaries, availability of product services and support
Technical	Technical compatibility Performance Complexity of installation, use and maintenance Energy savings	Compatibility with available infrastructure. Evidence of reliability, durability, performance metrics. Complexity for whom? Specialist or customer? These impact time and skill requirements. Energy usage in comparison to common alternatives.
Informational	Observability Trialability	Observability relates to the technology type. It relates to extent the potential customer becomes aware of it. Trialability enables the user to decide before investing in a product.
Externalities	Environmental and non-energy impacts	Energy savings, emissions etc including manufacture and operating the product. Non energy impacts are the more traditional marketing issues, the benefit of having the product for the user

Data adapted from Outcault *et al.* (2022)

The interplay between these factors can clearly be seen in the roll out of the electric vehicle (EV). Despite being promoted by governments and backed by well-respected brands, diffusion has been slow and fraught with difficulties which are explained in table 5.

Table 5. The factors influencing the adoption of the EV

Category	Factors influencing the adoption of EVs
Economic	The price of the EV is a barrier to purchase, although running costs are lower, and some governments offer aid to reduce either purchase or running costs or assist with the provision of charging infrastructure. Despite lower running costs, there is not always sufficient compensation for the hire purchase cost (Wang & Witlox, 2025). Maintenance costs are lower because there are far fewer moving parts, and obtaining spares were not reported to present a difficulty (Alessandro Augurio et al., 2024).
Technical	Being a paradigm innovation, EVs need a completely different infrastructure for refuelling. Charging was more inconvenient. It could take significantly longer than filling with petrol and the availability of charging points was potentially problematic, and not something the user could control. The availability of charging points close to residences and the workplace is one of the most critical considerations (Kristoffersson et al., 2025; Christensen et al., 2025). The new technology gave rise to performance and reliability concerns. Battery performance had to be improved, and such changes needed to be advertised. (Abbas Sheykhfard et al., 2024)
Informational	A lack of awareness of the benefits of the EV has impeded take-up in low observability that impedes diffusion (Singh & Ujjwal Kanti Paul, 2023) resulting in some regions, Car dealers did not have sufficient information to educate the customer and did not have display models in their showrooms limiting trialability, so customers were expected to "buy blind" (Trencher et al., 2020).
Externalities	The technology was clean at the point of use, providing a distinct advantage. However, there are environmental impacts. The electricity was not all renewable and there are concerns about the ongoing supply of cobalt for the batteries (Trencher et al., 2020).

The case of the EV illustrates the need for multiple stakeholders to be involved in the successful diffusion of an innovative product, not least because of a lack of market knowledge relating to its benefits. Involvement of actors such as the media to assist in educating the market through success stories of the application of a novel product can greatly assist, even more so when the innovation is being launched by a start-up or micro business. Skilful use of social media can also contribute to the innovation becoming recognised within the network of sustainable enterprises and technologies (Gebhardt & Bachmann, 2023).

Identifying The Founding Team

The product could be a perfect fit for the market, but if the founding team has problems, then it will undermine the success of the venture. There are five critical qualities the team should possess:

- A broad set of skills that addresses the scope of activities involved.
- A common entrepreneurial mindset.
- Committed to the venture and vision and the team coherence.
- Experienced in industry.
- Flexibility and prepared to take on a mix of roles.

(Roth, 2024)

In practice, founding teams are generally created by drawing on people within the founder's social network, and the outcome can result in a team that lacks the necessary spread of skills and experience. This is not detrimental in the very early stages of an enterprise where trust and cohesion are seen to be more important. A key skill that is required in the early growth stages is that of developing the team further. Advertising for team members during the infancy stage of an enterprise is not often successful because few applicants would be happy committing to a company with no track record (Klada, 2018).

Some aspects of developing the venture involve one-off activities and the skills will not be needed for running the enterprise such as those needed for logo design. These could legitimately be outsourced or undertaken through crowdsourcing. This could be in the form of a competition, a problem-solving challenge or brainstorming innovative solutions (Mishra & Maheshwari, 2024).

Scaling Up and Growth

Scaling up refers to the move towards achieving economies of scale in the operation that are typically missing at launch stage. It is essential if the product is to become competitive in the market. Whilst scaling up is likely to require some additional resources, it is not the same as growth which focuses on expansion of the operation and consequently requires further resources as a matter of course (Kruk, 2023).

Scaling up and growth can occur at different rates through the life of an innovation, increasing in speed as the innovation gets more accepted in the market. While rapid growth can offer advantages such as swift market penetration and investor interest, it also presents significant challenges, including operational strain and financial risks (Dwoskin, 2023). Conversely, a steady growth approach emphasizes sustainability, control, and the ability to adapt thoughtfully to market conditions. Ultimately, the optimal growth strategy depends on the specific context of the enterprise, including its industry, resources, and long-term objectives.

In addition to the novelty of the product and its compatibility with the infrastructure, the speed of successful scale up is also dependent on the network the entrepreneur has developed including connections with other successful ventures. The geographic region of the entrepreneur and that of the market is also influential (Startup Genome, 2023).

Scaling up requires a different set of skills to that of launching an enterprise. Indeed, the very skills that facilitate the launch of a product could hinder its growth (Hamm, 2002). The focus of the entrepreneur is to perfect the product and make it attract both the customer and financiers. Once the enterprise is established, there are far more issues to attend to and consequently, a broader skills base is needed.

Entrepreneurs do not make natural people-managers, but the human resource management element of the growing startup can make a significant difference to the success of the venture. Software can assist but care should be taken when selecting the platform to ensure that it will accommodate the degree of change a startup is likely to experience (Rosario, 2024). Attracting the right talent is a challenge because the enterprise does not necessarily have the reputation or finance to attract the specialist. The entrepreneur needs to have the ability to identify the features that could make the role attractive (Clark & Bradley, 2023).

Adding people to a team can disrupt the team dynamic, especially if the entrepreneur is a sole operator or with a very small team (Hamm, 2002) and as the focus changes, the necessary style of leadership changes. Not all entrepreneurs can manage this change successfully (Chandratreya, 2024)

Going Global

Before going global, the entrepreneur should critically assess options, considering the potential target markets, the ease with which sales can be managed and scaled up, understanding the culture, ensuring the founding team has the skill set and that the right support is in place to support the growth and logistics (Carton, n.d.).

In some industries geographic growth is a less sustainable model because the additional transport and packaging required adds to the carbon footprint of the entity (The Offsite Guide, 2024). In these instances, spawning new local operations in different regions can be the solution, but each time, it is faced with the same challenges as the start-up where the market is concerned, and the entity will need to scale up in each location for greater efficiencies. Enterprises do not need to grow, but they do need to scale up.

The entrepreneur should consider the prospect of moving to international markets, and if appropriate, determine the most appropriate approach early in the planning stages. This would ensure that the initial steps do not impede such development, and the team would be ready to move swiftly if the right opportunity opens before them. International expansion however complicates human resource management making the need for human resource management that much more important (G-P, 2020).

As with many aspects of running an enterprise, growth is challenging, the major issues being summarised in table 6.

Table 6. Addressing the challenge of scaling up

Challenge	Description	Examples and Mitigation
Resource Constraints	Limited financial, operational and human resources	Sustainable fashion companies encounter difficulties in consumer communication, resource limitations, sustainable sourcing, and production; however, collaborative strategies can help address these challenges (Hofmann et al., 2022) .
Lack of institutional support	Need for policies and financial incentives	With the regulation of eco-investment, systems and standards, as well as effective support from government in the form of "green investment" initiatives, the scale up becomes possible (Shkarupa et al., 2021) .
Technological and market barriers	Early-age financing and tailored commercialisation pathways	Solutions include creating collaborative ecosystems made of researchers, entrepreneurs, investors, and policymakers (Ngoc et al., 2024) .
Cultural and market adaptation	Degrowth attitudes prioritising sustainability over financial growth	Degrowth mindsets among entrepreneurs hinder fast venture scaling, while sustainable entrepreneurship promotes scaling slow strategies, with economic development level playing a crucial role in scaling decisions (Hinderer & Kuckertz, 2024).

SUCCESSFULLY ACCESSING FINANCE AND RESOURCES

Understanding the Financial Environment

Entrepreneurs have numerous sources of finance that are potentially available to them. In practice many start by looking to family and seeking a lean start-up, but when scaling up, most must seek it from elsewhere. Some will rely on bank overdrafts or credit cards, but these are costly and should be repaid as quickly as possible and are not a good choice for the longer-term investments (Craig, 2021). The options range from banks, business angels, venture capitalists (VCs), and crowdfunding platforms. Entrepreneurs should tailor their approach bearing in mind that each type of financier has distinct expectations, priorities, and criteria for investment as summarised in Table 7, (Walker, 2024).

Table 7. The different sources of start-up funding

Aspect	Banks	Business Angels	Venture Capitalists	Crowdfunding
Risk Tolerance	Low	Moderate	High	Moderate to High
Primary Concern	Ability to Repay	Personal passion & ROI	Scalability & exit potential	Public appeal & funding targets
Engagement style	Formal	Personal	Professional & data-driven	Engaging & community-focused

Data adapted from Walker (2024)

Biases

The entrepreneur is in a weak position when it comes to seeking finance if for no other reason than that they do not have a track record with the venture (Cassar, 2004). Augmenting this are various forms of biases, both cognitive and systemic, that can influence start-up success in obtaining finance:

- *Planning fallacy* results in over-optimisation of the profitability and success of a proposed venture. (Adomdza & Astebro, 2012) Financiers are aware this can occur and consequently take a cautious approach when approached by the entrepreneur.
- *Over-pessimism* on behalf of the entrepreneur that causes them to underestimate their potential success and consequently not seek the necessary funding in the first place (Bar-El et al., 2017).
- *Knowledge bias* occurs when entrepreneurs, deeply familiar with their ideas, technology, or business model, assume that others including financiers share the same level of understanding or enthusiasm, negatively affecting their ability to secure funding (Camerer et al., 1989).
- *Funding type bias* creating a preference for tradition funding over other types of funding (Graaf et al., 2018) could prevent a start-up from exploring potentially more accessible sources.

Entrepreneurs seeking finance should be aware of these biases and mitigate their power with careful preparation. Provision of realistic forecasting involving best-case and worst-case scenarios will demonstrate their understanding of both risks and opportunities. They should carefully consider which source is best suited to their needs. Other biases however originate with the lender and require a different approach:

- *Age, and education* of the entrepreneurial team (Zhang, 2020)
- *Gender bias* (Kanze et al., 2018)

- *Home bias* – the tendency to favour local players (Lin & Viswanathan, 2013)

The response to address these may be as simple as looking for funding that is addressed to a similar demographic. Relevant information can be found on the OECD Platform or Angel lists on LinkedIn. Another mitigation strategy is to research previous funded businesses in the region or by the chosen institution and see how they have secured their success.

Seeking Funding: The Preparation Stages

Preparation is not just about creating documents or pitches, but the process equips the entrepreneur with the tools, knowledge, and confidence to make a compelling case for their business. Whether applying to a bank, pitching to investors, or launching a crowdfunding campaign, thorough preparation is the foundation for success (Walsack, 2019). The process is challenging and regardless of the approach it takes, a growth mindset and the associated resilience and assurance are necessary attributes that contribute to the confidence a financier needs to develop about the entrepreneur prior to offering funding.

- To develop a compelling sustainability business case, several steps should be followed (Yadav & Mankavil Kovil Veettil, 2021).
- *Analyse existing and external data and evidence.* Various guidelines, standards, and frameworks (Prashar, 2019; Malesios et al., 2020) are available.
- *Examine proofs* and benchmark against the performance of peers.
- *Create complementary, cross-functional teams.* For a compelling business case, the entrepreneur and the founding team should include an appropriate range of skills to underpin the successful running of the enterprise such as: communication, interpersonal skills and criticality along with experience in strategy, risk, finance, human resources, technology (Miloud et al., 2012).

Building a Brand Story

A brand story is a narrative that explains the essence of a brand, where it originates from, its values and its purpose. It is a compelling story which engages the stakeholders on a cognitive and emotional level. For green entrepreneurs, a powerful brand story is essential for getting the necessary funding as it demonstrated the company's authenticity, its capacity for differentiation, its potential for long-term success and its ability to make a positive impact.

Donald Miller (2017) offers a simple strategy that sustainable entrepreneurs could use when building their own brand stories:

- *Define Your Brand as the Guide:* Position your brand as the knowledgeable helper who can guide customers through their challenges.
- *Identify Your Customer as the Hero:* Focus on your ideal customer's desires and struggles, making them the protagonist of your brand's story.
- *Craft a Clear Message:* Use simple, customer-centric language to explain how your brand can help customers achieve their goals.
- *Emphasize a Call to Action:* Make it easy for stakeholders to take the next step, whether it's signing up for scheduling a consultation, or making a decision related to funding.
- *Identify the anticipated return on investment:* This is the most important for those seeking finance from a business angel or venture capitalists and it can also substantiate figures for a bank.

Figure 1. Donald Miller's Brand Story Strategy

By following these steps, green entrepreneurs can create a compelling brand story that resonates with their target audience and drives engagement. This is an important aspect because it is recognised that storytelling is fundamental to human nature, shaping understanding of the world, guiding social interactions, and influencing behaviour. Stories help navigate life's challenges, develop empathy, and find meaning in experiences (Gottschall, 2012).

Developing the Business Case

Whereas the brand story will engage interest, the business case will demonstrate how the venture will be operated and its financial feasibility in order to demonstrate that it would be a viable investment. A formal business case document is not always required, but it will provide the information needed in the business pitch. Again, not all financiers ask for a pitch, but the likelihood is that you would need some or all of the information at some stage in the process, so it is better to be prepared (Martins, 2022). Some investors are more interested in the entrepreneur than the enterprise itself. Having this data at hand demonstrates professional qualities and inspires confidence (Harroch, 2022). Like the brand story, the business case involves clarifying a wide range issues relating to the proposed enterprise, namely:

- Describe the gap in the market and any relevant background. Explain alternative solutions to addressing the gap and why the selected one is the preferred option.
- Evaluate the market need, including a competitor analysis and consideration of industry characteristics.
- Demonstrate how the proposed enterprise aligns with the mission and vision.
- Describe the operation including risks and their mitigation strategies, success criteria, and key KPIs. Include a timeline and an indication of what has already been achieved.
- Provide a financial case including a cost-benefit analysis, proposed budget, to demonstrate the anticipated return on investment. It is important to demonstrate how the requested funding will be used and the point at which the enterprise becomes sustainable.
- Explain the governance structure, identifying the key individuals, their roles and how decisions are made.

(Walsh, 2023)

The business case for sustainability is a complex picture that, in addition to the above, considers the social and environmental outcomes. The fundamental elements to be included in a business case for sustainability are:

- The sustainability issues prioritised by the entrepreneur together with the proposed activities which form the basis for determining the funding requirement.
- The main risks and opportunities presented by the environmental, social, and governance (ESG) choices with clear mitigations actions and action plans. These will guide the allocation of resources and setting clear timelines.
- The company's mission, vision, values, purpose, level of ambition, its goals, and metrics on how to assess its performance.

(Grayson et al., 2022)

Developing the Pitch

Pitching is often a critical process for entrepreneurs and intrapreneurs to secure funding and it is a requirement of many financiers. A compelling pitch is essential if it is to attract investors, whether they are venture capitalists, angel investors, impact investors, or grant-making organisations. It is normally a short 2-minute presentation that showcases the potential for high returns while aligning with their goals.

The 4H Framework is a structured approach to crafting a compelling pitch, designed to guide entrepreneurs through the process of effectively communicating their startup's value proposition. It emphasizes storytelling, clarity, and understanding the audience's perspective (Kleiman, 2020). The elements and structure are as follows:

1. *Start with a hook:* An opening statement that grabs the audience's attention and piques their interest. It should be concise, intriguing, and relevant to the startup's core value proposition.
2. *Develop a heart:* Delving into the problem the startup is addressing and the motivation behind the venture, it connects with the audience on an emotional level by emphasising the significance of the problem and potential impact of the solution.
3. *Explain the hands:* Demonstrating the unique features of the solution with a clear and concise explanation of the venture, its key differentiators, and how it addresses the problem outlined in the heart.
4. *Finish with hope:* The future vision and potential of the startup and its desired outcomes, anticipated growth trajectory, and potential for success. It inspires the audience and leaves them with a sense of optimism about the venture's future.

The 4H Framework enables entrepreneurs to create a structured and engaging pitch that resonates with their audience and effectively communicates the value of their startup. The pitch needs to be tailored according to the intended sources of funding.

Common Sources of Finance

Grants

Entrepreneurs and startups are advised to see if there are any grants their venture is eligible for before approaching institutions that will be looking for a return on their investment. The ability to obtain a grant can give the entrepreneur greater credibility when approaching other financiers (Frimanslund et al., 2022).

However, it does take significant time. The startup must be careful to comply with set conditions and produce interim reports to the grant provider and it could mean disclosing information that leaves the startup vulnerable to competition (S3 Solutions, 2021).

Even small grants are of value because they are tax free, can be used to fund the initial stages of getting established and do not need to be repaid (Greaves, 2024). Table 8 outlines the manner in which skills support the successful application.

Table 8. The skills that support a successful application for a grant

Skillset	What it means and why it is important
Research	Find grants relevant to the enterprise, their eligibility criteria and funding priorities as well as deadlines and application process. This investment in time pays off as time will not be wasted on unsuccessful claims (Crawford, 2021).
Analytical and data presentation	Having identified the necessary criteria, it is necessary to collate data to support the application, including presenting a mix of metrics and qualitative comment. It will be necessary to show how progress and impact can be measured (Grantify.2024).
Written Communication	Facilitates producing a compelling case that includes a concise and clear description of the proposed enterprise, demonstrating how its goals align with the funder's priorities. It is also necessary to communicate budgets and timelines effectively (van den Besselaar & Mom, 2022).
Strategic thinking	Identifying the enterprise's competitive advantage, establishing how the grant can be effectively used to further the goals of the enterprise, and anticipate the grant provider's expectations so that the application can be tailored accordingly (Cherry, 2024).
Communication and networking	Enables the development and maintenance of valuable relationships, including engaging with funders at different events. It is also important to facilitate clarification of processes involved in the application (Kaufman, 2024).
Financial Management	Enables the development of realistic and detailed budgets, and management of any grant awarded. Its demonstration engenders confidence in the lender (WPAB, 2024).
Attention to detail	The application process can be complex, and it is important to follow instructions implicitly, ensuring there are no errors or omissions (Neal, 2024).
Organisational and project management	Grant applications come with deadlines that must be met. It is important to develop and manage realistic timelines and monitor the process closely (Floersch, 2019).

In conclusion, a successful grant application demands skills similar to those required for running a successful enterprise, although applied quite differently. In addition, the need to craft a concise and compelling application is essential. It is time-consuming but can prove highly beneficial.

Formal Banking Systems

Traditional banking schemes include loans, overdrafts credit facilities, and government-backed schemes. Bank financing is demonstrated to improve the performance of the SME because the relationship focuses on the need for financial management skills. (Burchi et al., 2021).

Public and private financial institutions are increasingly offering a variety of green and sustainable finance products designed to support ventures aiding the transition to Net 0 (OECD, 2025). Three-quarters of finance providers had already introduced such options by 2023 (OECD, 2023). Similarly, 63% of banks in the EU had launched products, services, or initiatives aligned with a broader range of SDGs and other sustainability standards (European Banking Federation, 2021). It is estimated that green finance presents a $23 trillion investment opportunity over the next five to seven years (Stein et al., 2024).

Governments also provide affordable financing, such as the UK Start-Up Loans programme, which offers unsecured loans of up to £25,000 per person (£100,000 per business) at a fixed 6% interest rate, with repayment terms of 1–5 years. Managed by the British Business Bank, it has funded over 100,000 entrepreneurs since 2012, contributing £1 billion to economic growth. The programme includes free mentoring and supports all sectors, including eco-friendly ventures, evaluating applications based on business plan viability (British Business Bank, 2021).

The UK Start-Up Loans programme supports businesses across all sectors, including eco-friendly ventures. Entrepreneurs can leverage the programme's funding and free mentoring to integrate sustainable practices into their businesses. SMEs focusing on circular economy (Toxopeus et al., 2021) can secure bank financing for circular business model innovation by demonstrating future cash flow potential, fostering strong relationships, and creating standardized, durable circular assets to use as collateral. Table 8 indicates how the necessary skills can be utilised to develop a successful bid.

Table 9. The skills that support the development of business qualities recognised by banks

Skillset	What it means and why it is important
Financial literacy Communication skills Problem-solving abilities	Bankers want to be sure that the entrepreneur will be able to pay interest on the loan. This group of skills will build budgeting, bookkeeping, and credit management and facilitate enterprise promotion and risk mitigation (Burchi et al., 2021).
Communication and networking	Build trust, foster relationships with financiers and enhance entrepreneurial performance (Dimitriadis & Koning, 2022).
Entrepreneurial competency	This will demonstrate the skills needed to build trust with the financier, with resource alignment, strategic planning, and efficient operations management (Kumar, 2023).

continued on following page

Table 9. Continued

Skillset	What it means and why it is important
Innovative problem-solving	If the banker can see evidence of this skill there would be a greater confidence of the entrepreneur's ability to pivot and thrive when change demands it, and to justify their potential success to lenders (Inglis 2022).
English Language	Most financiers are English speakers. The entrepreneur needs to be able to communicate effectively with global partners and potential financiers (Rajović et al., 2024),

In conclusion, entrepreneurs seeking bank loans should prioritise financial literacy, communication, strategic planning, and innovation. Engaging in targeted training and formal education programmes can further enhance their chances of securing financing and achieving long-term success.

Venture Capital

Venture capital (VC) is private equity funding that supports startups and early-stage companies with high growth potential, providing both financial backing and valuable expertise in exchange for ownership stakes (First-Citizens Bank & Trust Company, 2025). This form of funding is highly competitive, and entrepreneurs need a strong skillset to succeed in securing venture capital funding including deep understanding of the Venture Capitalist, their values, and specialisms. These skills are explained in table 10.

Table 10. Skills that support the development of business qualities recognised by Venture Capitalists

Skillset	What it means and why it is important
Brand Storytelling	A compelling and concise story around the business idea, its potential impact, and the team's vision is crucial to arouse a VC's interest and connect with them as a person (Rea, 2019; Segreto, 2023).
Financial Acumen	A strong grasp of financial modelling, projections, and key financial metrics (e.g., unit economics, customer acquisition cost, lifetime value) is essential. VCs scrutinize financial data, so be prepared to present a well-researched and realistic financial plan (Johnson, 2021).
Market knowledge and competitive advantage	VCs want to invest in businesses with a strong market position and a clear path to dominance. Entrepreneurs need to demonstrate deep understanding of the target market, including market size, growth potential, competitive landscape, and customer needs (Economic Development Collaborative, 2024).
Networking and building relationships	Building strong relationships with potential investors is key. Networking also supports the entrepreneur's ability to stay on top of market trends which supports long term success, a key characteristic that the venture capitalist is looking for (Elevate, 2022).

continued on following page

Table 10. Continued

Skillset	What it means and why it is important
Communication and Presentation Skills	The ability to clearly and concisely communicate the vision, answer questions, and present their pitch in a compelling and engaging manner is essential. Communication also involves listening. The venture capitalist is going to want to build a relationship with the entrepreneur and will need to see that the qualities needed for a two-way conversation are evident (Obrebowska, 2020).
Negotiation Skills	Once the entrepreneur secures a term sheet, they will need to negotiate the terms of the investment, including valuation, ownership stake, and board representation (Glade et al., 2025).

In conclusion, the character of the entrepreneur is as important as the venture itself, because the venture capitalist will be working with the entrepreneur and needs to be confident that it will be a prosperous relationship. The entrepreneur must not only demonstrate a strong understanding of their business but also show a willingness to listen in order to increase their chances of securing the funding.

Business Angels

Business angels (BA), also known as angel investors, are a crucial source of funding for entrepreneurs, particularly in the early stages of a startup.

Business angels are high-net-worth individuals who provide financial backing to startups in exchange for equity or convertible debt. They typically invest their own money and often bring valuable industry experience, mentorship, and networking opportunities (Kleiman, 2020, b).

Table 11. Skills that support successful funding from business angels

Skillset	What it means and why it is important
Choosing the optimal equity sharing	Before approaching business angels, the entrepreneur needs to decide how much of the future equity they are willing sacrifice and determine the precise benefits they are seeking. These decisions are essential for the future of the enterprise. The entrepreneur should also critically analyse the previous experience of the angel concerned as well as their future role in decision-making and management should they be successful (Arya et al., 2021).
Former Education and Prior Entrepreneurial experience	A positive correlation has been established between entrepreneurs with a formal education and founding experience and the likelihood of receiving equity funding from Business Angels (Pierrakis & Owen, 2022)
Pitching Skills	Pitching skills are very important because the competence of the presenter can influence the decision at both conscious and sub conscious levels (Polcz, 2021).

continued on following page

Table 11. Continued

Skillset	What it means and why it is important
"A Foot in the Door": Network activation	Entrepreneurs select contacts from their personal network to provide referrals to access specific investors. Selecting investor-centric contacts and using reciprocity-based persuasion tactics were found to increase referral success (Nai et al., 2021). The centrality of a Business Angel within a network impacts the likelihood of a company receiving investments from the BA group, with experience and geographical proximity also influencing this relationship (Vincenzo et al., 2020).
Technical expertise, managerial experience, and business model strength	Angel investors prioritise managerial features and resources in startups over financial aspects, potentially due to start-ups limited financial stability (Kim, 2023).

In conclusion, securing funding from business angels requires more than just a promising business idea—it demands a strategic approach that incorporates key skills and expertise. Entrepreneurs must carefully consider equity sharing, leverage their education and experience, refine their pitching abilities, and activate their networks to gain investor interest. Additionally, the strength of a startup's management team and business model plays a critical role in attracting angel investment. By developing these competencies, startups can enhance their chances of successfully securing financial backing and long-term support from business angels.

Crowdfunding

Different types of crowdfunding, as outlined in table 11, offer sustainable entrepreneurs access to capital, foster community engagement, and drive innovation (Hargrave, 2022). These approaches leverage the collective intelligence of the crowd, align financial incentives with social and environmental goals, and provide funding options beyond traditional sources (Sendpulse, 2023). As such, crowd funding has been seen to be highly effective in supporting sustainable enterprise (Arvila et al., 2020). While challenges like regulatory hurdles and competition exist, these methods hold significant potential for supporting the growth of the sustainable entrepreneurship sector.

Table 12. The different types of crowdsourcing

Type	Description	Example
Reward based Crowdfunding	Funders are rewarded with a non-financial return such as products or services.	The SME Solar Roadways launched a compelling campaign with a goal of raising $1m, in return of merchandising such as T shirts and personalised solar road tiles. It achieved nearly $2.5m, having reached their target in 22 hours. It funded their testing and initial installations (Start Engine, 2020).
Equity-based Crowdfunding	Investors receive a share in the enterprise.	Oddbox, an SME marketing boxes of misshapen fruit and veg that supermarkets would not sell raised £3.5m in its first two funding rounds for shares in the company (Reffell, 2024).
Donation based Crowdfunding	Donors receive nothing for their gift.	Mymizu, a Japanese SME with a mission to "to help people live more sustainably" (Mymizu, 2024), are campaigning for supporters to pay anything from 500 yen ($3.5) a month, with a tag line of "Mymizu needs you" (Mymizu, 2023).

It should be noted that a successful campaign does not certify long term success of a venture, but it can assist an organisation achieve the next step in its development. The skills that are needed to develop a successful campaign are listed in table 13, and finding an appropriate platform can help hone these further.

Table 13. Skills that support successful crowdfunding campaigns

Skillset	What it means and why it is important
Communication and Storytelling	There is a need for a compelling hook to attract the attention of the public, so it is important to communicate the benefit the enterprise will have and clearly explain how the funds will be used as well as potential pitfalls (Palmieri et al., 2022).
Marketing and effective use of social media	The communication must be tailored to an appropriate target audience using the same techniques as that used in digital marketing (NextCrowd, 2024).
Project Management and organisation.	The campaign is just that. It must be run with clear goals, timelines. It must be run in the same way as any project (Lerro et al., 2023).
Graphic Design and Visual Communication	A campaign is more likely to succeed when it contains a mix of video and images along with the text (Chen et al., 2024). When well produced, it helps to communicate professionalism and embed the brand (Forrest, 2024).
Network and community building	This will help create relationships with potential backers that will help get the campaign launched as well as maintain progress (Peng & Zhang, 2024).
Persuasiveness and Reward strategy	Understanding the target market will also help establish appropriate rewards. It will help attract influencers, and other businesses (Allison et al., 2017).
Financial Acumen	Needed to establish realistic funding goals. They need to be sufficient to finance the next steps as advertised and also be achievable. This includes establishing the costs of the platform used, rewards and production of the campaign itself (Anderson, 2023). In that crowdfunding can generate significantly more than the immediate need, financial judgement is needed to ensure that it is used judiciously
Understanding the Law	Unlike other forms of funding, Crowdfunding need not involve large institutions, but it is important to understand any legal requirements of the process (Legal Foundations, 2024).

In conclusion, crowdfunding is becoming a popular means to finance new ventures. Whilst they can prove to be highly successful, it is necessary to consider the target market and the style of communication including graphical elements. Consequently, a wider range of skills are required than those for other routes to raising revenue.

Developing Skills for the Successful Leverage of Finance

It is clear that without finance, few ventures will reach maturity. Consequently, investment in the time and effort to secure the necessary skills for success is essential. It has already been suggested that some can be outsourced or obtained through crowdsourcing, but the entrepreneur still needs to retain oversite of the activity.

To get the necessary skills, entrepreneurs could use **structured training programmes** that focus on financial and managerial education and contribute to better outcomes. Entrepreneurs who undergo such training demonstrate improved capabilities in managing their ventures and accessing funding (Singh & Verma, 2023).

- *Participate in Online courses:* Platforms like Coursera, edX, LinkedIn Learning, Udemy, and Skillshare offer numerous courses on communication, community management, project management, marketing, and data analysis, all relevant to developing crowdfunding skills, reading relevant books and articles, attending workshops, engaging in online communities, and gaining practical experience (Nawaz, 2023).
- *Research Books & Articles* on crowdsourcing, community building, social media marketing, and project management. It is important to find a crowdfunding platform that is a good fit for their purposes (NextCrowd, 2024).
- *Attend Workshops, Conferences & industry events:* Attending workshops and conferences focused on crowdsourcing, community management, and social media marketing can provide valuable insights and networking opportunities (Peng & Zhang, 2024).
- *Join Online Communities & Forums:* Engage in online communities and forums related to crowdsourcing and specific areas of interest. These platforms offer opportunities to learn from others, share experiences, and gain valuable insights (Peng & Zhang, 2024).
- *Develop Practical Experience:* The most effective way to learn is through hands-on experience. Start with small-scale projects, gradually increasing complexity as you gain confidence and refine your skills.

SUPPORT SYSTEMS IN THE ENVIRONMENT

In addition to financiers, other stakeholders in the wider environment have a significant role in facilitating the move to a more sustainable pattern of living, and in doing so, support the entrepreneurs in their endeavours.

The Role of Governments and Institutions

Entrepreneurs frequently work in very small teams, providing necessary agility but this can limit their breadth of knowledge and expertise and consequently could miss further opportunities to create a truly sustainable offering. Governments can facilitate NGOs and bridge the gap between the enterprise and the resources that are offered locally as well as provide opportunities for knowledge exchange.

Collaboration among stakeholders, including governments, technology providers, academic institutions, and industry associations, can foster innovation and accessibility (Imanto et al., 2019; Wasim et al, 2023). Government incentives, public-private partnerships, and customised training programs all hold an important role in assisting companies.

Table 14 details the areas that entrepreneurs need that have been identified by SEED, a division established by the United Nations Environment Programme (UNEP), and Global Opportunities for Sustainable Development Goals (Go4SDGs).

Table 14. The challenges faced by green innovators

Aspect of the enterprise	Challenge
Innovation	Can be highly resource intensive at both the development and testing stage. Start-ups must compete with larger well-resourced organisations
Non-financial support	Support is often offered to more mainstream activities and larger organisations. It is also needed for the remote entrepreneur working on specific green issues that require novel technologies for R&D.
Finance	Some sustainable endeavours have less profit potential and/or higher risks, offering little leverage.
Policy	SMEs are not sufficiently substantial to have the documentation or recognition, and their needs are not addressed.
Market	Start-ups are often competing with MNEs that already dominate the market. They are often in rural regions with a poor infrastructure.

(Hoballah et al., 2022)

Recognising the above challenges in conjunction with those experienced in launching disruptive innovations, the project has identified a range of interventions that can be provided by central and local governments. These are summarised in table 15:

Table 15. Government support recommended by SEED and examples

Approach (Hoballah et al., 2022).	Example
• Build up the capacity to innovate o Enhance the capacity of Green SMEs to continue to innovate. o Promote the need for green innovation to financiers and customers.	The EU's Horizon 2020 has supported the European Bank for Reconstruction and Development (EBRD) in the development of a Green Innovation Programme, open to support innovation in the twelve EU Member States where the bank currently operates (EBRD Fintecc, 2020).
• Increase innovation capacity o Collate information about innovators achievements and green SMEs. o Encourage innovators and green SMEs to network, share stories and consequently innovate further.	Cambridge Cleantech is the largest innovation network in the UK that has taken this concept further by bringing together innovators, academics, financiers and larger businesses, facilitating collaboration, pooling ideas and scouting for technology solutions (Cambridge Cleantech, 2024).
• Support scaling up. o Encourage collaboration between universities and researchers with Green SMEs o Support the development of science parks and technology centres	Benefitting from a grant awarded by Newham's Royal Docks Enterprise Zone's Good Growth Fund, The University of East London established the Royal Docks Centre for Sustainability, a hub enabling researchers, and business to support green start-ups, offering both access to equipment as well as incubators, accelerators, mentorship and grants (The Royal Docks Team, 2016).

AI-Enabled Support Ecosystems

Artificial Intelligence (AI) has emerged as a transformative force across industries, reshaping how businesses operate, innovate, and sustain themselves in an increasingly competitive and complex global economy (Antoncic, 2020). Using natural language processing (NLP), AI presents unprecedented opportunities for entrepreneurs to build resilient and sustainable business models. By leveraging AI-driven tools and insights, entrepreneurial ecosystems are becoming more dynamic, inclusive, and effective in addressing the multifaceted challenges of sustainability.

AI can assist entrepreneurs in identifying new opportunities, reducing risks, and developing innovative solutions that support ESG goals. The ability to process vast complex data that would normally require human understanding is a key feature that enables it to make predictions that can transform the sustainable enterprises' landscape. It could also help in managing energy systems, integration of renewable energy, resource usage, efficient smart transportation, and other sustainable practices (Olawade et al., 2024; Guo, et al., 2022; Kamalov, et al. 2023).

Many businesses now use ESG analytics to quantify, report, and control risks related to corporate sustainability. AI can contribute to sustainability through administrative integration, technical innovations, and processing advances which can influence sustainable business models that align with the UN SDGs (Di Vaio, 2020). By collecting and analysing data sets from tracking specific SDGs, businesses can enhance their financial metrics as well as their ESG and SDG footprints (Antoncic, 2020). Hence, entrepreneurs can also optimise resource use, reduce their environmental impact, and allow SDG objectives to be achieved. The combination of AI and Big Data can provide practical advice which can assist businesses in making informed decisions and support them in achieving sustainable results by optimising resource use and improving productivity (Bickley, et al., 2024).

Leveraging AI for Sustainable Entrepreneurship

The potential of AI technologies typically falls into three areas: assisting people in breaking away from relevant but monotonous and time-consuming responsibilities, receiving new perceptions that were only available to big unstructured data sets and integrating the capacity of several computers and other means to find the solutions to fundamental issues, including the climate crisis and environmental degradation. This includes facilitating collaborations by linking entrepreneurs with mentors, investors, and partners whose objectives are congruent with their own (Sipola et al., 2023).

Common Applications of AI

Predictive Analytics for Market Trends

AI-powered predictive analytics help entrepreneurs anticipate market changes and consumer preferences. Patagonia, a certified B Corporation uses AI to predict demand and ensure the right number of products are manufactured, hence, minimising excess manufacturing and waste (Patagonia 2022). Tools such as Google Trends provides a direct insight into consumer buying intention by analysing the frequency and timing of specific searches which allow it to gain insight into the link between the searches and actual purchases (Jun et al., 2018). Salesforce Einstein 1 Platform aims to improve productivity and customer engagement by combining both internal and external corporate data with generative AI technologies resulting in improved analytics, automation and provision of predictive suggestions for marketing campaigns, sales opportunities and customer service interactions (Kramer, 2023).

Resource Optimization for Supply Chains

The implementation of AI in supply chain logistics resulted in a 30-50% improvement in the use of assets and 10-20% reduction of inventory (Abhijith Suboyin et al., 2023) and can offer SME similar cost-effective solutions. For instance, Patagonia, is known for its environmental and sustainability efforts. It used AI to reduce greenhouse gas emissions by 12% within three years, and digital technologies have been embedded in its operations to empower its circular supply chain-focused model. Additionally, IoT-equipped items, including wearable sensors are used to monitor product performance and condition, facilitating overhauling, refurbishment, and recycling (Patagonia 2022). Platforms like IBM Watson Supply Chain analyse logistics, forecast disruptions, and recommend efficient pathways to minimize waste and costs, ensuring eco-friendly operations (supplychaindigital.com. 2020).

Skills Needed to Prompt AI Effectively

As the use of digital information and communication technologies increases, AI literacy is gradually becoming important for dealing with the universal AI systems in both personal and professional lives (Ng et al., 2023; Long & Magerko, 2020). It facilitates productive interaction with AI systems and the capacity to understand their limitations, evaluate ethical implications associated with AI applications, and the ability to learn and adapt to emerging AI technologies. This requires self-efficacy and problem-solving skills (Li et al., 2024; Cetindamar et al., 2022).

Prompt Engineering

Prompt engineering needs a strong conceptual and practical knowledge base and is vital because it improves AI tool accuracy (Federiakin et al., 2024). It improves data analysis, content production, and problem-solving, and generates more accurate and contextually relevant outcomes (Korzyński et al., 2023). Effective prompting requires imagination, strategic thinking, and a deep knowledge of generative AI's ability and reliability (Bozkurt, 2024) as well as critical thinking and logic (Barden, 2024). In addition to this it requires good communication skills to frame the prompts clearly and concisely (Loughran, 2024).

Entrepreneurial Mindset

It is suggested that the characteristics of an entrepreneurial mindset include drive and resilient, independence, resourcefulness, solutions-oriented creativity, and a thirst for knowledge (UAGC, 2021; Somers, 2022) align with the qualities that are essential for navigating complex and evolving technological landscapes (Somers, 2022) which includes AI integration. Further skills typical of the entrepreneur are also required as follows:

Critical Thinking

Critical thinking skill is an essential 21st century soft skill enabling the filtering through AI-generated information, in order to evaluate accuracy, identify what is relevant, and then make decisions based on accurate interpretations, as well as being prepared to challenge perceived weaknesses (Spector & Ma, 2019).

The ability to analyse and interpret complex information critically, make informed decisions based on data, helps in designing effective prompts, assessing the quality of AI-generated responses, and enables the questioning of assumptions ensuring that conclusions are backed by concrete evidence (Duong, et al, 2024).

Existing Platforms for Tailored AI Tool Development

Entrepreneurs can use various platforms to develop customized AI tools that meet their unique business needs. In addition, such platforms have significantly reduced the time-to-market for customized AI solutions, empowering smaller businesses to compete in AI-driven markets (Haleem et al., 2022).

Table 16 outlines key platforms, primary functions and their strengths and weaknesses:

Table 16. The strengths and weaknesses of popular platforms

Platform	Functions	Strengths	Weaknesses
TensorFlow (TechVidvan, 2020)	Open-source platform for building and deploying machine learning models, enabling customization for specific business objectives.	Highly flexible; vast community support; extensive documentation.	Steep learning curve for beginners; requires significant coding expertise.
Microsoft Azure AI (Jebaraj, 2024)	Offers pre-built AI models and tools for creating tailored applications, with support for various industries such as retail, healthcare, and finance.	Scalable; strong integration with Microsoft tools; robust security.	Expensive for small businesses; less customization compared to open-source platforms. Steep learning curve.
Hugging Face (Scalenut, 2025)	Specializes in fine-tuning AI models for niche applications like sentiment analysis, natural language processing, and sustainability monitoring.	User-friendly interfaces; excellent for NLP tasks; active community.	Limited support for non-NLP tasks; less scalable for high-demand enterprise-level applications.

continued on following page

Table 16. Continued

Platform	Functions	Strengths	Weaknesses
Amazon SageMaker (PeerSpot, 2021)	Provides an integrated environment for building, training, and deploying machine learning models, simplifying the AI development process.	Automated workflows; strong cloud integration; supports diverse use cases.	High cost for extended usage; reliance on Amazon Web Services infrastructure. Complex and not user friendly.
DataRobot (Lalitha Natraj, 2021)	Focuses on automated machine learning (AutoML), allowing users to create AI models without deep technical expertise.	Ideal for non-experts; fast model creation; provides actionable insights.	Limited customization options; expensive enterprise pricing. Steep learning curve at outset.
Google Cloud AI (CRM Masters, 2022)	Offers a versatile suite of AI tools, including natural language processing and computer vision, with robust integration capabilities.	Powerful algorithms; Facilitates collaboration Secure Google ecosystem & backups; Competitive pricing tiers; Reliable.	Limited support for highly specialized use cases; dependency on Google services; Innovation slow; complex pricing structure; documentation confusing.
PyTorch (Sharma, 2024)	Known for its flexibility and dynamic computation graph, making it suitable for research and development of experimental AI applications.	Preferred by researchers; supports advanced model experimentation; fast prototyping.	Smaller community compared to TensorFlow; challenging for production-level deployment. No visual interface.

Encouraging AI Usage by Entrepreneurs

Entrepreneurs can be supported in choosing an AI platforms through a combination of educational initiatives, social support networks, and AI-driven tools that enhance decision-making and business operations.

Alignment with Legislation and Ethical Standards

Governments and regulatory bodies must ensure AI legislation is accessible and comprehensible. Entrepreneurs should be provided with resources, such as online guides and workshops, to understand compliance requirements. This requires a well-designed and implemented regulation, including assurance tools which can encourage safe use and development and adoption of AI (Department for Science, Innovation & Technology, 2025).

Networking and Collaboration

Using AI is not intuitive, not only requiring digital literacy, but its successful employment also demands creativity in the manner in which it is used (Moravec et al., 2024). Consequently, entrepreneurs and SMEs benefit from a support network where collaboration can enhance their AI skills in a favourable environment with robust infrastructure, beneficial laws, and financial access opportunities. In 2025, The British Government suggested the establishment of 'AI Growth Zones' (AIGZs) to facilitate the accelerated build-out of AI data centres which will offer guidance, create a tailored planning use-class. It will also consider the creation of AI data centres that will provide relevant support that encourage investment in AI such as assisting top AI talents to move to the UK to work with UK-based partnered companies (Department for Science, Innovation & Technology, 2025).

Educational Workshops and Training

Interactive workshops can help entrepreneurs understand and use generative AI platforms effectively. The workshops should focus on better understanding of different types of AI technologies, their application by entrepreneurship and digital skills needed for successful application and (Kumar et al., 2024; Giuggioli & Pellegrini, 2022).

Social Support Networks

Entrepreneurs benefit from actively engaging with their local networks which provide a social environment (Imanto et al., 2019) and can use these to develop the incorporation of AI into business systems. It can provide opportunities to learn about new ways of using AI use and manage the stress that might be caused by addressing a new technology.

AI-Driven Tools and Platforms

AI can assist in assessing business models and predicting business performance, aiding entrepreneurs to make informed decisions and respond swiftly to market needs. This can be done by using AI to provide insights from large data volumes, thus, enhancing decision-making capabilities (Muhammad & Sagatovna, 2024).

Advisory Services

The rapid increase in different AI tools can make it difficult for businesses to decide on the AI tools to adopt. This is especially true for small firms without committed resources. AI consultants or business advisors can guide entrepreneurs based on their industry, budget, and goals, by giving advice about the AI platforms and tools that are available in the market, their costs, and how to implement them effectively and ethically (Singh & Kumar, 2024).

Platform Reviews and Comparisons

Comprehensive, independent reviews and feature comparisons can help entrepreneurs evaluate platforms based on functionality, scalability, and ease of use.

Incubators and Accelerators

Many startup hubs and incubators provide access to AI tools, mentoring, and practical training to help entrepreneurs experiment with platforms in a low-risk environment. AI platforms can also be used in in analysing video pitches for startup accelerators and incubators, which can help entrepreneurs modify their presentation strategies and enhance their prospects of securing funding (Giuggioli et al., 2024).

Pilot testing and Feedback

Businesses may use free trial environments to test platforms before committing to them. This is because the business might not be clear about the precise characteristics they are seeking to gain through using them. Hence, companies should create pilot projects for testing applications before introducing them across the entire enterprise. This approach companies to obtain useful feedback and build the required technology skills and abilities within the organisation (Davenport & Ronanki, 2018).

Many AI platforms offer open-access or free versions with limited features which allows entrepreneurs especially small business owners to explore their capabilities with minimal financial investment and they can later be upgraded to paid versions.

Ethical Considerations

AI users must emphasize ethical considerations, helping entrepreneurs understand the implications of AI misuse such as biased algorithms or data privacy breaches. Having a good understanding of ethical considerations including fairness, socio-economic impacts, and data privacy, and addressing them, is likely to increase trust, transparency, and fairness withing the supply chain consequently leading to a reduction in potential harms (Abhulimen & Ejike, 2024).

The Chart below illustrates some of the main ethical implications related to the use of AI by social entrepreneurs.

Figure 2. Ethical Implications of AI for Social Entrepreneurs

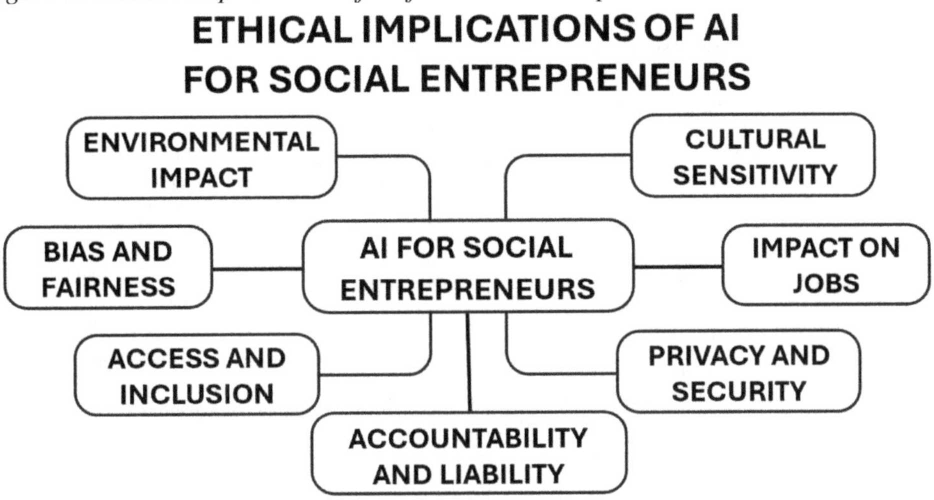

The ethical implications of AI use are especially critical for social entrepreneurs, who often serve vulnerable and diverse communities.

Table 17 below outlines key concerns such as bias, privacy, and cultural sensitivity, along with practical actions to mitigate risks. For instance, AI systems can amplify discrimination if built on biased data, as highlighted by Obermeyer et al. (2019), calling for fairness audits and inclusive design. Similarly, privacy and transparency issues require adherence to regulations like GDPR and the EU AI Act (2024), alongside explainable AI tools. Table 17 also stresses the need to address job displacement (WEF, 2023), ensure equitable access (UNESCO, 2021), and reduce environmental impact (Bender et al., 2021). Notably, cultural sensitivity, a growing concern, urges AI developers to co-create with local communities and adapt systems to diverse contexts (Zhu et al., 2024). Together, these guidelines offer a roadmap for ethically grounded innovation.

Table 17. Ethical Implications and Actions for Social Entrepreneurs

Ethical Implication	Brief Explanation	Relevant References	Actions for Social Entrepreneurs
Bias and Fairness	AI systems can replicate or intensify biases in data, leading to discrimination in areas like hiring or health.	Obermeyer et al., *Science* (2019)	Conduct fairness audits, diversify datasets, and include marginalized groups in system design.
Privacy and Security	Large-scale data processing increases risks of breaches and unauthorized data use.	ICO (UK), 2023: AI and Data Protection	Use encryption, get informed consent, comply with GDPR or local data laws, regularly audit data usage.
Transparency	AI systems are often "black boxes," making it difficult for users to understand or question outputs.	EU AI Act (2024): Artificial Intelligence Act	Use explainable AI (XAI), document decision-making processes, and provide clear user communication.
Impact on Jobs	AI may replace certain roles, affecting employment and economic security.	WEF (2023): Future of Jobs Report	Develop upskilling programs, use AI to augment rather than replace humans, engage workers in tech transition planning.
Access and Inclusion	AI technologies may be inaccessible due to language, cost, or connectivity barriers.	UNESCO (2021): AI and Inclusion	Localize tools linguistically and culturally, reduce costs via partnerships, and ensure access in remote areas.
Environmental Impact	AI model training requires high energy, contributing to carbon emissions.	Bender et al. (2021): Stochastic Parrots	Use energy-efficient models, cloud providers with green credentials, and carbon offsetting initiatives.
Accountability and Liability	Ambiguity over who is responsible for AI outcomes can delay redress or reforms.	OECD (2023): AI Principles	Set up governance frameworks, assign clear roles, maintain human oversight in automated processes.
Cultural Sensitivity	AI designed in one cultural context may be inappropriate or offensive in another.	Zhu et al.(2024)	Co-create with local communities, adapt AI to cultural norms, use multilingual training data.

Source: Developed by authors

CONCLUSION

In recognition that the entrepreneurs hold such a critical role in moving towards a sustainable future, this chapter has explored the challenges that need to be understood together with the skillsets and tools required to enable the entrepreneur leverage success. When incorporating the demands of sustainability into an enterprise, additional challenges are created. Firstly, the entrepreneur needs to consider a much wider range of activities, increasing the complexity of the process. it can demand a more radical solution that introduces a greater challenge in diffusion of the solution. These challenges sit alongside the difficulties faced by the average entrepreneur where success is never a given.

Important tools and skills that can support success are reviewed. Systems thinking and its tools are explored to support the development of a thorough understanding of the problem being addressed along with its environment. These can assist in identifying and communicating logical points of intervention and be used to predict the impact of the solution. Building on the learning gained from analysing the problem, classic idea generation techniques are explored to equip the would-be entrepreneur with robust steps that can help to generate a range of solutions before deciding on the one to be adopted.

Important characteristics and approaches of the successful entrepreneur are discussed, starting with the need for a positive entrepreneurial mindset against the backdrop of classic errors that have prevented success in the past. This includes understanding characteristics that must be built into the enterprise in order to mitigate the additional challenges because of the radical nature of an innovation. These are put into context against the case study of the diffusion of the electric car, where there was a need to ensure that it was made compatible with the supporting infrastructure, that it could be seen and tested by the purchaser and be affordable.

To achieve success the entrepreneur needs to gather a team of people who have the skills to launch the enterprise at a time when the market is ready to accept it, but also to carry it through the process of scaling up to achieve economies of scale, and if part of the plan, to grow its geographical footprint along with the associated challenges. These are different from those experienced at launch, but equally as demanding.

One of the most demanding elements of the enterprise is securing funds. Here the entrepreneur needs to first understand the priorities of the financier, whether it is institutional, crowd sourcing or seeking finance from a parent company. There is a need to match the source of finance with the enterprise type, recognising that not all sustainable projects are inherently profitable. Consequently, there is a need to identify the brand story and write the business case which should emphasise the qualities that would be of interest to the financier. Pitching is another skill that the entrepreneur must refine as a good pitch can be powerful in leveraging the desired results. Whilst applying for finance appears to demand the same skills regardless of the type of lender, their application is subtly different for each one. These are explored for bankers, venture capitalists and crowd funding, and approaches that can help their development are identified.

The entrepreneur has much support in the environment that has been structured to assist their success. These range from local to international level, and include networks involving academia, governments and larger businesses that can offer advice, workshops, mentoring and grants. The greatest development in such support is the evolution of artificial intelligence which offers a significant range of analytical and predictive resources for the entrepreneur. As with all resources, AI needs to be understood and the tools for its successful use need to be mastered. Of great relevance to the sustainable entrepreneur is its ability to manage the complexity imposed by the requirements of a successful sustainable solution.

REFERENCES

S3 Solutions. (2021, August 9). *Government Grants: Advantages and Disadvantages*. S3solutions. https://www.s3solutions.co.uk/post/government-grants-advantages-and-disadvantages

Abhulimen, A. O., & Ejike, O. G. (2024). Ethical considerations in AI use for SMEs and supply chains: Current challenges and future directions. *International Journal of Applied Research in Social Sciences*, *6*(8), 1653–1679. DOI: 10.51594/ijarss.v6i8.1391

Adomdza, G. K., & Astebro, T. B. (2012). The Effect of Entrepreneurial Cognition on Investments for Commercialization Success. SSRN *Electronic Journal*. https://doi.org/DOI: 10.2139/ssrn.2061022

AIContentfy. (2024, December 12). *The Importance of Entrepreneurial Resilience*. https://aicontentfy.com/en/blog/importance-of-entrepreneurial-resilience

Allison, T. H., Davis, B. C., Webb, J. W., & Short, J. C. (2017). Persuasion in crowdfunding: An elaboration likelihood model of crowdfunding performance. *Journal of Business Venturing*, *32*(6), 707–725. DOI: 10.1016/j.jbusvent.2017.09.002

Amoako, G., Omari, P., Kumi, D. K., Agbemabiase, G. C., & Asamoah, G. (2021). Conceptual Framework—Artificial Intelligence and Better Entrepreneurial Decision-Making: The Influence of Customer Preference, Industry Benchmark, and Employee Involvement in an Emerging Market. *Journal of Risk and Financial Management*, *14*(12), 604. DOI: 10.3390/jrfm14120604

Anderson, B. (2023). *How to Create a Budget and Goal for Your Crowdfunding Campaign*. Patronicity.com. https://resources.patronicity.com/blog/2023/02/creating-a-budget-and-goal-for-your-crowdfunding-campaign/

Antoncic, M. (2020). Uncovering hidden signals for sustainable investing using Big Data: Artificial intelligence, machine learning and natural language processing. *Journal of Risk Management in Financial Institutions*, *13*(2), 106–113. https://www.ingentaconnect.com/content/hsp/jrmfi/2020/00000013/00000002/art00002

Arvila, N., Winschiers-Theophilus, H., Keskinen, P., Laurikainen, R., & Nieminen, M. (2020). *Enabling successful crowdfunding for entrepreneurs in marginalized communities*. 45–54. https://doi.org/DOI: 10.1145/3377290.3377303

Arya, A., Mittendorf, B., & Pfeiffer, T. (2021). Incentive Provision in Light of Expertise and Operational Involvement of Angel Investors. *Production and Operations Management*, *30*(9), 2890–2909. DOI: 10.1111/poms.13409

Association for Project Management. (2024). *What is systems thinking? | APM*. Www.apm.org.uk. https://www.apm.org.uk/resources/find-a-resource/what-is-systems-thinking/

Augurio, Alessandro, Castaldi, L., Mazzoni, C., & Matarazzo, O. (2024). EV purchase intention in Italy, Germany, France, and Denmark: Comparative analysis after the approval of the 2035 ban. *Journal of Cleaner Production*, *486*, 144212–144212. DOI: 10.1016/j.jclepro.2024.144212

Bar-El, R., Gavious, I., Kaufmann, D., & Schwartz, D. (2017). Under-Investments in Innovative SMEs: The Effect of Entrepreneurial Cognitive Bias. *Human Capital and Assets in the Networked World*, 385–422. https://doi.org/DOI: 10.1108/978-1-78714-827-720171012

Barden, K. S. (2024, February 27). *Prompting engineering or AI literacy? How to develop a critical awareness of Generative AI in education*. #ALTC Blog. https://altc.alt.ac.uk/blog/2024/02/prompting-engineering-or-ai-literacy-how-to-develop-a-critical-awareness-of-generative-ai-in-education/#gref

Bender, E., McMillan-Major, A., Shmitchell, S., & Gebru, T. (2021). On the Dangers of Stochastic Parrots: Can Language Models Be Too Big? *FAccT '21: Proceedings of the 2021 ACM Conference on Fairness, Accountability, and Transparency*, 610–623. DOI: 10.1145/3442188.3445922

Bickley, S. J., Macintyre, A., & Torgler, B. (2024). Artificial Intelligence and Big Data in Sustainable Entrepreneurship. *Journal of Economic Surveys*, *39*(1). Advance online publication. DOI: 10.1111/joes.12611

Boldyreva, E. L. (2018). Cambridge Analytica: Ethics And Online Manipulation With Decision-Making Process. *The European Proceedings of Social & Behavioural Sciences*. DOI: 10.15405/epsbs.2018.12.02.10

Bora, G. (2019, September 12). *Donatekart gives us a glimpse of how charity can be made more "meaningful."* The Economic Times; Economic Times. https://economictimes.indiatimes.com/small-biz/startups/features/donatekart-gives-us-a-glimpse-of-how-charity-can-be-made-more-meaningful/articleshow/71091858.cms

Boyles, M. (2022, February 1). *What Is Creative Problem-Solving & Why Is It Important?* Business Insights Blog. https://online.hbs.edu/blog/post/what-is-creative-problem-solving

Bozkurt, A. (2024). Tell Me Your Prompts and I Will Make Them True: The Alchemy of Prompt Engineering and Generative AI. *Open Praxis*, *16*(2), 111–118. DOI: 10.55982/openpraxis.16.2.661

British Business Bank. (2021). *Start Up Loans - small businesses can borrow up to £25,000*. Start up Loans Company. https://www.startuploans.co.uk/

Bryant, S. (2024, June 24). *How many startups fail and why?* Investopedia. https://www.investopedia.com/articles/personal-finance/040915/how-many-startups-fail-and-why.asp

Build Plus, K. K. (2025). *10 Mission Driven Startups from Japan*. Wahl+Case; Build Plus K.K. https://www.wahlandcase.com/blog/10-sustainable-startups-japan

Burbano, V. (2020, April 4). *Scaling the Revolution: Patagonia CEO Rose Marcario Charts Path for Sustainable Business | Columbia Business School*. Columbia Business School. https://business.columbia.edu/leadership-and-ethics-news/bernstein-center-leadership-and-ethics/scaling-revolution-patagonia-ceo

Burchi, A., Włodarczyk, B., Szturo, M., & Martelli, D. (2021). The Effects of Financial Literacy on Sustainable Entrepreneurship. *Sustainability*, *13*(9), 5070. DOI: 10.3390/su13095070

Camerer, C., Loewenstein, G., & Weber, M. (1989). The Curse of Knowledge in Economic Settings: An Experimental Analysis. *Journal of Political Economy*, *97*(5), 1232–1254. DOI: 10.1086/261651

Carpineanu, S. (2022, December 12). *Multi Flow Map - Perfect tool for illustrating Causes and Effects*. Blog Mindomo. https://www.mindomo.com/blog/multi-flow-map/

Carton, E. (n.d.). *Five questions startups need to ask before going international*. PwC. https://www.pwc.com/gx/en/services/entrepreneurial-private-business/small-business-solutions/five-questions-startups-need-to-ask-before-going-international.html

Cassar, G. (2004). The financing of business start-ups. *Journal of Business Venturing*, *19*(2), 261–283. DOI: 10.1016/s0883-9026(03)00029-6

Cetindamar, D., Kitto, K., Wu, M., Zhang, Y., Abedin, B., & Knight, S. (2022). Explicating AI Literacy of Employees at Digital Workplaces. *IEEE Transactions on Engineering Management*, *71*, 1–14. DOI: 10.1109/tem.2021.3138503

Chandratreya, A. (2024). From Start-Up to Scale-Up Leadership Dynamics in Entrepreneurial Ventures. *Advances in Business Strategy and Competitive Advantage Book Series*, 454–486. DOI: 10.4018/979-8-3693-7903-5.ch019

Chen, Y., Hu, T., & Law, R. (2024). The impact of visual, auditory, textual stimuli on crowdfunding: Evidence from tourism projects. *Current Issues in Tourism*, 1–19. DOI: 10.1080/13683500.2024.2378608

Cherry, S. (2024, May 15). *What is "grantsmanship"? How strategic thinking improves your chances of success in the grant application process - CareerVolt*. CareerVolt. https://career-volt.com/grant-funding/what-is-grantsmanship-the-importance-of-strategic-thinking-in-the-grant-application-process/

Christensen, K., Ma, Z. G., & Jørgensen, B. N. (2025). A scoping review on electric vehicle charging strategies with a technical, social, and regulatory feasibility evaluation. *Renewable & Sustainable Energy Reviews*, *211*, 115300. DOI: 10.1016/j.rser.2024.115300

Clark, D. (2021, September 3). *Global companies 2020*. Statista. https://www.statista.com/statistics/1260686/global-companies/

Clark, D. R., & Bradley, K. J. (2023). Entrepreneurial leadership: Putting the "U" in team. *Business Horizons*, *67*(2), 183–198. DOI: 10.1016/j.bushor.2023.11.004

Cambridge Cleantech. (2024). Clean Technologies for a Sustainable Future | Cambridge Cleantech. *Cambridgecleantech.org.uk*. DOI: 1008220/1710514078318

Cohen, S. (2021, May 10). *The Role of Individual Responsibility in the Transition to Environmental Sustainability*. State of the Planet. https://news.climate.columbia.edu/2021/05/10/the-role-of-individual-responsibility-in-the-transition-to-environmental-sustainability/

Craig, R. (2021, December 29). *7 types of funding for startups and scaleups*. Rapid Formations Blog. https://www.rapidformations.co.uk/blog/funding-startups-scaleups/

Crawford, A. (2021). *12 top tips for writing a grant application*. Www.ukri.org. https://www.ukri.org/blog/12-top-tips-for-writing-a-grant-application/

da Silva, B. A., Constantino, M., de Moraes, P. M., Herrera, G. P., de Oliveira, O. S., dos Santos, S. A. L., Kulevicz, R. A., Porfírio, G., & da Costa, R. B. (2021). Econometric analysis of IPAT-e: A new tool for the environmental impact assessment of publicly traded companies. *Environmental Impact Assessment Review*, *89*, 106586. DOI: 10.1016/j.eiar.2021.106586

Dam, R. F., & Teo Yu Siang. (2016a, November 26). *Learn How to Use the Best Ideation Methods: Brainstorming, Braindumping, Brainwriting, and Brainwalking*. The Interaction Design Foundation; Interaction Design Foundation. https://www.interaction-design.org/literature/article/learn-how-to-use-the-best-ideation-methods-brainstorming-braindumping-brainwriting-and-brainwalking?srsltid=AfmBOoo3q1-7WVIYQHttAiDNT3RXRqUzEkV7bWgK9KY7j1Dh6I-bbjoS#7._be_visual-8

Dam, R. F., & Teo Yu Siang. (2016b, November 26). *Scamper: How to Use the Best Ideation Methods*. The Interaction Design Foundation; Interaction Design Foundation. https://www.interaction-design.org/literature/article/learn-how-to-use-the-best-ideation-methods-scamper?srsltid=AfmBOoqEt3K1sKzpINm7lDGn9v_ZqLgqtgI_jesH02Occt6fmISZfBV4#example_%E2%80%93_mcdonald%E2%80%99s-2

Daniels, M. (2024, January 3). *Why 2023 saw a boom in B Corp certifications*. Modern Retail. https://www.modernretail.co/operations/why-2023-saw-a-boom-in-b-corp-certifications/

Davenport, T., Guha, A., Grewal, D., & Bressgott, T. (2020). How Artificial Intelligence Will Change the Future of Marketing. *Journal of the Academy of Marketing Science, 48*(1), 24–42. Springer. https://doi.org/DOI: 10.1007/s11747-019-00696-0

Davenport, T. H. (2018). *Artificial Intelligence for the Real World*. Harvard Business Review. https://hbr.org/webinar/2018/02/artificial-intelligence-for-the-real-world

Department for Science. Innovation & Technology. (2025, January 13). *AI Opportunities Action Plan: government response*. GOV.UK. https://www.gov.uk/government/publications/ai-opportunities-action-plan-government-response/ai-opportunities-action-plan-government-response

Di Vaio, A., Palladino, R., Hassan, R., & Escobar, O. (2020). Artificial Intelligence and Business Models in the Sustainable Development Goals perspective: A Systematic Literature Review. *Journal of Business Research, 121*(1), 283–314. DOI: 10.1016/j.jbusres.2020.08.019

Dimitriadis, S., & Koning, R. (2022). Social Skills Improve Business Performance: Evidence from a Randomized Control Trial with Entrepreneurs in Togo. *Management Science, 68*(12). Advance online publication. DOI: 10.1287/mnsc.2022.4334

Duong, C. D. Viet, T., The Anh Khuc, Nhat Minh Tran, & Phuong, T. (2024). Unraveling the dark side of ChatGPT: A moderated mediation model of technology anxiety and technostress. *Information Technology & People*. Advance online publication. DOI: 10.1108/itp-11-2023-1151

Duong, C. D., Le, T. T., Dang, N. S., Do, N. D., & Vu, A. T. (2024). Unraveling the determinants of digital entrepreneurial intentions: Do performance expectancy of artificial intelligence solutions matter? *Journal of Small Business and Enterprise Development, 31*(2), 1327–1356. DOI: 10.1108/jsbed-02-2024-0065

Dweck, C. (2017). *Mindset: Changing the way you think to fulfil your potential.* Robinson.

Dwoskin, J. (2023, April 17). *It seems as though every day the world is beginning to move faster and faster. Often times, in my career, I have seen entrepreneurs or business people with great products or ideas, but they lack one specific quality: patience.* Linkedin.com. https://www.linkedin.com/pulse/start-slow-grow-big-slowing-down-best-way-get-ahead-jon-dwoskin-/

Economic Development Collaborative. (2024, September 4). *5 Keys to Attract Venture Capital Funding*. Economic Development Collaborative. https://edcollaborative.com/blog/compelling-business-plan-raising-venture-capital/

ECOVER. (2024, July 24). *Ecover Timeline*. Ecover. https://uk.ecover.com/mission/history/

Elevate. (2022, September 8). *The Power of Networking for Entrepreneurs*. Elevate Ventures. https://elevateventures.com/the-power-of-networking-for-entrepreneurs

EMBROKER. (2020, February 2). 106 Must-Know Startup. https://www.embroker.com/blog/startup-statistics/

Engine, S. (2020). *Solar Roadways® | StartEngine*. StartEngine. https://www.startengine.com/offering/solar-roadways

European Banking Federation. (2021, June 24). *Banks prioritize SDGs requiring greatest financing impact, study finds*. European Banking Federation. https://www.ebf.eu/financing-growth/banks-prioritize-sdgs-requiring-greatest-financing-impact-study-finds/

European Environment Agency. (2024, December 5). *Europe's circular economy in facts and figures*. Europa.eu. https://www.eea.europa.eu/en/analysis/publications/europes-circular-economy-in-facts

European Union. (2024). *The EU Artificial Intelligence Act*. The Artificial Intelligence Act. https://artificialintelligenceact.eu/

Fairphone. (2024). *About us | Fairphone*. Fairphone BV. https://shop.fairphone.com/about-us

Fairphone. (2025, January 13). *Fairphone's next chapter starts now. - Fairphone.* Fairphone. https://www.fairphone.com/en/2025/01/13/fairphones-next-chapter-starts-now/

Federiakin, D., Molerov, D., Zlatkin-Troitschanskaia, O., & Maur, A. (2024). Prompt engineering as a new 21st century skill. *Frontiers in Education, 9*. Advance online publication. DOI: 10.3389/feduc.2024.1366434

Ferrara, E. (2023). Fairness and Bias in Artificial Intelligence: A Brief Survey of Sources, Impacts, and Mitigation Strategies. *Sci, 6*(1), 3. DOI: 10.3390/sci6010003

Fintecc, E. B. R. D. (2020). *Green Innovation Programme | EBRD FINTECC.* Ebrd.com. https://fintecc.ebrd.com/greeninnovationprogramme

First-Citizens Bank & Trust Company. (2025). *What is Venture Capital? | Silicon Valley Bank.* Www.svb.com. https://www.svb.com/startup-insights/vc-relations/what-is-venture-capital/

Fisher, R., & Ury, W. (2012). *Getting to yes: Negotiating an agreement without giving in.* Random House Business Books.

Floersch, B. (2019, August 6). *Grant Proposal Development as Project Management.* The Grantsmanship Center. https://www.tgci.com/blog/2019/08/grant-proposal-development-project-management

Forrest, M. (2024, August 9). *10 reasons Graphic Design is the foundation for great Web Design - Access Creative.* Access Creative College. https://www.accesscreative.ac.uk/blog/10-reasons-graphic-design-is-foundation-for-web-design/

Frimanslund, T., Kwiatkowski, G., & Oklevik, O. (2022). The role of finance in the literature of entrepreneurial ecosystems. *European Planning Studies, 31*(2), 1–20. DOI: 10.1080/09654313.2022.2055962

G-P. (2020, March 10). *Tips on Expanding a Startup Internationally | Globalization Partners.* Globalization-Partners.com. https://www.globalization-partners.com/blog/tips-on-expanding-a-startup-internationally/?utm_keyword=&utm_device=c&utm_source=Adwords&utm_medium=cpc&utm_campaign=uk__search__dynamic__

Galea-Pace, S. (2020, May 17). *IBM Watson: how AI is transforming the supply chain.* Supplychaindigital.com. https://supplychaindigital.com/technology/ibm-watson-how-ai-transforming-supply-chain

Gebhardt, L., & Bachmann, N. (2023). Entrepreneurial contributions to sustainability transitions—A longitudinal study of their representation and enactment through topic modeling and thematic analysis. *Journal of Cleaner Production, 420*, 138255. DOI: 10.1016/j.jclepro.2023.138255

Genome, S. (2023). *What Makes a Startup Succeed? Identifying Scaling Success Factors*. Startup Genome. https://startupgenome.com/article/what-makes-a-startup-succeed-identifying-scaling-success-factors

Gibson, K. (2024, August 14). *5 Ethical Considerations of AI in Business*. Business Insights Blog. https://online.hbs.edu/blog/post/ethical-considerations-of-ai

Giuggioli, G., & Pellegrini, M. M. (2022). Artificial intelligence as an enabler for entrepreneurs: A systematic literature review and an agenda for future research. *International Journal of Entrepreneurial Behaviour & Research, 29*(4), 816–837. DOI: 10.1108/ijebr-05-2021-0426

Glade, C., Kesting, P., Smolinski, R., & Kanbach, D. K. (2025). Start-up funding negotiations with venture capitalists: Understanding the behaviors and strategies of experienced entrepreneurs. *International Journal of Entrepreneurial Behaviour & Research, 1*(1). Advance online publication. DOI: 10.1108/ijebr-06-2024-0615

Global Footprint Network. (2022). *How many Earths? How many countries?* Earth Overshoot Day. https://overshoot.footprintnetwork.org/how-many-earths-or-countries-do-we-need/

Gompers, P. A., & Lerner, J. (2004). *The venture capital cycle*. Mit.

Gottschall, J. (2012). *The storytelling animal: how stories make us human*. Houghton Mifflin Harcourt.

Granstrand, O., & Holgersson, M. (2020). Innovation ecosystems: A conceptual review and a new definition. *Technovation, 90-91*, 102098. https://doi.org/DOI: 10.1016/j.technovation.2019.102098

Grantify. (2024). *How to Use Data to Win Grants and Attract Investors | Grantify*. Grantify.io. https://www.grantify.io/articles/how-to-use-data-to-win-grants-and-attract-investors

Grayson, D., Coulter, C., & Lee, M. (2022). *The sustainable business handbook: a guide to becoming more innovative, resilient and successful*. Kogan Page Inc.

Greaves, K. (2024, August 20). *If Grants for Black-Owned Businesses Are Eliminated, Your Favorite Beauty Brands Could Be Too*. Allure. https://www.allure.com/story/grants-for-black-owned-beauty-businesses

Gregersen, H. (2018, March 1). *Better Brainstorming*. Harvard Business Review. https://hbr.org/2018/03/better-brainstorming

Groner, T., & Moradi, A. (2024). Sacrificing Sustainability for a Higher GDP Growth Rate. *Development and Sustainability in Economics and Finance, 2-4*, 100015–100015. DOI: 10.1016/j.dsef.2024.100015

Guglielmo, G., Pellegrini, M. M., & Giannone, G. (2024). Artificial intelligence as an enabler for entrepreneurial finance: A practical guide to AI-driven video pitch evaluation for entrepreneurs and investors. *Management Decision, 29*, 816–837. DOI: 10.1108/md-10-2023-1926

Guo, K., Wang, J., & Chu, S. K. W. (2022). Using chatbots to scaffold EFL students' argumentative writing. *Assessing Writing, 54*, 100666. DOI: 10.1016/j.asw.2022.100666

Hagberg, R. (2020, August 13). *Building Startup Teams: The Challenge for Entrepreneurs*. Www.hagbergconsulting.com. https://www.hagbergconsulting.com/building-startup-teams-the-challenge-for-entrepreneurs

Haleem, A., Javaid, M., Qadri, M. A., Singh, R. P., & Suman, R. (2022). Artificial Intelligence (AI) Applications for marketing: a literature-based Study. *International Journal of Intelligent Networks, 3*(3), 119–132. DOI: 10.1016/j.ijin.2022.08.005

Hamm, J. (2002, December). *Why Entrepreneurs Don't Scale*. Harvard Business Review. https://hbr.org/2002/12/why-entrepreneurs-dont-scale?registration=success

Hargrave, M. (2022, November 20). *How Crowdsourcing Works*. Investopedia. https://www.investopedia.com/terms/c/crowdsourcing.asp

Harroch, R. (2022). *What Angel Investors Want To Know Before Investing In Your Startup*. Forbes. https://www.forbes.com/sites/allbusiness/2020/12/13/what-angel-investors-want-to-know-before-investing-in-your-startup/

Hinderer, S., & Kuckertz, A. (2024). Degrowth attitudes among entrepreneurs hinder fast venture scaling. *Business Strategy and the Environment, 33*. Advance online publication. DOI: 10.1002/bse.3735

Hoballah, A., Mühlbauer, S., & Zürker, M. (2022). *Sustainable SME Action Agenda Scaling Green SME Support for 2030 2 YEARS*. https://adelphi.de/system/files/mediathek/bilder/Sustainable-SME-Action-Agenda-Scaling-Green-SME-Support-for-2030_0.pdf?utm_source=chatgpt.com

Hofmann, K. H., Jacob, A., & Pizzingrilli, M. (2022). Overcoming Growth Challenges of Sustainable Ventures in the Fashion Industry: A Multinational Exploration. *Sustainability*, *14*(16), 10275. DOI: 10.3390/su141610275

Horatio Alger Association. (2007). *News & Announcements*. Horatio Alger. https://horatioalger.org/members/detail/howard-schultz/

ICO. (2025, June 13). *Guidance on AI and data protection*. Ico.org.uk. https://ico.org.uk/for-organisations/guide-to-data-protection/key-dp-themes/guidance-on-ai-and-data-protection/

IEA. (2022). *Net Zero Emissions by 2050 Scenario (NZE) – Global Energy and Climate Model – Analysis*. IEA. https://www.iea.org/reports/global-energy-and-climate-model/net-zero-emissions-by-2050-scenario-nze

Imanto, Y., Prijadi, R., & Dyah, R. (2019). Innovation Ecosystem for SMEs in the Creative Industry. *International Journal of Business*, *24*(4), 2019.

Inglis, I. (2022). Formation of Entrepreneurial Skills and Protection of Intellectual Property. *Intellectus*, *2*(2), 61–73. DOI: 10.56329/1810-7087.22.2.06

IPCC. (2014). *AR5 Climate Change 2014: Mitigation of Climate Change — IPCC*. Ipcc.ch; IPCC. https://www.ipcc.ch/report/ar5/wg3/

Jebaraj, K. (2024, March 18). *Microsoft Azure Advantages and Disadvantages*. Www.knowledgehut.com. https://www.knowledgehut.com/blog/cloud-computing/microsoft-azure-advantages-and-disadvantages

Johnson, E. (2021, December 5). *IntelliGENZ Magazine*. IntelliGENZ Magazine. https://www.intelligenzmag.com/articles/3gudz2xq31a48paw4lr4v2t26s3a9j

Josić, K. (2024). *Creativity*. The Engines of Our Ingenuity. https://engines.egr.uh.edu/episode/2817

Jun, S.-P., Yoo, H. S., & Choi, S. (2018). Ten years of research change using Google Trends: From the perspective of big data utilizations and applications. *Technological Forecasting and Social Change, 130*, 69–87. DOI: 10.1016/j.techfore.2017.11.009

Kamalov, F., Calonge, D. S., & Gurrib, I. (2023). New Era of Artificial Intelligence in Education: Towards a Sustainable Multifaceted Revolution. *Sustainability*, *15*(16), 12451. DOI: 10.3390/su151612451

Kanze, D., Huang, L., Conley, M. A., & Higgins, E. T. (2018). We Ask Men to Win and Women Not to Lose: Closing the Gender Gap in Startup Funding. *Academy of Management Journal*, *61*(2), 586–614. DOI: 10.5465/amj.2016.1215

Kapoor, K. (2024, November 4). *Celebrating Green Entrepreneurs: Meet Three Young Innovators Leading Solutions for a Greener World.* Generationunlimited.org. https://www.generationunlimited.org/stories/celebrating-green-entrepreneurs-meet-three-young-innovators-leading-solutions-greener-world

Kaufman, T. (2024, May 7). *Communicating program impact in a grant proposal.* Candid Insights. https://blog.candid.org/post/communicating-program-impact-in-a-grant-proposal/

Khanin, D., Rosenfield, R., Mahto, R. V., & Singhal, C. (2021). Barriers to entrepreneurship: Opportunity recognition vs. opportunity pursuit. *Review of Managerial Science, 16*(4). Advance online publication. DOI: 10.1007/s11846-021-00477-6

Kienapple, B. (2020, August 21). *40+ Amazing Mind Map Templates You Can Use Now.* Venngage. https://venngage.com/blog/mind-map-templates/

Kim, K.-Y. (2023). A Study on the Decision-making Factors of Angel Investment to Revitalize Local Startup: Focusing on. *Hanguk Jibang Jachi Yeongu/Han'gug Ji'bang Jachi Yeon'gu/Han-Guk Jibang Jachi Yeon-Gu, 25*(2), 195–224. DOI: 10.38134/klgr.2023.25.2.195

Kim, W. C., & Mauborgne, R. (2005). *Blue Ocean Strategy: How to Create Uncontested Market Space and Make the Competition Irrelevant.* Havard Business School Publishing Corporation.

Kiradoo, G. (2023, March). *Unlocking the Potential of AI in Business: Challenges and Ethical Considerations.* https://papers.ssrn.com/sol3/papers.cfm?abstract_id=4387922

Klada, T.-V. (2018). Unraveling Entrepreneurial Team Formation: A Qualitative Study Among Funded Ventures. *SAGE Open, 8*(2). DOI: 10.1177/2158244018776700

Kleiman, D. (2020). *First pitch: winning money, mentors, and more for your startup.* Babson College Publishing.

Korzyński, P., Mazurek, G., Krzypkowska, P., & Kurasiński, A. (2023). Artificial intelligence prompt engineering as a new digital competence: Analysis of generative AI technologies such as ChatGPT. *Entrepreneurial Business and Economics Review, 11*(3), 25–37. DOI: 10.15678/eber.2023.110302

Kramer, R. (2023, September 27). *Salesforce Leans On Enterprise Data With The Einstein 1 AI Platform.* Forbes. https://www.forbes.com/sites/moorinsights/2023/09/27/salesforce-leans-on-enterprise-data-with-the-einstein-1-ai-platform/

Kruk, E. (2023, October 18). *The Challenges of Scaling Tech Teams and How to Overcome Them*. Codigee.com; Codigee. https://codigee.com/blog/the-challenges-of-scaling-tech-teams-and-how-to-overcome-them?utm_source=chatgpt.com

Kulkov, I., Kulkova, J., Rohrbeck, R., Menvielle, L., Kaartemo, V., & Makkonen, H. (2023). Artificial intelligence - driven sustainable development: Examining organizational, technical, and processing approaches to achieving global goals. *Sustainable Development, 32*(3). Advance online publication. DOI: 10.1002/sd.2773

Kumar, S. (2023). Evaluating performance of SMEs using structure equation modeling. *International Journal of Financial Engineering, 11*(02). Advance online publication. DOI: 10.1142/s2424786323500421

Kumar, V., Ashraf, A. R., & Nadeem, W. (2024). AI-powered marketing: What, where, and how? *International Journal of Information Management, 77*, 102783–102783. DOI: 10.1016/j.ijinfomgt.2024.102783

Lab, B. (2025). *What is the average size of a Certified B Corp?* Www.bcorporation.net. https://www.bcorporation.net/en-us/faqs/what-average-size-certified-b-corp/

Learn, F. (n.d.). *Sign graphs*. FutureLearn. https://www.futurelearn.com/info/courses/systems-thinking-complexity/0/steps/20382

Legal Foundations. (2024, February 10). *The Legal Framework of Crowdfunding for Startups - Legal Foundations*. Legal Foundations -. https://legalfoundations.org.uk/blog/the-legal-framework-of-crowdfunding-for-startups/

Lerro, A., Santarsiero, F., Schiuma, G., & Bartuseviciene, I. (2023). Mapping knowledge assets categories for successful crowdfunding strategies. *European Journal of Innovation Management*. Advance online publication. DOI: 10.1108/ejim-03-2022-0138

Li, Y., Wu, B., Huang, Y., & Luan, S. (2024). Developing trustworthy artificial intelligence: Insights from research on interpersonal, human-automation, and human-AI trust. *Frontiers in Psychology, 15*. Advance online publication. DOI: 10.3389/fpsyg.2024.1382693 PMID: 38694439

Lin, M., & Viswanathan, S. (2013). Home Bias in Online Investments: An Empirical Study of an Online Crowd Funding Market. SSRN *Electronic Journal*. https://doi.org/DOI: 10.2139/ssrn.2219546

Long, D., & Magerko, B. (2020). What is AI Literacy? Competencies and Design Considerations. *Proceedings of the 2020 CHI Conference on Human Factors in Computing Systems*, 1–16. DOI: 10.1145/3313831.3376727

Lopez, N. (2024, January). *Copernicus: 2023 is the hottest year on record, with global temperatures close to the 1.5°C limit | Copernicus*. Climate.copernicus.eu. https://climate.copernicus.eu/copernicus-2023-hottest-year-record

Loughran, M. (2024, August 14). *Communicating with AI: The Art of Prompting — A Guide for SMBs | by Matthew Loughran, EMBA | Craftsman AI*. Medium; Craftsman AI. https://medium.com/craftsman-ai/communicating-with-ai-the-art-of-prompting-a-guide-for-smbs-015856bba9b4

MacCarthy, J., Tyukavina, S., Weisse, M., & Harris, N. (2024, August). *New data confirms: Forest fires are getting worse*. https://www.wri.org/insights/global-trends-forest-fires

Malesios, C., De, D., Moursellas, A., Dey, P. K., & Evangelinos, K. (2020). Sustainability performance analysis of small and medium sized enterprises: Criteria, methods and framework. *Socio-Economic Planning Sciences*, *75*, 100993. DOI: 10.1016/j.seps.2020.100993

Marks, A. P. (1989). The Sinclair C5 – An Investigation into its Development, Launch, and Subsequent Failure. *European Journal of Marketing*, *23*(1), 61–71. DOI: 10.1108/eum0000000000542

Martins, J. (2022, October 5). *The beginner's guide to writing an effective business case • asana*. Asana. https://asana.com/resources/business-case

Masters, C. R. M. (2022, August 4). *Google Cloud Platform – Advantages and Disadvantages*. CRM Masters. https://crm-masters.com/google-cloud-platform-advantages-and-disadvantages/

May, R. (2019, January 24). *Start-ups across the UK are going bust - they need more careful management for our economy to boom*. The Telegraph. https://www.telegraph.co.uk/politics/2019/01/24/start-ups-across-uk-going-bust-need-careful-management-economy/

Meadows, D., Randers, J., & Meadows, D. (2004). *Limits to growth: The 30-Year update*. Chelsea Green Publishing Company.

Miller, D. (2017). *Building a storybrand: clarify your message so customers will listen*. Harpercollins Leadership, An Imprint of Harpercollins.

Miloud, T., Aspelund, A., & Cabrol, M. (2012). Startup valuation by venture capitalists: An empirical study. *Venture Capital*, *14*(2-3), 151–174. DOI: 10.1080/13691066.2012.667907

Miquel. (2023, August 30). *Is the Fairphone 5 the most sustainable phone in the world?* Fairphone. https://www.fairphone.com/en/2023/08/30/is-the-fairphone-5-the-most-sustainable-phone-in-the-world/

Mishra, D., & Maheshwari, N. (2024). Crowdsourcing-based social linkage and organizational innovation competence: Knowledge transfer effectiveness and absorptive capacity as serial mediators. *Journal of Knowledge Management, 28*(7), 2013–2037. DOI: 10.1108/jkm-07-2023-0583

Mitchell, I. K., & Walinga, J. (2017). The creative imperative: The role of creativity, creative problem solving and insight as key drivers for sustainability. *Journal of Cleaner Production, 140*(3), 1872–1884. DOI: 10.1016/j.jclepro.2016.09.162

Moravec, V., Hynek, N., Gavurova, B., & Rigelsky, M. (2024). Who uses it and for what purpose? The role of digital literacy in ChatGPT adoption and utilisation. *Journal of Innovation & Knowledge, 9*(4), 100602–100602. DOI: 10.1016/j.jik.2024.100602

Muhammad, N., & Sagatovna, M. (2024). The impact of Artificial Intelligence in decision making: A comprehensive review. *EPRA International Journal of Economics. Business and Management, 11*(2), 27–38. DOI: 10.36713/epra15747

Mulder, P. (2015, March 17). *Influence Mapping, a great stakeholder management tool | ToolsHero.* Toolshero. https://www.toolshero.com/project-management/influence-mapping/

Mymizu. (2023). *mymizu.* Mymizu. https://www.mymizu.co/en/monthly-supporter

Mymizu. (2024). *Home (EN).* Mymizu. https://www.mymizu.co/home-en

Nai, J., Lin, Y., Kotha, R., & Vissa, B. (2021). A foot in the door: Field experiments on entrepreneurs' network activation strategies for investor referrals. *Strategic Management Journal, 43*(2), 323–339. DOI: 10.1002/smj.3341

Natraj, L. (2021, March 24). *DataRobot — An end to end AI platform - Lalitha Natraj - Medium.* Medium. https://lnatraj.medium.com/data-robot-5a0efa279d48

Nawaz, H. R. (2023, April 28). *Introduction Being an entrepreneur is tough, and learning how to do it is even tougher. What's the best way to learn about entrepreneurship? Well, there are lots of ways! We've put together this list of the top ten platforms that will help you understand what it takes to be a successful entrepreneur.* https://www.linkedin.com/pulse/9-best-platforms-learn-entrepreneurship-hamid-rab-nawaz/

Neal, M. (2024, January 8). *Expectations and Success Factors When Writing for Grants*. Medium. https://medium.com/@marcneal/expectations-and-success-factors-when-writing-for-grants-77236ed15b3c

Nemko, M. N. (2016, July 20). *An Interview with Tony Robbins*. Psychology Today. https://www.psychologytoday.com/us/blog/how-to-do-life/201607/an-interview-with-tony-robbins?msockid=2177f2f48c4c63ed0e9ce7d98d5962f4

NextCrowd. (2024). *Effective Crowdfunding Marketing Strategies to Boost Your Campaign*. Nextcrowd.co.uk. https://nextcrowd.co.uk/blog/effective-crowdfunding-marketing-strategies-to-boost-your-campaign

Ng, K., Su, J., & Kai, S. (2023). Fostering Secondary School Students' AI Literacy through Making AI-Driven Recycling Bins. *Education and Information Technologies*, *29*(8). Advance online publication. DOI: 10.1007/s10639-023-12183-9

Ngoc, T. H. (2024). *Green Innovation: Strategies for Commercializing Environmental Technologies and Solutions*. 151–156. DOI: 10.1109/atigb63471.2024.10717780

Nishant, R., Kennedy, M., & Corbett, J. (2020). Artificial intelligence for sustainability: Challenges, opportunities, and a research agenda. *International Journal of Information Management*, *53*(53), 102104. DOI: 10.1016/j.ijinfomgt.2020.102104

Now, O. (2023). *Sinclair C5 electric car: The future too soon?* Www.footmanjames.co.uk. https://www.footmanjames.co.uk/blog/sinclair-c5-electric-car-the-future-too-soon

NPC. (2024, February 15). *Systems Mapping - NPC*. Think NPC. https://www.thinknpc.org/resource-hub/systems-practice-toolkit/systems-mapping/?utm_source=chatgpt.com

Obermeyer, Z., Powers, B., Vogeli, C., & Mullainathan, S. (2019). Dissecting Racial Bias in an Algorithm Used to Manage the Health of Populations. *Science*, *366*(6464), 447–453. DOI: 10.1126/science.aax2342 PMID: 31649194

Obrebowska, E. (2020, June 25). *The role of communication in the VC and start-ups universe*. Market One Capital Corner. https://medium.com/market-one-capital-corner/the-role-of-communication-in-the-vc-and-startups-universe-51a19a1bbf75

OECD. (2019). *The OECD Artificial Intelligence (AI) Principles*. Oecd.ai; OECD. https://oecd.ai/en/ai-principles

OECD. (2023). Financing SMEs for sustainability – Financial institution strategies and approaches financing SMEs for sustainability. Results of an OECD survey of public and private financial institutions. In *OECD*. OECD. https://www.oecd.org/content/dam/oecd/en/about/programmes/cfe/oecd-platform-on-financing-smes-for-sustainability/Financing-SMEs-for-sustainability-Survey-report.pdf

OECD. (2024). *Survey shows households are willing to shift to greener lifestyles but that cost and convenience are key*. OECD. https://www.oecd.org/en/about/news/press-releases/2023/06/survey-shows-households-are-willing-to-shift-to-greener-lifestyles-but-that-cost-and-convenience-are-key-.html

OECD. (2025). OECD Platform on Financing SMEs for Sustainability Activity Report 2024. In *OECD Platform on Financing SMEs for Sustainability*. OECD. https://www.oecd.org/en/about/programmes/oecd-platform-on-financing-smes-for-sustainability.html

Olawade, D. B., Wada, O. Z., Ige, A. O., Egbewole, B. I., Olojo, A., & Oladapo, B. I. (2024). Artificial Intelligence in Environmental Monitoring: Advancements, Challenges, and Future Directions. *Hygiene and Environmental Health Advances*, *12*, 100114–100114. DOI: 10.1016/j.heha.2024.100114

Onetti, A. (2021, March 23). *Why most intrapreneurship programmes fail | Sifted*. Sifted. https://sifted.eu/articles/why-intrapreneurship-programmes-fail

Open University. (2024). *Mastering systems thinking in practice*. Open Learning. https://www.open.edu/openlearn/mod/oucontent/view.php?id=65668&section=4

Ottinger, R. (2021, April 2). *Create Sustainable Success with the 4 Types of Innovation*. Fresh Consulting. https://www.freshconsulting.com/insights/blog/the-4-types-of-innovation/

Outcault, S., Sanguinetti, A., & Nelson, L. (2022). Technology characteristics that influence adoption of residential distributed energy resources: Adapting Rogers' framework. *Energy Policy*, *168*, 113153. DOI: 10.1016/j.enpol.2022.113153

Palmieri, R., Mercuri, C., & Mazzali-Lurati, S. (2022). Persuasive Reasons in Crowdfunding Campaigns: Comparing Argumentative Strategies in Successful and Unsuccessful Projects on Kickstarter. *International Journal of Strategic Communication*, *16*(2), 332–355. DOI: 10.1080/1553118x.2021.2008942

Patagonia. (2022). *Core values*. Patagonia. https://www.patagonia.com/core-values/

PeerSpot. (2021, August 30). *Pros and Cons of Amazon SageMaker 2025 | PeerSpot*. Peerspot.com. https://www.peerspot.com/products/amazon-sagemaker-pros-and-cons

Peng, L., & Zhang, L. (2024). Unleashing the Crowd: The Effect of Social Networks in Crowdfunding Markets. *Management Science*. Advance online publication. DOI: 10.1287/mnsc.2022.01364

Phelon, P. (2021, July 13). *The path to growth - Get Funded to Grow Your Business*. LinkedIn. https://www.linkedin.com/learning/get-funded-to-grow-your-business/the-path-to-growth?u=56744289

Pierrakis, Y., & Owen, R. (2022). Startup ventures and equity finance: How do Business Accelerators and Business Angels' assess the human capital of socio-environmental mission led entrepreneurs? *Innovation*, 1–25. DOI: 10.1080/14479338.2022.2029706

Polcz, K. (2021). Pitching as an Entrepreneurial Soft Skill in the World of Startups. *GiLE Journal of Skills Development*, *1*(2), 5–6. DOI: 10.52398/gjsd.2021.v1.i2.pp5-6

Pollman, E. (2023, September 29). *Startup Failure*. The Harvard Law School Forum on Corporate Governance. https://corpgov.law.harvard.edu/2023/09/29/startup-failure/

Prashar, A. (2019). Towards sustainable development in industrial small and Medium-sized Enterprises: An energy sustainability approach. *Journal of Cleaner Production*, *235*, 977–996. DOI: 10.1016/j.jclepro.2019.07.045

Purdue Global. (2024, January 8). *What Is a Growth Mindset and How Can You Develop One?* Purdue Global. https://www.purdueglobal.edu/blog/careers/develop-growth-mindset/

Rajović, J., Jovanović, M., Denić, N., & Bogdanovic, I. B. (2024). English Language as one of the key entrepreneurial competences. *Science International Journal*, *3*(2), 127–131. DOI: 10.35120/sciencej0302127r

Ratanavanich, M., & Charoensukmongkol, P. (2024). The interaction effect of goal orientation and mindfulness of entrepreneurs on firm innovation capability and its impact on firm performance. *VINE Journal of Information and Knowledge Management Systems*. Advance online publication. DOI: 10.1108/vjikms-06-2023-0135

Ratcliffe, S. (2016). *Oxford Essential Quotations* (4th ed.). Oxford University Press.

Rea, A. (2019, July 10). *Storytelling in Life, Startups, and Venture Capital*. Medium. https://medium.com/%40andrew.twoclarify/storytelling-in-life-startups-and-venture-capital-da01ea89b09c

Reddy, S. (2023). Translational Application of Artificial Intelligence in Healthcare. In *Chapman and Hall/CRC eBooks*. Informa., DOI: 10.1201/9781003262152

Reffell, C. (2024). *Big Investor Returns from Equity Crowdfunding in the UK*. Crowdsourcing Week. https://crowdsourcingweek.com/blog/equity-crowdfunding-big-returns/

Riani, A. (2023). *The 5 Key Success Factors For Startup Founders*. Forbes. https://www.forbes.com/sites/abdoriani/2023/06/30/the-5-key-success-factors-for-startup-founders/

Rogers, E. M. (2003). *Diffusion of Innovations* (5th ed.). Free Press.

Rosario, R. (2024, July 12). *The Ultimate Guide to HR Management in Startups - ProfitLeap*. ProfitLeap - Supercharge Your Financial Control with Huxley. https://profitleap.com/human-resource-management-in-startups/?utm_source=chatgpt.com

Roth, G. (2024, January 23). *3 Deadly Mistakes Early-Stage Startups Can Make Building Their Founding Teams*. Startup Stockpile. https://startup.unitelvoice.com/building-founding-teams

Scalenut. (2025, January 20). *Hugging Face AI Detector: In-Depth Review*. Scalenut.com; Scalenut. https://www.scalenut.com/blogs/hugging-face-ai-detector-review

Schultz, H. (2014). *Pour your heart into it: how Starbucks built a company one cup at a time*. Hachette. (Original work published 1997)

Segreto, P. (2023, August 12). *The Balancing Act: The Entrepreneurial Mindset Between Innovation and Sustainable Success*. Medium. https://paulsegreto.medium.com/the-balancing-act-the-entrepreneurial-mindset-between-innovation-and-sustainable-success-4b3bf5a532c5

Sendpulse. (2023, March 22). *What is Crowdsourcing: Types and Examples - Definition*. SendPulse. https://sendpulse.com/support/glossary/crowdsourcing

Seshadri, D. V. R. (2007). Understanding New Venture Failure due to Entrepreneur-Organization Goal Dissonance. *Vikalpa*, *32*(1), 55–74. DOI: 10.1177/0256090920070105

Sha, Q. (2023). Application of positive psychology to study the root of psychological anxiety of innovative entrepreneurs. *CNS Spectrums*, *28*(S1), S24–S24. DOI: 10.1017/s1092852923000949

Sharma, J. (2024, December 31). *All About Pytorch: Features and Advantages*. Shiksha.com; Shiksha Online. https://www.shiksha.com/online-courses/articles/all-about-pytorch-features-and-advantages-blogId-186266

Sheykhfard, , Azmoodeh, Das, & Kutela. (2024). Analyzing Purchase Intentions of Used Electric Vehicles Through Consumer Experiences: A Structural Equation Modeling Approach. *Transport Policy*, *160*, 125–137. DOI: 10.1016/j.tranpol.2024.10.038

Shkarupa, O. V., Ignatchenko, A. S., & Vlasenko, K. A. (2021). *Mechanisms of investment support for scaling eco-innovations for sustainable development*. Vìsnik Sums'kogo Deržavnogo Unìversitetu, *2021*(2). DOI: 10.21272/1817-9215.2021.2-9

Sigmundsson, H., & Haga, M. (2024). Passion and grit in individuals with high levels of growth mindset are different than in individuals who have low growth mindset. *Acta Psychologica*, *250*, 104480. DOI: 10.1016/j.actpsy.2024.104480 PMID: 39265349

Singh & Paul. (2023). Impact of Awareness on the Adoption of Electric Vehicles: A Systematic Literature Review. *Emerald Publishing Limited EBooks*, 331–357. DOI: 10.1108/978-1-83753-060-120231023

Singh, M., & Verma, J. (2023). The Effect of Entrepreneurship Education on Micro-entrepreneurial Outcomes Funded by MFIs. *European Conference on Innovation and Entrepreneurship, 18*(2), 822–830. DOI: 10.34190/ecie.18.2.1486

Singh, S., & Kumar, A. (2024). Investing in the future: An integrated model for analysing user attitudes towards Robo-advisory services with AI integration. *Vilakshan – XIMB. Journal of Management*, *21*. Advance online publication. DOI: 10.1108/xjm-03-2024-0046

Sipola, J., Saunila, M., & Ukko, J. (2023). Adopting artificial intelligence in sustainable business. *Journal of Cleaner Production*, *426*, 139197. DOI: 10.1016/j.jclepro.2023.139197

Smith, R. (2024, April 9). *The Power of Positivity: The Benefits of a Positive Mindset at Work - Thrive4Life*. Thrive4Life. https://www.thrive4life.co.uk/blog/the-power-of-positivity-the-benefits-of-a-positive-mindset-at-work/

Somers, M. (2022, November 23). *3 traits of an entrepreneurial mindset*. MIT Sloan. https://mitsloan.mit.edu/ideas-made-to-matter/3-traits-entrepreneurial-mindset

Spector, J. M., & Ma, S. (2019). Inquiry and critical thinking skills for the next generation: From artificial intelligence back to human intelligence. *Smart Learning Environments*, *6*(1). Advance online publication. DOI: 10.1186/s40561-019-0088-z

Stein, P. B. W., Rooprai, G., & Kludovac, T. (2024). *Raising United States (U.S.) 23 Trillion Dollars Greening Banks and Capital Markets for Growth: G20 Input Paper on Emerging Markets*. World Bank. https://documents.worldbank.org/curated/en/995131540533377620/Raising-United-States-U-S-23-Trillion-Dollars-Greening-Banks-and-Capital-Markets-for-Growth-G20-Input-Paper-on-Emerging-Markets

Suboyin, Eldred, Thatcher, Rehman, Gee, & Anjum. (2023). *Environomics Framework for Sustainable Business Practices: Industrial Case Studies on True Impact Reduction and Process Optimization Through AI*. DOI: 10.2118/214459-ms

Swartz, T. (2024, December 10). *Scientists pinpoint key attribute of people who have more willpower — how to get it yourself*. New York Post. https://nypost.com/2024/12/10/health/scientists-pinpoint-key-attribute-of-people-with-willpower

TechVidvan. (2020, August). *Advantages and Disadvantages of TensorFlow*. TechVidvan. https://techvidvan.com/tutorials/pros-and-cons-of-tensorflow

Tennekoon, C. E. (2023, June 23). *The 4 P's of Innovation: Exploring the Dimensions of Change*. Www.linkedin.com

The Offsite Guide. (2024). *Local vs. Global: Is Local Sourcing Always the Most Sustainable Option in Construction?* The Offsite Guide. https://theoffsiteguide.com/articles/local-vs-global-is-local-sourcing-always-the-most-sustainable-option-in-construction

The Royal Docks Team. (2016). *Launching the Royal Docks Centre for Sustainability*. The Royal Docks. https://royaldocks.london/whats-on/launching-the-royal-docks-centre-for-sustainability

Tidd, J., & Bessant, J. (2020). *Managing innovation: Integrating technological, market and organizational change* (7th ed.). Wiley.

Toxopeus, H., Achterberg, E., & Polzin, F. (2021). How can firms access bank finance for circular business model innovation? *Business Strategy and the Environment*, *30*(6), 2773–2795. DOI: 10.1002/bse.2893

Trencher, G., Taeihagh, A., & Yarime, M. (2020). Overcoming barriers to developing and diffusing fuel-cell vehicles: Governance strategies and experiences in Japan. *Energy Policy*, *142*, 111533. DOI: 10.1016/j.enpol.2020.111533

UAGC. (2021, December 8). *9 Characteristics of the Entrepreneurial Mindset*. The University of Arizona Global Campus. https://www.uagc.edu/blog/9-characteristics-of-the-entrepreneurial-mindset

UNEP. (2021, July 6). Five young entrepreneurs embracing sustainable business models. *Unep.org*. https://www.unep.org/news-and-stories/story/five-young-entrepreneurs-embracing-sustainable-business-models

UNESCO. (2025). https://unesdoc.unesco.org/ark:/48223/pf0000379936

Unlimited, G. (2024, November 4). *Naglaa's Green Solution for Environmental Restoration*. YouTube. https://www.youtube.com/watch?v=Y2aQDBrjWVc

van den Besselaar, P., & Mom, C. (2022). The effect of writing style on success in grant applications. *Journal of Informetrics*, *16*(1), 101257. DOI: 10.1016/j.joi.2022.101257

Vincenzo, B., Annalisa, C., & Elisa, U. (2020). Network dynamics in business angel group investment decisions. *Journal of Corporate Finance*, *66*(101812), 101812. DOI: 10.1016/j.jcorpfin.2020.101812

Voulvoulis, N., Giakoumis, T., Hunt, C., Kioupi, V., Petrou, N., Souliotis, I., & Vaghela, C., & binti Wan Rosely, WIH. (2022). Systems Thinking as a Paradigm Shift for Sustainability Transformation. *Global Environmental Change*, *75*(102544), 102544. DOI: 10.1016/j.gloenvcha.2022.102544

Walker, J. (2024, June 4). *Understanding Different Types of Startup Funding | Rooled*. Rooled. https://rooled.com/resources/understanding-different-types-of-startup-funding/

Walsack, J. (2019, July 23). *How to Prepare Your Business to Raise Funding*. Https://Www.uschamber.com/Co. https://www.uschamber.com/co/run/business-financing/how-to-prepare-to-raise-funding

Walsh, N. (2023). *Business Bites: Writing a business case - ABDO*. ABDO. https://www.abdo.org.uk/news/business-bites-writing-a-business-case/

Wang, Y., & Witlox, F. (2025). Global trends in electric vehicle adoption and the impact of environmental awareness, user attributes, and barriers. *Energy Reports*, *13*, 1125–1137. DOI: 10.1016/j.egyr.2024.12.054

Wasim, J., Youssef, M. H., Christodoulou, I., & Reinhardt, R. (2023). The Path to Entrepreneurship: The Role of Social Networks in Driving Entrepreneurial Learning and Education. *Journal of Management Education*, *48*(3). Advance online publication. DOI: 10.1177/10525629231219235

Williamson, M. (2021, September 26). *Clive Sinclair: Visionary who helped create the first home computers*. The Independent. https://www.independent.co.uk/news/obituaries/clive-sinclair-pc-computer-c5-obituary-death-b1926557.html

WMO. (2024a). *State of the Climate 2024 update for COP 2029*. Wmo.int; WMO. https://library.wmo.int/viewer/69075/?offset=#page=4&viewer=picture&o=bookmarks&n=0&q=

WMO. (2024b, October). *WMO report highlights growing shortfalls and stress in global water resources*. World Meteorological Organization. https://wmo.int/news/media-centre/wmo-report-highlights-growing-shortfalls-and-stress-global-water-resources

World Economic Forum. (2023, April 30). *The Future of Jobs Report 2023*. World Economic Forum. https://www.weforum.org/publications/the-future-of-jobs-report-2023/

WPAB. (2024, November 20). *Creating a Financial Management Plan for Your Grant Proposal - fundsforNGOs - Grants and Resources for Sustainability*. FundsforNGOs - Grants and Resources for Sustainability - Grants and Resources for Sustainability. https://www.fundsforngos.org/how-to-write-a-proposal/creating-a-financial-management-plan-for-your-grant-proposal/

Yadav, N., & Mankavil Kovil Veettil, N. (2021). Developing a comprehensive business case for sustainability: an inductive study. *International Journal of Organizational Analysis, ahead-of-print*(ahead-of-print). https://doi.org/DOI: 10.1108/ijoa-04-2020-2146

Yasir, N., Babar, M., Mehmood, H. S., Xie, R., & Guo, G. (2023). The Environmental Values Play a Role in the Development of Green Entrepreneurship to Achieve Sustainable Entrepreneurial Intention. *Sustainability*, *15*(8), 6451. DOI: 10.3390/su15086451

Zamfir Cristina Mihaela. (2018). Reprogramming Mind for Business Success. *Ovidius University Annals: Economic Sciences Series, 18*(2), 372–375. https://doaj.org/article/3e51bd939b1f4e5fbedbca7d1fedfa4a

Zao, S. (2024). Intrapreneurship Examples. https://www.studiozao.com/knowledge/intrapreneurship-examples

Zhang, Y. (2020). How Venture Capitalists Bet: Evidence from Two Randomized Controlled Trials. SSRN *Electronic Journal*. DOI: 10.2139/ssrn.3724424

Zhu, L., Mou, W., Lai, Y., Lin, J., & Luo, P. (2024). Language and cultural bias in AI: Comparing the performance of large language models developed in different countries on Traditional Chinese Medicine highlights the need for localized models. *Journal of Translational Medicine*, *22*(1). Advance online publication. DOI: 10.1186/s12967-024-05128-4 PMID: 38553705

Chapter 7
Ethical Entrepreneurship:
Navigating the Path to Responsible Business

Mustafa Kayyali
https://orcid.org/0000-0003-3300-262X
Maaref University of Applied Sciences, Idlib, Syria

ABSTRACT

This chapter examines the developing notion of ethical entrepreneurship concerning AI-driven business strategies and sustainability ideals. As artificial intelligence transforms sectors and business models, entrepreneurs encounter substantial opportunities and considerable ethical dilemmas. The incorporation of AI into entrepreneurial operations requires a responsible strategy to guarantee that innovation does not compromise social, environmental, or economic welfare. The chapter provides insights into how entrepreneurs can establish businesses that are both profitable and socially and environmentally responsible by examining ethical dilemmas in AI decision-making, the significance of a responsible business culture, and the incorporation of sustainability principles. The chapter finishes by delineating solutions to surmount the hurdles of adopting ethical AI and the course for promoting responsible, sustainable enterprise in the AI epoch.

INTRODUCTION

The fast growth of artificial intelligence (AI) has provided tremendous potential across every sector of modern business (Michael, 2024). AI's potential to automate procedures, analyze enormous quantities of data and make predictive judgments is revolutionizing industries—from healthcare and banking to manufacturing and retail. As AI becomes more embedded in corporate processes, it is transforming the

DOI: 10.4018/979-8-3373-1107-4.ch007

interactions companies have with their customers, workers, and partners. However, with these improvements comes a rising need for organizations to negotiate the ethical, social, and environmental aspects of employing AI technology. AI is not only a tool for innovation but a strong force that demands serious consideration of its greater influence on society and the planet at large (Goralski & Tan, 2020). As AI's influence rises, so too does the obligation of businesses to ensure that their AI-driven initiatives are not only efficient and lucrative but also ethical and sustainable. Entrepreneurs must struggle with a complicated landscape where technical possibilities interact with moral considerations, legal requirements, and society expectations. The convergence of AI and business necessitates that entrepreneurs identify and handle the ethical concerns and possible hazards connected with these advances while working to maximize their beneficial consequences. For organizations to survive in this AI-driven era, they must discover methods to utilize AI's capabilities without sacrificing principles such as justice, openness, responsibility, and sustainability.

This chapter tries to study the ethical and sustainable integration of AI into business models, with a special focus on how entrepreneurs may develop responsible AI-driven companies that benefit both their organizations and society. Ethical entrepreneurship, in the context of AI, includes more than conforming to a set of norms or regulations. It demands a basic commitment to establishing systems that accord with social ideals and contribute to the greater good. AI has great promise, but the route to reaching its potential in a way that is ethical and sustainable is plagued with problems. From issues of prejudice and discrimination in algorithmic decision-making to worries about the environmental effect of AI research, businesses must negotiate these challenges carefully and responsibly.

One of the most crucial components of responsible AI entrepreneurship is ensuring that AI technologies are employed in ways that promote human well-being, justice, and equity (Chang & Ke, 2024). The ethical consequences of AI are not merely theoretical problems; they have real-world effects. For example, biased algorithms might perpetuate inequality in hiring practices, loan choices, and criminal justice outcomes. Lack of transparency in AI systems can damage confidence in companies and lead to consumer unhappiness. Furthermore, AI systems that emphasize business over humans might deepen societal differences, producing riches and opportunities for some while leaving others behind. Addressing these concerns demands a deliberate effort by entrepreneurs to emphasize ethical considerations in their AI plans, ensuring that their solutions are not just creative but also aligned with social norms. Equally crucial is the notion of sustainability. As AI continues to progress, the environmental effect of its research and implementation is becoming a crucial problem. The energy consumption necessary for training big AI models and maintaining data centers may be enormous, contributing to the rising environmental issues linked with technology. Entrepreneurs must not only examine the long-term impact of their company activities but also research methods to build AI technologies that reduce their ecological imprint. Sustainable AI solutions are those that combine technology advancement with environmental responsibility, ensuring that AI contributes to global sustainability goals rather than increasing environmental deterioration.

Moreover, the significance of openness and accountability in AI-driven corporate operations cannot be emphasized. The opacity of AI decision-making processes has prompted concerns about accountability, particularly when AI systems make vital judgments that affect people's lives (Cheong, 2024). From driverless automobiles to predictive police, the consequences of AI-driven judgments can be substantial. For companies to preserve confidence with their stakeholders—customers, workers, investors, and society at large—they must guarantee that their AI systems are visible, explainable, and responsible. Clear information about how AI systems make choices, as well as the capacity to hold companies accountable for the results of those decisions, is vital for sustaining the ethical integrity of AI-driven organizations. This chapter will dive into the ethical difficulties and possibilities that exist at the nexus of AI, entrepreneurship, and sustainability. By analyzing the concepts of ethical AI, the necessity of justice, the role of transparency and accountability, and the need for sustainable business practices, the chapter attempts to give a comprehensive framework for entrepreneurs looking to integrate AI into their enterprises ethically.

Figure 1. Ethical AI Entrepreneurship Framework

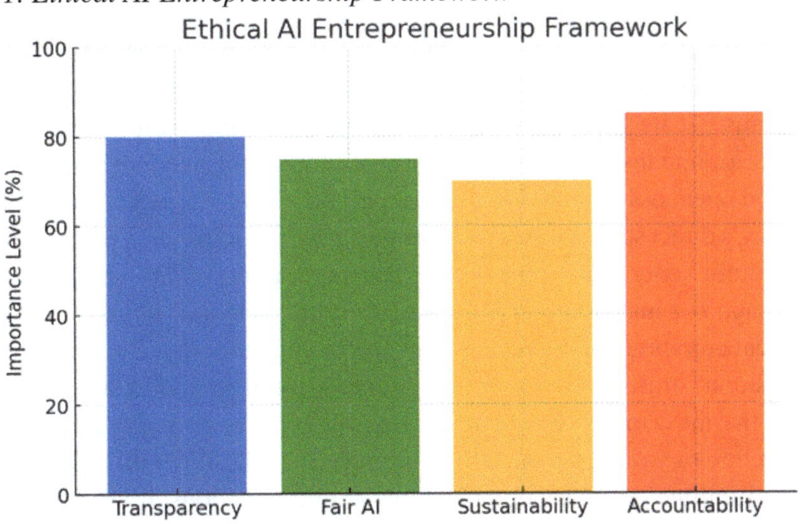

Furthermore, it will address how organizations may utilize AI to promote innovation while ensuring that their operations are aligned with ethical norms and environmental goals. Through this research, the chapter will give vital insights into how entrepreneurs may establish AI-driven companies that are not only lucrative but also socially responsible and morally sound. As businesses continue to grow in the age of AI, entrepreneurs must examine the larger consequences of their actions. The stakes are enormous, and the consequences of immoral or unsustainable AI techniques can be far-reaching. Yet, with deliberate study and a commitment to responsible innovation, AI has the potential to be a revolutionary force for good. By developing a culture of ethical AI entrepreneurship, organizations may not only win in the marketplace but also contribute to the construction of a more equal, just, and sustainable society. The road toward responsible AI entrepreneurship is not without its hurdles, but it provides great benefits for those who approach it with a profound sense of duty and a determination to have a positive effect.

DEFINING ETHICAL ENTREPRENEURSHIP IN THE AGE OF AI

Ethical entrepreneurship is a notion that has grown dramatically over the past few decades, particularly as companies have become more conscious of the social, environmental, and economic implications of their activities (Crane et al, 2019). This transition has grown even more obvious in the era of artificial intelligence (AI) when technology has begun to play an increasingly dominating role in defining business models and decision-making processes. In this age of fast technology innovation, ethical entrepreneurship today needs a deeper assessment of how AI might be integrated into business activities while keeping a strong commitment to ethical norms. At its foundation, ethical entrepreneurship includes founding and maintaining a company that values not just profitability but also social responsibility, fairness, and openness (Ahsan, 2020). This obligation extends beyond the bounds of the company's direct stakeholders to cover the broader community, the environment, and even future generations. It is about ensuring that corporate operations do not create damage but instead contribute positively to society at large. In the context of AI, ethical entrepreneurship implies incorporating modern technical capabilities into commercial strategy without abandoning essential ethical ideals.

One of the most important difficulties for entrepreneurs today is the interplay between technology progress and ethical concerns (Vallaster et al, 2019). AI, as an emerging discipline, provides organizations with tremendous tools that may boost productivity, improve customer experience, and drive development. However, these benefits typically come with major hazards. From data privacy difficulties to algorithmic biases, AI poses new ethical dilemmas that entrepreneurs must handle carefully. For example, AI algorithms are widely employed in employment, marketing, and decision-making processes, and without proper control, these systems might unwittingly perpetuate prejudices and injustices. Therefore, ethical entrepreneurship in the age of AI demands a full grasp of how technology interacts with human behavior and society standards. In the classic sense, entrepreneurship has always been about spotting possibilities, taking risks, and inventing in ways that provide value for consumers and profit for enterprises. However, the definition of value in ethical entrepreneurship is wider. Entrepreneurs must now consider how their ideas contribute to society and the environment. Do they create inclusion, justice, and equal opportunity? Do they assist solve important global concerns such as climate change, poverty, and inequality? Ethical entrepreneurs are individuals who mix the drive for financial success to generate meaningful social change.

When it comes to AI, this balancing gets much more challenging. AI technologies can dramatically affect society, both favorably and badly (Acemoglu, 2021). On the one hand, AI may empower organizations to solve complicated issues, expedite processes, and make better-informed decisions. For example, AI is being utilized in healthcare to produce individualized treatment plans, in agriculture to maximize crop yields, and in energy to enhance efficiency and decrease waste. On the other hand, AI raises worries about the loss of employment due to automation, the consolidation of power in the hands of a few tech companies, and the possibility of privacy violations through data exploitation. Ethical entrepreneurship in the era of AI demands organizations to proactively address these difficulties by implementing responsible practices that stress justice, transparency, and accountability (Buhmann & Fieseler, 2021). Entrepreneurs must not just guarantee that their AI systems are built to be efficient and productive but also that they are fair, unbiased, and respectful of privacy. This implies designing AI systems that are transparent in their decision-making processes, allowing users to understand how and why particular conclusions are obtained. It also entails developing controls to avoid the exploitation of data and ensuring that AI algorithms do not propagate negative prejudices or discrimination.

At the same time, ethical entrepreneurship also requires comprehending the larger implications of AI for society as a whole (Du & Xie, 2021). Entrepreneurs must examine the long-term consequences of AI on jobs, economic inequality, and social dynamics. For instance, AI has the potential to displace labor in areas such as manufacturing, retail, and transportation, resulting in job losses and economic instability. Ethical entrepreneurs must think about how to offset these consequences by investing in reskilling programs, generating new employment in growing areas, and ensuring that the advantages of AI are dispersed equitably. Ethical entrepreneurship in the AI era requires developing a culture of accountability inside companies. AI systems, like any other technology, are only as ethical as the humans who create and implement them. Therefore, entrepreneurs must establish a culture that supports ethical decision-making and guarantees that workers, stakeholders, and AI developers are held accountable for their activities. This may be done by defining clear ethical rules for the use of AI, supporting open debates about the ethical implications of AI technologies, and ensuring that ethical concerns are integrated into every level of the AI development process.

Another key facet of ethical entrepreneurship in the era of AI is the significance of collaboration and participation with a broad variety of stakeholders (Häußermann & Lütge, 2022). In the past, companies could generally operate inside their circles of influence, making decisions that affected just their immediate stakeholders. However, the interwoven structure of today's global economy means that the activities of one company can have far-reaching effects on society, the environment, and the economy. As such, ethical entrepreneurs must engage with a wide range of stakeholders, including consumers, workers, regulators, and civil society groups, to ensure that their company operations correspond with larger social goals. This partnership extends to the development and usage of AI technology. Entrepreneurs must collaborate closely with AI academics, politicians, and other important stakeholders to ensure that AI systems are created and deployed in ways that are socially acceptable and aligned with the public good. This can involve pushing for regulations that encourage ethical AI development, supporting projects that address the possible social and economic implications of AI, and ensuring that AI technologies are available to all, not just a privileged few.

Furthermore, the ethical entrepreneur in the era of AI must also be forward-thinking. AI is a field of fast technical growth, and what appears like an ethical answer now may not remain so in the future (Stahl, 2021). As AI continues to advance, ethical entrepreneurs must stay fluid and adaptive, continually reassessing the effect of their business practices and technology. They must be prepared to handle new ethical concerns as they occur and ensure that their business plans stay consistent with the key values of fairness, openness, and accountability. Ethical entrepreneurship in the era of AI is about more than just embracing new technology; it is about ensuring that these technologies are employed in ways that benefit society as a whole. It demands a profound awareness of the ethical implications of AI and a dedication to developing enterprises that are not just lucrative but also socially responsible and sustainable. Entrepreneurs must combine the urge for innovation with a dedication to justice, openness, and responsibility, knowing that the future of business is closely related to the principles we support today. As AI continues to transform the world of business, ethical entrepreneurship will be vital to ensuring that this technology is utilized for good, building a more inclusive, sustainable, and equitable future for all.

THE INTERSECTION OF ETHICS, SUSTAINABILITY, AND ENTREPRENEURSHIP

The convergence of ethics, sustainability, and entrepreneurship has become one of the most critical topics in modern business (Azmat et al, 2023). As global challenges continue to mount, particularly around environmental degradation, social inequality, and economic instability, business leaders and entrepreneurs are increasingly recognizing the importance of integrating ethical considerations and sustainable practices into their business models. This increased awareness is not only a response to public demands or legal needs; it is a reflection of a profound, fundamental shift in how businesses understand their position in society. For decades, traditional company strategies were constructed solely around the notion of profit maximization, with little concern for the larger social or environmental consequences of their activities. The ultimate objective was to create returns for shareholders, frequently at the expense of workers, customers, or the environment. However, as the world has evolved, this limited concentration on profit has increasingly been challenged. Consumers, workers, and other stakeholders today demand corporations to show corporate social responsibility (CSR), transparency, and a commitment to ethical conduct and sustainability. In this setting, the junction of ethics, sustainability, and entrepreneurship creates a strong new paradigm that aims to balance the pursuit of profit with the larger objective of achieving beneficial societal and environmental benefits.

At its foundation, ethical entrepreneurship entails making business decisions that correspond with moral principles, respect human rights, and promote fairness and justice (Arnold et al, 2020). Entrepreneurs are no longer just concerned with financial success; they are also focused on ensuring that their actions contribute positively to society. This may mean promoting the well-being of employees, helping local communities, or investing in ecologically sustainable technology. In many respects, ethical entrepreneurship represents a more holistic approach to business—one that acknowledges the interconnection of social, environmental, and economic aspects. Sustainability, on the other hand, refers to the capacity to fulfill the demands of the present without compromising the ability of future generations to meet their requirements. It is an idea that has acquired substantial support in recent decades, particularly in response to rising worries about climate change, resource depletion, and environmental degradation. Sustainability in business means adopting strategies that limit harm to the environment, promote social fairness, and maintain long-term economic success. This may take various forms, from decreasing carbon emissions and waste to procuring materials sustainably and ensuring fair labor standards across the supply chain. Entrepreneurship, in its classic sense, has always been about innovation, risk-taking, and producing value. However, the growth of ethical entrepreneurship has brought a new dimension to this notion. It is no longer enough for entrepreneurs to build enterprises that just generate profit; they must now examine the social and environmental repercussions of their ventures. This shift in thinking is particularly crucial in the age of globalization and rapid technology breakthroughs, where companies can influence whole sectors and modify cultural standards. Entrepreneurs nowadays are entrusted not just with recognizing market possibilities but also with ensuring that their enterprises are contributing to the greater good.

The convergence of ethics, sustainability, and entrepreneurship becomes more crucial when we examine the larger context in which companies operate (Crane et al, 2019). The difficulties of the modern world—climate change, inequality, and resource scarcity—require corporations to go beyond basic compliance with laws and regulations. Instead, they must proactively seek out methods to produce value while simultaneously tackling these global concerns. This is where the role of entrepreneurship becomes so vital. Entrepreneurs are typically at the vanguard of innovation and change, producing new goods, services, and business models that may create positive development. One of the primary ways in which entrepreneurship may interact with sustainability is through the development of green technology and environmentally friendly business practices. As the globe grapples with the pressing need to cut carbon emissions and prevent climate change, entrepreneurs have a unique chance to establish businesses that offer answers to these concerns (Lisniak, 2024). This can entail researching renewable energy technology, making goods that are manufactured from sustainable materials, or giving services that assist other companies lessen their environmental effect. The emergence of the green economy has spawned a new surge of entrepreneurial activity, with startups and established corporations alike seeking to discover innovative solutions to global environmental concerns.

However, sustainability is not only about environmental issues; it also covers social and economic elements. Ethical entrepreneurs must also evaluate how their companies influence the communities in which they operate. This can mean assuring fair salaries and working conditions for employees, supporting local suppliers, or investing in community development programs. In a worldwide economy, it is simple for companies to exploit inexpensive labor and resources from poor countries, frequently at the price of workers' rights and environmental sustainability. Ethical entrepreneurship challenges this paradigm by highlighting the necessity of fair and ethical business practices that benefit all stakeholders, not just shareholders. Sustainability also extends to the economic effect of enterprises. A truly sustainable company plan must be economically viable in the long run. This challenges entrepreneurs to go beyond short-term profit maximization and focus on establishing companies that can survive over the long haul. This can mean reinvesting revenues into innovation, diversifying income streams, or maintaining strong connections with consumers and suppliers. Entrepreneurs that embrace sustainability are frequently more robust in the face of economic problems because they have established companies that are adaptive and focused on long-term value generation, rather than merely chasing the next big profit opportunity.

The ethical dimension of entrepreneurship entails making choices that accord with core moral beliefs (Wittmer, 2019). This involves operating with integrity, being truthful in company procedures, and treating workers, customers, and other stakeholders with respect and fairness. Ethical entrepreneurs are individuals who value the well-being of people and the earth before personal or corporate gain. In practice, this involves making decisions that reflect a commitment to social justice, human rights, and environmental sustainability. For example, an ethical entrepreneur could opt to pay their workers a fair salary, even if it means compromising short-term earnings. They could prefer to get goods from suppliers who adhere to ethical labor standards, even if it means paying a premium for such items. Ethical entrepreneurship also entails responsibility. In an increasingly connected world, businesses are under greater scrutiny than ever before. Consumers, investors, and other stakeholders want companies to be open about their methods and to accept responsibility for the consequences of their activities (Barauskaite & Streimikiene, 2021). Ethical entrepreneurs acknowledge that they must be accountable not only to their shareholders but also to the larger community and the environment. This might entail providing information about corporate practices, participating in communication with stakeholders, and taking meaningful efforts to remediate any negative affects their company may have produced. The convergence of ethics, sustainability, and entrepreneurship is not without its obstacles. One of the primary hurdles is the friction between profitability and social responsibility. Many entrepreneurs find it challenging to combine the necessity to earn profit with the desire to create a beneficial social or environmental effect. This conflict may be particularly problematic in businesses where competition is severe and margins are small. However, research has shown that companies that embrace ethical and sustainable practices are generally more profitable in the long term. By creating good relationships with consumers, workers, and other stakeholders, ethical entrepreneurs may generate a devoted customer base that recognizes their commitment to social and environmental responsibility.

In addition to the obstacles of integrating profitability with sustainability, ethical entrepreneurs also confront the task of negotiating complicated global supply networks and regulatory contexts. In many circumstances, corporations are operating in countries with poor labor laws or environmental standards, which might generate a temptation to take shortcuts to minimize expenses. However, ethical entrepreneurs know that this short-term thinking can have long-term detrimental effects, both for their company and for society. By choosing to act responsibly and ethically, entrepreneurs may help raise standards in the sectors and places where they do business, producing a ripple effect that encourages others to follow suit. The convergence of ethics, sustainability, and entrepreneurship creates a great potential for entrepreneurs to establish companies that are not only successful but also contribute to a better society. By embracing these values, entrepreneurs can promote good change, solve important global concerns, and establish companies that are not just successful but also meaningful. The future of entrepreneurship depends on the ability to establish companies that balance the pursuit of profit with a commitment to social and environmental responsibility. As the globe faces increasingly complex issues, the role of entrepreneurs in building a sustainable and ethical future has never been more crucial.

AI-DRIVEN BUSINESS MODELS: OPPORTUNITIES FOR ETHICAL INNOVATION

AI-driven business models are quickly altering sectors throughout the world (Soni et al, 2019). From customer service chatbots to predictive analytics, artificial intelligence (AI) is revolutionizing how organizations operate, engage with consumers, and create value. As the technology continues to improve, its potential to promote ethical innovation in business has become increasingly obvious. AI can offer new approaches to improve company operations, increase consumer experiences, and address social concerns. Yet, for AI to effectively support ethical innovation, organizations must embrace AI-driven models that value transparency, justice, and sustainability. By employing AI in responsible ways, businesses may achieve not just economic outcomes but also significant societal effects, creating a new benchmark for ethical entrepreneurship in the digital age. The incorporation of AI into business models brings up various prospects for innovation, efficiency, and customization. AI systems can examine massive volumes of data to reveal insights that would be hard for humans to perceive. By automating procedures, companies may boost productivity, cut operating expenses, and strengthen decision-making skills. AI can improve supply chains, expedite customer service operations, and generate individualized marketing tactics that fit specific consumer demands. The potential of AI to forecast trends, actions, and results can also help organizations design novel goods and services suited to specific market demands. In this approach, AI can deliver extraordinary corporate development, efficiency, and consumer delight.

However, with tremendous promise comes responsibility. As AI becomes increasingly integrated into commercial operations, companies must confront the ethical consequences of its use. Ethical AI refers to the development and implementation of AI systems that correspond with moral concepts, such as justice, responsibility, transparency, and respect for privacy. One of the primary issues around AI is the possibility of bias in algorithms (Panch et al, 2019). If AI systems are educated on biased data, they might perpetuate inequality and reinforce existing social prejudices. For example, face recognition technology has been challenged for its racial biases, which can lead to discriminatory consequences. Similarly, AI systems employed in recruiting procedures might unwittingly favor certain demographic groups over others, perpetuating prejudice and inequality in the workforce. To solve these concerns, organizations must ensure that their AI models are created with fairness in mind. This requires carefully selecting and curating training material, routinely evaluating AI systems for bias, and being open about how AI judgments are made. By doing so, companies can ensure that their AI-driven models are not just successful but also ethical. Moreover, corporations must be committed to constant monitoring and adjustment of AI systems to guarantee that they continue to act fairly as social norms and values develop.

Beyond justice, another crucial ethical factor is privacy. AI-driven business models rely significantly on data, and much of this data might be personal or sensitive (Selvarajan, 2021). Companies that collect and analyze consumer data must be honest about how it is used and guarantee that data privacy is maintained. This requires organizations to develop comprehensive data protection procedures and comply with legislation such as the General Data Protection Regulation (GDPR) in the European Union. Consumers nowadays are more aware than ever of the value of their data and want companies to manage it appropriately. Businesses that respect client privacy and are honest about their data practices may generate trust and loyalty, leading to long-term success. AI also gives chances for corporations to contribute to social and environmental sustainability. One of the biggest concerns confronting the globe today is climate change, and companies have a crucial role to play in minimizing its consequences. AI can help organizations minimize their carbon footprint by optimizing energy consumption, eliminating waste, and boosting supply chain efficiency. For example, AI may be used to forecast energy consumption trends and offer solutions to cut energy use during peak hours.

Figure 2. AI's Carbon Footprint in Data Centers

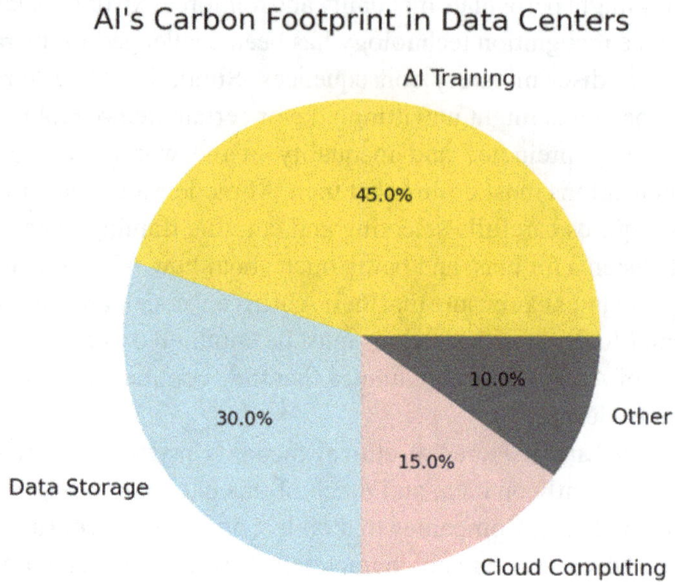

AI may also assist companies locate more sustainable suppliers, optimize transportation routes to decrease fuel usage, and produce eco-friendly products and services. In this approach, AI may be a strong tool for advancing sustainability and decreasing the environmental effect of company operations. AI-driven business models may potentially contribute to social good by solving important global concerns such as poverty, inequality, and access to healthcare (Madavarapu et al, 2024). AI has the potential to enhance healthcare outcomes by providing more accurate diagnoses, tailored treatments, and better resource allocation. For example, AI can analyze medical data to uncover trends and predict health outcomes, allowing for earlier identification of illnesses and more effective therapies. In developing countries, AI-powered mobile health apps can deliver remote healthcare services to underserved groups, enhancing access to medical care and lowering health inequities. By adopting AI to address these difficulties, organizations may produce good social impact while simultaneously producing value for their stakeholders.

In addition to enhancing sustainability and social effects, AI-driven business models may stimulate creativity by enabling organizations to explore new goods and services. The capacity of AI to scan big datasets and identify new patterns can help organizations remain ahead of the curve and design solutions that fit shifting client demands. For instance, AI may be used to forecast consumer preferences and produce personalized products or services suited to individual desires. AI may also assist organizations uncover new market possibilities by monitoring customer behavior and detecting holes in the market (Aaker & Moorman, 2023). By embracing AI in this way, organizations can drive innovation and create goods and services that are not just lucrative but also meaningful to their consumers. While the potential for AI to drive ethical innovation is great, organizations must also address the possible dangers and obstacles connected with its usage. One of the biggest threats is the influence of AI on jobs. As AI automates jobs and processes, there is fear that technology might lead to job displacement and worsen economic inequality. This is particularly true in businesses that rely significantly on physical labor or repetitive operations. However, AI also creates chances for businesses to generate new jobs and skills. For example, companies that employ AI may need to recruit data scientists, AI engineers, and other technical expertise to create, install, and manage AI systems. Moreover, AI can generate new positions in areas like as customer service, content production, and product development. To guarantee that AI-driven business models are morally appropriate, corporations must engage in training and reskilling initiatives to assist workers adjust to the changing labor market.

Another problem is the possibility for AI to be used unethically, such as in monitoring or manipulation (Veluru et al, 2024). AI technologies that track staff productivity or consumer behavior might raise issues about privacy and autonomy. Similarly, AI algorithms applied in marketing or advertising may be misused to control customer behavior, leading to unethical actions such as deceptive advertising or exploitation of vulnerable populations. To avoid these concerns, companies must create explicit ethical norms for the development and use of AI. This involves ensuring that AI technologies are utilized in ways that respect individual rights, promote justice, and avoid damage. To support ethical AI innovation, companies must also cooperate with other stakeholders, including governments, regulators, and civil society groups. Governments have a significant role in setting legislation and policies that ensure the proper use of AI. For example, the European Union has suggested legislation to guarantee that AI is created and utilized in ways that are ethical, transparent, and compatible with human rights. Collaboration between companies and government is crucial to building a regulatory environment that supports innovation while preserving public interests (Torfing, 2019). Furthermore, corporations should work with civil society groups, academia, and other stakeholders to ensure that AI is created in ways that are inclusive, diverse, and egalitarian.

The convergence of AI and ethical innovation is a fascinating and dynamic sector that has great potential for businesses to produce value in ways that match social aspirations. By adopting AI-driven business models that stress justice, transparency, and sustainability, organizations may contribute to beneficial social and environmental results while still attaining financial success. The key to unleashing the full potential of AI is to guarantee that its usage is governed by ethical standards that emphasize the well-being of people and the world. As AI continues to alter the future of business, entrepreneurs, business leaders, and legislators must work together to establish AI-driven models that support innovation, accountability, and good change. In this approach, AI may become a tremendous force for good, pushing both ethical corporate practices and profound societal reform.

NAVIGATING ETHICAL DILEMMAS IN AI AND BUSINESS DECISION-MAKING

Navigating ethical challenges in AI and corporate decision-making is a key and more difficult topic that companies must handle as artificial intelligence becomes more thoroughly integrated into the commercial environment (Rezaei et al, 2024). AI-driven solutions are transforming decision-making processes across sectors, enabling organizations to make faster, data-driven choices with unparalleled levels of accuracy and efficiency. However, with these breakthroughs come major ethical problems that deserve serious attention. In many circumstances, AI systems might accidentally add prejudices, breach privacy, and contribute to inequities. This raises a unique issue for corporate executives who must balance the great potential of AI with the requirement for ethical integrity, fairness, and openness in their decision-making processes. At the heart of these ethical problems is the increased dependence on algorithms to make judgments that can have substantial consequences for persons and society (Whittlestone et al, 2019). Whether it's a recruiting algorithm screening candidates, a loan approval system judging creditworthiness, or an AI tool anticipating consumer behavior, these systems are increasingly controlling who gets opportunities, resources, or access to services. Because AI systems are based on enormous databases, their judgments typically mirror trends in past data. While this might make choices look more impartial, it also implies that AI can perpetuate and even magnify existing biases in the data. For example, if an AI system used in recruiting is trained on data that indicates a history of gender or racial biases in hiring, it may unwittingly favor certain groups over others, perpetuating injustice. This raises challenges about the fairness and transparency of AI-driven decision-making, and it is up to business leaders to ensure that these technologies are created and used in ways that promote justice and fairness.

One of the fundamental ethical challenges in AI and commercial decision-making is the challenge of guaranteeing fairness in automated conclusions (Kirat et al, 2023). Traditional decision-making methods, especially when led by human judgment, can be prejudiced and subjective. In many circumstances, these biases are subtle and unintended yet can nonetheless lead to unfair consequences. AI, however, offers the potential to remove human bias from decision-making by employing data-driven models to find trends and make predictions. But the truth is more convoluted. AI systems themselves might inherit biases from the data on which they are taught. If the training data represents social prejudices—such as racial or gender biases—then the AI system will learn and reproduce these biases. This can result in biased actions, whether it's in hiring practices, lending, healthcare, or criminal justice systems. The question then becomes: how can corporations verify that their AI systems are free from these biases? This is not a straightforward process. First, companies must be proactive in finding and removing bias in their data. This includes thoroughly reviewing the data that goes into AI systems, ensuring that it is varied, representative, and free from discriminating trends. For instance, organizations must avoid utilizing past data that indicates unjust practices or systematic imbalances, since they would simply help to perpetuate current disadvantages. They must also routinely audit their AI systems to check for biases and guarantee that the judgments produced by the algorithms fit with ethical norms. Additionally, organizations should aim for openness in how AI systems are built and deployed. This includes properly conveying to stakeholders how AI models function, what data is being used, and how choices are being made. This transparency creates trust and guarantees that individuals can understand and dispute decisions that may negatively influence them. A related challenge emerges from the topic of responsibility (Borenstein & Howard, 2021). When AI systems are responsible for making decisions, it might be difficult to establish who is ultimately accountable for the consequences. If an AI system makes an immoral or prejudiced choice, who should be held accountable—the developer who designed the algorithm, the business that deployed it, or the AI system itself? In certain circumstances, the absence of clear accountability can lead to a diffusion of responsibility, when no one takes ownership of the problem. This is especially troubling when AI judgments damage vulnerable persons or groups. To overcome this difficulty, companies must create clear lines of responsibility and guarantee that there is human monitoring in AI-driven decision-making processes. Even if an AI system is capable of making choices independently, there should always be a mechanism in place for human involvement and responsibility.

Furthermore, there are ethical problems around privacy and data security. AI systems are typically driven by large quantities of personal data, and corporations must be cautious in preserving the privacy of individuals. The use of personal data in AI decision-making processes creates substantial privacy concerns, particularly when users are uninformed of how their data is being used or when agreement is not effectively sought (Felzmann et al, 2019). For instance, in industries like healthcare, AI systems that analyze medical data might give useful insights for improving patient outcomes, but they also raise issues about data protection and the possibility of unwanted access to sensitive information. In the sphere of business, organizations must ensure that their AI systems comply with data protection standards, such as the General Data Protection Regulation (GDPR) in Europe, which imposes tight criteria for how personal data is acquired, kept, and utilized. Businesses must be upfront with consumers about how their data is being used and provide them control over their information. This includes offering clients the choice to opt out of data collecting or to have their data anonymized. Another ethical challenge that corporations confront when using AI is the impact on jobs and employment (Kriebitz & Lütge, 2020). As AI systems grow more capable of performing jobs traditionally done by people, there is worry about job displacement and the loss of livelihood for workers. Automation through AI has the potential to dramatically reduce the demand for physical labor and routine activities, but it can also lead to the obsolescence of whole job categories. While AI generates new possibilities in tech, data science, and AI-related industries, it can also worsen economic inequality if displaced workers are not supplied with the required training and assistance to move into other professions. This raises a moral problem for companies that must weigh the cost-saving benefits of AI automation with the ethical duty of preserving workers' employment and lives. Ethical organizations must evaluate how they can help their workforce through reskilling programs and give opportunities for employees to develop new skills in keeping with the changing needs of the labor market.

The ethical challenge of job displacement is further aggravated by the rising usage of AI in decision-making linked to hiring and promotions (Rawashdeh, 2023). AI is routinely used to go through resumes, rate prospects, and even offer suggestions for hiring or promotion choices. While AI can enhance efficiency and reduce human bias in many processes, it also raises questions about fairness and transparency. If AI systems are used to select who gets employed or promoted, there must be explicit restrictions on how the systems are taught and what data they use to make choices. Additionally, companies must ensure that AI-driven recruiting procedures do not unwittingly perpetuate prejudice or bias, such as preferring candidates from particular demographic groups over others. Furthermore, there is a rising worry regarding the dehumanization of recruiting choices, as AI algorithms, rather than human recruiters, select who is most fit for a post. This can damage trust in the recruiting process and make applicants feel as though their credentials and experiences are not being adequately examined. Businesses must carefully assess the benefits of AI in recruiting and promotion against the ethical consequences of diminishing human involvement in these key choices. One of the most urgent ethical challenges in AI and commercial decision-making is the question of openness and explainability (McDermid et al, 2021). AI algorithms are sometimes dubbed "black boxes" because their decision-making processes may be difficult to grasp, even for the humans who designed them. This lack of openness can make it difficult for companies to explain to consumers or stakeholders how certain decisions were taken. For example, in the situation of an

AI system that refuses a loan application, how can the business defend the decision if the reasons behind it are not immediately understood? AI systems that function without explicit explanations can damage confidence and create issues about justice, especially if customers believe that they have been treated unfairly or discriminated against. To solve this challenge, organizations must emphasize the explainability of their AI systems. This entails building algorithms that are not only effective but also transparent, allowing decision-makers and customers to understand how and why choices are being made. By offering transparent explanations of AI choices, organizations can create confidence and guarantee that their AI systems are being utilized ethically and responsibly.

The ethical challenges in AI and commercial decision-making are not easy to overcome, and there is no one-size-fits-all answer (Qiang et al, 2024). However, organizations may overcome these issues by embracing ethical concepts such as fairness, responsibility, openness, and respect for privacy. By emphasizing these principles in the design, implementation, and monitoring of AI systems, organizations may guarantee that AI is utilized to benefit society while limiting harm.

Figure 3. Ethical AI Implementation Timeline

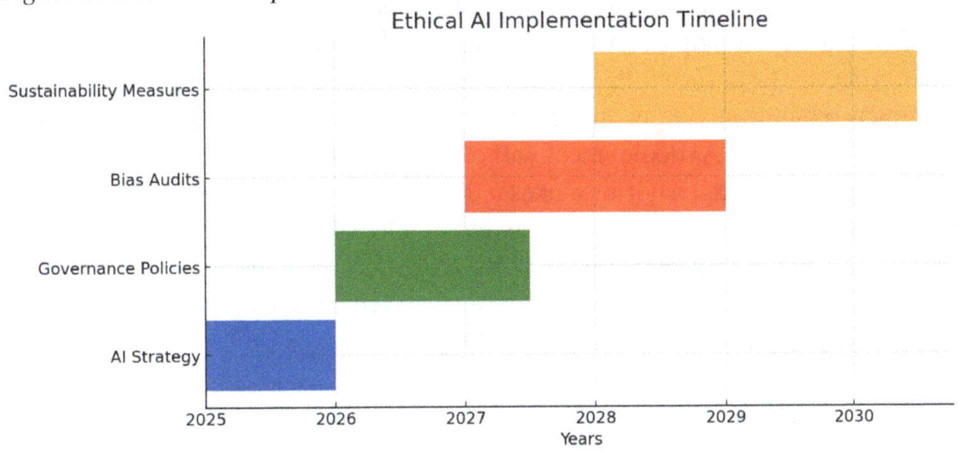

Moreover, organizations must acknowledge that the ethical use of AI is not a one-time effort but an ongoing process that requires regular examination and change. As AI technology improves, so too will the ethical challenges connected with its usage, and organizations must be alert in addressing these issues as they occur. Ultimately, resolving ethical challenges in AI and commercial decision-making needs a dedication to doing what is right, especially when presented with tough choices or conflicting agendas. By taking a proactive, ethical approach to AI, organizations can design AI-driven models that not only drive innovation and profitability but also contribute to the greater benefit of society.

CHALLENGES AND BARRIERS TO IMPLEMENTING ETHICAL AI IN ENTREPRENEURSHIP

The integration of artificial intelligence (AI) into business strategy has the potential to change industries and promote innovation (Reim et al, 2020). However, despite these potentials, AI also brings substantial obstacles and ethical issues, especially when it comes to ensuring that AI systems are created and deployed in ways that accord with ethical norms. As entrepreneurs enter into the AI-driven business environment, they meet a range of problems that make the adoption of ethical AI a complicated and, at times, frightening endeavor. These problems are complex, coming from technical limits, company culture, regulatory frameworks, and cultural expectations. To comprehend the entire magnitude of these problems, it is crucial to explore them in detail and assess the larger implications for the future of entrepreneurship in an AI-driven world. One of the major problems in integrating ethical AI in entrepreneurship is the absence of established frameworks and rules (Du & Xie, 2021). AI technologies are growing at a rapid speed, frequently exceeding the creation of clear legal and ethical norms. This gap between technological innovation and ethical monitoring creates ambiguity for entrepreneurs, forcing them to pass over the uncharted seas of AI deployment without a clear set of regulations. The absence of globally acknowledged norms makes it difficult for entrepreneurs to examine the ethical consequences of their AI systems, especially when such systems are used in high-stakes domains like healthcare, criminal justice, or finance.

Furthermore, even when rules do exist, they typically lack the clarity needed to meet the particular issues brought by AI. Ethical issues in AI are not one-size-fits-all; they vary based on the application, the type of data being utilized, and the possible influence on different stakeholders. For example, an AI system employed in a recruiting process may raise issues about discrimination and bias, while an AI-powered financial service may demand further examination for data protection and security. AI systems are commonly trained on enormous datasets, and if those datasets contain prejudices—whether they be based on race, gender, socioeconomic position, or other factors—the AI system will inherit those biases and may perpetuate them in its decision-making processes (Prince & Schwarcz, 2019). This is particularly troublesome in fields like recruiting, financing, and law enforcement, where biased AI systems can have substantial repercussions, increasing existing inequities and perpetuating discriminatory behaviors. Entrepreneurs who build AI technologies have an ethical obligation to ensure that their systems do not perpetuate or magnify social prejudices, but doing this is no simple undertaking. Identifying and reducing bias in AI systems needs access to varied, high-quality datasets that are representative of the community being served (Hanna et al, 2024). Unfortunately, getting such datasets might be problematic. In many circumstances, the data available for training AI models is inadequate, distorted, or unrepresentative, making it challenging to construct fair and impartial systems. Moreover, even when unbiased data is available, it may not always be adequate to eliminate all sources of bias. AI systems are inherently complicated, and even slight biases can develop through the interplay between numerous factors in a dataset. Entrepreneurs must devote substantial efforts to ensuring that their AI systems are fair, which can be particularly difficult for small enterprises and startups with limited funds and experience in AI ethics.

In addition to issues about fairness, data privacy, and security are other important hurdle to integrating ethical AI in entrepreneurship. AI systems sometimes rely on huge volumes of data, much of which may be personal or sensitive. Whether it's data relating to health, money, or user behavior, AI technologies have the potential to jeopardize privacy if not handled with caution. As AI systems get more proficient, they are increasingly able to gather, evaluate, and make judgments based on sensitive personal data. Entrepreneurs must ensure that their AI systems are created with rigorous data protection safeguards in place to prevent breaches and abuse of personal information. The difficulty of maintaining privacy becomes significantly more challenging in light of AI's ability to learn from data. Machine learning algorithms generally work by finding patterns in vast datasets, and this process may mistakenly divulge private information about individuals. For example, an AI system trained on health data could be able to deduce someone's medical state, even if that information was not explicitly included in the dataset. Entrepreneurs must consequently design AI systems that respect privacy rights, comply with data protection requirements, and prevent unintentional exposures of sensitive information. Achieving this degree of security and privacy is a big issue, especially considering the rising complexity of cyber attacks.

Furthermore, the complexity and opacity of many AI systems represent a considerable obstacle to ethical deployment (Felzmann et al, 2020). Machine learning models, particularly deep learning algorithms, are sometimes referred to as "black boxes" since their decision-making processes are not clearly understood or interpretable. This lack of openness makes it difficult for entrepreneurs to explain how their AI systems arrive at certain conclusions, which in turn presents issues when it comes to enforcing responsibility. For example, if an AI system makes an error or generates biased results, it may be difficult to determine the origin of the problem or to take corrective action. The lack of explainability in AI is especially troublesome in domains such as healthcare, where decisions made by AI systems can have life-or-death effects. If an AI system suggests a certain therapy or diagnosis, healthcare practitioners must understand the reasons behind that choice. However, the complexity of many AI models makes it tough to offer clear and intelligible explanations of their behavior. As a result, entrepreneurs creating AI solutions in high-stakes industries must prioritize efforts to increase the transparency and interpretability of their systems. This is no minor effort since it entails balancing the trade-off between model accuracy and explainability, which may be particularly tough in deep-learning models.

Another key difficulty to integrating ethical AI in entrepreneurship is the push to prioritize profitability and scalability over ethical considerations (Moro-Visconti, 2024). In a competitive business climate, entrepreneurs are typically under pressure to provide results rapidly and to expand their AI systems to meet rising demand. This pressure can often lead to shortcuts in the development process, with ethical issues taking a backseat to financial goals. For example, entrepreneurs may be enticed to deploy AI systems without fully analyzing their potential societal effect or to favor speed above justice when training models. This propensity can result in the creation of AI systems that are not just immoral but also unsustainable in the long run. Entrepreneurs must know that the quest for profitability should not come at the price of ethical responsibility. Building a successful AI-driven company demands a long-term view that combines financial aims with the larger societal implications of the technology. Ethical AI deployment is not only helpful for society but also for businesses themselves, as it helps develop trust with consumers, investors, and other stakeholders. By balancing ethics alongside economics, entrepreneurs may design AI systems that are both ethical and financially feasible.

The absence of appropriate talent and resources in AI ethics constitutes a significant impediment to the successful deployment of ethical AI in entrepreneurship (Faqihi & Miah, 2023). While AI is a fast-emerging discipline, the ethical questions surrounding its research and application are still relatively new and complicated. Many entrepreneurs, particularly those in small enterprises and startups, may not have the technical understanding or skills to negotiate the ethical problems of AI. Additionally, the lack of availability of specialist expertise in AI ethics might make it difficult for entrepreneurs to develop teams that can handle these concerns successfully. Entrepreneurs must invest in education and training to obtain the essential skills and knowledge to manage the ethical challenges of AI. This requires comprehending the technological elements of AI, as well as the social, legal, and moral consequences of its application. The adoption of ethical AI in entrepreneurship is riddled with hurdles and barriers that originate from technology limits, organizational pressures, regulatory uncertainty, and social concerns. Entrepreneurs confront the challenging problem of designing AI systems that are not just creative and profitable but also fair, transparent, and responsible. Overcoming these problems demands a commitment to ethical values, a willingness to engage in responsible AI research, and an awareness that ethical AI is crucial for the long-term success of enterprises and society. While the route to ethical AI in entrepreneurship is not simple, it is a vital one if we are to ensure that AI technologies are employed in ways that benefit mankind and contribute to a sustainable, fair, and egalitarian future.

CHARTING A SUSTAINABLE AND ETHICAL PATH FORWARD FOR AI-DRIVEN BUSINESSES

As the integration of artificial intelligence (AI) into business models becomes increasingly popular, the need for a sustainable and ethical approach to AI-driven entrepreneurship has never been more critical. The capacity of AI to change businesses, simplify processes, and provide new avenues for creativity is evident (Sjödin et al, 2021). However, as organizations employ AI technology, they must also tackle the huge ethical problems that accompany these developments. Navigating these issues demands a commitment to sustainability, not just in environmental terms but also in the social, economic, and ethical elements of corporate operations. Charting a sustainable and ethical way ahead for AI-driven organizations is vital for ensuring that the advantages of AI are achieved while reducing the risks and negative repercussions. The first step in charting a sustainable and ethical route forward for AI-driven enterprises requires understanding the necessity of responsible AI development and deployment. While AI provides great promise for increasing efficiency and addressing complicated issues, it is not without the ability to harm. The fast speed of AI advancement frequently outstrips the ability of corporations and regulatory authorities to set comprehensive rules for ethical AI use. This regulatory gap can result in the creation of AI systems that are prejudiced, opaque, or otherwise destructive. For businesses to stay responsible, they must prioritize the invention of AI technologies that are created with ethical ideals at the forefront.

One of the most critical issues in building ethical AI is maintaining fairness (Modi, 2023). AI systems are routinely trained on enormous datasets, and if these datasets are insufficient, obsolete, or biased, the resultant AI models might propagate harmful preconceptions or unfair behaviors. In many circumstances, AI systems may unwittingly perpetuate existing societal disparities, whether in hiring procedures, loan approvals, or law enforcement. Businesses must acknowledge that the data used to train their AI systems is not neutral, and the potential for bias must be properly minimized. This needs not just a careful examination of the data utilized in AI development but also a commitment to diversity and inclusiveness in the design process. By making measures to guarantee that AI systems are trained on diverse and representative data, organizations may avoid the danger of propagating systemic prejudice. Equally crucial is the problem of openness in AI systems. Many

AI models, particularly those constructed utilizing deep learning approaches, are exceedingly sophisticated and function as “black boxes,” making it impossible for even the architects of these systems to comprehend how they arrive at certain judgments. In commercial applications where decisions have substantial effects, such as healthcare or banking, openness is vital. Customers, clients, and stakeholders need to understand how AI-driven choices are being made to guarantee responsibility. Moreover, openness in AI may create trust, which is vital for the long-term success of any organization. By making their AI systems more interpretable and explainable, organizations may ensure that they are held accountable for the decisions made by their technology.

Accountability is another fundamental value that must be included in the development and deployment of AI systems (Raji et al, 2020). AI systems must not only be transparent but also accountable for the consequences they create. If an AI system makes an error or causes harm, corporations must accept responsibility and seek to remedy the situation. This includes creating clear lines of responsibility inside enterprises so that choices made by AI are traceable to specific persons or teams. Without explicit responsibility, corporations face the danger of permitting AI systems to function in ways that are immoral or destructive without any remedy for the individuals impacted. Entrepreneurs must grasp the necessity of keeping control over AI systems, especially as these technologies become more independent. Sustainability, in the context of AI-driven organizations, goes beyond environmental issues and extends to the social and economic consequences of AI. Businesses must guarantee that their AI systems are created and deployed in ways that contribute to the well-being of society (Feijóo et al, 2020). This requires examining the potential for AI to generate new economic possibilities while simultaneously reducing its potential to aggravate current disparities. For example, while AI has the potential to create employment in new industries, it also threatens to displace people in conventional businesses. To overcome this difficulty, businesses must make efforts to guarantee that the advantages of AI are shared equally, both inside the corporation and throughout society.

One strategy to enhance sustainability in AI-driven organizations is through the creation of AI applications that solve social and environmental concerns (Kulkov et al, 2024). AI has the potential to make major contributions to sustainability goals by helping companies lower their carbon footprints, enhance resource efficiency, and optimize supply chains. By applying AI to sectors such as renewable energy, waste management, and sustainable agriculture, businesses may not only enhance their operations but also contribute to greater social goals. For example, AI-powered systems can assist optimize energy use in buildings, cutting water usage in agriculture, or find possibilities for decreasing waste in industrial processes. These sorts of AI applications combine commercial goals with sustainability aims, offering a win-win outcome for both corporations and society. While the potential for AI to help sustainability is immense, it is equally vital that businesses take responsibility for the environmental effects of their own AI systems. The energy consumption involved with training and operating big AI models may be enormous, and organizations must be cognizant of the environmental cost of AI research. In this context, organizations may implement tactics to offset the environmental effects of their AI systems, such as maximizing the efficiency of their algorithms, employing renewable energy sources for data centers, and ensuring that their AI infrastructure is as energy-efficient as feasible. By including sustainability concerns in the development process, organizations may assist limit the carbon impact of their AI systems.

In addition to justice, transparency, accountability, and sustainability, organizations must also address the ethical implications of data privacy and security while deploying AI. AI systems rely on large volumes of data, most of which are sensitive. Whether it is personal information, financial data, or health-related records, AI systems must be developed to respect the privacy of individuals and guarantee that data is utilized responsibly. As AI systems get more advanced, they can access and analyze more granular data, which raises worries about the potential for privacy abuses. Businesses must establish robust data protection procedures and adhere to rigorous privacy standards to preserve the information entrusted to them (Martin et al, 2019). Ethical AI adoption also demands enterprises to examine the possible influence of their AI systems on society at large. This involves ensuring that AI does not promote injustice, exploitation, or harm to vulnerable communities. For instance, AI systems that are used in hiring or lending procedures must be properly built to avoid discrimination based on race, gender, or other protected characteristics. Similarly, AI applications in law enforcement must be evaluated to ensure that they do not unfairly target marginalized populations or perpetuate institutional prejudices. By examining the larger social consequences of their AI systems, corporations may endeavor to ensure that their technologies are utilized for good and contribute to a more fair and equal society.

Charting a sustainable and ethical way ahead for AI-driven companies demands a shift in mentality (Fernandes et al, 2024). Entrepreneurs must consider AI not simply as a tool for business maximization but as a powerful technology that carries with it substantial ethical obligations. By putting sustainability and ethics into the core of their AI plans, businesses can help guarantee that AI is deployed in ways that benefit both their enterprises and society. This requires a commitment to developing AI systems that are transparent, accountable, fair, and respectful of privacy, as well as a recognition that the long-term success of AI-driven businesses depends on their ability to align their business goals with the broader social and environmental goals of the world. As the AI ecosystem continues to change, organizations must stay watchful and agile (Bozkus, 2023). The difficulties and opportunities posed by AI are continually changing, and companies must be prepared to respond to new ethical concerns as they occur. By retaining a commitment to sustainability and ethical standards, businesses can help guarantee that AI stays a force for good in the world and a driving force for positive change in the corporate landscape. In doing so, they will not only develop trust with consumers, workers, and stakeholders but also pave the path for a more responsible and ethical future for AI in entrepreneurship.

BRIDGING ETHICS AND ACTION: TOWARD A PRACTICAL FRAMEWORK FOR RESPONSIBLE AI ENTREPRENEURSHIP

One of the most persistent challenges in writing about ethics and innovation is the tendency to remain in the realm of abstract ideals. Discussions often orbit around values—justice, fairness, transparency—without ever quite landing on how these are translated into action. But entrepreneurs navigating the age of artificial intelligence do not have the luxury of theory alone. They are faced with daily decisions that require moral clarity and strategic foresight. This chapter, up to now, has made the case for ethical entrepreneurship in AI as a moral imperative and a social necessity. But to move beyond intention, we must now explore how ethical commitments are translated into operational strategies, informed by existing regulatory landscapes, collaborative initiatives, and the lived experience of entrepreneurs who have wrestled with these dilemmas in the real world. The emergence of binding and soft-law regulatory frameworks offers both a constraint and a compass. For instance, the European Union's Artificial Intelligence Act—arguably the most comprehensive legal response to date—lays out a risk-based classification of AI systems, outlining obligations for transparency, human oversight, robustness, and data governance. Its very structure invites entrepreneurs to rethink their product pipelines not just in terms of efficiency or profitability, but also in terms of social risk and public accountability. Importantly, the AI Act moves beyond punitive logic and offers a blueprint for building trust: companies that comply not only avoid fines—they gain legitimacy in a skeptical marketplace.

Parallel to this, initiatives like CDREurope (Collaborative Digital Responsibility) foster cross-border cooperation around digital ethics, especially among SMEs and startups. CDREurope doesn't merely advocate for ethics—it builds the capacity to implement it (Shaw et al, 2024). Through stakeholder workshops, public-private partnerships, and practical toolkits, the initiative helps companies move ethical intention into organizational routines. This convergence of law and collaborative ethics is vital: one offers the minimum threshold, the other helps raise the bar.

Still, no regulation or white paper will capture the messiness of real decisions made under pressure, where trade-offs are inevitable and consequences are not always clear. This is why the inclusion of lived entrepreneurial case studies is crucial—not as anecdotes, but as evidence of what ethical practice can look like in motion. One instructive case is that of a Berlin-based fintech startup, which developed an AI-driven loan assessment model. From the outset, the team recognized the risk of replicating historical financial biases, particularly those affecting immigrants and low-income populations. They responded by assembling an advisory board of social scientists, conducting intersectional audits of their training data, and baking explainability into their user interface—so applicants could see, in plain language, why their application was accepted or denied. While this transparency slowed down deployment, it ultimately enhanced public trust and helped the firm secure a partnership with a municipal bank focused on inclusive finance.

In contrast, a health-tech startup in Nairobi approached AI implementation with a community-first lens. Designing a diagnostic tool for early disease detection, the founders recognized that Western medical datasets could not be uncritically applied to African populations. They partnered with local doctors and public health institutions to co-develop culturally attuned diagnostic models. The resulting AI not only performed with greater accuracy, but it also preserved patient dignity and trust in contexts where algorithmic authority might otherwise provoke suspicion or resistance. These examples make it clear that ethics is not an external constraint—it's an integral part of product-market fit, brand identity, and long-term sustainability.

From these cases, and from the broader institutional landscape, a set of guiding principles begins to emerge. Though no single framework can encompass all ethical dimensions, there are recurring patterns—touchstones for entrepreneurs trying to navigate complexity. Ethical entrepreneurship in the AI era requires first and foremost a commitment to embedding social values into the design phase, not as an afterthought but as a fundamental design constraint. Second, it demands a deep integration with regulatory structures—not simply reacting to rules, but anticipating them and participating in their evolution. Third, ethical entrepreneurship must be dialogic. Entrepreneurs cannot act in isolation; they must co-create with affected communities, domain experts, and regulatory bodies to ensure that their innovations reflect not just technical brilliance, but social legitimacy. Equally important is the notion of adaptive governance. Ethics is not static. As technologies evolve, so too do their risks, benefits, and unintended consequences (Ategeka, 2021). Startups need governance structures that evolve with them—ethics committees, internal audit mechanisms, continuous learning systems—that can pivot when new challenges arise. This is particularly crucial for AI systems, which can drift in behavior over time as they ingest new data. Without a living feedback loop, initial safeguards become obsolete. Finally, there must be a way to measure what matters. Financial metrics are ubiquitous—but how do we measure ethical performance? Some startups are now experimenting with dual-ledger reporting: one for fiscal outcomes, another for ethical KPIs—like algorithmic bias audits, environmental footprint, or equity of access. These metrics are not perfect, but they signal an organizational will to be accountable for more than just the bottom line.

In many ways, the shift from abstract ethics to applied frameworks mirrors the entrepreneurial journey itself—from vision to execution, from idea to iteration. Ethics is not a fixed destination, but a practice—a way of asking better questions, making better decisions, and building better futures. As AI becomes more autonomous, more powerful, and more deeply woven into the fabric of our lives, entrepreneurs are not just writing lines of code or building business models. They are, quite literally, coding the future. And with that power comes a responsibility to ensure that the future being written is one that includes all of us—not just the privileged, not just the profitable, but the public in its full, diverse, and vulnerable reality. The path forward is not paved with perfect solutions but with deliberate, ethically conscious steps. Strategic guidance—rooted in law, lived practice, and collective intelligence—offers entrepreneurs the tools they need to meet the moral demands of the AI age. Ethics is not a constraint on innovation. It is the discipline that makes innovation worth pursuing.

CONCLUSION

In conclusion, as artificial intelligence continues to impact the future of entrepreneurship, companies need to approach the incorporation of AI with a sense of responsibility and ethical mindfulness. The fast speed of technology growth has created a unique crossroads where innovation, ethics, and sustainability combine, pushing entrepreneurs to negotiate an increasingly complicated landscape. Throughout this chapter, we have studied the important concepts that drive ethical AI integration in business, from ensuring fairness and transparency to addressing environmental issues and fostering an accountable company culture. These aspects are not only theoretical ideals; they are actual demands for companies seeking long-term profitability and meaningful societal influence. At the heart of ethical AI entrepreneurship is the awareness that technology is a potent force that determines the destiny of mankind. Entrepreneurs have a vital role in influencing how AI is implemented inside their businesses and the larger community. This job is not confined to technological skill or business savvy; it extends to the moral and ethical duty of building systems that match human values and social demands. Ethical entrepreneurship in the age of AI is about more than compliance with regulations; it is about proactively identifying and addressing potential harms, ensuring that AI benefits all stakeholders equitably, and safeguarding against unintended consequences that could exacerbate inequality or discrimination.

One of the major lessons from this chapter is that ethical AI is not a homogenous or static idea. It is dynamic and context-dependent, influenced by the individual difficulties and possibilities given by each industry, each company, and each society setting. There is no one-size-fits-all approach, but rather a collection of guiding principles that can be tweaked and implemented when organizations engage with AI in diverse ways. For example, the ethical implications of AI in healthcare may differ greatly from those in banking or transportation, although the essential ideals of justice, openness, accountability, and sustainability remain universal. Entrepreneurs must be prepared not just with the technical skills to apply AI efficiently but also with the ethical framework to make informed, responsible decisions at every stage of the AI lifecycle—from design and development to deployment and assessment. As organizations continue to implement AI-driven models, they must embrace a forward-thinking strategy that promotes the well-being of both individuals and communities. The potential for AI to change sectors and provide new commercial possibilities is tremendous, but so too is the potential for harm. The challenge for entrepreneurs is to achieve the correct balance between innovation and responsibility, ensuring that the pursuit of profit does not come at the price of social good or environmental sustainability. By incorporating ethical concerns into the core of their AI plans, companies may not only avoid risks but also unleash new possibilities for development, consumer trust, and social influence.

Another essential takeaway from this chapter is the significance of openness and accountability in AI systems. As AI gets more deeply ingrained in business decision-making processes, there is a growing need for companies to be honest about how these systems function and the impact they have. Transparency fosters confidence and allows consumers, workers, and other stakeholders to understand and assess AI systems. Accountability, on the other hand, guarantees that corporations accept responsibility for the results of their AI-driven decisions, particularly when these outcomes influence humans' lives in major ways. Whether it is in employment practices, loan approvals, healthcare diagnoses, or criminal justice judgments, AI systems must be held accountable for their activities, and companies must be willing to recognize and remedy any harm caused by defective or biased algorithms. Sustainability also plays a vital role in influencing the future of AI-driven enterprises. The environmental effect of AI technologies—particularly in terms of energy consumption and resource use—cannot be disregarded. As AI continues to advance, so too must our awareness of its ecological imprint. Entrepreneurs have a responsibility to address the long-term sustainability of their AI systems, ensuring that they are not just efficient but also ecologically responsible. This involves investing in energy-efficient technology, lowering carbon emissions, and examining the larger environmental consequences of AI development. Sustainable AI solutions not only connect with global environmental goals but also position organizations as leaders in the emerging field of green technology.

Moreover, the ethical problems of AI are not restricted to technical or operational considerations but extend to the larger societal consequences of AI deployment. Issues of social justice, fairness, and inclusion are intrinsically tied to the ethical use of AI. AI systems that perpetuate prejudice or reinforce existing inequities can have disastrous effects on underprivileged people, further entrenching social disparities. As businesses develop and implement AI technologies, they must be attentive to finding and reducing biases in their algorithms, ensuring that these systems support justice and equity rather than worsen existing imbalances. Ethical AI is about ensuring that no group is left behind and that technological advancement is shared equally across society. As we look to the future, it is apparent that ethical AI entrepreneurship is not simply a passing trend—it is the basis upon which the next generation of companies will be formed. As AI technologies continue to progress, the necessity for ethical, responsible innovation will only get stronger. Entrepreneurs who embrace these principles will be better positioned to lead their companies through the difficulties and possibilities of an AI-driven future. They will establish trust with their consumers, empower their staff, and contribute to the larger societal good. Ethical AI is not a burden; it is an opportunity—a chance to develop enterprises that are not only lucrative but also have a good influence in the world. The road toward ethical AI entrepreneurship is a complicated and varied one, but it is also a highly gratifying one. By incorporating ethics, sustainability, transparency, and accountability into the core of AI-driven business strategies, entrepreneurs have the chance to design a future that is not just technologically sophisticated but also socially responsible. The route forward demands careful analysis, continuing conversation, and a commitment to building AI systems that work for everyone, not just a chosen few. As organizations continue to navigate this quickly changing world, they must remain company in their commitment to ethical standards, ensuring that AI acts as a force for good and not as a tool for harm. In doing so, companies will not only ensure their place in the market but also contribute to the building of a more fair, sustainable, and equitable world for future generations.

REFERENCES

Aaker, D. A., & Moorman, C. (2023). *Strategic market management.* John Wiley & Sons.

Acemoglu, D. (2021). *Harms of AI (No. w29247).* National Bureau of Economic Research.

Ahsan, M. (2020). Entrepreneurship and ethics in the sharing economy: A critical perspective. *Journal of Business Ethics, 161*(1), 19–33.

Arnold, D. G., Beauchamp, T. L., & Bowie, N. E. (2020). *Ethical theory and business.* Cambridge University Press.

Ategeka, C. (2021). *The Unintended Consequences of Technology: Solutions, Breakthroughs, and the Restart We Need.* John Wiley & Sons.

Azmat, F., Lim, W. M., Moyeen, A., Voola, R., & Gupta, G. (2023). Convergence of business, innovation, and sustainability at the tipping point of the sustainable development goals. *Journal of Business Research, 167*, 114170.

Barauskaite, G., & Streimikiene, D. (2021). Corporate social responsibility and financial performance of companies: The puzzle of concepts, definitions and assessment methods. *Corporate Social Responsibility and Environmental Management, 28*(1), 278–287.

Borenstein, J., & Howard, A. (2021). Emerging challenges in AI and the need for AI ethics education. *AI and Ethics, 1*(1), 61–65. PMID: 38624388

Bozkus, K. (2023). Organizational culture change and technology: Navigating the digital transformation. In *Organizational Culture-Cultural Change and Technology.* IntechOpen.

Buhmann, A., & Fieseler, C. (2021). Towards a deliberative framework for responsible innovation in artificial intelligence. *Technology in Society, 64*, 101475.

Chang, Y. L., & Ke, J. (2024). Socially responsible artificial intelligence empowered people analytics: A novel framework towards sustainability. *Human Resource Development Review, 23*(1), 88–120.

Cheong, B. C. (2024). Transparency and accountability in AI systems: Safeguarding wellbeing in the age of algorithmic decision-making. *Frontiers in Human Dynamics, 6*, 1421273.

Crane, A., Matten, D., Glozer, S., & Spence, L. J. (2019). *Business ethics: Managing corporate citizenship and sustainability in the age of globalization*. Oxford university press.

Du, S., & Xie, C. (2021). Paradoxes of artificial intelligence in consumer markets: Ethical challenges and opportunities. *Journal of Business Research*, *129*, 961–974.

Faqihi, A., & Miah, S. J. (2023). Artificial intelligence-driven talent management system: Exploring the risks and options for constructing a theoretical foundation. *Journal of Risk and Financial Management*, *16*(1), 31.

Feijóo, C., Kwon, Y., Bauer, J. M., Bohlin, E., Howell, B., Jain, R., & Xia, J. (2020). Harnessing artificial intelligence (AI) to increase wellbeing for all: The case for a new technology diplomacy. *Telecommunications Policy*, *44*(6), 101988. PMID: 32377031

Felzmann, H., Fosch-Villaronga, E., Lutz, C., & Tamò-Larrieux, A. (2020). Towards transparency by design for artificial intelligence. *Science and Engineering Ethics*, *26*(6), 3333–3361. PMID: 33196975

Felzmann, H., Villaronga, E. F., Lutz, C., & Tamò-Larrieux, A. (2019). Transparency you can trust: Transparency requirements for artificial intelligence between legal norms and contextual concerns. *Big Data & Society*, *6*(1), 2053951719860542.

Fernandes, S., Sheeja, M. S., & Parivara, S. (2024). Potential of AI for a Sustainable, Inclusive, and Ethically Responsible Future. *Fostering Multidisciplinary Research for Sustainability*, 196.

Goralski, M. A., & Tan, T. K. (2020). Artificial intelligence and sustainable development. *International Journal of Management Education*, *18*(1), 100330.

Hanna, M., Pantanowitz, L., Jackson, B., Palmer, O., Visweswaran, S., Pantanowitz, J., & Rashidi, H. (2024). Ethical and Bias considerations in artificial intelligence (AI)/machine learning. *Modern Pathology*, 100686. PMID: 39694331

Häußermann, J. J., & Lütge, C. (2022). Community-in-the-loop: Towards pluralistic value creation in AI, or—why AI needs business ethics. *AI and Ethics*, 1–22.

Kirat, T., Tambou, O., Do, V., & Tsoukiàs, A. (2023). Fairness and Explainability in Automatic Decision-Making Systems. A challenge for computer science and law. *EURO Journal on Decision Processes, 11*, 100036.

Kriebitz, A., & Lütge, C. (2020). Artificial intelligence and human rights: A business ethical assessment. *Business and Human Rights Journal*, *5*(1), 84–104.

Kulkov, I., Kulkova, J., Rohrbeck, R., Menvielle, L., Kaartemo, V., & Makkonen, H. (2024). Artificial intelligence-driven sustainable development: Examining organizational, technical, and processing approaches to achieving global goals. *Sustainable Development, 32*(3), 2253–2267.

Lisniak, B. A. (2024). *Global environmental problems and their impact on international business*. Academic Press.

Madavarapu, J. B., Kasula, B. Y., Whig, P., & Kautish, S. (2024). AI-Powered Solutions Advancing UN Sustainable Development Goals: A Case Study in Tackling Humanity's Challenges. In *Digital Technologies to Implement the UN Sustainable Development Goals* (pp. 47–67). Springer Nature Switzerland.

Martin, N., Matt, C., Niebel, C., & Blind, K. (2019). How data protection regulation affects startup innovation. *Information Systems Frontiers, 21*(6), 1307–1324.

McDermid, J. A., Jia, Y., Porter, Z., & Habli, I. (2021). Artificial intelligence explainability: The technical and ethical dimensions. *Philosophical Transactions of the Royal Society A, 379*(2207), 20200363. PMID: 34398656

Michael, O. (2024). of Artificial Intelligence. *The Future of Small Business in Industry 5.0*, 215.

Modi, T. B. (2023). Artificial Intelligence Ethics and Fairness: A study to address bias and fairness issues in AI systems, and the ethical implications of AI applications. *Revista Review Index Journal of Multidisciplinary, 3*(2), 24–35.

Moro-Visconti, R. (2024). Artificial Intelligence-Driven Digital Scalability and Growth Options. In *Artificial Intelligence Valuation: The Impact on Automation, BioTech, ChatBots, FinTech, B2B2C, and Other Industries* (pp. 131–204). Springer Nature Switzerland.

Panch, T., Mattie, H., & Atun, R. (2019). Artificial intelligence and algorithmic bias: Implications for health systems. *Journal of Global Health, 9*(2), 020318. PMID: 31788229

Prince, A. E., & Schwarcz, D. (2019). Proxy discrimination in the age of artificial intelligence and big data. *Iowa Law Review, 105*, 1257.

Qiang, V., Rhim, J., & Moon, A. (2024). No such thing as one-size-fits-all in AI ethics frameworks: A comparative case study. *AI & Society, 39*(4), 1975–1994.

Raji, I. D., Smart, A., White, R. N., Mitchell, M., Gebru, T., Hutchinson, B., & Barnes, P. (2020, January). Closing the AI accountability gap: Defining an end-to-end framework for internal algorithmic auditing. In *Proceedings of the 2020 conference on fairness, accountability, and transparency* (pp. 33-44).

Rawashdeh, A. (2023). The consequences of artificial intelligence: an investigation into the impact of AI on job displacement in accounting. *Journal of Science and Technology Policy Management.*

Reim, W., Åström, J., & Eriksson, O. (2020). Implementation of artificial intelligence (AI): A roadmap for business model innovation. *AI, 1*(2), 11.

Rezaei, M., Pironti, M., & Quaglia, R. (2024). AI in knowledge sharing, which ethical challenges are raised in decision-making processes for organisations? *Management Decision.*

Selvarajan, G. P. (2021). Harnessing AI-Driven Data Mining for Predictive Insights: A Framework for Enhancing Decision-Making in Dynamic Data Environments. *International Journal of Creative Research Thoughts*, *9*(2), 5476–5486.

Shaw, P., Price, R., Elliott, K., Copilah-Ali, J., Huntingford, J., & Ionescu, O. (2024). White Paper-Corporate Digital Responsibility (CDR) Securing Our Digital Futures. *Corporate Digital Responsibility (CDR) Securing Our Digital Futures*, 1-35.

Sjödin, D., Parida, V., Palmié, M., & Wincent, J. (2021). How AI capabilities enable business model innovation: Scaling AI through co-evolutionary processes and feedback loops. *Journal of Business Research, 134*, 574–587.

Soni, N., Sharma, E. K., Singh, N., & Kapoor, A. (2019). Impact of artificial intelligence on businesses: from research, innovation, market deployment to future shifts in business models. arXiv preprint arXiv:1905.02092.

Stahl, B. C. (2021). *Artificial intelligence for a better future: an ecosystem perspective on the ethics of AI and emerging digital technologies*. Springer Nature.

Torfing, J. (2019). Collaborative innovation in the public sector: The argument. *Public Management Review*, *21*(1), 1–11.

Vallaster, C., Kraus, S., Lindahl, J. M. M., & Nielsen, A. (2019). Ethics and entrepreneurship: A bibliometric study and literature review. *Journal of Business Research*, *99*, 226–237.

Veluru, C. S. (2024). Responsible Artificial Intelligence on Large Scale Data to Prevent Misuse, Unethical Challenges and Security Breaches. *Journal of Artificial Intelligence & Cloud Computing*. DOI: 10.47363/JAICC/2024

Whittlestone, J., Nyrup, R., Alexandrova, A., Dihal, K., & Cave, S. (2019). *Ethical and societal implications of algorithms, data, and artificial intelligence: a roadmap for research*. Nuffield Foundation.

Wittmer, D. P. (2019). Ethical decision-making. In *Handbook of administrative ethics* (pp. 481–507). Routledge.

KEY TERMS AND DEFINITIONS

Accountability: The obligation of businesses and AI developers to take responsibility for ethical considerations and consequences of their decisions.

AI-Driven Strategies: Business approaches utilizing artificial intelligence to enhance decision-making, efficiency, and innovation.

Algorithmic Bias: The presence of systematic errors in AI systems that result in unfair outcomes, often due to biased training data.

Corporate Social Responsibility (CSR): A business model integrating social and environmental concerns into corporate governance and operations.

Ethical Entrepreneurship: The practice of creating and managing businesses that prioritize social, environmental, and economic responsibility alongside profitability.

Sustainability Principles: Guidelines ensuring business operations do not harm the environment and promote long-term societal well-being.

Transparency: The practice of openly sharing business policies, AI decision-making processes, and data usage with stakeholders.

Chapter 8
Personality Traits and AI-Driven Strategies for Sustainable Growth Among Women Entrepreneurs in Bangalore

Jyothsna Thimmaiah B.
https://orcid.org/0009-0009-2825-5770
Periyar University, Salem, India

V.R. Palanivelu
https://orcid.org/0000-0003-0607-7570
Periyar University, Salem, India

ABSTRACT

In this chapter, the authors explore whether strong personality traits also shape the entrepreneurial mindset of women entrepreneurs in Bangalore, as well as how AI-driven interventions create sustainability in their business growth. It's about perseverance, and it's about creativity, and it's about being bold, and it's about how those things end up affecting one's personal decision-making and business outcomes. Finally, the chapter reviews AI tools for strategic planning, market analysis, resource allocation, and environmental sustainability. A framework for the alchemical integration of entrepreneurial behaviour, AI breakthroughs, and sustainability principles is presented with prescriptive relevance to policymakers, scholars, and business practitioners. When we combine technology passion points

DOI: 10.4018/979-8-3373-1107-4.ch008

and sustainable goals, we can afford to help women entrepreneurs fast-track stand-out growth and contribute to creating the world's best-in-class inclusive and responsible entrepreneur community.

INTRODUCTION

Female entrepreneurship is increasingly recognized as influential for economic development, innovation and social change (Brush, 2006; Fernández-Ruiz et al., 2016). In rapid-paced cosmopolitan cities, for example, Bangalore, popularly referred to as the "Silicon Valley of India," women entrepreneurs are at the forefront of challenging hegemonic business ideals and promoting technology and responsible growth (Rai et al., 2021). While much interest has focused on environmental considerations, such as access to finance, policy facilitation, and technological advancement, there are underlying drivers, including personality traits, that are responsible for entrepreneurial outcomes. Personality factors, including risk-taking propensity, resilience, innovation orientation, and self-efficacy, have a profound effect not only on the decision to start a venture but also on sustaining and succeeding with one. These inner motivating factors are often as important as the external capabilities (Singha & Sivarethinamohan, 2022).

Personal characteristics such as resilience and adaptability and the capacity for and openness to innovating and risk-taking have a significant impact on how entrepreneurs frame cognitively problems, spot potential for opportunity, and act on critical decisions under uncertainty (Rauch and Frese, 2007; Zhao and Seibert, 2006). For female entrepreneurs, these characteristics are intervened by contextual factors such as cultural norms, network embeddedness, and systemic gender bias, which could have the capability of either crossing or strengthening women's entrepreneurial trajectory and sustainability impact (Brush et al.

At the same time , the ongoing 4th Industrial Revolution is reflected in the combination of new and emerging technologies, such as artificial intelligence (AI), radically transforming entrepreneurial ecosystems (McKinsey Global Institute, 2018). Business owners get predictive analytics, resource optimization, customer segmentation, and process automation at their disposal once they adopt AI-enhanced solutions. These technologies are not only enhancing the efficiency of operations but also providing platforms to harmonize business with fundamentals of sustainability and good governance that focus, among other things, on environmental care, ecologically sustainable governance and inclusive social conduct (Brundtland Commission, 1987).

In this chapter, we discuss the personality dimensions, AI model, and female entrepreneurs in Bangalore. It outlines how personal variables impact the acceptance and use of AI and further how AI technologies can allow businesswomen to scale their enterprises on time and in a sustainable way. This chat is lined up as follows, as the root question is this: How do personalities affect AI when it comes to being entrepreneurs? How can AI be used to support and create a business that is as socially and environmentally responsible as possible? What is the place of a crowd model that consists of both human potential and technological capability in a more inclusive and sustainable entrepreneurship ecosystem?

Where these intersections are explored, the chapter provides intriguing possibilities of what women entrepreneurs can leverage in the space of diversity and technological evolution to create scalable and viable business models based on their unique traits and technological discontinuities. It also shows the columns corresponding to the spillover inputs. This description aims to investigate the influence of incentives, barriers, and drivers towards the adoption of AI for sustainable entrepreneurship, which can have the potential to offer practical implications to entrepreneurs, academics, policymakers , and enterprise managers who aim to foster inclusive economic growth.

BACKGROUND

Women-owned businesses have captured the fancy of the Indian social landscape, which is manifesting no more in the innovation ecosystems of cities like Bangalore. While differences in access to finance or education by gender are fundamental structural determinants, the personal characteristics of entrepreneurs can also play a significant role. Simultaneously, the proliferation of artificial Intelligence (AI) and sustainability-related aspirations is altering the start-up ecosystems, with both barriers and opportunities for women-led ventures (Woywode & Schreyögg, 2008) (Brush et al., 2007; Rai et al., 2021).

While AI has become more of a game changer for them now, with data analytics, automation and machine learning helping them shape strategies not just to cushion themselves for the high seas but to make their businesses meaner and leaner and to leave sustainable practices embedded in the operations, in the banking sector in Bengaluru, we find that women are instrumental in creating inclusive organizational climates characterized by safety, commitment, and equity features that can be transferred to entrepreneurial leadership. Their strong commitment with poor support and recognition proves they could bring about transformation in any sector (Singha & Sivarethinamohan, 2021). However, despite SDG 5's progress marker, the persistent existence of gender biases in leadership, particularly in the banking industry in India, calls for systemic changes—which include inducting more women with a global perspective that conceive the spirit of SDG 5 and make available opportunities to create a genuinely diverse and future-ready ecosystem to bolster entrepreneurship (Singha & Sivarethinamohan, 2022a). However, the linkage of psycho factors to technology adoption on sustainable behaviour is one of the less studied concepts in an Indian environment.

THEORETICAL FRAMEWORK

Three interrelated theoretical frames are also used in this chapter to explore the factors driving women entrepreneurs toward business growth. First, based on the Trait Theory of Entrepreneurship, the most stable personality traits included in the model that have been found to be essential for carrying out the model in entrepreneurship (e.g., resilience, openness to experience and risk propensity) influence the behaviour and decision making of entrepreneurs (Rauch & Frese, 2007). These traits may explain the manner in which women entrepreneurs address challenges and innovation and capitalize on opportunities. Secondly, the Technology Acceptance Model (TAM) (Davis, 1989) is applicable as it addresses how perceived usefulness and ease of use influence people's acceptance of new technology. TAM is, in this context, described to explain women's entrepreneurial intention in using and integrating AI tools in their businesses. Finally, the Theory of Sustainable Development emphasizes the importance of reconciling economic growth with environmental and social care (Brundtland Commission 1987). The model portrays the significance of ethical as well as sustainable business endeavours. Taken together, these theories provide a firm foundation for understanding how personality traits, AI adoption and sustainability interact with each other in relation to entrepreneurial success.

CONCEPTUAL FRAMEWORK

The theoretical model developed in this chapter brings together three key interfaces—personality traits, AI strategies and sustainability principles—so as to account for the mechanisms by which women entrepreneurs realize sustainable growth. Adopting new technologies: The first concept relates to the personality of entrepreneurs, who are thought to possess traits such as resilience, openness to innovation, risk-taking, and adaptability, which make up the entrepreneur's mindset and influence the willingness to adopt and the ability to use new technologies (Rauch & Frese, 2007). Automation, data analytics, customer relationship management (CRM), and forecasting tools fall under the AI strategies umbrella that helps in making informed decisions, improving operational efficiency, reaching the broader market and contributing to the sustainability goals of data-driven decision-making (Davis,

1989). Important for strategic management researchers, sustainability principles (including environmental achievements, social equality, circular economy models, etc.) are 'ethical and strategic reference systems' that position business activities in line with long-term societal and ecological objectives (Brundtland Commission, 1987). Incorporating humanistic values such as Ubuntu into organizational sustainability can foster inclusive workplace climates, especially in sectors like banking, where emotional well-being and unity are often overlooked due to operational pressures. Ubuntu, grounded in empathy and mutual respect, complements sustainability's ethical core by encouraging collective resilience and social harmony (Singha & Sivarethinamohan, 2022b). The dynamic relationship between these three components plays out in more innovative, responsible, and resilient business practices, particularly in urban entrepreneurial ecosystems such as Bangalore, where both technology and sustainability are essential points of competitive position.

UNDERSTANDING PERSONALITY TRAITS IN WOMEN ENTREPRENEURS

Personality characteristics Personality characteristics reflect relatively permanent, trait-like individual differences in how one perceives, interprets, and responds to the environment. They are essential factors influencing entrepreneurial behaviours and outcomes (Rauch & Frese, 2007). In women entrepreneurs, some of the key behavioural traits such as resilience, openness to novelty, risk-taking propensity, self-efficacy, and adaptability have been shown to have a strong relationship with business performance. The attribute of resilience is a psychological trwww.ccsenet.org/ibr International Business Research Vol.11, No.1 2018 out of the coping for entrepreneurs to endure market instability, financial limitations and social adversity which imply that entrepreneurs with resilient personality and perceived failures as learning lessons would seem to be a star in the eye of the market. Experience serves to develop a readiness to accept and implement new ideas and technology. One of the most significant features of women who are willing to use new tool applications such as AI is similar to Male (Zhao & Seibert, 2006). Proposition 4 (risk-taking propensity–enterprise success): Female entrepreneurs who have a high propensity for risk-taking are able to make more calculated risks than risk-takers and take strategic leaps in terms of business decisions in environments where risk is always part of any investment in new technologies such as AI, which hold the promise of long-term efficiency and competitive advantages. By helping peers in SAN develop self-efficacy: 'Expectation of personal capability to perform required behaviour to produce desired outcome', or confidence in one's ability to learn things and to do what is necessary to cope with a task demand, one can cultivate competencies for problem-solving, negotiating, and showing perseverance, particularly in the traditionally male-dominated field of business (Bandura, 1997). The malleability of grit equips entrepreneurs with the ability to adjust to shifts in market demands, customer trends, and technological developments — the exact characteristics that mark fast-moving urban geographies such as Bangalore. These are 'inclined planes' for decision-making, where innovation, scaling and sustainability possibilities are adjudged. These capabilities, supplemented by data-led strategies such as data analytics, automation, prediction modelling, and AI, play an essential role in women entrepreneurs making intelligent, future-ready decisions. Entrepreneurs who exhibit greater levels of resilience and openness are more likely to adopt AI tools to enhance their business' operability and sustainability and thereby leverage (technological disruption to gain a competitive edge (Sharma & Menon, 2022). In addition, women contribute to creating the climate of an organization. In sectors such as banking, they make professional spaces that are safe and committed, within which individuals can feel a sense of security and cohesion, even systemically driven ones. The evidence gleaned from banks in Bengaluru shows the ways in which female leaders could impact the workplace culture and efforts to reconcile institutional demands with personal obligations (Singha & Sivarethinamohan, 2021).

CASE STUDIES FROM WOMEN ENTREPRENEURS IN BANGALORE

Case Study 1: Resilience and Tech Adoption

AR, a new young women entrepreneur in the busy start-up scene in Bangalore, started a sustainable fashion label that sourced ethically and promoted artisan empowerment, with a concentration on eco options. Her product first caught on with urban buyers who were beginning to care about their environmental footprints. However, once the COVID-19 pandemic turned global supply chains, consumer habits, and retail logistics upside down, AR's fledgling business encountered an untested foe. The shuttering of storefronts, cancelled orders and uncertain inventory flows all threatened to upend years of labour.

AR does not give in and instead shows extraordinary strength and tactical vision. The answer: artificial intelligence (AI) will help stabilize and future-proof her business operations. Working with a nearby tech consultancy, she implemented AI-powered inventory management systems that kept track of materials, streamlined production and cut down on waste. That's how she was able to shift from a reactive to a predictive approach, adjusting stock levels by predicting customer patterns and seasonal shifts.

With machine learning programs, the company could predict demand for consumer products—things based on thousands of data points, including social media sentiment, search engine trends, and purchase history at e-commerce portals. The AI tools also allowed her to segment her customer base and provide personalized marketing strategies and product recommendations that increased customer engagement and loyalty.

AR also employed chatbot automation tools on her site to deliver better customer service. They adopted AI into her CRM in order to identify high-value clients and adjust loyalty programs accordingly. The new services not only helped the brand survive the economic hurricane, but it also found new ways to grow through those digital channels. In less than six months, online sales expanded by over 40%, and the label went international with curated digital pop-ups and sustainable e-retail platforms.

The case of AR is a powerful illustration of the interaction among personality components (e.g., resilience, openness to novelty, strategic risk-taking) and AI-mediated strategies. It was thanks to this ability to embrace the technological disruption of her business model and rapidly acclimatize to the new environment her sustainable fashion start-up was able to turn the tide of adversity into opportunity. It is a tale of how digital tools, combined with psychological fortitude and inspired leadership, can help women entrepreneurs sustain and grow their businesses in a time of crisis.

Case Study 2: Openness to Innovation

In the fast-evolving landscape of eco-conscious entrepreneurship, M.S., a forward-thinking woman entrepreneur based in Pune, launched a start-up dedicated to creating biodegradable and recyclable packaging alternatives. Recognizing the environmental toll of conventional packaging—especially plastic and Styrofoam—she was determined to offer businesses a sustainable yet cost-effective solution. What set her apart early on was not just her commitment to sustainability but her remarkable openness to innovation.

Unlike many start-ups that delay technological adoption until a later growth phase, M.S. incorporated artificial intelligence (AI) tools into her operational framework from the outset. Specifically, she implemented AI-based supply chain optimization software that allowed real-time tracking of raw materials, production schedules, logistics, and delivery outcomes. This strategic move enabled her to address a fundamental challenge in the packaging industry: inefficiencies in material procurement and distribution that often lead to unnecessary waste and higher emissions.

Using AI-powered geolocation and route optimization features, M.S. could map the most efficient transportation routes, reducing fuel consumption and lowering the carbon footprint of each shipment. Furthermore, the system provided predictive analytics that helped anticipate delays, adjust delivery routes, and manage customer expectations proactively. The enhanced transparency also allowed her to share real-time tracking data with her clients, increasing customer trust and satisfaction.

The platform also offered insights into supplier performance, helping her negotiate better contracts and ensure timely, ethical sourcing. As a result, operational costs were reduced without compromising on her sustainability principles. M.S. regularly utilized dashboard analytics to monitor key performance indicators (KPIs), such as emission reductions per shipment, material wastage percentages, and on-time delivery rates.

Her technological approach attracted the attention of large retail brands looking to reduce their environmental impact, leading to high-profile partnerships. Within 18 months, her company experienced a 60% increase in demand, expanded into two new regional markets, and received recognition at a national green innovation summit.

M.S.'s story illustrates how openness to innovation, especially in the form of early AI adoption, can transform not only a business model but also its ecological footprint. Her case underscores the value of combining sustainability goals with technological foresight. It exemplifies how personality traits like adaptability and innovation readiness can empower women entrepreneurs to thrive in modern, competitive markets.

Case Study 3: Risk-taking and Strategic Pivot

P.M. is a driven Kolkata-born entrepreneur who had previously made a name for herself by opening one of Bengaluru's first boutique coworking spaces dedicated to women-run start-ups and freelancers. Her model of business was about building cooperative, respectful, and engaging physical workspaces—a concept that had great resonance in an emerging gig economy across urban India. In 2019, her enterprise had three sites, with a mini-ecosystem of start-ups, creatives and social enterprises in each locale.

But then the COVID-19 pandemic of early 2020 came along and suddenly imploded the system. Suddenly empty due to widespread national lockdowns and a wholesale switch to remote work, the burgeoning properties behind these coworking companies stopped cash flowing in. As others in the industry either shuttered production or scaled-down, P.M. pursued a very different path, one that would become characteristic of entrepreneurial risk-taking and strategic foresight.

Instead of sitting back and waiting for the physical space market to bounce back, she entirely shifted her business to remote work infrastructure. Having not seen a lot of tech solutions around, she spent time and money checking out AI-based collaboration platforms. She introduced a new service vertical: remote office management and virtual coworking ecosystems. There were customizable digital workspaces, virtual team-building games, AI-driven project monitoring, and mental health resources, all baked into an intuitive online dashboard.

This metamorphosis demanded fundamental changes: retraining her core team, investing in unfamiliar technology and educating her existing clientele. It was a risky decision — in terms of finances and strategy — but it paid off handsomely. By mid-2021, her company had adopted more than 120 remote-first startups and mid-size organizations in India and Southeast Asia. The platforms, which use AI to mimic coworking environments for remote teams, include features such as intelligent scheduling, mood monitoring during meetings and performance-feedback loops.

P.M.'s Gambling paid off in terms of doors and also in terms of respect in the industry. She was profiled in a national business magazine as a "Digital Workplace Pioneer" and invited to speak at a large tech conference about women-led digital transformation.

The way she's been able to pivot under pressure, take smart risks, and innovate her core business with AI-driven solutions is all about what we call entrepreneurial agility. P.M.'s story offers a blueprint of how resilience, courage and strategic thinking — particularly among women entrepreneurs — can transform crises into opportunities. Her travel reveals how risk-taking developed in a context of vision and adaptability opens up new markets and secures long-term value.

.These cases have demonstrated that specific crucial personality attributes give womenpreneurs the keys to navigate business challenges, manoeuvre the way to exploit AI-based innovations and create a sustainable growth path. They underline the need to develop these elements through mentoring activities, policies and educational programmes, and support for women entrepreneurs.

AI-DRIVEN STRATEGIES FOR BUSINESS GROWTH

The emergence of artificial intelligence (AI) is transforming the environment for entrepreneurship by enabling better decision-making, automating operations, and allowing the development of innovative business models (McKinsey Global Institute, 2018). Artificial intelligence as an enabler for Female Entrepreneurs in Bangalore Based on the information in the existing literature, in fast-paced environments like that of Bangalore, there is a unique opportunity for AI to close the gap for women, enabling them to drive sustainable growth and compete more effectively (Rai, Agarwal, & Agarwal, 2021). AI in Entrepreneurship The major AI use cases in entrepreneurship are predictive analytics for predicting markets and consumer patterns, the AI-powered CRM that augments personalization that improves retention, and the chatbots and virtual assistants that handle admin and customer service so that employees can focus more on driving strategies. Additionally, voluntary AI-driven marketing automation helps companies manage campaigns, social media, and financial forecasting, leading to budgeting and fraud discovery to promote economic growth and stability (McKinsey Global Institute, 2018). This will play a significant role in the negotiations between the bank and FDIC for Morgan Stanley to get to Witches Hill, as well as the strategic planning. These are the capabilities that enable entrepreneurs to identify nascent opportunities and discover nascent threats so that they can develop a business strategy with foresight and mitigate risk in advance (Davenport & Ronanki, 2018). It also encourages operational efficiency, automatically taking over repetitive tasks, such as inventory management and invoicing, along with improving the use of resources while at the same time reducing operational spending. AI has been harnessed to transform hiring, firing and employee reviews in human resources so that predictive analytics can match job seekers to corporate cultures and values. AI-powered dashboards that keep customers in the loop at all times. In addition to on-demand market insights, real-time dashboards are empowering entrepreneurs to monitor KPIs, customer feedback and bottlenecks. So they can react immediately and no longer sit passively in the face of market changes. Women entrepreneurs who use AI tools are more ideally placed to scale their businesses responsibly, introduce sustainable practices, and lead innovation-driven growth (Rai et al., 2021; Sharma & Menon, 2022). It is not just about making women's businesses profitable; AI empowers companies that are ethical and future-ready.

INTEGRATING SUSTAINABILITY PRINCIPLES IN ENTREPRENEURIAL VENTURES

In our ever-evolving economic landscape of today, sustainability has transformed from being an 'add on' to being a core business issue, particularly for entrepreneurs who want to remain a competitive, purposeful driving force of the future as well as responsible (Brundtland Commission, 1987). For woman entrepreneurs in IBKI such as Bangalore, integrating sustainability into the business not only builds brand equity and trust, it also gives them a competitive edge which future-proofs their business, and these women will now have access to a growing number of impact investors and customers (Brush et al. It's not just about the environment -- it is also about responsible innovation, ethical labour practices, and genuine partnerships with communities. Be proactive. An organization that absorbs this way of thinking is more prepared to adapt to new regulations, consumer preference changes and worldwide sustainability benchmarks like the United Nation's Sustainable Development Goals (SDGS). AI can act as the boomerang that can return years of sustainability efforts and betterment for the environment by means of data-driven optimization and smart resource utilization. As an example, AI-based energy management systems can reduce operating and environmental costs by optimizing the energy efficiency of individual systems (McKinsey Global Institute, 2018). Similarly, AI-powered innovative inventory systems help reduce waste and spoilage by better aligning production with demand forecasts. AI also contributes to sustainability in supply chains in that it enables traceability that's monkey-business proof, companies can choose a more ethical supplier, and it decreases the emissions in logistics (Davenport & Ronanki, 2018). Second, AI-based decision-making will create circular economy programs where products and processes are designed to be constantly reused, up-cycled and recycled. This is particularly the case in states such as Assam, where traditional sectors like Muga, Pat, and Eri silk weaving -which women dominate - are being upended by automation and competition from the market. Combining Web 2.0-based AI tools with traditional sustainability models can fuel the local weavers, sustain indigenous craftsmanship and guarantee a long-lasting existence (Singha & Singha, 2020). A case for sustainable entrepreneurship can only be made if deliberate efforts are made to incorporate sustainability into entrepreneurial activities. This involves integrating sustainability into the business model from the outset, setting explicit ESG (economic, social and governance) goals, using AI-based real-time assessment for impact, and reading stakeholders in a co-creation journey to sustainability (Rai et al., 2021). Women entrepreneurs also need to continue to invest in sustainable innovation and experiment with new raw materials processes, as well as technologies that deliver environmental or social good. With the help of AI-enabled tools, WOLCFs can scale profitably and create a more equitable and environmentally friendly world- a beautiful future- by combining the above strategies (Sharma & Menon, 2022).

INTERPLAY BETWEEN PERSONALITY, AI, AND SUSTAINABILITY

The fusion of entrepreneurial qualities / character and AI power provide a fertile ground for the Sustainable Business Innovation. “Personal traits such ss resilience, adaptivity, openness to new experience and the willingness to take risks then shape how entrepreneurs engage with new technology,” the researchers said. Resilience provides business leaders with the capacity to respond and react to this trial-and-error mechanism of AI testing, absorbing knocks and iterating strategies quickly. Ability to innovate Being open to innovation makes it possible to creatively reimagine business processes throughout an enterprise, from customer relationship management to supplier relationship management, and apply AI tools creatively to do just that. By taking risks, we empower women entrepreneurs to take bold bets in AI, while holding their hands as the early adopters that can claim and dominate profitable market spaces. Moreover, insofar as strategic anticipation (typically part of the profile of successful entrepreneurs) is concerned as a source of data to empower AI predictive abilities to even make data-consumed forward-looking-enough decisions which trade off operation performance against environmental or social impact. Based in the neuroscience of stress, this link highlights a mechanism by which chronic stress undermines cognitive flexibility, emotional regulation and decision-making ability. Resilience, by contrast, is a neurobiological armour that boosts creativity, cognitive flexibility, and problem-solving.

Singha (2024a) emphasizes that evidence-based stress management and resiliency training can enable leaders to face the vagaries and complexities of the modern world of work with greater clarity and certainty. The chapter provides illustrative cases to show how organizations that embed resilient practices into leadership paradigms are best placed to enable adaptability and longer-term sustainability. These results contribute to the broader neuro leadership conversation, which underscores the importance of cognitive well-being in influencing novel, responsible and future-proof entrepreneurial responses. Singha and Singha (2024) demonstrate the complex interplay between employee well-being and organizational sustainability, documenting how fostering employee experiences, resilience, and a growth-oriented mindset produces strength and positive engagement in the form of productivity and longevity. Based on their substantial academic research and practical experience, they show that building a favourable psychological climate at work is not just an ethical obligation; it is also an investment in creating sustainable organizational outcomes.

By harnessing the interplay between personality traits, AI competencies, and sustainability principles, a systematic approach can assist women entrepreneurs in developing this ecopreneur orientation congruent with environmental, social, and ethical concerns. These elements of the integrated framework are connected, consisting of personality traits like resilience, creativity, risk-taking, and adaptability; AI competencies like predictive analytics, automation, and impact measurement; and sustainability goals for environmental conservation, social responsibility, and ethical governance. All are essential for an entrepreneur to cultivate a growth mindset and an entrepreneur's ethical mind. The framework starts with a self-assessment, in which entrepreneurs evaluate their strengths and areas for improvement as they relate to innovation and sustainability. The next level is AI technology being applied to strategy , which means AI-relevant technology will be used to the business vision and impact goals. 3d) Goals are the third step: In this step, an E is explicitly included, and in their strategic mileposts, entrepreneurs have to place transparent and small measurable ESG (Environmental, Social and Governance) targets. Hence, a culture of lifelong learning is fostered to cater for the flexibility and reactivity of the newly emerging AI and sustainability dynamic. Finally, impact evaluation deploys

AI-focused analysis to measure successes and refine strategies to make a more substantial positive impact. All these factors, combined, introduce a woman entrepreneur to the world of the then founding her personality strengths with technology and an ethical route map to develop competitive and socially responsible ventures.

Challenges and Opportunities in the Integration Process

Challenges

But, there are still some hurdles that stand in the way of mass adoption of this fusion of AI and sustainability for women entrepreneurs. There are several root causes of this, and lack of technical skills is probably the most significant – too many entrepreneurs do not know very much about AI. Hence, they are unable to select, implement, and manage the right tech tools. All of this is compounded by a significant cost barrier–the upfront cost of purchasing AI tools and getting sustainability initiatives off the ground, which both can be prohibitively expensive, particularly for early-stage start-ups that are working with small amounts of capital. Moreover, cultural resistance, whether at the level of companies or, more generally, can blunt or delay the assimilation of new practices into such spaces, particularly when prevailing attitudes or gender biases are discouraging them from engaging in technological experimentation or environmentally responsible action. Privacy and ethics are yet another autonomous challenge; ethical use of AI needs to treat the data with protection while fair, transparent and secure algorithms need to be developed. Navigating these ethical quandaries involves operational burden, more resources and compliance knowledge. These various barriers can be overcome by targeted policy support, education and inclusive innovation ecosystems for women entrepreneurs to unleash AI's full potential for sustainable growth.

Opportunities

Not only do the challenges exist, but there are also immense prospects for women entrepreneurs to use AI and sustainability to achieve success. Early adopters of such approaches will be able to give themselves a considerable competitive edge, being able to differentiate themselves in crowded markets where they increasingly cannot rely on simplicity alone in order to stand out but instead need to provide comprehensive solutions that are novel and efficient at the same time. Furthermore, new markets will be a lot more accessible as a growing mass of ethical consumers and forward-thinking international partners look to do business with companies that value these principles more than the bottom line. AI- and sustainability-savvy entrepreneurs will also get to tap into ever-increasing funding and support ecosystems: more and more governments support projects to enhance impact and impact investors, and NGOs prioritize the most dedicated social and eco innovators. "Better still, by combining such approaches, we have a path to scale the impact, as entrepreneurs can profit from doing well for the environment and society. Recognizing these opportunities for women entrepreneurs in Bangalore and taking the challenges head-on rather than shying from them, women entrepreneurs in Bangalore can shape the move to an era of AI-led and green-focused business in the new decade.

POLICY AND EDUCATIONAL IMPLICATIONS

Diversity is not just a moral obligation but a strategic advantage to forming more inclusive and sustainable entrepreneurial ecosystems. As Singha and Singha (2023) argue, diversity is an essential ingredient of our world, including racial, ethnic, gender, sexual, age, ability/disability, religious, or cultural. To them, understanding and valuing diversity is vital in creating inclusive environments and in fostering life-affirming personal and professional relationships. Their study highlights how different perspectives lead to improved problem-solving, creativity, and decision-making, which can help ensure more innovative and resilient organizations. They also emphasize the need for inclusive leadership, fair policies and ongoing education to address unconscious biases and systemic impediments. "Through the encouragement of transparent and empathetic environments, both people and organizations can make a significant contribution to social equity and sustainable development.

Structural public health and gender equity issues also need to be addressed because economic and technological empowerment is insufficient. Singha and Kanna S (2022) have emphasized the revolutionary nature of mindfulness and women's bottom-up leadership in social change. Moreover, with this historical perspective, it is crucial to acknowledge that women's access to land in India is marginalized, given that it is mainly owned by men who make decisions on land use, including in tobacco cultivation. Tobacco, a well-known carcinogen, is grown extensively in rural and remote areas where there are little or no facilities for cancer treatment, particularly in the case of North-East India, where there is only one cancer hospital providing services to eight states.

Closing this gap through mindfulness training and tobacco education in school programming and in community settings can serve an important role. "But in areas where high-speed internet is not provided- North-East, A&N Islands and J&K- community spread driven communications through radio, TV, audio files, print materials or mobile for dissemination is the most suitable outreach." It would take a concerted effort among NGOs, language and culture specialists, healthcare professionals, and local volunteers for customized, on-the-ground relevance and timely deployment (particularly in light of the waking nightmare we're all still in).

The government can also help nudge an ecosystem for female entrepreneurs forward, particularly in emerging sectors such as AI and sustainability. CV Structurally removing obstacles, supporting gender equity, and driving innovation-led growth. There are, however, policy initiatives that may be successful in addressing structural impediments, encouraging gender parity, and propelling innovation-led growth. Besides structural interventions and policy changes in addressing social evils, grassroots women's organizations in India are also leading by example, using empowerment and compassion-centric approaches. Singha and Kanna S (2022a) state that women's empowerment and self-help groups are operational and mostly effective in India. However, there is a long way to go by formally introducing standardized quality parameters in the ongoing training programs. Although many empowerment cells conduct successful skill-building efforts, often in the hinterland or the insurgency-ridden areas, there is a need to follow protocols, clearly define the characteristics of the trainers, and have a clear curriculum in place, which conforms to the best practices available internationally. They also note that there are social barriers, such as substance abuse or social norms, which interfere with TI's empowerment. Among the noteworthy is the effort of local organizations such as the Naga Mothers' Association and the women's wing of the Koch Rajbongshi student union, which have had commendable success in combating substance abuse by generating awareness and building consensus at the community level. Their mindful, compassionate, and situational leadership is a model for how to deal with complex public issues. Mindfulness based on contemplation, awareness in the present moment, and ethical action—is introduced as a new way to ground women's social reform movements.

Policy needs to be pushed even further to help create an ecosystem where women entrepreneurs can drive AI and sustainability. Fiscal grants and incentives are an effective way of providing targeted funding to offers driven by women, both incorporating sustainability and new technologies and lowering the financial barriers to starting and scaling. Key support will take place in other forms: developing infrastructure, creating innovation hubs, incubators and digital training centres tailored to women entrepreneurs, and providing them with resources, mentoring and an enabling environment. A strong regulatory atmosphere is necessary to foster responsible AI usage, encourage sustainable and compliant deployment, and minimize red tape, which often impedes the growth of small firms. Public–private partnerships, meanwhile, can do their part by convening government, corporate and academia to provide women with training, market access and skills-building programs tailored to women entrepreneurs. Then, girl, we need to invest, and invest and invest still more, in fighting back — in courts, in legislatures, in board rooms and everywhere else — against intellectual theft, against systemic gender discrimination and for greater numbers of young women in policy-making spaces. These policy recommendations, taken together, can advance entrepreneurship and position women as leaders within sustainable and technology-enabled business innovation. When formulating inclusive policies and education reforms to facilitate women's entrepreneurship, it is as essential to engage in lessons learned from around the world and the past. Similar and equally valuable lessons can be learnt by revisiting the contributions of African women to social, economic, and political development.

Singha and Singha (2024) have made the point that 'African historical narratives reveal the persistent impact of gendered power relations and the strategies women have employed to contest and transform those relations, first, in Indigenous societies, second, in resistance to colonial domination, and third, in the construction of post-colonial states'. Such pieces of knowledge, or knowledge-making practices, based on oral histories and archives, feminist historiography, demand for re-entering women's voices and agency when we look at our past futures as well as think about policy-making. These African lessons have deep resonance for the current struggle for gender equity and social justice in India as well as globally. In the spirit of global feminism, the perspective of Afro-feminism places the indispensable place of indigenous knowledge systems in the Ford to get women's liberation in the spotlight. As previously highlighted, the critique of gender inequalities in Africa from an intersection crosscutting approach necessitates a feminist dialect that pays homage to varied cultural orientations and historical experiences. Singha (2024) maintains that intergenerational learning, traditional medicine and advocacy of laws based on indigenous wisdom are essential in the prevention and empowerment of indigenous women. Community-based feminist movements and indigenous organizations are crucial to legislative and policy influence. Cross-cultural exchange and global solidarity are the underpinnings of Afro-feminist solidarity—linking movements across, lording over traditions, and moving beyond geographical boundaries. In this tangled terrain of digital capitalism, we now stand at a crossroads marked by vast opportunities and daunting challenges. In order to successfully manage this transition, one must be cognizant of the hurdles and the possibilities for social change within new media technologies.

Singha (2024b) has underscored that such a time demands policies of inclusion, strategic frameworks, and multi-sectoral partnerships that would optimize the transformative power of digital capitalism to favour socially relevant change. The future we envision of the digital worlds we inhabit is seeping beyond the labels and stereotypes into a virtual existence based on intrinsic worth and not stereotypes. By strategically harnessing technology to address and reshape long-entrenched gender biases, we can create a digital world where equality is not just an aspiration but a reality, one that provides infinite possibilities for every citizen. Such policies do not just lead to the empowerment of the individual entrepreneur—they also serve to bolster the larger economy by enabling more inclusive, sustainable innovation.

Integrating AI and Sustainability Concepts in Entrepreneurship Education

Consequently, entrepreneurship education needs to integrate the two AI and sustainability topics into the core education process in a way that business decision-makers of the future are better able to comprehend and shape the evolving digital and ecological complexity. Education is a cornerstone of training future entrepreneurs, especially women so that they can thrive and do well while doing good. This integration can begin with multidisciplinary coursework in the curriculum that weaves business strategy together with AI technology, ethics, and sustainable frameworks. Experiential learning further enhances understanding with collaborative project work, case studies and real-world problems rooted in business issues with a sustainability focus. Students then tackle these through AI Plus skill-building workshops, such as AI literacy, EIA & sustainable innovation levels that seed the capabilities you need to succeed as an entrepreneur. Mentoring and networking with role models and AI & sustainability leaders provide students with the support, inspiration and hands-on science they need. Finally, and most importantly, it is about creating inclusive education environments where we are free of bias and supportive of multiple backgrounds so we all women feel empowered to look at the intersection of entrepreneurship, technology, and sustainability. "By integrating this as a subject for schools and universities, the next generation of AI-powered socially responsible female entrepreneurs could be trained to build ethical society-enabling businesses.

RECOMMENDATIONS AND SOLUTIONS

Several interventions are required to help women entrepreneurs in Bangalore and elsewhere successfully use AI to grow sustainably in areas related to education, policy, ecosystem, and ethics. The first step is to introduce AI literacy to entrepreneurship education. Many of these women entrepreneurs could just as easily have been laying a foundation for applications built on top of AI methods and leveraging them strategically. Tailor-made workshops and mentorship programs equip business owners with the necessary, practical instruments to apply AI to their business, market predictions, customer engagement and sustainability. These training programmes should be gender-sensitive and context-specific and should be linked to the practical reality that women-owned enterprises can relate to and experience.

Second, policy-based financial incentives can lower the barrier for women-owned start-ups when adopting AI. For these, governments and financial institutions can design nuanced programmes of grants, subsidies, and tax breaks that are targetable against projects that can demonstrate their 'green and innovative' nature as well as ESG (Environmental, Social, and Governance) compliance. They are not only encouraging investments in new technologies, but at the level of the wider society, they help to redress the social economy for the broader social and ecological function played by women entrepreneurs. Capital support should zero in on early-stage start-ups and disenfranchised groups who may not have the usual kind of capital or collateral for it.

A third critical piece of advice is to establish collaborative ecosystems involving all leading actors in the field—entrepreneurs, AI technology developers, researchers in academia, sustainability experts, investors, and policymakers. These ecosystems can manifest as innovation hubs, incubators or digital collaboration platforms, all helping people to learn together and experiment and solve common problems. These networks nurtured through public-private partnerships, have the potential to catalyse the co-creation of scalable AI-based solutions to local issues like waste management, water conservation, or women's access to healthcare. But the fact that the battle isn't quite so solitary for women entrepreneurs (and they don't need to walk the innovation path all by themselves), given that they form part of a support group, can potentially make them a more potent force to be reckoned with.

Embedding ESG into business plans is also a strategic approach that could ensure that technological adoption is consistent with sustainability goals. Through mentorship and coaching, women entrepreneurs can be encouraged to factor in measurable ESG indicators into their business, such as reducing carbon emissions, hiring for diversity or sourcing responsibly. AI services that offer immediate analytics, scenario simulation, or impact analysis can promote this system and help entrepreneurs stay current with the news and better align their plans. Open tools/ templates and advisory services to make ESG integration practical and feasible for startups/SMEs should also be provided by policymakers and incubators.

In addition to Artificial Intelligence (AI) based approaches, virtual immersive technologies, such as Virtual Reality and Augmented Reality, are also emerging as great tools for improving mental health support to entrepreneurs and society in general.

According to Singha and Singha (2024a), AR and VR have the potential to provide patients and clinicians with immersive, personalized and captivating treatment sessions that can alter the landscape of mental health treatment. Immersion technologies can offer proper instruments for exposure therapy, can be combined with standard treatment techniques, help to reduce the stigma of mental health treatment, and improve the therapeutic alliance. AR and VR make the delivery of mental health services more accessible and compelling through better-targeted interventions.

Yet, responsible avenues for their integration would require the appropriate training of mental health practitioners, the protection of privacy and common data security standards, and the implementation of scientific investigations. With the cost of these technologies continuing to decrease, AR/VR applications also offer great potential for providing greater access to quality mental health care—something that the underserved population of women entrepreneurs experiencing high levels of stress and a lack of support systems could benefit significantly from. Besides technological solutions, HR has an important role to play when it comes to embedding sustainability in organizations. HR is a strategic enabler that helps embed environmental and social responsibilities more deeply into HR processes such as recruitment, training, leadership development, and internal communications. Singha (2024c) highlights that the sustainability principles in HR practices guide and motivate to leverage a gamut of resources and reinforce the cultural issue of creativity. Focused training programs aimed at creating sustainable changemakers are a way to help sustain and ensure that the organization is committed to sustainability in the long run and , at the same time, give employees a stake in the game in achieving sustainability goals. Transparency, partnership, and access are all by-products of a well-engaged workforce. In addition, the adoption of defined indicators, performance-based rewards and public acknowledgement of sustainability success create a strong framework for ongoing change to ensure businesses are on the leading edge of responsibility and future readiness at the global scale.

Last but not least, ethical dimension and privacy cannot be ignored in AI for the industry. As women entrepreneurs eye AI to gather data, make decisions, and automate, expectations are for clear rules and protocols on ethical use. That means protecting customers' data, avoiding algorithmic bias and being transparent about how AI-powered insights are being used. Regulators and trainers need to produce literature, guidelines, etc., that entrepreneurs can use to understand these RATS consider the mitigation strategy, and put in 347 place policies that enable them to be trusted by other stakeholders and comply with international standardization. Collectively, women-led entrepreneurs can chart a course towards inclusive, tech-savvy and sustainable businesses that will be at the forefront of responsible innovation.

FUTURE RESEARCH DIRECTIONS

She left too many resources for future research on the intersection of traits, AI, and sustainability in women's enterprise at the AI moment. The increasing role of technology in reconfiguring entrepreneurial ecosystems, especially in a developing economy like India, calls for a more fine-grained, empirically based understanding of how these dynamics evolve across regions and in different social settings.

Future work may include a longitudinal study on AI adoption to determine the influence on business resilience and sustainability outcomes. The literature in place mainly discusses the short-run or cross-sectional behaviour. However, it does little to reveal how sustained usage of AI impacts the expansion, agility and ethical positioning of women-led firms over multiple years. Researchers might want to investigate Why early responders have sustained competitive advantages with AI, what makes AI adoption garner long-term gains on something as finicky as environmental and social measures, and what contributes to significant outcomes, including initial personality factors in such things as resilience or openness to innovation. The longitudinal approach can enable the monitoring of the evolution of decision-making capability, technological maturity, and integration of sustainability goals into business practice.

Another critical avenue for future work is to compare science among cities, regions, and even countries to investigate differential geographical and cultural environments that may influence personality and technology usage. "In Bangalore, the so-called Singapore of India, there is a unique tech-enabled environment cluster that enables supportive mechanisms to be enveloped around. Yet (female) entrepreneurs in smaller cities or rural areas are also confronted with a different set of barriers and incentives for embracing AI. Cross-country comparisons are new and will tell us what social norms, how much infrastructure access, digital literacy and regional policy would affect entrepreneurial behaviour. Moreover, an international comparative study could explore the behaviour of women entrepreneurs in similar developing paths, such as Brazil5, South Africa1 and Indonesia4, around AI used in DL for SI to contribute with valuable information shedding light on not only the global trends but also the country specificities.

Second, the potential effects of emotional intelligence and related psychological variables on AI integration might be an engaging narrative for future investigations. While resilience and openness are common personality aspects that are researched among entrepreneurs, EI, with its focus on self-awareness, empathy, social skills and the regulation of feelings, could arguably be more related to the ways in which entrepreneurs engage with stakeholders, lead their teams through technological change and grapple with the ethical challenges of AI. Higher EI might help foster trust, team decision-making, and responsible innovation, which are all critical in green businesses. Moreover, empirical studies aimed at finding the relationship between EI and business sustainability and the rate of AI adoption may offer helpful psychological explanations for these entrepreneurial dimensions. Third, the intersectional analysis involving caste, class and socio-economic backgrounds of women entrepreneurs could be of significance in knowing who is more likely to adopt AI. The digital divide, as discussed earlier, does not affect everyone equally as the disadvantage or privilege varies with social identities, which reflect caste, class and other signifiers. As an analysis tool, the intersectionality principle might, therefore, assist in understanding to what extent disadvantages or privileges intersect to explain entrepreneurial behaviour and outcomes. At the most, this investigation might result in policy or intervention suggestions that can support the incorporation of women from different social states, such as India and the Global South. As such, this study will contribute to a more integrated, fair and context-embedded knowledge of how personality, AI and sustainability converge in the construction of the future of women's entrepreneurship.

DISCUSSION

There is empirical and anecdotal evidence that while women entrepreneurs in Bangalore are using AI technologies to conduct their businesses more efficiently, they are also leveraging AI to innovate in the long run. But in such a rapidly moving ecosystem as Israel, with a tech environment that remakes startup culture on a constant basis, these entrepreneurs are finding that AI is a value add to what they are already doing and a match for what they see as longer-term sustainability goals. In business processes, women-led companies can leverage AI to address traditional gaps in access to resources, decision-making, and scale. However, the successful adoption of AI is often personality dependent on factors such as resiliency, openness for innovativeness, and adoptiveness.

Internal motives such as personality traits play a vital role in the opportunity and challenge recognition and response of women entrepreneurs. Flexibility - perhaps as in the case of such wild market behaviour and given the socio-cultural resistance barriers - is just the thing. Examples demonstrate that more resilient organizations recover from setbacks such as a pandemic by adopting AI-based inventory management, supply chain improvement, and demand prediction solutions, as they did in the case of COVID-19 (Sharma & Menon, 2022). This rebound or adaptation to these changes is not a mental fortitude but a willingness to embrace new technologies that help improve operational efficiency and reduce waste, which is a key part of sustainability.

Openness to innovation is also another key attribute for the embrace of AI. The more genuinely curious and open to experimenting entrepreneurs are regarding new technologies, the more capable they become of introducing AI in different areas of their business. They have served even the playing field in markets where lots of female entrepreneurs are doing business in the shadow of their male competitors.

Take the women in tech who AI, along with CRMs, marketing automation and the ability to give a personalized service to your clients, has enabled to level the playing field for those women who would have been working in a highly saturated market; except that it's much better to be in a saturated market and have tools like AI that can make you more competitive. This information is helpful in contributing to strategic and tactical decision-making in order to increase customer commitment (McKinsey Global Institute, 2018). If used thoughtfully, those strategies will do businesses well while helping to minimize waste, maximize resource use, and encourage responsible consumption.

Finally, AI transforms it into a vehicle for greater accountability and transparency – two foundational principles of sustainable entrepreneurship. Data Presentation: Real-time impact metrics, KPI, and social engagement results can be visualized on dashboards and AI analytical tools, which help entrepreneurs keep track of the same 24/7." It enables data-driven decision-making, which is suitable for businesses and communities. Entrepreneurs who are nimble enough to experiment with these tools will be better positioned to track consumer trends and satisfy gathering regulatory norms around sustainability.

It is imperative that, for as long as AI is a part of development towards sustainability, an ethics-grounded foundation is an obligation. Women entrepreneurs want to ACT with social conscience and ethics. In regards to women who are treated from the perspective of their social responsibility and moral considerations, it is more probable that they will use AI in order to create beneficial social and environmental impacts and not only for monetary gain. This convergence of technology and purpose is a downpayment on a shift toward a new entrepreneurial model – an entrepreneurial model oriented toward transformation, towards harnessing innovation for public benefit. Multiply the personality traits in point 1 with access to AI tools to change the world, a commitment to sustainability, and a dedication to sustainability. That quartet of psychology, AI, and sustainability has grown to be a swaddle that holds entrepreneurs in Bangalore, and beyond.

The first point I would like to make here is that AI is not a single solution but rather a strategic enabler. Analyzing AI through the lens of entrepreneurial traits and the sustainability value system reveals that AI is a radical innovation driver. They're not just adopting techy, though - they're leading sustainable business forward.

CONCLUSION

AI-enabled methodologies and sustainable principles- the intersection of capabilities are indeed the best nurturing ground to promote strong and impactful women entrepreneurs in Bangalore. When we realize what resilience, adaptability, being open to ideas and being prepared to take risks have in common, then that's how we start to identify the potential friction, duplication, and edge cases of our built-in capabilities (and how we can prime them even better) with a well-rounded blend of technology and purpose-led leadership.

However, AI, as an enabler of efficiency and planning strategies, can also catalyze a better future. Used wisely, AI can empower women entrepreneurs to more effectively leverage resources, identify market needs, and achieve broader social and environmental aims.

By embedding sustainability at the heart of startups and business ideas, growth can not only be profitable but also responsible, inclusive, and future-proof. The mix of identity, technology and sustainability also demands not entrepreneurship, but NEW entrepreneurship, which is all about educational free fall, never stop innovating and responsibility!

But systemic supports, including forward-looking policy, an LGBTQ-inclusive educational curriculum and a supportive entrepreneurial ecosystem, are vital if it is to achieve its potential. By empowering women entrepreneurs with the right tools, knowledge and opportunities, we can kickstart a transformational wave of AI-empowered, sustainable growth in Bangalore and beyond!

In doing so, we don't just pursue success—we aspire to change the industry for the better and, in the process, shape the future e. that we want to live in.

REFERENCES

Bandura, A. (1997). *Self-efficacy: The exercise of control.* W.H. Freeman. https://www.amazon.com/Self-Efficacy-Exercise-Albert-Bandura/dp/0716726262

Brundtland Commission. (1987). *Our common future.* Oxford University Press. https://sustainabledevelopment.un.org/content/documents/5987our-common-future.pdf

Brush, C. G., Greene, P. G., Balachandra, L., & Davis, A. (2018). The gender gap in venture capital: Progress, problems, and perspectives. *Venture Capital, 20*(2), 115–136. DOI: 10.1080/13691066.2017.1349266

Davenport, T. H., & Ronanki, R. (2018). Artificial intelligence for the real world. *Harvard Business Review, 96*(1), 108–116. https://hbr.org/2018/01/artificial-intelligence-for-the-real-world

Davis, F. D. (1989). Perceived usefulness, perceived ease of use, and user acceptance of information technology. *Management Information Systems Quarterly, 13*(3), 319–340. DOI: 10.2307/249008

Hayward, M. L., Forster, W. R., Sarasvathy, S. D., & Fredrickson, B. L. (2010). Beyond hubris: How highly confident entrepreneurs rebound to venture again. *Journal of Business Venturing, 25*(6), 569–578. DOI: 10.1016/j.jbusvent.2009.03.002

McKinsey Global Institute. (2018). *Artificial Intelligence: The next digital frontier?* https://www.mckinsey.com/mgi/overview/2018-in-review/ai-the-next-digital-frontier

Rai, R. K., Agarwal, S., & Agarwal, U. A. (2021). Artificial intelligence in business: Insights from women entrepreneurs in India. *Technological Forecasting and Social Change, 171*, 120990. DOI: 10.1016/j.techfore.2021.120990

Rauch, A., & Frese, M. (2007). Let us put the person back into entrepreneurship research: A meta-analysis on the relationship between business owners' personality traits, business creation, and success. *European Journal of Work and Organizational Psychology, 16*(4), 353–385. DOI: 10.1080/13594320701595438

Sharma, M., & Menon, P. (2022). Women entrepreneurs and AI adoption in post-pandemic India. *Journal of Entrepreneurship and Innovation in Emerging Economies, 8*(2), 150–169. DOI: 10.1177/23939575221096845

Singha, R. (2024). Centring African Indigenous Knowledge: Afro-Feminist Perspectives on Women's Empowerment. In Musingafi, M., & Hungwe, C. (Eds.), *African Womanhood and the Feminist Agenda* (pp. 208–226). IGI Global Scientific Publishing. DOI: 10.4018/979-8-3693-1999-4.ch013

Singha, R. (2024a). Stress, Resilience, and Brain Performance. In Saluja, S., Kukreja, J., & Sharma, S. (Eds.), *Building Organizational Resilience With Neuroleadership* (pp. 14–29). IGI Global Scientific Publishing. DOI: 10.4018/979-8-3693-1785-3.ch002

Singha, R., & Kanna, S. Y. (2022). Tobacco farming, addiction, promotion of gender equality, well-being and monopoly of the Indian market. *Journal of International Women's Studies, 23*(5), 11. https://vc.bridgew.edu/jiws/vol23/iss5/11

Singha, R., & Kanna, S. Y. (2022a). Women's empowerment, mindfulness, and role of women in eradicating alcohol and drug addiction from Indian society. *Journal of International Women's Studies, 24*(7), 7. https://vc.bridgew.edu/jiws/vol24/iss7/7

Singha, R., & Singha, S. (2020). Women's empowerment through the silk industry of Assam, India, and its underlying economy. *Journal of International Women's Studies, 21*(5), 3. https://vc.bridgew.edu/jiws/vol21/iss5/3

Singha, R., & Singha, S. (2024). Positive Interventions at Work: Enhancing Employee Well-Being and Organizational Sustainability. In Baykal, E. (Ed.), *Fostering Organizational Sustainability With Positive Psychology* (pp. 151–179). IGI Global Scientific Publishing. DOI: 10.4018/979-8-3693-1524-8.ch007

Singha, R., & Singha, S. (2024a). Mental Health Treatment: Exploring the Potential of Augmented Reality and Virtual Reality. In Hiran, K., Doshi, R., & Patel, M. (Eds.), *Applications of Virtual and Augmented Reality for Health and Well-being* (pp. 91–110). IGI Global Scientific Publishing. DOI: 10.4018/979-8-3693-1123-3.ch006

Singha, S. (2024b). Unveiling Gender Dynamics in Digital Capitalism: Navigating the Path to Social Gender Equality. In Topçu, Ç. (Ed.), *Digital Capitalism in the New Media Era* (pp. 161–186). IGI Global Scientific Publishing. DOI: 10.4018/979-8-3693-1182-0.ch009

Singha, S. (2024c). Fostering a Culture of Sustainability Through Human Resources Practices. In Popescu, C., Martínez-Falcó, J., Marco-Lajara, B., Sánchez-García, E., & Millán-Tudela, L. (Eds.), *Building Sustainable Human Resources Management Practices for Businesses* (pp. 107–124). IGI Global Scientific Publishing. DOI: 10.4018/979-8-3693-1994-9.ch007

Singha, S., & Singha, R. (2023). Understanding Diversity: The Power of Differences. In Even, A., & Christiansen, B. (Eds.), *Enhancing Employee Engagement and Productivity in the Post-Pandemic Multigenerational Workforce* (pp. 297–313). IGI Global Scientific Publishing. DOI: 10.4018/978-1-6684-9172-0.ch015

Singha, S., & Singha, R. (2024). Revisiting African Womanhood: Historical Archives. In Musingafi, M., & Hungwe, C. (Eds.), *African Womanhood and the Feminist Agenda* (pp. 186–207). IGI Global Scientific Publishing. DOI: 10.4018/979-8-3693-1999-4.ch012

Singha, S., & Sivarethinamohan, R. (2021). The role of women in the formation of organizational climates in various workspaces in Bengaluru, India. *Journal of International Women's Studies*, *22*(6), 13. https://vc.bridgew.edu/jiws/vol22/iss6/13

Singha, S., & Sivarethinamohan, R. (2022a). Social inclusion, equality, leadership, and diversity to attain Sustainable Development Goal 5 in the Indian banking industry. *Journal of International Women's Studies*, *23*(5), 9. https://vc.bridgew.edu/jiws/vol23/iss5/9

Singha, S., & Sivarethinamohan, R. (2022b). Formation of positive organizational climate: Integration of Ubuntu diversity management in banks. *Journal of International Women's Studies*, *24*(4), 10. https://vc.bridgew.edu/jiws/vol24/iss4/10

Zhao, H., & Seibert, S. E. (2006). The Big Five personality dimensions and entrepreneurial status: A meta-analytical review. *The Journal of Applied Psychology*, *91*(2), 259–271. DOI: 10.1037/0021-9010.91.2.259 PMID: 16551182

KEY TERMS AND DEFINITIONS

AI-Driven Strategies: This term may be new, but the technologies are not, and companies have been dabbling with machine learning, predictive analytics and automation to make better decisions, move faster and innovate. These tactics allow entrepreneurs to streamline operations, forecast market trends, personalize customer experience, and align with sustainability objectives.

Bangalore: Bangalore, also known as Bengaluru, is a significant name when it comes to Indian city spaces and is often referred to as India's tech and startup centre. Known as the "Silicon Valley of India," it is a breeding ground for change, enabling technology innovation. It is an ideal location for women-led, AI-enabled and sustainability-focused ventures.

Entrepreneurial Mindset: Entrepreneurial mindset: An entire set of attitudes, skills and behaviours that, together, enable individuals to identify opportunities, take calculated risks, innovate and sustain the effort required to bring new ideas to the market within a wide variety of contexts. It comprises qualities such as creativity, flexibility, judgment and the capacity to be proactive in identifying and solving problems—attributes needed to traverse landscapes of AI and sustainability.

Personality Traits: Personality traits are stable individual differences that have an impact on how people think, feel, and behave. In entrepreneurship, personal characteristics such as resilience, openness to innovation, risk taking, adaptability, and self-efficacy are strongly associated with distinguishing characteristics of entrepreneurial success and the successful adoption of AI and sustainability.

Sustainable Growth: Sustainable development is business growth that leverages profitability with environmental protection, social fairness, and ethical conduct. It focuses on long-term value creation that does not diminish the ability of future generations to meet their needs, and is backed by AI-powered tools to monitor, measure and manage sustainability performance.

Sustainability Principles: The guiding "processes" which require ethical and operational standards are the principles of sustainability, which reflect that businesses, as part of society, must embrace the new paradigm of sustainable development – progressive, environmentally friendly, socially responsive and commercially viable. These principles drive the incorporation of sustainability into the baseline business model, guaranteeing that the businesses will deliver on the Sustainable Development Goals (SDGS) alongside profit.

Women Entrepreneurs: Lady entrepreneurs are not just females who have started and already own and manage businesses. They are at the heart of innovation, job creation and tackling societal challenges. Women entrepreneurs in places like Bangalore are turning to AI and do-gooder models for building businesses that are so inclusive and impactful.

Compilation of References

Aaker, D. A., & Moorman, C. (2023). *Strategic market management*. John Wiley & Sons.

Abhulimen, A. O., & Ejike, O. G. (2024). Ethical considerations in AI use for SMEs and supply chains: Current challenges and future directions. *International Journal of Applied Research in Social Sciences*, *6*(8), 1653–1679. DOI: 10.51594/ijarss.v6i8.1391

Accenture & MIT Sloan Management Review. (2022). Responsible AI: Driving business value and trust. https://www.accenture.com

Accenture. (2016). The Promise of Artificial Intelligence: Redefining Management in the Workforce of the Future. https://www.accenture.com/us-en/insight-promise-artificial-intelligence

Acemoglu, D. (2021). *Harms of AI (No. w29247)*. National Bureau of Economic Research.

Acs, Z. J., & Varga, A. (2005). Entrepreneurship, agglomeration and technological change. *Small Business Economics*, *24*, 323–334.

Adoli, H. L., & Kilika, J. M. (2020). Conceptualizing the role of leadership strategy in the context of strategic management process: A review of literature. *Journal of Economics and Business*, *3*(4), 1598–1623.

Adomdza, G. K., & Astebro, T. B. (2012). The Effect of Entrepreneurial Cognition on Investments for Commercialization Success. SSRN *Electronic Journal*. https://doi.org/DOI: 10.2139/ssrn.2061022

Agrawal, S., Chatterjee, K., & Novotný, P. (2017). Lexicographic ranking supermartingales: an efficient approach to termination of probabilistic programs. *Proceedings of the ACM on Programming Languages, 2*(POPL), 1-32.

Ahmed, N., Abbasi, M. S., Zuberi, F., Qamar, W., Halim, M. S. B., Maqsood, A., & Alam, M. K. (2021). Artificial intelligence techniques: Analysis, application, and outcome in dentistry—a systematic review. *BioMed Research International, 2021*(1), 1–15. PMID: 34258283

Ahsan, M. (2020). Entrepreneurship and ethics in the sharing economy: A critical perspective. *Journal of Business Ethics, 161*(1), 19–33.

AIContentfy. (2024, December 12). *The Importance of Entrepreneurial Resilience.* https://aicontentfy.com/en/blog/importance-of-entrepreneurial-resilience

Al Hadwer, A., Tavana, M., Gillis, D., & Rezania, D. (2021). A systematic review of organizational factors impacting cloud-based technology adoption using technology-organization-environment framework. *Internet of Things : Engineering Cyber Physical Human Systems, 15*, 1–10.

Alblushi, A. (2021). Face recognition based on artificial neural network: A review. *Artificial Intelligence & Robotics Development Journal, 1*(2), 116–131.

Alegre, J., & Chiva, R. (2013). Linking entrepreneurial orientation and firm performance: The role of organizational learning capability and innovation performance. *Journal of Small Business Management, 51*(4), 491–507.

Alghamdi, A., & Alharbi, F. (2025). Strategic oversight of AI adoption in Saudi Arabian SMEs: A mixed-method study. *Journal of AI and Entrepreneurship, 3*(1), 45–62.

Ali, D. M. T. E., Motuzienė, V., & Džiugaitė-Tumėnienė, R. (2024). Ai-driven innovations in building energy management systems: A review of potential applications and energy savings. *Energies, 17*(17), 4277.

Al-Jabri, I., & Sohail, M. S. (2012). Mobile banking adoption: Application of diffusion of innovation theory. *Journal of Electronic Commerce Research, 13*(4), 379–391.

Allison, T. H., Davis, B. C., Webb, J. W., & Short, J. C. (2017). Persuasion in crowdfunding: An elaboration likelihood model of crowdfunding performance. *Journal of Business Venturing, 32*(6), 707–725. DOI: 10.1016/j.jbusvent.2017.09.002

Alsheibani, S., Cheung, Y., & Messom, C. (2018). Artificial intelligence adoption: AI-readiness at firm-level. *Twenty-Second Pacific Asia Conference on Information Systems,* Japan 2018 (pp. 1-8). Association for Information Systems.

Amaghouss, J., & Ibourk, A. (2013). Entrepreneurial activities, innovation and economic growth: The role of cyclical factors evidence from OECD countries for the period 2001-2009. *International Business Research, 6*(1), 153–162.

Ammar, M., Haleem, A., Javaid, M., Walia, R., & Bahl, S. (2021). Improving material quality management and manufacturing organizations system through Industry 4.0 technologies. *Materials Today: Proceedings*, *45*, 5089–5096.

Amoako, G., Omari, P., Kumi, D. K., Agbemabiase, G. C., & Asamoah, G. (2021). Conceptual Framework—Artificial Intelligence and Better Entrepreneurial Decision-Making: The Influence of Customer Preference, Industry Benchmark, and Employee Involvement in an Emerging Market. *Journal of Risk and Financial Management*, *14*(12), 604. DOI: 10.3390/jrfm14120604

Anderson, B. (2023). *How to Create a Budget and Goal for Your Crowdfunding Campaign*. Patronicity.com. https://resources.patronicity.com/blog/2023/02/creating-a-budget-and-goal-for-your-crowdfunding-campaign/

Antoncic, M. (2020). Uncovering hidden signals for sustainable investing using Big Data: Artificial intelligence, machine learning and natural language processing. *Journal of Risk Management in Financial Institutions*, *13*(2), 106–113. https://www.ingentaconnect.com/content/hsp/jrmfi/2020/00000013/00000002/art00002

Arner, D. W., Zetzsche, D. A., & Buckley, R. P. (2019). The Identity Challenge in Finance: From Analogue Identity to Digitized Identification to Digital KYC Utilities. *European Business Organization Law Review*, *20*, 55–80. DOI: 10.1007/s40804-019-00135-1

Arnold, D. G., Beauchamp, T. L., & Bowie, N. E. (2020). *Ethical theory and business*. Cambridge University Press.

Arrieta, A. B., Díaz-Rodríguez, N., Del Ser, J., Bennetot, A., Tabik, S., Barbado, A., & Herrera, F. (2020). Explainable Artificial Intelligence (XAI): Concepts, taxonomies, opportunities and challenges toward responsible AI. *Information Fusion*, *58*, 82–115.

Arucu, M. (2021). Industry 4.0–holistic perspective: Modeling and simulation implementations in manufacturing systems. *Journal of Innovative Science and Engineering*, *5*(1), 50–63.

Arvila, N., Winschiers-Theophilus, H., Keskinen, P., Laurikainen, R., & Nieminen, M. (2020). *Enabling successful crowdfunding for entrepreneurs in marginalized communities*. 45–54. https://doi.org/DOI: 10.1145/3377290.3377303

Arya, A., Mittendorf, B., & Pfeiffer, T. (2021). Incentive Provision in Light of Expertise and Operational Involvement of Angel Investors. *Production and Operations Management*, *30*(9), 2890–2909. DOI: 10.1111/poms.13409

Association for Project Management. (2024). *What is systems thinking? | APM*. Www.apm.org.uk. https://www.apm.org.uk/resources/find-a-resource/what-is-systems-thinking/

Ategeka, C. (2021). *The Unintended Consequences of Technology: Solutions, Breakthroughs, and the Restart We Need*. John Wiley & Sons.

Augurio, Alessandro, Castaldi, L., Mazzoni, C., & Matarazzo, O. (2024). EV purchase intention in Italy, Germany, France, and Denmark: Comparative analysis after the approval of the 2035 ban. *Journal of Cleaner Production*, *486*, 144212–144212. DOI: 10.1016/j.jclepro.2024.144212

Awa, H. O., Ojiabo, O. U., & Orokor, L. E. (2017). Integrated technology-organization-environment (TOE) taxonomies for technology adoption. *Journal of Enterprise Information Management*, *30*(6), 893–921.

Aydemir, E. (2018). Weka ile yapay zeka. *Seçkin Yayınevi*.

Azmat, F., Lim, W. M., Moyeen, A., Voola, R., & Gupta, G. (2023). Convergence of business, innovation, and sustainability at the tipping point of the sustainable development goals. *Journal of Business Research*, *167*, 114170.

Babu, K. E. K. (2021b). Artificial intelligence, its applications in different sectors and challenges: Bangladesh context. In *Artificial intelligence in cyber security: Impact and implications: Security challenges, technical and ethical issues, forensic investigative challenges* (pp. 103–119).

Babu, K. E. K. (2021a). Artificial intelligence in Bangladesh, its applications in different sectors and relevant challenges for the government: An analysis. *International Journal of Public Law and Policy*, *7*(4), 319–333.

Bag, S., & Pretorius, J. H. C. (2022). Relationships between industry 4.0, sustainable manufacturing and circular economy: Proposal of a research framework. *The International Journal of Organizational Analysis*, *30*(4), 864–898.

Bail, C. A. (2014). The cultural environment: Measuring culture with big data. *Theory and Society*, *43*, 465–482.

Bandura, A. (1997). *Self-efficacy: The exercise of control*. W.H. Freeman. https://www.amazon.com/Self-Efficacy-Exercise-Albert-Bandura/dp/0716726262

Bansal, P., & DesJardine, M. R. (2014). Business sustainability: It is about time. *Strategic Organization*, *12*(1), 70–78.

Barauskaite, G., & Streimikiene, D. (2021). Corporate social responsibility and financial performance of companies: The puzzle of concepts, definitions and assessment methods. *Corporate Social Responsibility and Environmental Management, 28*(1), 278–287.

Barden, K. S. (2024, February 27). *Prompting engineering or AI literacy? How to develop a critical awareness of Generative AI in education.* #ALTC Blog. https://altc.alt.ac.uk/blog/2024/02/prompting-engineering-or-ai-literacy-how-to-develop-a-critical-awareness-of-generative-ai-in-education/#gref

Bar-El, R., Gavious, I., Kaufmann, D., & Schwartz, D. (2017). Under-Investments in Innovative SMEs: The Effect of Entrepreneurial Cognitive Bias. *Human Capital and Assets in the Networked World*, 385–422. https://doi.org/DOI: 10.1108/978-1-78714-827-720171012

Batool, S., Gill, S. A., Javaid, S., & Khan, A. J. (2021). Good governance via E-Governance: moving towards digitalization for a digital economy. *Review of Applied Management and Social Sciences, 4*(4), 823-836.

Beer, S. (1972). *Brain of the firm*. John Wiley & Sons.

Bender, E., McMillan-Major, A., Shmitchell, S., & Gebru, T. (2021). On the Dangers of Stochastic Parrots: Can Language Models Be Too Big? *FAccT '21: Proceedings of the 2021 ACM Conference on Fairness, Accountability, and Transparency*, 610–623. DOI: 10.1145/3442188.3445922

Bernoster, I., Mukerjee, J., & Thurik, R. (2020). The role of affect in entrepreneurial orientation. *Small Business Economics, 54*(1), 235–256.

Bessant, J., & Tidd, J. (2007). *Innovation and entrepreneurship*. John Wiley & Sons.

Bharadiya, J. P. (2023). A comparative study of business intelligence and artificial intelligence with big data analytics. *American Journal of Artificial Intelligence, 7*(1), 24–30.

Bharadwaj, A., El Sawy, O. A., Pavlou, P. A., & Venkatraman, N. V. (2013). Digital business strategy: Toward a next generation of insights. *Management Information Systems Quarterly*, 471–482.

Bickley, S. J., Macintyre, A., & Torgler, B. (2024). Artificial Intelligence and Big Data in Sustainable Entrepreneurship. *Journal of Economic Surveys, 39*(1). Advance online publication. DOI: 10.1111/joes.12611

Bocken, N. M. P., Short, S. W., Rana, P., & Evans, S. (2014). A literature and practice review to develop sustainable business model archetypes. *Journal of Cleaner Production*, *65*, 42–56.

Boehmer, E., Grammig, J., & Theissen, E. (2007). Estimating the probability of informed trading—Does trade misclassification matter? *Journal of Financial Markets*, *10*(1), 26–47.

Boiral, O., & Henri, J. F. (2012). Modelling the impact of ISO 14001 on environmental performance: A comparative approach. *Journal of Environmental Management*, *99*, 84–97. PMID: 22326757

Boldyreva, E. L. (2018). Cambridge Analytica: Ethics And Online Manipulation With Decision-Making Process. *The European Proceedings of Social & Behavioural Sciences*. DOI: 10.15405/epsbs.2018.12.02.10

Bora, G. (2019, September 12). *Donatekart gives us a glimpse of how charity can be made more "meaningful."* The Economic Times; Economic Times. https://economictimes.indiatimes.com/small-biz/startups/features/donatekart-gives-us-a-glimpse-of-how-charity-can-be-made-more-meaningful/articleshow/71091858.cms

Borenstein, J., & Howard, A. (2021). Emerging challenges in AI and the need for AI ethics education. *AI and Ethics*, *1*(1), 61–65. PMID: 38624388

Boston Consulting Group. (2024). *Global AI adoption and value realization report*. https://www.bcg.com

Boyles, M. (2022, February 1). *What Is Creative Problem-Solving & Why Is It Important?* Business Insights Blog. https://online.hbs.edu/blog/post/what-is-creative-problem-solving

Bozkurt, A. (2024). Tell Me Your Prompts and I Will Make Them True: The Alchemy of Prompt Engineering and Generative AI. *Open Praxis*, *16*(2), 111–118. DOI: 10.55982/openpraxis.16.2.661

Bozkus, K. (2023). Organizational culture change and technology: Navigating the digital transformation. In *Organizational Culture-Cultural Change and Technology*. IntechOpen.

Braun, D., Han, Y., & Wang, H. E. (2023). The application of feed forward neural networks to merger arbitrage: A return-based analysis. *Finance Research Letters*, *58*, 104391.

British Business Bank. (2021). *Start Up Loans - small businesses can borrow up to £25,000*. Start up Loans Company. https://www.startuploans.co.uk/

Brundtland Commission. (1987). *Our common future*. Oxford University Press. https://sustainabledevelopment.un.org/content/documents/5987our-common-future.pdf

Brush, C. G., Greene, P. G., Balachandra, L., & Davis, A. (2018). The gender gap in venture capital: Progress, problems, and perspectives. *Venture Capital, 20*(2), 115–136. DOI: 10.1080/13691066.2017.1349266

Bryant, S. (2024, June 24). *How many startups fail and why?* Investopedia. https://www.investopedia.com/articles/personal-finance/040915/how-many-startups-fail-and-why.asp

Brynjolfsson, E., & McAfee, A. (2014). *The second machine age: Work, progress, and prosperity in a time of brilliant technologies*. W.W. Norton & Company.

Buhmann, A., & Fieseler, C. (2021). Towards a deliberative framework for responsible innovation in artificial intelligence. *Technology in Society*, *64*, 101475.

Build Plus, K. K. (2025). *10 Mission Driven Startups from Japan*. Wahl+Case; Build Plus K.K. https://www.wahlandcase.com/blog/10-sustainable-startups-japan

Buolamwini, J., & Gebru, T. (2018). Gender shades: Intersectional accuracy disparities in commercial gender classification. *Proceedings of Machine Learning Research*, *81*, 77–91.

Burbano, V. (2020, April 4). *Scaling the Revolution: Patagonia CEO Rose Marcario Charts Path for Sustainable Business | Columbia Business School*. Columbia Business School. https://business.columbia.edu/leadership-and-ethics-news/bernstein-center-leadership-and-ethics/scaling-revolution-patagonia-ceo

Burchi, A., Włodarczyk, B., Szturo, M., & Martelli, D. (2021). The Effects of Financial Literacy on Sustainable Entrepreneurship. *Sustainability*, *13*(9), 5070. DOI: 10.3390/su13095070

Cambridge Cleantech. (2024). Clean Technologies for a Sustainable Future | Cambridge Cleantech. *Cambridgecleantech.org.uk*. DOI: 1008220/1710514078318

Camerer, C., Loewenstein, G., & Weber, M. (1989). The Curse of Knowledge in Economic Settings: An Experimental Analysis. *Journal of Political Economy*, *97*(5), 1232–1254. DOI: 10.1086/261651

Cammack, P. (2022). *The politics of global competitiveness*. Oxford University Press.

Canhoto, A. I., & Clear, F. (2020). Artificial intelligence and machine learning as business tools: A framework for diagnosing value destruction potential. *Business Horizons*, *63*(2), 183–193.

Carlsson, C., & Walden, P. (1997). More effective strategic management with hyperknowledge: The Woodstrat case. *Journal of Decision Systems*, *6*(1), 23–44.

Carpineanu, S. (2022, December 12). *Multi Flow Map - Perfect tool for illustrating Causes and Effects*. Blog Mindomo. https://www.mindomo.com/blog/multi-flow-map/

Carroll, A. B. (1991). The pyramid of corporate social responsibility: Toward the moral management of organizational stakeholders. *Business Horizons*, *34*(4), 39–48. DOI: 10.1016/0007-6813(91)90005-G

Carroll, A. B., & Shabana, K. M. (2010). The business case for corporate social responsibility: A review of concepts, research, and practice. *International Journal of Management Reviews*, *12*(1), 85–105.

Carton, E. (n.d.). *Five questions startups need to ask before going international*. PwC. https://www.pwc.com/gx/en/services/entrepreneurial-private-business/small-business-solutions/five-questions-startups-need-to-ask-before-going-international.html

Cassar, G. (2004). The financing of business start-ups. *Journal of Business Venturing*, *19*(2), 261–283. DOI: 10.1016/s0883-9026(03)00029-6

Cetindamar, D., Kitto, K., Wu, M., Zhang, Y., Abedin, B., & Knight, S. (2022). Explicating AI Literacy of Employees at Digital Workplaces. *IEEE Transactions on Engineering Management*, *71*, 1–14. DOI: 10.1109/tem.2021.3138503

Chandratreya, A. (2024). From Start-Up to Scale-Up Leadership Dynamics in Entrepreneurial Ventures. *Advances in Business Strategy and Competitive Advantage Book Series*, 454–486. DOI: 10.4018/979-8-3693-7903-5.ch019

Chang, Y. L., & Ke, J. (2024). Socially responsible artificial intelligence empowered people analytics: A novel framework towards sustainability. *Human Resource Development Review*, *23*(1), 88–120.

Chen, W., He, W., Shen, J., Tian, X., & Wang, X. (2023). Systematic analysis of artificial intelligence in the era of industry 4.0. *Journal of Management Analytics*, *10*(1), 89–108.

Chen, Y., Hu, T., & Law, R. (2024). The impact of visual, auditory, textual stimuli on crowdfunding: Evidence from tourism projects. *Current Issues in Tourism*, 1–19. DOI: 10.1080/13683500.2024.2378608

Cheong, B. C. (2024). Transparency and accountability in AI systems: Safeguarding wellbeing in the age of algorithmic decision-making. *Frontiers in Human Dynamics*, *6*, 1421273.

Cherry, S. (2024, May 15). *What is "grantsmanship"? How strategic thinking improves your chances of success in the grant application process - CareerVolt*. CareerVolt. https://career-volt.com/grant-funding/what-is-grantsmanship-the-importance-of-strategic-thinking-in-the-grant-application-process/

Chota, M. C. (2020). *Entrepreneurial orientation and it's effects on micro, small and medium enterprises (MSME's) business performance in Lusaka district* (Doctoral dissertation, The University of Zambia).

Christensen, K., Ma, Z. G., & Jørgensen, B. N. (2025). A scoping review on electric vehicle charging strategies with a technical, social, and regulatory feasibility evaluation. *Renewable & Sustainable Energy Reviews*, *211*, 115300. DOI: 10.1016/j.rser.2024.115300

Cielen, A., Peeters, L., & Vanhoof, K. (2004). Bankruptcy prediction using a data envelopment analysis. *European Journal of Operational Research*, *154*(2), 526–532.

Cioffi, R., Travaglioni, M., Piscitelli, G., Petrillo, A., & De Felice, F. (2020). Artificial intelligence and machine learning applications in smart production: Progress, trends, and directions. *Sustainability*, *12*(2), 1–26.

Clark, D. (2021, September 3). *Global companies 2020*. Statista. https://www.statista.com/statistics/1260686/global-companies/

Clark, D. R., & Bradley, K. J. (2023). Entrepreneurial leadership: Putting the "U" in team. *Business Horizons*, *67*(2), 183–198. DOI: 10.1016/j.bushor.2023.11.004

Codini, A. P., Abbate, T., & Petruzzelli, A. M. (2023). Business Model Innovation and exaptation: A new way of innovating in SMEs. *Technovation*, *119*, 1–16.

Cohen, S. (2021, May 10). *The Role of Individual Responsibility in the Transition to Environmental Sustainability*. State of the Planet. https://news.climate.columbia.edu/2021/05/10/the-role-of-individual-responsibility-in-the-transition-to-environmental-sustainability/

Cohen, B., & Winn, M. I. (2007). Market imperfections, opportunity and sustainable entrepreneurship. *Journal of Business Venturing*, *22*(1), 29–49.

Corrêa, V. S., Queiroz, M. M., Cruz, M. A., & Shigaki, H. B. (2022). Entrepreneurial orientation far beyond opportunity: The influence of the necessity for innovativeness, proactiveness and risk-taking. *International Journal of Entrepreneurial Behaviour & Research, 28*(4), 952–979.

Costa, A. (2024). *Navigating the twin transition: digital transformation and sustainability in low-tech industries: a small and medium-sized companies' perspective.* Academic Press.

Covin, J. G., & Lumpkin, G. T. (2011). Entrepreneurial orientation theory and research: Reflections on a needed construct. *Entrepreneurship Theory and Practice, 35*(5), 855–872.

Covin, J. G., & Slevin, D. P. (1989). Strategic management of small firms in hostile and benign environments. *Strategic Management Journal, 10*(1), 75–87.

Covin, J. G., & Wales, W. J. (2012). The measurement of entrepreneurial orientation. *Entrepreneurship Theory and Practice, 36*(4), 677–702.

Craig, R. (2021, December 29). *7 types of funding for startups and scaleups.* Rapid Formations Blog. https://www.rapidformations.co.uk/blog/funding-startups-scaleups/

Crane, A., Matten, D., Glozer, S., & Spence, L. J. (2019). *Business ethics: Managing corporate citizenship and sustainability in the age of globalization.* Oxford university press.

Crawford, A. (2021). *12 top tips for writing a grant application.* Www.ukri.org. https://www.ukri.org/blog/12-top-tips-for-writing-a-grant-application/

Cubric, M. (2020). Drivers, barriers and social considerations for AI adoption in business and management: A tertiary study. *Technology in Society, 62*, 101257.

Cui, Y., Kara, S., & Chan, K. C. (2020). Manufacturing big data ecosystem: A systematic literature review. *Robotics and Computer-integrated Manufacturing, 62*, 1–20.

da Silva, B. A., Constantino, M., de Moraes, P. M., Herrera, G. P., de Oliveira, O. S., dos Santos, S. A. L., Kulevicz, R. A., Porfírio, G., & da Costa, R. B. (2021). Econometric analysis of IPAT-e: A new tool for the environmental impact assessment of publicly traded companies. *Environmental Impact Assessment Review, 89*, 106586. DOI: 10.1016/j.eiar.2021.106586

Dam, R. F., & Teo Yu Siang. (2016a, November 26). *Learn How to Use the Best Ideation Methods: Brainstorming, Braindumping, Brainwriting, and Brainwalking*. The Interaction Design Foundation; Interaction Design Foundation. https://www.interaction-design.org/literature/article/learn-how-to-use-the-best-ideation-methods-brainstorming-braindumping-brainwriting-and-brainwalking?srsltid=AfmBOoo3q1-7WVIYQHttAiDNT3RXRqUzEkV7bWgK9KY7j1Dh6I-bbjoS#7._be_visual-8

Dam, R. F., & Teo Yu Siang. (2016b, November 26). *Scamper: How to Use the Best Ideation Methods*. The Interaction Design Foundation; Interaction Design Foundation. https://www.interaction-design.org/literature/article/learn-how-to-use-the-best-ideation-methods-scamper?srsltid=AfmBOoqEt3K1sKzpINm7lDGn9v_ZqLgqtgI_jesH02Occt6fmISZfBV4#example_%E2%80%93_mcdonald%E2%80%99s-2

Daniels, M. (2024, January 3). *Why 2023 saw a boom in B Corp certifications*. Modern Retail. https://www.modernretail.co/operations/why-2023-saw-a-boom-in-b-corp-certifications/

Dastin, J. (2018). *Amazon scraps secret AI recruiting tool that showed bias against women*. Reuters.

Daugherty, P. R., & Wilson, H. J. (2018). *Human+ machine: Reimagining work in the age of AI*. Harvard Business Press.

Dauvergne, P. (2020). *AI in the Wild: Sustainability in the Age of Artificial Intelligence*. MIT Press.

Davenport, T. H. (2018). *Artificial Intelligence for the Real World*. Harvard Business Review. https://hbr.org/webinar/2018/02/artificial-intelligence-for-the-real-world

Davenport, T., Guha, A., Grewal, D., & Bressgott, T. (2020). How Artificial Intelligence Will Change the Future of Marketing. *Journal of the Academy of Marketing Science, 48*(1), 24–42. Springer. https://doi.org/DOI: 10.1007/s11747-019-00696-0

Davenport, T. H., & Ronanki, R. (2018). Artificial intelligence for the real world. *Harvard Business Review*, *96*(1), 108–116.

Davidsson, P. (2015). Entrepreneurial opportunities and the entrepreneurship nexus: A re-conceptualization. *Journal of Business Venturing*, *30*(5), 674–695.

Davis, F. D. (1989). Perceived usefulness, perceived ease of use, and user acceptance of information technology. *Management Information Systems Quarterly, 13*(3), 319–340. DOI: 10.2307/249008

De Marcellis-Warin, N., Marty, F., Thelisson, E., & Warin, T. (2022). Artificial intelligence and consumer manipulations: From consumer's counter algorithms to firm's self-regulation tools. *AI and Ethics*, *2*(2), 259–268.

Deloitte Insights. (2023). *The rise of AI in corporate sustainability: Leveraging AI for transparent and impactful CSR initiatives*. Deloitte LLP.

Demirel, P., & Kesidou, E. (2019). Sustainability-oriented capabilities for eco-innovation: Meeting the regulatory, technology, and market demands. *Business Strategy and the Environment*, *28*(5), 847–857.

Department for Science. Innovation & Technology. (2025, January 13). *AI Opportunities Action Plan: government response*. GOV.UK. https://www.gov.uk/government/publications/ai-opportunities-action-plan-government-response/ai-opportunities-action-plan-government-response

Di Vaio, A., Palladino, R., Hassan, R., & Escobar, O. (2020). Artificial Intelligence and Business Models in the Sustainable Development Goals perspective: A Systematic Literature Review. *Journal of Business Research*, *121*(1), 283–314. DOI: 10.1016/j.jbusres.2020.08.019

Díaz-Rodríguez, N., Del Ser, J., Coeckelbergh, M., de Prado, M. L., Herrera-Viedma, E., & Herrera, F. (2023). Connecting the dots in trustworthy Artificial Intelligence: From AI principles, ethics, and key requirements to responsible AI systems and regulation. *Information Fusion*, *99*, 101896.

Dimitriadis, S., & Koning, R. (2022). Social Skills Improve Business Performance: Evidence from a Randomized Control Trial with Entrepreneurs in Togo. *Management Science*, *68*(12). Advance online publication. DOI: 10.1287/mnsc.2022.4334

Dmuchowski, P., Dmuchowski, W., Baczewska-Dąbrowska, A. H., & Gworek, B. (2023). Environmental, social, and governance (ESG) model; impacts and sustainable investment–Global trends and Poland's perspective. *Journal of Environmental Management*, *329*, 117023. PMID: 36571952

Doyle, G., Srivastava, S. B., Goldberg, A., & Frank, M. C. (2017). Alignment at Work: Using Language to Distinguish the Internalization and Self-Regulation Components of Cultural Fit in Organizations. *IRLE Working Paper*, pp. 102-110. https://irle.berkeley.edu/files/2017/Alignment-At-Work.pdf

Drucker, P. F. (1985). Entrepreneurial strategies. *California Management Review*, *27*(2), 9–25.

Drucker, P. F. (1998). The discipline of innovation. *Harvard Business Review*, *76*(6), 149–157. PMID: 10187245

Duong, C. D. Viet, T., The Anh Khuc, Nhat Minh Tran, & Phuong, T. (2024). Unraveling the dark side of ChatGPT: A moderated mediation model of technology anxiety and technostress. *Information Technology & People*. Advance online publication. DOI: 10.1108/itp-11-2023-1151

Duong, C. D., Le, T. T., Dang, N. S., Do, N. D., & Vu, A. T. (2024). Unraveling the determinants of digital entrepreneurial intentions: Do performance expectancy of artificial intelligence solutions matter? *Journal of Small Business and Enterprise Development*, *31*(2), 1327–1356. DOI: 10.1108/jsbed-02-2024-0065

Du, S., & Xie, C. (2021). Paradoxes of artificial intelligence in consumer markets: Ethical challenges and opportunities. *Journal of Business Research*, *129*, 961–974.

Dutz, M. A., Ordover, J. A., & Willig, R. D. (2000). Entrepreneurship, access policy and economic development: Lessons from industrial organization. *European Economic Review*, *44*(4-6), 739–747.

Dweck, C. (2017). *Mindset: Changing the way you think to fulfil your potential.* Robinson.

Dwivedi, Y. K., Hughes, L., Ismagilova, E., Aarts, G., Coombs, C., Crick, T., & Williams, M. D. (2021). Artificial Intelligence (AI): Multidisciplinary perspectives on emerging challenges, opportunities, and agenda for research, practice and policy. *International Journal of Information Management*, *57*, 1–47.

Dwivedi, Y. K., Hughes, L., Kar, A. K., Baabdullah, A. M., Grover, P., Abbas, R., & Wade, M. (2022). Climate change and COP26: Are digital technologies and information management part of the problem or the solution? An editorial reflection and call to action. *International Journal of Information Management*, *63*, 102456.

Dwoskin, J. (2023, April 17). *It seems as though every day the world is beginning to move faster and faster. Often times, in my career, I have seen entrepreneurs or business people with great products or ideas, but they lack one specific quality: patience.* Linkedin.com. https://www.linkedin.com/pulse/start-slow-grow-big-slowing-down-best-way-get-ahead-jon-dwoskin-/

Eccles, R. G., Ioannou, I., & Serafeim, G. (2012). The impact of a corporate culture of sustainability on corporate behavior and performance. *Management Science*, *60*(11), 2835–2857.

Economic Development Collaborative. (2024, September 4). *5 Keys to Attract Venture Capital Funding*. Economic Development Collaborative. https://edcollaborative.com/blog/compelling-business-plan-raising-venture-capital/

ECOVER. (2024, July 24). *Ecover Timeline*. Ecover. https://uk.ecover.com/mission/history/

Editorial, P. W. C. (2016). https://www.pwc.com/gx/en/industries/industries-4.0/landing-page/industry-4.0-building-your-digital-enterprise-april-2016.pdf

El Miedany, Y. (2019). Virtual reality and augmented reality. *Rheumatology teaching: the art and science of medical education*, 403-427.

Elevate. (2022, September 8). *The Power of Networking for Entrepreneurs*. Elevate Ventures. https://elevateventures.com/the-power-of-networking-for-entrepreneurs

Elkington, J. (1997). *Cannibals with forks: The triple bottom line of 21st century business*. Capstone.

Elkington, J. (1997). *Cannibals with forks: The triple bottom line of 21st-century business*. Capstone Publishing.

Ellen MacArthur Foundation. (2019). *Artificial intelligence and the circular economy*.

EMBROKER. (2020, February 2). 106 Must-Know Startup. https://www.embroker.com/blog/startup-statistics/

Engine, S. (2020). *Solar Roadways® | StartEngine*. StartEngine. https://www.startengine.com/offering/solar-roadways

Ensmenger, N. (2012). Is chess the drosophila of artificial intelligence? A social history of an algorithm. *Social Studies of Science*, *42*(1), 5–30. PMID: 22530382

European Banking Federation. (2021, June 24). *Banks prioritize SDGs requiring greatest financing impact, study finds*. European Banking Federation. https://www.ebf.eu/financing-growth/banks-prioritize-sdgs-requiring-greatest-financing-impact-study-finds/

European Commission. (2021). *Proposal for a regulation laying down harmonized rules on Artificial Intelligence*. Artificial Intelligence Act.

European Commission. (2024). The AI Act: Regulation of artificial intelligence. https://digital-strategy.ec.europa.eu/en/policies/european-approach-artificial-intelligence

European Environment Agency. (2024, December 5). *Europe's circular economy in facts and figures*. Europa.eu. https://www.eea.europa.eu/en/analysis/publications/europes-circular-economy-in-facts

European Union. (2024). *The EU Artificial Intelligence Act*. The Artificial Intelligence Act. https://artificialintelligenceact.eu/

Fairphone. (2024). *About us | Fairphone*. Fairphone BV. https://shop.fairphone.com/about-us

Fairphone. (2025, January 13). *Fairphone's next chapter starts now. - Fairphone*. Fairphone. https://www.fairphone.com/en/2025/01/13/fairphones-next-chapter-starts-now/

Faqihi, A., & Miah, S. J. (2023). Artificial intelligence-driven talent management system: Exploring the risks and options for constructing a theoretical foundation. *Journal of Risk and Financial Management*, *16*(1), 31.

Farghali, M., Osman, A. I., Mohamed, I. M., Chen, Z., Chen, L., Ihara, I., & Rooney, D. W. (2023). Strategies to save energy in the context of the energy crisis: A review. *Environmental Chemistry Letters*, *21*(4), 2003–2039. PMID: 37362011

Favaretto, M., De Clercq, E., Schneble, C. O., & Elger, B. S. (2020). What is your definition of Big Data? Researchers' understanding of the phenomenon of the decade. *PLoS One*, *15*(2), 1–20. PMID: 32097430

Federiakin, D., Molerov, D., Zlatkin-Troitschanskaia, O., & Maur, A. (2024). Prompt engineering as a new 21st century skill. *Frontiers in Education*, *9*. Advance online publication. DOI: 10.3389/feduc.2024.1366434

Feijóo, C., Kwon, Y., Bauer, J. M., Bohlin, E., Howell, B., Jain, R., & Xia, J. (2020). Harnessing artificial intelligence (AI) to increase wellbeing for all: The case for a new technology diplomacy. *Telecommunications Policy*, *44*(6), 101988. PMID: 32377031

Felicetti, A. M., Corvello, V., & Ammirato, S. (2024). Digital innovation in entrepreneurial firms: A systematic literature review. *Review of Managerial Science*, *18*(2), 315–362.

Felzmann, H., Fosch-Villaronga, E., Lutz, C., & Tamò-Larrieux, A. (2020). Towards transparency by design for artificial intelligence. *Science and Engineering Ethics*, *26*(6), 3333–3361. PMID: 33196975

Felzmann, H., Villaronga, E. F., Lutz, C., & Tamò-Larrieux, A. (2019). Transparency you can trust: Transparency requirements for artificial intelligence between legal norms and contextual concerns. *Big Data & Society*, *6*(1), 2053951719860542.

Fernandes, S., Sheeja, M. S., & Parivara, S. (2024). Potential of AI for a Sustainable, Inclusive, and Ethically Responsible Future. *Fostering Multidisciplinary Research for Sustainability*, 196.

Ferrara, E. (2023). Fairness and Bias in Artificial Intelligence: A Brief Survey of Sources, Impacts, and Mitigation Strategies. *Sci*, *6*(1), 3. DOI: 10.3390/sci6010003

Ferràs-Hernández, X., Tarrats-Pons, E., & Arimany-Serrat, N. (2017). Disruption in the automotive industry: A Cambrian moment. *Business Horizons*, *60*(6), 855–863.

Ferreras-Méndez, J. L., Olmos-Penuela, J., Salas-Vallina, A., & Alegre, J. (2021). Entrepreneurial orientation and new product development performance in SMEs: The mediating role of business model innovation. *Technovation*, *108*, 1–13.

Fintecc, E. B. R. D. (2020). *Green Innovation Programme | EBRD FINTECC*. Ebrd. com. https://fintecc.ebrd.com/greeninnovationprogramme

First-Citizens Bank & Trust Company. (2025). *What is Venture Capital? | Silicon Valley Bank*. Www.svb.com. https://www.svb.com/startup-insights/vc-relations/what-is-venture-capital/

Fisher, R., & Ury, W. (2012). *Getting to yes: Negotiating an agreement without giving in*. Random House Business Books.

Fleck, J. (2018). Development and establishment in artificial intelligence. In *The Question of Artificial Intelligence* (pp. 106–164). Routledge.

Floersch, B. (2019, August 6). *Grant Proposal Development as Project Management*. The Grantsmanship Center. https://www.tgci.com/blog/2019/08/grant-proposal-development-project-management

Floridi, L. (2019). What the near future of artificial intelligence could be. *Philosophy & Technology*, *32*, 1–15.

Forrest, M. (2024, August 9). *10 reasons Graphic Design is the foundation for great Web Design - Access Creative*. Access Creative College. https://www.accesscreative.ac.uk/blog/10-reasons-graphic-design-is-foundation-for-web-design/

Freeman, R. E., Harrison, J. S., Wicks, A. C., Parmar, B. L., & De Colle, S. (2010). *Stakeholder theory: The state of the art*. Cambridge University Press.

Frimanslund, T., Kwiatkowski, G., & Oklevik, O. (2022). The role of finance in the literature of entrepreneurial ecosystems. *European Planning Studies*, *31*(2), 1–20. DOI: 10.1080/09654313.2022.2055962

Galea-Pace, S. (2020, May 17). *IBM Watson: how AI is transforming the supply chain*. Supplychaindigital.com. https://supplychaindigital.com/technology/ibm-watson-how-ai-transforming-supply-chain

Gangwani, D., & Zhu, X. (2024). Modeling and prediction of business success: A survey. *Artificial Intelligence Review, 57*(2), 1–51.

Gebhardt, L., & Bachmann, N. (2023). Entrepreneurial contributions to sustainability transitions—A longitudinal study of their representation and enactment through topic modeling and thematic analysis. *Journal of Cleaner Production, 420*, 138255. DOI: 10.1016/j.jclepro.2023.138255

Genome, S. (2023). *What Makes a Startup Succeed? Identifying Scaling Success Factors*. Startup Genome. https://startupgenome.com/article/what-makes-a-startup-succeed-identifying-scaling-success-factors

Ghoreishi, M., & Happonen, A. (2020, May). Key enablers for deploying artificial intelligence for circular economy embracing sustainable product design: Three case studies. In *AIP conference proceedings* (Vol. 2233, No. 1). AIP Publishing.

Ghoreishi, M., Treves, L., Teplov, R., & Pynnönen, M. (2023). The Impact of Artificial Intelligence on Circular Value Creation for Sustainable Development Goals. In Mazzi, F., & Floridi, L. (Eds.), *The Ethics of Artificial Intelligence for the Sustainable Development Goals. Philosophical Studies Series* (Vol. 152). Springer.

Gibson, K. (2024, August 14). *5 Ethical Considerations of AI in Business*. Business Insights Blog. https://online.hbs.edu/blog/post/ethical-considerations-of-ai

Giuggioli, G., & Pellegrini, M. M. (2022). Artificial intelligence as an enabler for entrepreneurs: A systematic literature review and an agenda for future research. *International Journal of Entrepreneurial Behaviour & Research, 29*(4), 816–837. DOI: 10.1108/ijebr-05-2021-0426

Glade, C., Kesting, P., Smolinski, R., & Kanbach, D. K. (2025). Start-up funding negotiations with venture capitalists: Understanding the behaviors and strategies of experienced entrepreneurs. *International Journal of Entrepreneurial Behaviour & Research, 1*(1). Advance online publication. DOI: 10.1108/ijebr-06-2024-0615

Global Footprint Network. (2022). *How many Earths? How many countries?* Earth Overshoot Day. https://overshoot.footprintnetwork.org/how-many-earths-or-countries-do-we-need/

Gompers, P. A., & Lerner, J. (2004). *The venture capital cycle*. Mit.

Goodell, J. W., Kumar, S., Lim, W. M., & Pattanaik, D. (2023). Artificial intelligence and machine learning in finance: Identifying foundations, themes, and research clusters from bibliometric analysis. *Journal of Behavioral and Experimental Finance, 32*, 100577.

Goralski, M. A., & Tan, T. K. (2020). Artificial intelligence and sustainable development. *International Journal of Management Education, 18*(1), 100330.

Gottschall, J. (2012). *The storytelling animal: how stories make us human*. Houghton Mifflin Harcourt.

G-P. (2020, March 10). *Tips on Expanding a Startup Internationally | Globalization Partners*. Globalization-Partners.com. https://www.globalization-partners.com/blog/tips-on-expanding-a-startup-internationally/?utm_keyword=&utm_device=c&utm_source=Adwords&utm_medium=cpc&utm_campaign=uk__search__dynamic__

Granstrand, O., & Holgersson, M. (2020). Innovation ecosystems: A conceptual review and a new definition. *Technovation, 90-91*, 102098. https://doi.org/DOI: 10.1016/j.technovation.2019.102098

Grantify. (2024). *How to Use Data to Win Grants and Attract Investors | Grantify*. Grantify.io. https://www.grantify.io/articles/how-to-use-data-to-win-grants-and-attract-investors

Grayson, D., Coulter, C., & Lee, M. (2022). *The sustainable business handbook: a guide to becoming more innovative, resilient and successful*. Kogan Page Inc.

Greaves, K. (2024, August 20). *If Grants for Black-Owned Businesses Are Eliminated, Your Favorite Beauty Brands Could Be Too*. Allure. https://www.allure.com/story/grants-for-black-owned-beauty-businesses

GreenRoutes. (2024). GreenRoutes: Open-source sustainable route planning. https://github.com/GreenRoutes

Gregersen, H. (2018, March 1). *Better Brainstorming*. Harvard Business Review. https://hbr.org/2018/03/better-brainstorming

Groner, T., & Moradi, A. (2024). Sacrificing Sustainability for a Higher GDP Growth Rate. *Development and Sustainability in Economics and Finance, 2-4*, 100015–100015. DOI: 10.1016/j.dsef.2024.100015

Guerrero, M., Liñán, F., & Cáceres-Carrasco, F. R. (2021). The influence of ecosystems on the entrepreneurship process: A comparison across developed and developing economies. *Small Business Economics, 57*(4), 1733–1759.

Guglielmo, G., Pellegrini, M. M., & Giannone, G. (2024). Artificial intelligence as an enabler for entrepreneurial finance: A practical guide to AI-driven video pitch evaluation for entrepreneurs and investors. *Management Decision, 29*, 816–837. DOI: 10.1108/md-10-2023-1926

Guo, K., Wang, J., & Chu, S. K. W. (2022). Using chatbots to scaffold EFL students' argumentative writing. *Assessing Writing, 54*, 100666. DOI: 10.1016/j.asw.2022.100666

Haefner, N., Wincent, J., Parida, V., & Gassmann, O. (2021). Artificial intelligence and innovation management: A review, framework, and research agenda . *Technological Forecasting and Social Change, 162*, 1–10.

Haenlein, M., & Kaplan, A. (2021). Artificial intelligence and robotics: Shaking up the business world and society at large. *Journal of Business Research, 124*(C), 405–407.

Hagberg, R. (2020, August 13). *Building Startup Teams: The Challenge for Entrepreneurs.* Www.hagbergconsulting.com. https://www.hagbergconsulting.com/building-startup-teams-the-challenge-for-entrepreneurs

Hagerty, A., & Rubinov, I. (2019). Global AI ethics: a review of the social impacts and ethical implications of artificial intelligence. arXiv preprint arXiv:1907.07892.

Haleem, A., Javaid, M., Qadri, M. A., Singh, R. P., & Suman, R. (2022). Artificial Intelligence (AI) Applications for marketing: a literature-based Study. *International Journal of Intelligent Networks, 3*(3), 119–132. DOI: 10.1016/j.ijin.2022.08.005

Hall, J. K., Daneke, G. A., & Lenox, M. J. (2010). Sustainable development and entrepreneurship: Past contributions and future directions. *Journal of Business Venturing, 25*(5), 439–448.

Hamm, J. (2002, December). *Why Entrepreneurs Don't Scale.* Harvard Business Review. https://hbr.org/2002/12/why-entrepreneurs-dont-scale?registration=success

Hanna, M., Pantanowitz, L., Jackson, B., Palmer, O., Visweswaran, S., Pantanowitz, J., & Rashidi, H. (2024). Ethical and Bias considerations in artificial intelligence (AI)/machine learning. *Modern Pathology*, 100686. PMID: 39694331

Hannan, M. A., Begum, R. A., Al-Shetwi, A. Q., Ker, P. J., Al Mamun, M. A., Hussain, A., & Mahlia, T. M. I. (2020). Waste collection route optimisation model for linking cost saving and emission reduction to achieve sustainable development goals. *Sustainable Cities and Society, 62*, 102393.

Hargrave, M. (2022, November 20). *How Crowdsourcing Works.* Investopedia. https://www.investopedia.com/terms/c/crowdsourcing.asp

Hariram, N. P., Mekha, K. B., Suganthan, V., & Sudhakar, K. (2023). Sustainalism: An integrated socio-economic-environmental model to address sustainable development and sustainability. *Sustainability, 15*(13), 10682.

Harroch, R. (2022). *What Angel Investors Want To Know Before Investing In Your Startup*. Forbes. https://www.forbes.com/sites/allbusiness/2020/12/13/what-angel-investors-want-to-know-before-investing-in-your-startup/

Hart, S. L., & Dowell, G. (2011). A natural-resource-based view of the firm: Fifteen years after. *Journal of Management*, *37*(5), 1464–1479.

Hassan, A., Anwar, I., Saleem, I., Islam, K. B., & Hussain, S. A. (2021). Individual entrepreneurial orientation, entrepreneurship education and entrepreneurial intention: The mediating role of entrepreneurial motivations. *Industry and Higher Education*, *35*(4), 403–418.

Häußermann, J. J., & Lütge, C. (2022). Community-in-the-loop: Towards pluralistic value creation in AI, or—why AI needs business ethics. *AI and Ethics*, 1–22.

Hayward, M. L., Forster, W. R., Sarasvathy, S. D., & Fredrickson, B. L. (2010). Beyond hubris: How highly confident entrepreneurs rebound to venture again. *Journal of Business Venturing*, *25*(6), 569–578. DOI: 10.1016/j.jbusvent.2009.03.002

He, H., Gray, J., Cangelosi, A., Meng, Q., McGinnity, T. M., & Mehnen, J. (2021). The challenges and opportunities of human-centered AI for trustworthy robots and autonomous systems. *IEEE Transactions on Cognitive and Developmental Systems*, *14*(4), 1398–1412.

Hinderer, S., & Kuckertz, A. (2024). Degrowth attitudes among entrepreneurs hinder fast venture scaling. *Business Strategy and the Environment*, *33*. Advance online publication. DOI: 10.1002/bse.3735

Hoballah, A., Mühlbauer, S., & Zürker, M. (2022). *Sustainable SME Action Agenda Scaling Green SME Support for 2030 2 YEARS*. https://adelphi.de/system/files/mediathek/bilder/Sustainable-SME-Action-Agenda-Scaling-Green-SME-Support-for-2030_0.pdf?utm_source=chatgpt.com

Hofmann, K. H., Jacob, A., & Pizzingrilli, M. (2022). Overcoming Growth Challenges of Sustainable Ventures in the Fashion Industry: A Multinational Exploration. *Sustainability*, *14*(16), 10275. DOI: 10.3390/su141610275

Horatio Alger Association. (2007). *News & Announcements*. Horatio Alger. https://horatioalger.org/members/detail/howard-schultz/

Hua, H., Li, Y., Wang, T., Dong, N., Li, W., & Cao, J. (2023). Edge computing with artificial intelligence: A machine learning perspective. *ACM Computing Surveys*, *55*(9), 1–35.

Hughes, C., Robert, L., Frady, K., & Arroyos, A. (2019). Artificial intelligence, employee engagement, fairness, and job outcomes. In *Managing technology and middle-and low-skilled employees* (pp. 61–68). Emerald Publishing Limited.

Hult, G. T. M., Hurley, R. F., & Knight, G. A. (2004). Innovativeness: Its antecedents and impact on business performance. *Industrial Marketing Management*, *33*(5), 429–438.

Humble, K. P., & Altun, D. (2020). Artificial Intelligence and the threat to human rights. *Journal of Internet Law*, *24*(3), 1–19.

IBM. (2024). AI adoption trends in business: 2024 report. https://www.ibm.com

ICO. (2025, June 13). *Guidance on AI and data protection*. Ico.org.uk. https://ico.org.uk/for-organisations/guide-to-data-protection/key-dp-themes/guidance-on-ai-and-data-protection/

IEA. (2022). *Net Zero Emissions by 2050 Scenario (NZE) – Global Energy and Climate Model – Analysis*. IEA. https://www.iea.org/reports/global-energy-and-climate-model/net-zero-emissions-by-2050-scenario-nze

Imanto, Y., Prijadi, R., & Dyah, R. (2019). Innovation Ecosystem for SMEs in the Creative Industry. *International Journal of Business*, *24*(4), 2019.

Inglis, I. (2022). Formation of Entrepreneurial Skills and Protection of Intellectual Property. *Intellectus*, *2*(2), 61–73. DOI: 10.56329/1810-7087.22.2.06

IPCC. (2014). *AR5 Climate Change 2014: Mitigation of Climate Change — IPCC*. Ipcc.ch; IPCC. https://www.ipcc.ch/report/ar5/wg3/

IPCC. (2021). *Climate change 2021: The physical science basis. Contribution of Working Group I to the Sixth Assessment Report*. Cambridge University Press.

Ireland, R. D., Hitt, M. A., & Sirmon, D. G. (2003). A model of strategic entrepreneurship: The construct and its dimensions. *Journal of Management*, *29*(6), 963–989.

Jarrahi, M. H. (2018). Artificial intelligence and the future of work: Human-AI symbiosis in organizational decision making. *Business Horizons*, *61*(4), 577–586.

Jean, N., Burke, M., Xie, M., Davis, W. M., Lobell, D. B., & Ermon, S. (2016). Combining satellite imagery and machine learning to predict poverty. *Science*, *353*(6301), 790–794. PMID: 27540167

Jebaraj, K. (2024, March 18). *Microsoft Azure Advantages and Disadvantages*. Www.knowledgehut.com. https://www.knowledgehut.com/blog/cloud-computing/microsoft-azure-advantages-and-disadvantages

Jobin, A., Ienca, M., & Vayena, E. (2019). The global landscape of AI ethics guidelines. *Nature Machine Intelligence, 1*(9), 389–399. DOI: 10.1038/s42256-019-0088-2

Jöhnk, J., Weißert, M., & Wyrtki, K. (2021). Ready or not, AI comes—An interview study of organizational AI readiness factors. *Business & Information Systems Engineering, 63*(1), 5–20.

Johnson, E. (2021, December 5). *IntelliGENZ Magazine*. IntelliGENZ Magazine. https://www.intelligenzmag.com/articles/3gudz2xq31a48paw4lr4v2t26s3a9j

Johnson, J., Whittington, R., Regnér, P., Angwin, D., Johnson, G., & Scholes, K. (2020). Exploring strategy. Academic Press.

Johnson, P. C., Laurell, C., Ots, M., & Sandström, C. (2022). Digital innovation and the effects of artificial intelligence on firms' research and development–Automation or augmentation, exploration or exploitation? *Technological Forecasting and Social Change, 179*, 121636.

Jones, R. (2020). The role of Artificial Intelligence in regulatory compliance. *Journal of Compliance and Regulation, 12*(2), 87-104.

Jose, R., Panigrahi, S. K., Patil, R. A., Fernando, Y., & Ramakrishna, S. (2020). Artificial intelligence-driven circular economy as a key enabler for sustainable energy management. *Materials Circular Economy, 2*, 1–7.

Josić, K. (2024). *Creativity*. The Engines of Our Ingenuity. https://engines.egr.uh.edu/episode/2817

Journeault, M., Perron, A., & Vallières, L. (2021). The collaborative roles of stakeholders in supporting the adoption of sustainability in SMEs. *Journal of Environmental Management, 287*, 112349. PMID: 33735683

Julmi, C. (2019). When rational decision-making becomes irrational: A critical assessment and re-conceptualization of intuition effectiveness. *Business Research, 12*(1), 291–314.

Jun, S.-P., Yoo, H. S., & Choi, S. (2018). Ten years of research change using Google Trends: From the perspective of big data utilizations and applications. *Technological Forecasting and Social Change, 130*, 69–87. DOI: 10.1016/j.techfore.2017.11.009

Kadwa, I., & Barnard, B. (2019). The impact of leadership on entrepreneurship and innovation: Perceptions of entrepreneurs. *IUP Journal of Entrepreneurship Development, 16*(4), 7–43.

Kaggwa, S., Eleogu, T. F., Okonkwo, F., Farayola, O. A., Uwaoma, P. U., & Akinoso, A. (2024). AI in decision making: Transforming business strategies. *International Journal of Research and Scientific Innovation, 10*(12), 423–444.

Kamalov, F., Calonge, D. S., & Gurrib, I. (2023). New Era of Artificial Intelligence in Education: Towards a Sustainable Multifaceted Revolution. *Sustainability, 15*(16), 12451. DOI: 10.3390/su151612451

Kanze, D., Huang, L., Conley, M. A., & Higgins, E. T. (2018). We Ask Men to Win and Women Not to Lose: Closing the Gender Gap in Startup Funding. *Academy of Management Journal, 61*(2), 586–614. DOI: 10.5465/amj.2016.1215

Kapoor, K. (2024, November 4). *Celebrating Green Entrepreneurs: Meet Three Young Innovators Leading Solutions for a Greener World.* Generationunlimited.org. https://www.generationunlimited.org/stories/celebrating-green-entrepreneurs-meet-three-young-innovators-leading-solutions-greener-world

Karami, M., Ojala, A., & Saarenketo, S. (2023). Entrepreneurial orientation and international opportunity development by SMEs: The mediating role of decision-making logic. *Journal of Small Business Management, 61*(2), 994–1022.

Karantza, P. (2017). *The impact of economic crises on the development of innovation and entrepreneurship* (Doctoral dissertation, Business Administration Programm, School of Economic Sciences and Business, Neapolis University Pafos).

Kar, S., Kar, A. K., & Gupta, M. P. (2021). Modeling drivers and barriers of artificial intelligence adoption: Insights from a strategic management perspective. *Intelligent Systems in Accounting, Finance & Management, 28*(4), 217–238.

Kaufman, T. (2024, May 7). *Communicating program impact in a grant proposal.* Candid Insights. https://blog.candid.org/post/communicating-program-impact-in-a-grant-proposal/

Keding, C. (2021). Understanding the interplay of artificial intelligence and strategic management: Four decades of research in review. *Management Review Quarterly, 71*(1), 91–134.

Khanin, D., Rosenfield, R., Mahto, R. V., & Singhal, C. (2021). Barriers to entrepreneurship: Opportunity recognition vs. opportunity pursuit. *Review of Managerial Science, 16*(4). Advance online publication. DOI: 10.1007/s11846-021-00477-6

Kienapple, B. (2020, August 21). *40+ Amazing Mind Map Templates You Can Use Now.* Venngage. https://venngage.com/blog/mind-map-templates/

Kim, K.-Y. (2023). A Study on the Decision-making Factors of Angel Investment to Revitalize Local Startup: Focusing on. *Hanguk Jibang Jachi Yeongu/Han'gug Ji'bang Jachi Yeon'gu/Han-Guk Jibang Jachi Yeon-Gu, 25*(2), 195–224. DOI: 10.38134/klgr.2023.25.2.195

Kim, W. C., & Mauborgne, R. (2005). *Blue Ocean Strategy: How to Create Uncontested Market Space and Make the Competition Irrelevant*. Havard Business School Publishing Corporation.

Kiradoo, G. (2023, March). *Unlocking the Potential of AI in Business: Challenges and Ethical Considerations*. https://papers.ssrn.com/sol3/papers.cfm?abstract_id=4387922

Kirat, T., Tambou, O., Do, V., & Tsoukiàs, A. (2023). Fairness and Explainability in Automatic Decision-Making Systems. A challenge for computer science and law. *EURO Journal on Decision Processes, 11*, 100036.

Kiyabo, K., & Isaga, N. (2020). Entrepreneurial orientation, competitive advantage, and SMEs' performance: Application of firm growth and personal wealth measures. *Journal of Innovation and Entrepreneurship, 9*(1), 1–15.

Klada, T.-V. (2018). Unraveling Entrepreneurial Team Formation: A Qualitative Study Among Funded Ventures. *SAGE Open, 8*(2). DOI: 10.1177/2158244018776700

Kleiman, D. (2020). *First pitch: winning money, mentors, and more for your startup*. Babson College Publishing.

Koivusalo, S. (2023). *Digital entrepreneurship: challenges faced by Finnish professional service business owners during venture launch in online business environments*. Master's Thesis, School of Business and Economics, Jyväskylä University.

Kokotović, F., Kurečić, P., & Mjeda, T. (2019). Accomplishing the sustainable development goal 13–climate action and the role of the European Union. *Interdisciplinary Description of Complex Systems: INDECS, 17*(1-B), 132–145.

Komal Singh, K., Hasan, M., & Rajendran, R. P. (2023). Opportunities and challenges of AI/ML in finance. In Irfan, M., Elmogy, M., Majid, M. S. A., & El-Sappagh, S. (Eds.), *The impact of AI innovation on financial sectors in the era of industry 5.0* (pp. 238–260). IGI Global. DOI: 10.4018/979-8-3693-0082-4.ch014

Korzyński, P., Mazurek, G., Krzypkowska, P., & Kurasiński, A. (2023). Artificial intelligence prompt engineering as a new digital competence: Analysis of generative AI technologies such as ChatGPT. *Entrepreneurial Business and Economics Review, 11*(3), 25–37. DOI: 10.15678/eber.2023.110302

Kramer, R. (2023, September 27). *Salesforce Leans On Enterprise Data With The Einstein 1 AI Platform.* Forbes. https://www.forbes.com/sites/moorinsights/2023/09/27/salesforce-leans-on-enterprise-data-with-the-einstein-1-ai-platform/

Kreiser, P. M., & Davis, J. (2010). Entrepreneurial orientation and firm performance: The unique impact of innovativeness, proactiveness, and risk-taking. *Journal of Small Business and Entrepreneurship*, *23*(1), 39–51.

Kriebitz, A., & Lütge, C. (2020). Artificial intelligence and human rights: A business ethical assessment. *Business and Human Rights Journal*, *5*(1), 84–104.

Kruk, E. (2023, October 18). *The Challenges of Scaling Tech Teams and How to Overcome Them.* Codigee.com; Codigee. https://codigee.com/blog/the-challenges-of-scaling-tech-teams-and-how-to-overcome-them?utm_source=chatgpt.com

Kubanek, A., & Szymoniak, M. (2022). Ethical governance in AI integration: A system-wide approach. *AI Ethics Journal*, *1*(2), 101–115.

Kulkov, I., Kulkova, J., Rohrbeck, R., Menvielle, L., Kaartemo, V., & Makkonen, H. (2023). Artificial intelligence - driven sustainable development: Examining organizational, technical, and processing approaches to achieving global goals. *Sustainable Development*, *32*(3). Advance online publication. DOI: 10.1002/sd.2773

Kulkov, I., Kulkova, J., Rohrbeck, R., Menvielle, L., Kaartemo, V., & Makkonen, H. (2024). Artificial intelligence-driven sustainable development: Examining organizational, technical, and processing approaches to achieving global goals. *Sustainable Development*, *32*(3), 2253–2267.

Kumar, V., Ashraf, A. R., & Nadeem, W. (2024). AI-powered marketing: What, where, and how? *International Journal of Information Management*, *77*, 102783–102783. DOI: 10.1016/j.ijinfomgt.2024.102783

Kumar, S. (2023). Evaluating performance of SMEs using structure equation modeling. *International Journal of Financial Engineering*, *11*(02). Advance online publication. DOI: 10.1142/s2424786323500421

Laaksonen, S., Virtanen, T., & Hämäläinen, M. (2025). Regional and cultural influences on AI adoption in Finnish SMEs. *Nordic Journal of Innovation*, *12*(1), 78–95.

Lab, B. (2025). *What is the average size of a Certified B Corp?* Www.bcorporation.net. https://www.bcorporation.net/en-us/faqs/what-average-size-certified-b-corp/

Labanauskaitė, D., Župerkienė, E., Kumpf, A., Šimanskienė, L., & Koller, S. M. (2021). Development of digital and entrepreneurial competences for the future labour market needs. *Entrepreneurship and Sustainability Issues*, *8*(3), 565-581.

Le Blanc, D. (2015). Towards integration at last? The Sustainable Development Goals as a network of targets. *Sustainable Development, 23*(3), 176–187.

Learn, F. (n.d.). *Sign graphs*. FutureLearn. https://www.futurelearn.com/info/courses/systems-thinking-complexity/0/steps/20382

Lee, J., Suh, T., Roy, D., & Baucus, M. (2019). Emerging technology and business model innovation: The case of artificial intelligence. *Journal of Open Innovation, 5*(3), 44.

Legal Foundations. (2024, February 10). *The Legal Framework of Crowdfunding for Startups - Legal Foundations*. Legal Foundations -. https://legalfoundations.org.uk/blog/the-legal-framework-of-crowdfunding-for-startups/

Lerro, A., Santarsiero, F., Schiuma, G., & Bartuseviciene, I. (2023). Mapping knowledge assets categories for successful crowdfunding strategies. *European Journal of Innovation Management*. Advance online publication. DOI: 10.1108/ejim-03-2022-0138

Liang, D., Tsai, C. F., & Wu, H. T. (2015). The effect of feature selection on financial distress prediction. *Knowledge-Based Systems, 73*, 289–297.

Liberatore, M. J., & Wagner, W. P. (2021). Virtual, mixed, and augmented reality: A systematic review for immersive systems research. *Virtual Reality (Waltham Cross), 25*(3), 773–799.

Lichtenthaler, U. (2020). Extremes of acceptance: Employee attitudes toward artificial intelligence. *The Journal of Business Strategy, 41*(5), 39–45.

Lin, M., & Viswanathan, S. (2013). Home Bias in Online Investments: An Empirical Study of an Online Crowd Funding Market. SSRN *Electronic Journal*. https://doi.org/DOI: 10.2139/ssrn.2219546

Lisniak, B. A. (2024). *Global environmental problems and their impact on international business*. Academic Press.

Liu, R. (2023). Innovative research on synergistic development of digital integrated media and visual design based on kruskal algorithm. *Applied Mathematics and Nonlinear Sciences, 9*(1), 1–13.

Liu, Y., Dai, W., Liao, M., & Wei, J. (2021). AI-driven CSR initiatives: A review of sustainability, transparency, and ethical challenges. *Sustainability, 13*(6), 3450. DOI: 10.3390/su13063450

Li, X., Li, J., Yuan, C., Guo, S., & Wang, Z. (2022). Digital infrastructure. In *Development practice of digital business environment in China* (pp. 39–55). Springer Nature Singapore.

Li, Y., Wu, B., Huang, Y., & Luan, S. (2024). Developing trustworthy artificial intelligence: Insights from research on interpersonal, human-automation, and human-AI trust. *Frontiers in Psychology, 15*. Advance online publication. DOI: 10.3389/fpsyg.2024.1382693 PMID: 38694439

Long, D., & Magerko, B. (2020). What is AI Literacy? Competencies and Design Considerations. *Proceedings of the 2020 CHI Conference on Human Factors in Computing Systems*, 1–16. DOI: 10.1145/3313831.3376727

Lopez, N. (2024, January). *Copernicus: 2023 is the hottest year on record, with global temperatures close to the 1.5°C limit | Copernicus*. Climate.copernicus.eu. https://climate.copernicus.eu/copernicus-2023-hottest-year-record

Loughran, M. (2024, August 14). *Communicating with AI: The Art of Prompting — A Guide for SMBs | by Matthew Loughran, EMBA | Craftsman AI*. Medium; Craftsman AI. https://medium.com/craftsman-ai/communicating-with-ai-the-art-of-prompting-a-guide-for-smbs-015856bba9b4

Lumpkin, G. T., & Dess, G. G. (1996). Clarifying the entrepreneurial orientation construct and linking it to performance. *Academy of Management Review, 21*(1), 135–172.

Lumpkin, G. T., & Dess, G. G. (2001). Linking two dimensions of entrepreneurial orientation to firm performance: The moderating role of environment and industry life cycle. *Journal of Business Venturing, 16*(5), 429–451.

MacCarthy, J., Tyukavina, S., Weisse, M., & Harris, N. (2024, August). *New data confirms: Forest fires are getting worse*. https://www.wri.org/insights/global-trends-forest-fires

Madavarapu, J. B., Kasula, B. Y., Whig, P., & Kautish, S. (2024). AI-Powered Solutions Advancing UN Sustainable Development Goals: A Case Study in Tackling Humanity's Challenges. In *Digital Technologies to Implement the UN Sustainable Development Goals* (pp. 47–67). Springer Nature Switzerland.

Makhloufi, L., Laghouag, A. A., Ali Sahli, A., & Belaid, F. (2021). Impact of entrepreneurial orientation on innovation capability: The mediating role of absorptive capability and organizational learning capabilities. *Sustainability, 13*(10), 1–20.

Makridakis, S. (2017). The forthcoming Artificial Intelligence (AI) revolution: Its impact on society and firms. *Futures, 90*, 46–60.

Malesios, C., De, D., Moursellas, A., Dey, P. K., & Evangelinos, K. (2020). Sustainability performance analysis of small and medium sized enterprises: Criteria, methods and framework. *Socio-Economic Planning Sciences*, *75*, 100993. DOI: 10.1016/j.seps.2020.100993

Malik, S., Chadhar, M., Vatanasakdakul, S., & Chetty, M. (2021). Factors affecting the organizational adoption of blockchain technology: Extending the technology–organization–environment (TOE) framework in the Australian context. *Sustainability*, *13*(16), 1–31.

Mariotti, S., & Marzano, R. (2021). The effects of competition policy, regulatory quality and trust on inward FDI in host countries. *International Business Review*, *30*(6), 1–16.

Marks, A. P. (1989). The Sinclair C5 – An Investigation into its Development, Launch, and Subsequent Failure. *European Journal of Marketing*, *23*(1), 61–71. DOI: 10.1108/eum0000000000542

Martin, N., Matt, C., Niebel, C., & Blind, K. (2019). How data protection regulation affects startup innovation. *Information Systems Frontiers*, *21*(6), 1307–1324.

Martins, J. (2022, October 5). *The beginner's guide to writing an effective business case • asana*. Asana. https://asana.com/resources/business-case

Martos, V., Ahmad, A., Cartujo, P., & Ordoñez, J. (2021). Ensuring agricultural sustainability through remote sensing in the era of agriculture 5.0. *Applied Sciences (Basel, Switzerland)*, *11*(13), 5911.

Masters, C. R. M. (2022, August 4). *Google Cloud Platform – Advantages and Disadvantages*. CRM Masters. https://crm-masters.com/google-cloud-platform-advantages-and-disadvantages/

Matalamäki, M. J., & Joensuu-Salo, S. (2022). Digitalization and strategic flexibility–a recipe for business growth. *Journal of Small Business and Enterprise Development*, *29*(3), 380–401.

May, R. (2019, January 24). *Start-ups across the UK are going bust - they need more careful management for our economy to boom*. The Telegraph. https://www.telegraph.co.uk/politics/2019/01/24/start-ups-across-uk-going-bust-need-careful-management-economy/

McDermid, J. A., Jia, Y., Porter, Z., & Habli, I. (2021). Artificial intelligence explainability: The technical and ethical dimensions. *Philosophical Transactions of the Royal Society A*, *379*(2207), 20200363. PMID: 34398656

McKinsey & Company. (2023). AI and sustainability: Opportunities in logistics. https://www.mckinsey.com

McKinsey Global Institute. (2018). *Artificial Intelligence: The next digital frontier?* https://www.mckinsey.com/mgi/overview/2018-in-review/ai-the-next-digital-frontier

McKinsey Technology Council and McKinsey Digital. (2023). What Every CEO Should Know about Generative AI. https://www.mckinsey.com/capabilities/mckinsey-digital/ourinsights/what-every-ceo-should-know-about-generative-ai

Meadows, D. H., Meadows, D. L., Randers, J., & Behrens, W. W. (1972). *The limits to growth*. Potomac Associates.

Meadows, D., Randers, J., & Meadows, D. (2004). *Limits to growth: The 30-Year update*. Chelsea Green Publishing Company.

Merhi, M. I., & Harfouche, A. (2024). Enablers of artificial intelligence adoption and implementation in production systems. *International Journal of Production Research, 62*(15), 5457–5471.

Metawa, N., Hassan, M. K., & Metawa, S. (2022). *Artificial Intelligence and Big Data for Financial Risk Management*. Routledge.

Michael, O. (2024). of Artificial Intelligence. *The Future of Small Business in Industry 5.0*, 215.

Miikkulainen, R., Iscoe, N., Shagrin, A., Rapp, R., Nazari, S., McGrath, P., & Lamba, G. (2018, April). Sentient ascend: AI-based massively multivariate conversion rate optimization. In *Proceedings of the AAAI Conference on Artificial Intelligence* (Vol. 32, No. 1), 7696-7703.

Mikalef, P., Boura, M., Lekakos, G., & Krogstie, J. (2020). Big data analytics capabilities and innovation: The mediating role of dynamic capabilities and moderating effect of the environment. *British Journal of Management, 31*(2), 356–382.

Miller, D. (1983). The correlates of entrepreneurship in three types of firms. *Management Science, 29*(7), 770–791.

Miller, D. (2017). *Building a storybrand: clarify your message so customers will listen*. Harpercollins Leadership, An Imprint of Harpercollins.

Miller, D., & Friesen, P. H. (1982). Innovation in conservative and entrepreneurial firms: Two models of strategic momentum. *Strategic Management Journal, 3*(1), 1–25.

Miloud, T., Aspelund, A., & Cabrol, M. (2012). Startup valuation by venture capitalists: An empirical study. *Venture Capital, 14*(2-3), 151–174. DOI: 10.1080/13691066.2012.667907

Mintzberg, H. (1973). Strategy-making in three modes. *California Management Review, 16*(2), 44–53.

Miquel. (2023, August 30). *Is the Fairphone 5 the most sustainable phone in the world?* Fairphone. https://www.fairphone.com/en/2023/08/30/is-the-fairphone-5-the-most-sustainable-phone-in-the-world/

Misaros, M., Stan, O. P., Donca, I. C., & Miclea, L. C. (2023). Autonomous Robots for Services—State of the Art, Challenges, and Research Areas. *Sensors (Basel), 23*(10), 1–31. PMID: 37430875

Mishra, D., & Maheshwari, N. (2024). Crowdsourcing-based social linkage and organizational innovation competence: Knowledge transfer effectiveness and absorptive capacity as serial mediators. *Journal of Knowledge Management, 28*(7), 2013–2037. DOI: 10.1108/jkm-07-2023-0583

Mitchell, I. K., & Walinga, J. (2017). The creative imperative: The role of creativity, creative problem solving and insight as key drivers for sustainability. *Journal of Cleaner Production, 140*(3), 1872–1884. DOI: 10.1016/j.jclepro.2016.09.162

Modayil, J., & Kuipers, B. (2008). The initial development of object knowledge by a learning robot. *Robotics and Autonomous Systems, 56*(11), 879–890. PMID: 19953188

Modi, T. B. (2023). Artificial Intelligence Ethics and Fairness: A study to address bias and fairness issues in AI systems, and the ethical implications of AI applications. *Revista Review Index Journal of Multidisciplinary, 3*(2), 24–35.

Mohammed, I. B., & Isa, S. M. (2021). The role of internet of things (IoT) in the containment and spread of the novel COVID-19 pandemic. *Computational intelligence methods in COVID-19: surveillance, prevention, prediction and diagnosis*, 109-119.

Montgomery, R. M. (2024). The Rise of Inequality and Artificial Intelligence: Impacts, Challenges, and Opportunities in a Globalized Economy. *Challenges, and Opportunities in a Globalized Economy.*

Montiel, I., Cuervo-Cazurra, A., Park, J., Antolín-López, R., & Husted, B. W. (2021). Implementing the United Nations' sustainable development goals in international business. *Journal of International Business Studies, 52*(5), 999. PMID: 34054154

Moravec, V., Hynek, N., Gavurova, B., & Rigelsky, M. (2024). Who uses it and for what purpose? The role of digital literacy in ChatGPT adoption and utilisation. *Journal of Innovation & Knowledge*, *9*(4), 100602–100602. DOI: 10.1016/j.jik.2024.100602

Moro-Visconti, R. (2024). Artificial Intelligence-Driven Digital Scalability and Growth Options. In *Artificial Intelligence Valuation: The Impact on Automation, BioTech, ChatBots, FinTech, B2B2C, and Other Industries* (pp. 131–204). Springer Nature Switzerland.

Mostafiz, M. I., Hughes, M., & Sambasivan, M. (2022). Entrepreneurial orientation, competitive advantage and strategic knowledge management capability in Malaysian family firms. *Journal of Knowledge Management*, *26*(2), 423–458.

Muhammad, N., & Sagatovna, M. (2024). The impact of Artificial Intelligence in decision making: A comprehensive review. *EPRA International Journal of Economics. Business and Management*, *11*(2), 27–38. DOI: 10.36713/epra15747

Mulder, P. (2015, March 17). *Influence Mapping, a great stakeholder management tool | ToolsHero*. Toolshero. https://www.toolshero.com/project-management/influence-mapping/

Musendekwa, M. (2025). Unveiling the Foundations of Quality Research in Higher Education: A Contemporary Perspective. In *Higher Education and Quality Assurance Practices* (pp. 421-454). IGI Global Scientific Publishing.

Mymizu. (2023). *mymizu*. Mymizu. https://www.mymizu.co/en/monthly-supporter

Mymizu. (2024). *Home (EN)*. Mymizu. https://www.mymizu.co/home-en

Nai, J., Lin, Y., Kotha, R., & Vissa, B. (2021). A foot in the door: Field experiments on entrepreneurs' network activation strategies for investor referrals. *Strategic Management Journal*, *43*(2), 323–339. DOI: 10.1002/smj.3341

Naqvi, R., Soomro, T. R., Alzoubi, H. M., Ghazal, T. M., & Alshurideh, M. T. (2021). The nexus between big data and decision-making: A study of big data techniques and technologies. In *The international conference on artificial intelligence and computer vision* (pp. 838–853). Springer International Publishing.

National Institute of Standards and Technology. (2023). *AI risk management framework (AI RMF 1.0)*. U.S. Department of Commerce. https://www.nist.gov/itl/ai-risk-management-framework

Natraj, L. (2021, March 24). *DataRobot — An end to end AI platform - Lalitha Natraj - Medium*. Medium. https://lnatraj.medium.com/data-robot-5a0efa279d48

Nawaz, H. R. (2023, April 28). *Introduction Being an entrepreneur is tough, and learning how to do it is even tougher. What's the best way to learn about entrepreneurship? Well, there are lots of ways! We've put together this list of the top ten platforms that will help you understand what it takes to be a successful entrepreneur*. https://www.linkedin.com/pulse/9-best-platforms-learn-entrepreneurship-hamid-rab-nawaz/

Ndagi, A., & Salihu, A. A. (2019). Technology Entrepreneurship and Fourth Industrial Revolution Era. *LAPAI International Journal of Management and Social Sciences*, *11*(1), 142–153.

Neal, M. (2024, January 8). *Expectations and Success Factors When Writing for Grants*. Medium. https://medium.com/@marcneal/expectations-and-success-factors-when-writing-for-grants-77236ed15b3c

Nemko, M. N. (2016, July 20). *An Interview with Tony Robbins*. Psychology Today. https://www.psychologytoday.com/us/blog/how-to-do-life/201607/an-interview-with-tony-robbins?msockid=2177f2f48c4c63ed0e9ce7d98d5962f4

Neumann, T. (2021). The impact of entrepreneurship on economic, social and environmental welfare and its determinants: A systematic review. *Management Review Quarterly*, *71*(3), 553–584.

NextCrowd. (2024). *Effective Crowdfunding Marketing Strategies to Boost Your Campaign*. Nextcrowd.co.uk. https://nextcrowd.co.uk/blog/effective-crowdfunding-marketing-strategies-to-boost-your-campaign

Ng, K., Su, J., & Kai, S. (2023). Fostering Secondary School Students' AI Literacy through Making AI-Driven Recycling Bins. *Education and Information Technologies*, *29*(8). Advance online publication. DOI: 10.1007/s10639-023-12183-9

Ngoc, T. H. (2024). *Green Innovation: Strategies for Commercializing Environmental Technologies and Solutions*. 151–156. DOI: 10.1109/atigb63471.2024.10717780

Nishant, R., Kennedy, M., & Corbett, J. (2020). Artificial intelligence for sustainability: Challenges, opportunities, and a research agenda. *International Journal of Information Management*, *53*, 102104.

Nissen, M. E., & Sengupta, K. (2006). Incorporating software agents into supply chains: Experimental investigation with a procurement task. *Management Information Systems Quarterly*, *30*(1), 145–166.

Now, O. (2023). *Sinclair C5 electric car: The future too soon?* Www.footmanjames.co.uk. https://www.footmanjames.co.uk/blog/sinclair-c5-electric-car-the-future-too-soon

NPC. (2024, February 15). *Systems Mapping - NPC*. Think NPC. https://www.thinknpc.org/resource-hub/systems-practice-toolkit/systems-mapping/?utm_source=chatgpt.com

O'Kane, C., Zhang, J. A., Haar, J., & Cunningham, J. A. (2023). How scientists interpret and address funding criteria: Value creation and undesirable side effects. *Small Business Economics*, *61*(2), 799–826. PMID: 38625286

O'Neil, C. (2016). *Weapons of math destruction: How big data increases inequality and threatens democracy*. Crown Publishing.

Obermeyer, Z., Powers, B., Vogeli, C., & Mullainathan, S. (2019). Dissecting Racial Bias in an Algorithm Used to Manage the Health of Populations. *Science*, *366*(6464), 447–453. DOI: 10.1126/science.aax2342 PMID: 31649194

Obrebowska, E. (2020, June 25). *The role of communication in the VC and start-ups universe*. Market One Capital Corner. https://medium.com/market-one-capital-corner/the-role-of-communication-in-the-vc-and-startups-universe-51a19a1bbf75

OECD. (2019). *OECD principles on artificial intelligence*. Organisation for Economic Co-operation and Development.

OECD. (2019). *The OECD Artificial Intelligence (AI) Principles*. Oecd.ai; OECD. https://oecd.ai/en/ai-principles

OECD. (2023). AI incident trends and governance challenges. https://www.oecd.org

OECD. (2023). Financing SMEs for sustainability – Financial institution strategies and approaches financing SMEs for sustainability. Results of an OECD survey of public and private financial institutions. In *OECD*. OECD. https://www.oecd.org/content/dam/oecd/en/about/programmes/cfe/oecd-platform-on-financing-smes-for-sustainability/Financing-SMEs-for-sustainability-Survey-report.pdf

OECD. (2024). National AI strategies and governance principles. https://www.oecd.org

OECD. (2024). *Survey shows households are willing to shift to greener lifestyles but that cost and convenience are key*. OECD. https://www.oecd.org/en/about/news/press-releases/2023/06/survey-shows-households-are-willing-to-shift-to-greener-lifestyles-but-that-cost-and-convenience-are-key-.html

OECD. (2025). OECD Platform on Financing SMEs for Sustainability Activity Report 2024. In *OECD Platform on Financing SMEs for Sustainability*. OECD. https://www.oecd.org/en/about/programmes/oecd-platform-on-financing-smes-for-sustainability.html

Okoli, I. E. N., Nwosu, K. C., & Okechukwu, M. E. (2021). Entrepreneurial orientation and performance of selected SMEs in Southeast, Nigeria. *European Journal of Business and Management Research*, *6*(4), 108–115.

Olawade, D. B., Wada, O. Z., Ige, A. O., Egbewole, B. I., Olojo, A., & Oladapo, B. I. (2024). Artificial Intelligence in Environmental Monitoring: Advancements, Challenges, and Future Directions. *Hygiene and Environmental Health Advances*, *12*, 100114–100114. DOI: 10.1016/j.heha.2024.100114

Olimjonovich, D. B. (2024). The subscription economy: Transforming business models. Web of Discoveries. *Journal of Analysis and Inventions*, *2*(3), 71–76.

Onetti, A. (2021, March 23). *Why most intrapreneurship programmes fail | Sifted*. Sifted. https://sifted.eu/articles/why-intrapreneurship-programmes-fail

Onukwulu, E. C., Agho, M. O., & Eyo-Udo, N. L. (2023). Sustainable supply chain practices to reduce carbon footprint in oil and gas. *Global Journal of Research in Multidisciplinary Studies*, *1*(2), 24–43.

Open University. (2024). *Mastering systems thinking in practice*. Open Learning. https://www.open.edu/openlearn/mod/oucontent/view.php?id=65668&section=4

Otero-Neira, C., Arias, M. J. F., & Lindman, M. T. (2013). Market orientation and entrepreneurial proclivity: Antecedents of innovation. *Global Business Review*, *14*(3), 385–395.

Ottinger, R. (2021, April 2). *Create Sustainable Success with the 4 Types of Innovation*. Fresh Consulting. https://www.freshconsulting.com/insights/blog/the-4-types-of-innovation/

Outcault, S., Sanguinetti, A., & Nelson, L. (2022). Technology characteristics that influence adoption of residential distributed energy resources: Adapting Rogers' framework. *Energy Policy*, *168*, 113153. DOI: 10.1016/j.enpol.2022.113153

Pallathadka, H., Ramirez-Asis, E. H., Loli-Poma, T. P., Kaliyaperumal, K., Ventayen, R. J. M., & Naved, M. (2023). Applications of artificial intelligence in business management, e-commerce and finance. *Materials Today: Proceedings*, *80*, 1–4.

Palmieri, R., Mercuri, C., & Mazzali-Lurati, S. (2022). Persuasive Reasons in Crowdfunding Campaigns: Comparing Argumentative Strategies in Successful and Unsuccessful Projects on Kickstarter. *International Journal of Strategic Communication*, *16*(2), 332–355. DOI: 10.1080/1553118x.2021.2008942

Panch, T., Mattie, H., & Atun, R. (2019). Artificial intelligence and algorithmic bias: Implications for health systems. *Journal of Global Health, 9*(2), 020318. PMID: 31788229

Parviainen, P., Tihinen, M., Kääriäinen, J., & Teppola, S. (2017). Tackling the digitalization challenge: how to benefit from digitalization in practice. *International Journal of Information Systems and Project Management, 5*(1), 63-77.

Patagonia. (2022). *Core values*. Patagonia. https://www.patagonia.com/core-values/

PeerSpot. (2021, August 30). *Pros and Cons of Amazon SageMaker 2025 | PeerSpot*. Peerspot.com. https://www.peerspot.com/products/amazon-sagemaker-pros-and-cons

Peng, L., & Zhang, L. (2024). Unleashing the Crowd: The Effect of Social Networks in Crowdfunding Markets. *Management Science*. Advance online publication. DOI: 10.1287/mnsc.2022.01364

Perifanis, N. A., & Kitsios, F. (2023). Investigating the influence of artificial intelligence on business value in the digital era of strategy: A literature review. *Information (Basel), 14*(2), 1–42.

Pertusa-Ortega, E. M., Zaragoza-Sáez, P., & Claver-Cortés, E. (2010). Can formalization, complexity, and centralization influence knowledge performance? *Journal of Business Research, 63*(3), 310–320.

Phelon, P. (2021, July 13). *The path to growth - Get Funded to Grow Your Business*. LinkedIn. https://www.linkedin.com/learning/get-funded-to-grow-your-business/the-path-to-growth?u=56744289

Pierrakis, Y., & Owen, R. (2022). Startup ventures and equity finance: How do Business Accelerators and Business Angels' assess the human capital of socio-environmental mission led entrepreneurs? *Innovation*, 1–25. DOI: 10.1080/14479338.2022.2029706

Pillai, R., & Sivathanu, B. (2020). Adoption of artificial intelligence (AI) for talent acquisition in IT/ITeS organizations. *Benchmarking, 27*(9), 2599–2629.

Pinto Borges, A., Lopes, J. M., Carvalho, C., Vieira, B. M., & Lopes, J. (2021). Education as a key to provide the growth of entrepreneurial intentions. *Education + Training, 63*(6), 809–832.

Polcz, K. (2021). Pitching as an Entrepreneurial Soft Skill in the World of Startups. *GiLE Journal of Skills Development, 1*(2), 5–6. DOI: 10.52398/gjsd.2021.v1.i2.pp5-6

Pollman, E. (2023, September 29). *Startup Failure*. The Harvard Law School Forum on Corporate Governance. https://corpgov.law.harvard.edu/2023/09/29/startup-failure/

Porter, M. E., & Heppelmann, J. E. (2014). How smart, connected products are transforming competition. *Harvard Business Review*, *92*(11), 64–88.

Pournader, M., Ghaderi, H., Hassanzadegan, A., & Fahimnia, B. (2021). Artificial intelligence applications in supply chain management. *International Journal of Production Economics*, *241*, 1–16.

Prashar, A. (2019). Towards sustainable development in industrial small and Medium-sized Enterprises: An energy sustainability approach. *Journal of Cleaner Production*, *235*, 977–996. DOI: 10.1016/j.jclepro.2019.07.045

Prince, A. E., & Schwarcz, D. (2019). Proxy discrimination in the age of artificial intelligence and big data. *Iowa Law Review*, *105*, 1257.

Pulka, B. M., & Gawuna, M. S. (2022). Contributions of SMEs to employment, gross domestic product, economic growth and development. *Jalingo Journal of Social and Management Sciences*, *4*(1), 1–18.

Purdue Global. (2024, January 8). *What Is a Growth Mindset and How Can You Develop One?* Purdue Global. https://www.purdueglobal.edu/blog/careers/develop-growth-mindset/

Putniņš, T. J., & Sauka, A. (2020). Why does entrepreneurial orientation affect company performance? *Strategic Entrepreneurship Journal*, *14*(4), 711–735.

Qiang, V., Rhim, J., & Moon, A. (2024). No such thing as one-size-fits-all in AI ethics frameworks: A comparative case study. *AI & Society*, *39*(4), 1975–1994.

Qiu, L., Hu, D., & Wang, Y. (2020). How do firms achieve sustainability through green innovation under external pressures of environmental regulation and market turbulence? *Business Strategy and the Environment*, *29*(6), 2695–2714.

Rai, R. K., Agarwal, S., & Agarwal, U. A. (2021). Artificial intelligence in business: Insights from women entrepreneurs in India. *Technological Forecasting and Social Change*, *171*, 120990. DOI: 10.1016/j.techfore.2021.120990

Raisch, S., & Krakowski, S. (2021). Artificial intelligence and management: The automation–augmentation paradox. *Academy of Management Review*, *46*(1), 192–210.

Rajest, S. S., Singh, B., Obaid, A. J., Regin, R., & Chinnusamy, K. (Eds.). (2023). *Advances in artificial and human intelligence in the modern era*. IGI Global.

Raji, I. D., & Buolamwini, J. (2019). Actionable auditing: Investigating the impact of publicly naming biased performance results of commercial AI products. *Proceedings of the 2019 AAAI/ACM Conference on AI Ethics and Society*, 429–435.

Raji, I. D., Smart, A., White, R. N., Mitchell, M., Gebru, T., Hutchinson, B., & Barnes, P. (2020, January). Closing the AI accountability gap: Defining an end-to-end framework for internal algorithmic auditing. In *Proceedings of the 2020 conference on fairness, accountability, and transparency* (pp. 33-44).

Rajović, J., Jovanović, M., Denić, N., & Bogdanovic, I. B. (2024). English Language as one of the key entrepreneurial competences. *Science International Journal*, *3*(2), 127–131. DOI: 10.35120/sciencej0302127r

Ramachandran, K. K., Mary, A. A. S., Hawladar, S., Asokk, D., Bhaskar, B., & Pitroda, J. R. (2022). Machine learning and role of artificial intelligence in optimizing work performance and employee behavior. *Materials Today: Proceedings*, *51*, 2327–2331.

Rane, N. (2023). Enhancing customer loyalty through Artificial Intelligence (AI), Internet of Things (IoT), and Big Data technologies: improving customer satisfaction, engagement, relationship, and experience. *Internet of Things (IoT), and Big Data Technologies: Improving Customer Satisfaction, Engagement, Relationship, and Experience*.

Rashid, C. A. (2021). The efficiency of financial ratios analysis to evaluate company's profitability. *Journal of Global Economics and Business*, *2*(4), 119–132.

Ratanavanich, M., & Charoensukmongkol, P. (2024). The interaction effect of goal orientation and mindfulness of entrepreneurs on firm innovation capability and its impact on firm performance. *VINE Journal of Information and Knowledge Management Systems*. Advance online publication. DOI: 10.1108/vjikms-06-2023-0135

Ratcliffe, S. (2016). *Oxford Essential Quotations* (4th ed.). Oxford University Press.

Rauch, A., & Frese, M. (2007). Let us put the person back into entrepreneurship research: A meta-analysis on the relationship between business owners' personality traits, business creation, and success. *European Journal of Work and Organizational Psychology*, *16*(4), 353–385. DOI: 10.1080/13594320701595438

Rauch, A., Wiklund, J., Lumpkin, G. T., & Frese, M. (2009). Entrepreneurial orientation and business performance: An assessment of past research and suggestions for the future. *Entrepreneurship Theory and Practice*, *33*(3), 761–787.

Rawashdeh, A. (2023). The consequences of artificial intelligence: an investigation into the impact of AI on job displacement in accounting. *Journal of Science and Technology Policy Management*.

Rea, A. (2019, July 10). *Storytelling in Life, Startups, and Venture Capital.* Medium. https://medium.com/%40andrew.twoclarify/storytelling-in-life-startups-and-venture-capital-da01ea89b09c

Reddy, S. (2023). Translational Application of Artificial Intelligence in Healthcare. In *Chapman and Hall/CRC eBooks*. Informa., DOI: 10.1201/9781003262152

Reeves, M., & Ueda, D. (2016). Designing the machines that will design strategy. *Harvard Business Review Digital Articles*, 2–6. https://hbr.org/2016/04/welcoming-the-chief-strategy-robot

Reffell, C. (2024). *Big Investor Returns from Equity Crowdfunding in the UK*. Crowdsourcing Week. https://crowdsourcingweek.com/blog/equity-crowdfunding-big-returns/

Reim, W., Åström, J., & Eriksson, O. (2020). Implementation of artificial intelligence (AI): A roadmap for business model innovation. *AI*, *1*(2), 11.

Renieris, E. M., Kiron, D., & Mills, S. (2022). The responsible AI imperative: Aligning CSR with technological innovation. *MIT Sloan Management Review*, *64*(1), 45–59.

Rezaei, M., Pironti, M., & Quaglia, R. (2024). AI in knowledge sharing, which ethical challenges are raised in decision-making processes for organisations? *Management Decision.*

Riahi, Y., & Riahi, S. (2018). Big data and big data analytics: Concepts, types and technologies. *International Journal of Research and Engineering*, *5*(9), 524–528.

Riani, A. (2023). *The 5 Key Success Factors For Startup Founders*. Forbes. https://www.forbes.com/sites/abdoriani/2023/06/30/the-5-key-success-factors-for-startup-founders/

Ris, K., Stankovic, Z., & Avramovic, Z. (2020). Implications of Implementation of Artificial Intelligence in the Banking Business with Correlation to the Human Factor. *Journal of Computer and Communications*, *8*, 130–144.

Robertson, A., & Maccarone, M. (2023). AI narratives and unequal conditions. Analyzing the discourse of liminal expert voices in discursive communicative spaces. *Telecommunications Policy*, *47*(5), 102462.

Robinson, M. F. (2019). *Artificial intelligence in hiring: Understanding attitudes and perspectives of HR practitioners*. A dissertation submitted to the faculty of Wilmington University in partial fulfillment of the requirements for the degree of Doctor of Business Administration, Wilmington University (Delaware).

Robinson, C. V., Ahmad, F., & Simmons, J. E. (2021). Consolidation and fragmentation in environmental scanning: A review and research agenda. *Long Range Planning*, *54*(3), 1–18.

Rogers, E. M. (2003). *Diffusion of Innovations* (5th ed.). Free Press.

Rosario, R. (2024, July 12). *The Ultimate Guide to HR Management in Startups - ProfitLeap*. ProfitLeap - Supercharge Your Financial Control with Huxley. https://profitleap.com/human-resource-management-in-startups/?utm_source=chatgpt.com

Roth, G. (2024, January 23). *3 Deadly Mistakes Early-Stage Startups Can Make Building Their Founding Teams*. Startup Stockpile. https://startup.unitelvoice.com/building-founding-teams

Russell, S., & Norvig, P. (2020). *Artificial intelligence: A modern approach* (4th ed.). Pearson.

Ruzgas, T., Jakubeliene, K., & Buivyte, A. (2016). Big Data Mining and Knowledge Discovery. *Journal of Communications Technology. Electronics and Computer Science*, *9*, 5–9.

S3 Solutions. (2021, August 9). *Government Grants: Advantages and Disadvantages*. S3solutions. https://www.s3solutions.co.uk/post/government-grants-advantages-and-disadvantages

Sanders, N. R., Boone, T., Ganeshan, R., & Wood, J. D. (2019). Sustainable supply chains in the age of AI and digitization: Research challenges and opportunities. *Journal of Business Logistics*, *40*(3), 229–240.

Scalenut. (2025, January 20). *Hugging Face AI Detector: In-Depth Review*. Scalenut.com; Scalenut. https://www.scalenut.com/blogs/hugging-face-ai-detector-review

Schultz, H. (2014). *Pour your heart into it: how Starbucks built a company one cup at a time*. Hachette. (Original work published 1997)

Schumpeter, J. A. (1934). *The theory of economic development. An inquiry into profits, capital, credit, interest, and the business cycle*. Harvard University Press.

Sedkaoui, S. (Ed.). (2018). *Big data analytics for entrepreneurial success*. IGI Global.

Segreto, P. (2023, August 12). *The Balancing Act: The Entrepreneurial Mindset Between Innovation and Sustainable Success*. Medium. https://paulsegreto.medium.com/the-balancing-act-the-entrepreneurial-mindset-between-innovation-and-sustainable-success-4b3bf5a532c5

Selvarajan, G. P. (2021). Harnessing AI-Driven Data Mining for Predictive Insights: A Framework for Enhancing Decision-Making in Dynamic Data Environments. *International Journal of Creative Research Thoughts*, *9*(2), 5476–5486.

Sendpulse. (2023, March 22). *What is Crowdsourcing: Types and Examples - Definition*. SendPulse. https://sendpulse.com/support/glossary/crowdsourcing

Seshadri, D. V. R. (2007). Understanding New Venture Failure due to Entrepreneur-Organization Goal Dissonance. *Vikalpa*, *32*(1), 55–74. DOI: 10.1177/0256090920070105

Shahid, A., & Mushtaq, M. (2020, November). A survey comparing specialized hardware and evolution in TPUs for neural networks. In *2020 IEEE 23rd International Multitopic Conference (INMIC)* (pp. 1-6). IEEE.

Shane, S. A. (Ed.). (2007). *Economic development through entrepreneurship: Government, university and business linkages*. Edward Elgar Publishing.

Sha, Q. (2023). Application of positive psychology to study the root of psychological anxiety of innovative entrepreneurs. *CNS Spectrums*, *28*(S1), S24–S24. DOI: 10.1017/s1092852923000949

Sharma, J. (2024, December 31). *All About Pytorch: Features and Advantages*. Shiksha.com; Shiksha Online. https://www.shiksha.com/online-courses/articles/all-about-pytorch-features-and-advantages-blogId-186266

Sharma, M., & Menon, P. (2022). Women entrepreneurs and AI adoption in post-pandemic India. *Journal of Entrepreneurship and Innovation in Emerging Economies*, *8*(2), 150–169. DOI: 10.1177/23939575221096845

Shaw, P., Price, R., Elliott, K., Copilah-Ali, J., Huntingford, J., & Ionescu, O. (2024). White Paper-Corporate Digital Responsibility (CDR) Securing Our Digital Futures. *Corporate Digital Responsibility (CDR) Securing Our Digital Futures*, 1-35.

Sheehy, B., & Farneti, F. (2021). Corporate social responsibility, sustainability, sustainable development and corporate sustainability: What is the difference, and does it matter? *Sustainability*, *13*(11), 5965.

Shepherd, D. A., & Patzelt, H. (2011). The new field of sustainable entrepreneurship: Studying entrepreneurial action linking "what is to be sustained" with "what is to be developed.". *Entrepreneurship Theory and Practice*, *35*(1), 137–163.

Sheykhfard, , Azmoodeh, Das, & Kutela. (2024). Analyzing Purchase Intentions of Used Electric Vehicles Through Consumer Experiences: A Structural Equation Modeling Approach. *Transport Policy*, *160*, 125–137. DOI: 10.1016/j.tranpol.2024.10.038

Shkarupa, O. V., Ignatchenko, A. S., & Vlasenko, K. A. (2021). *Mechanisms of investment support for scaling eco-innovations for sustainable development*. Vìsnik Sums'kogo Deržavnogo Unìversitetu, *2021*(2). DOI: 10.21272/1817-9215.2021.2-9

Shneiderman, B. (2020). Bridging the gap between ethics and practice: Guidelines for reliable, safe, and trustworthy human-centered AI systems. *ACM Transactions on Interactive Intelligent Systems*, *10*(4), 1–31.

Shokri, R., & Shmatikov, V. (2015). Privacy-preserving machine learning. *Proceedings on Privacy Enhancing Technologies. Privacy Enhancing Technologies Symposium*, *2015*(2), 35–50.

Siddiqui, M. K., & Goyal, K. K. (2023). A Study the Use of E-Payment Systems Based on Artifical Intelligence. *Computing & Intellegent Systems (SCTS)*, 1063-1076.

Sigmundsson, H., & Haga, M. (2024). Passion and grit in individuals with high levels of growth mindset are different than in individuals who have low growth mindset. *Acta Psychologica*, *250*, 104480. DOI: 10.1016/j.actpsy.2024.104480 PMID: 39265349

Singh & Paul. (2023). Impact of Awareness on the Adoption of Electric Vehicles: A Systematic Literature Review. *Emerald Publishing Limited EBooks*, 331–357. DOI: 10.1108/978-1-83753-060-120231023

Singha, R. (2024). Centring African Indigenous Knowledge: Afro-Feminist Perspectives on Women's Empowerment. In Musingafi, M., & Hungwe, C. (Eds.), *African Womanhood and the Feminist Agenda* (pp. 208–226). IGI Global Scientific Publishing. DOI: 10.4018/979-8-3693-1999-4.ch013

Singha, R. (2024a). Stress, Resilience, and Brain Performance. In Saluja, S., Kukreja, J., & Sharma, S. (Eds.), *Building Organizational Resilience With Neuroleadership* (pp. 14–29). IGI Global Scientific Publishing. DOI: 10.4018/979-8-3693-1785-3.ch002

Singha, R., & Kanna, S. Y. (2022). Tobacco farming, addiction, promotion of gender equality, well-being and monopoly of the Indian market. *Journal of International Women's Studies*, *23*(5), 11. https://vc.bridgew.edu/jiws/vol23/iss5/11

Singha, R., & Kanna, S. Y. (2022a). Women's empowerment, mindfulness, and role of women in eradicating alcohol and drug addiction from Indian society. *Journal of International Women's Studies*, *24*(7), 7. https://vc.bridgew.edu/jiws/vol24/iss7/7

Singha, R., & Singha, S. (2020). Women's empowerment through the silk industry of Assam, India, and its underlying economy. *Journal of International Women's Studies*, *21*(5), 3. https://vc.bridgew.edu/jiws/vol21/iss5/3

Singha, R., & Singha, S. (2024). Positive Interventions at Work: Enhancing Employee Well-Being and Organizational Sustainability. In Baykal, E. (Ed.), *Fostering Organizational Sustainability With Positive Psychology* (pp. 151–179). IGI Global Scientific Publishing. DOI: 10.4018/979-8-3693-1524-8.ch007

Singha, R., & Singha, S. (2024a). Mental Health Treatment: Exploring the Potential of Augmented Reality and Virtual Reality. In Hiran, K., Doshi, R., & Patel, M. (Eds.), *Applications of Virtual and Augmented Reality for Health and Well-being* (pp. 91–110). IGI Global Scientific Publishing. DOI: 10.4018/979-8-3693-1123-3.ch006

Singha, S. (2024b). Unveiling Gender Dynamics in Digital Capitalism: Navigating the Path to Social Gender Equality. In Topçu, Ç. (Ed.), *Digital Capitalism in the New Media Era* (pp. 161–186). IGI Global Scientific Publishing. DOI: 10.4018/979-8-3693-1182-0.ch009

Singha, S. (2024c). Fostering a Culture of Sustainability Through Human Resources Practices. In Popescu, C., Martínez-Falcó, J., Marco-Lajara, B., Sánchez-García, E., & Millán-Tudela, L. (Eds.), *Building Sustainable Human Resources Management Practices for Businesses* (pp. 107–124). IGI Global Scientific Publishing. DOI: 10.4018/979-8-3693-1994-9.ch007

Singha, S., & Singha, R. (2023). Understanding Diversity: The Power of Differences. In Even, A., & Christiansen, B. (Eds.), *Enhancing Employee Engagement and Productivity in the Post-Pandemic Multigenerational Workforce* (pp. 297–313). IGI Global Scientific Publishing. DOI: 10.4018/978-1-6684-9172-0.ch015

Singha, S., & Sivarethinamohan, R. (2021). The role of women in the formation of organizational climates in various workspaces in Bengaluru, India. *Journal of International Women's Studies*, *22*(6), 13. https://vc.bridgew.edu/jiws/vol22/iss6/13

Singha, S., & Sivarethinamohan, R. (2022a). Social inclusion, equality, leadership, and diversity to attain Sustainable Development Goal 5 in the Indian banking industry. *Journal of International Women's Studies*, *23*(5), 9. https://vc.bridgew.edu/jiws/vol23/iss5/9

Singha, S., & Sivarethinamohan, R. (2022b). Formation of positive organizational climate: Integration of Ubuntu diversity management in banks. *Journal of International Women's Studies*, *24*(4), 10. https://vc.bridgew.edu/jiws/vol24/iss4/10

Singh, M., & Verma, J. (2023). The Effect of Entrepreneurship Education on Micro-entrepreneurial Outcomes Funded by MFIs. *European Conference on Innovation and Entrepreneurship, 18*(2), 822–830. DOI: 10.34190/ecie.18.2.1486

Singh, S., & Kumar, A. (2024). Investing in the future: An integrated model for analysing user attitudes towards Robo-advisory services with AI integration. *Vilakshan – XIMB. Journal of Management, 21*. Advance online publication. DOI: 10.1108/xjm-03-2024-0046

Sipola, J., Saunila, M., & Ukko, J. (2023). Adopting artificial intelligence in sustainable business. *Journal of Cleaner Production, 426*, 139197. DOI: 10.1016/j.jclepro.2023.139197

Si, S., Hall, J., Suddaby, R., Ahlstrom, D., & Wei, J. (2023). Technology, entrepreneurship, innovation and social change in digital economics. *Technovation, 119*, 102484.

Sjödin, D., Parida, V., Palmié, M., & Wincent, J. (2021). How AI capabilities enable business model innovation: Scaling AI through co-evolutionary processes and feedback loops. *Journal of Business Research, 134*, 574–587.

Smith, A. & Gupta, A. (2022). Adapting to regulatory changes with AI: Strategies for financial institutions. *Regulatory Compliance Journal, 28*(1), 22-39.

Smith, R. (2024, April 9). *The Power of Positivity: The Benefits of a Positive Mindset at Work - Thrive4Life*. Thrive4Life. https://www.thrive4life.co.uk/blog/the-power-of-positivity-the-benefits-of-a-positive-mindset-at-work/

Somers, M. (2022, November 23). *3 traits of an entrepreneurial mindset*. MIT Sloan. https://mitsloan.mit.edu/ideas-made-to-matter/3-traits-entrepreneurial-mindset

Soni, N., Sharma, E. K., Singh, N., & Kapoor, A. (2019). Impact of artificial intelligence on businesses: from research, innovation, market deployment to future shifts in business models. arXiv preprint arXiv:1905.02092.

Soni, N., Sharma, E. K., Singh, N., & Kapoor, A. (2020). Artificial intelligence in business: From research and innovation to market deployment. *Procedia Computer Science, 167*, 2200–2210.

Spector, J. M., & Ma, S. (2019). Inquiry and critical thinking skills for the next generation: From artificial intelligence back to human intelligence. *Smart Learning Environments, 6*(1). Advance online publication. DOI: 10.1186/s40561-019-0088-z

Stahl, B. C. (2021). *Artificial intelligence for a better future: an ecosystem perspective on the ethics of AI and emerging digital technologies*. Springer Nature.

Stein, P. B. W., Rooprai, G., & Kludovac, T. (2024). *Raising United States (U.S.) 23 Trillion Dollars Greening Banks and Capital Markets for Growth: G20 Input Paper on Emerging Markets*. World Bank. https://documents.worldbank.org/curated/en/995131540533377620/Raising-United-States-U-S-23-Trillion-Dollars-Greening-Banks-and-Capital-Markets-for-Growth-G20-Input-Paper-on-Emerging-Markets

Strohmeier, S., & Piazza, F. (2013). Domain driven data mining in human resource management: A review of current research. *Expert Systems with Applications*, *40*(7), 2410–2420.

Suboyin, Eldred, Thatcher, Rehman, Gee, & Anjum. (2023). *Environomics Framework for Sustainable Business Practices: Industrial Case Studies on True Impact Reduction and Process Optimization Through AI*. DOI: 10.2118/214459-ms

Suominen, A., Toivanen, H., & Seppänen, M. (2017). Firms' knowledge profiles: Mapping patent data with unsupervised learning. *Technological Forecasting and Social Change*, *115*, 131–142.

Svoboda, A. (2023). The impact of artificial intelligence on the banking industry. *Journal of Banking and Finance Management*, *4*(1), 7–13.

Swartz, T. (2024, December 10). *Scientists pinpoint key attribute of people who have more willpower — how to get it yourself*. New York Post. https://nypost.com/2024/12/10/health/scientists-pinpoint-key-attribute-of-people-with-willpower

Syed, R., Suriadi, S., Adams, M., Bandara, W., Leemans, S. J., Ouyang, C., & Reijers, H. A. (2020). Robotic process automation: Contemporary themes and challenges. *Computers in Industry*, *115*, 1–15.

TechVidvan. (2020, August). *Advantages and Disadvantages of TensorFlow*. TechVidvan. https://techvidvan.com/tutorials/pros-and-cons-of-tensorflow

Tekin, İ. Ç., & Küsbeci, P. (2021). Dijital dönüşüm sürecinde yükselen bir değer: Dijital girişimcilik. *Stratejik Yönetim Araştırmaları Dergisi*, *4*(1), 81–102.

Tennekoon, C. E. (2023, June 23). *The 4 P's of Innovation: Exploring the Dimensions of Change*. Www.linkedin.com

The Offsite Guide. (2024). *Local vs. Global: Is Local Sourcing Always the Most Sustainable Option in Construction?* The Offsite Guide. https://theoffsiteguide.com/articles/local-vs-global-is-local-sourcing-always-the-most-sustainable-option-in-construction

The Royal Docks Team. (2016). *Launching the Royal Docks Centre for Sustainability*. The Royal Docks. https://royaldocks.london/whats-on/launching-the-royal-docks-centre-for-sustainability

Thiele, L. P. (2024). *Sustainability*. John Wiley & Sons.

Thorpe, R. (2016). *Gower handbook of leadership and management development*. CRC Press.

Tidd, J., & Bessant, J. (2020). *Managing innovation: Integrating technological, market and organizational change* (7th ed.). Wiley.

Tien, J. M. (2017). Internet of things, real-time decision making, and artificial intelligence. *Annals of Data Science*, *4*, 149–178.

Todaro, M. P., & Smith, S. C. (2020). *Economic development*.

Tong, S., Jia, N., Luo, X., & Fang, Z. (2021). The Janus face of artificial intelligence feedback: Deployment versus disclosure effects on employee performance. *Strategic Management Journal*, *42*(9), 1600–1631.

Topol, E. (2019). *Deep medicine: How artificial intelligence can make healthcare human again*. Basic Books.

Torfing, J. (2019). Collaborative innovation in the public sector: The argument. *Public Management Review*, *21*(1), 1–11.

Tornatzky, L. G., & Fleischer, M. (1990). *The processes of technological innovation*. Lexington Books.

Torrado, R. R., Bontrager, P., Togelius, J., Liu, J., & Perez-Liebana, D. (2018, August). Deep reinforcement learning for general video game ai. In *2018 IEEE Conference on Computational Intelligence and Games (CIG)* (pp. 1-8). IEEE.

Toxopeus, H., Achterberg, E., & Polzin, F. (2021). How can firms access bank finance for circular business model innovation? *Business Strategy and the Environment*, *30*(6), 2773–2795. DOI: 10.1002/bse.2893

Trencher, G., Taeihagh, A., & Yarime, M. (2020). Overcoming barriers to developing and diffusing fuel-cell vehicles: Governance strategies and experiences in Japan. *Energy Policy*, *142*, 111533. DOI: 10.1016/j.enpol.2020.111533

Truong, Y., & Papagiannidis, S. (2022). Artificial intelligence as an enabler for innovation: A review and future research agenda. *Technological Forecasting and Social Change*, *183*, 1–6.

Tschang, F. T., & Almirall, E. (2021). Artificial intelligence as augmenting automation: Implications for employment. *The Academy of Management Perspectives*, *35*(4), 642–659.

Turienzo, J., Cabanelas, P., & Lampón, J. F. (2023). Business models in times of disruption: The connected and autonomous vehicles (uncertain) domino effect. *Journal of Business Research*, *156*, 1–12.

Turner, C. (2022). Augmented reality, augmented epistemology, and the real-world web. *Philosophy & Technology*, *35*(1), 19.

UAGC. (2021, December 8). *9 Characteristics of the Entrepreneurial Mindset*. The University of Arizona Global Campus. https://www.uagc.edu/blog/9-characteristics-of-the-entrepreneurial-mindset

Ukoba, K., Olatunji, K. O., Adeoye, E., Jen, T. C., & Madyira, D. M. (2024). Optimizing renewable energy systems through artificial intelligence: Review and future prospects. *Energy & Environment*, *35*(7), 3833–3879.

UNEP. (2021, July 6). Five young entrepreneurs embracing sustainable business models. *Unep.org*. https://www.unep.org/news-and-stories/story/five-young-entrepreneurs-embracing-sustainable-business-models

UNESCO. (2025). https://unesdoc.unesco.org/ark:/48223/pf0000379936

United Nations. (2015). *Transforming our world: The 2030 Agenda for Sustainable Development.*

Unlimited, G. (2024, November 4). *Naglaa's Green Solution for Environmental Restoration*. YouTube. https://www.youtube.com/watch?v=Y2aQDBrjWVc

Uralovich, K. S., Toshmamatovich, T. U., Kubayevich, K. F., Sapaev, I. B., Saylaubaevna, S. S., Beknazarova, Z. F., & Khurramov, A. (2023). A primary factor in sustainable development and environmental sustainability is environmental education. *Caspian Journal of Environmental Sciences*, *21*(4), 965–975.

Usman, F. O., Kess-Momoh, A. J., Ibeh, C. V., Elufioye, A. E., Ilojianya, V. I., & Oyeyemi, O. P. (2024). Entrepreneurial innovations and trends: A global review: Examining emerging trends, challenges, and opportunities in the field of entrepreneurship, with a focus on how technology and globalization are shaping new business ventures. *International Journal of Science and Research Archive*, *11*(1), 552–569.

Uzir, M. U. H., Al Halbusi, H., Lim, R., Jerin, I., Abdul Hamid, A. B., Ramayah, T., & Haque, A. (2021). Applied Artificial Intelligence and user satisfaction: Smartwatch usage for healthcare in Bangladesh during COVID-19. *Technology in Society*, *67*, 101780. PMID: 34697510

Vallaster, C., Kraus, S., Lindahl, J. M. M., & Nielsen, A. (2019). Ethics and entrepreneurship: A bibliometric study and literature review. *Journal of Business Research*, *99*, 226–237.

van den Besselaar, P., & Mom, C. (2022). The effect of writing style on success in grant applications. *Journal of Informetrics*, *16*(1), 101257. DOI: 10.1016/j.joi.2022.101257

Van Doorn, S., Heyden, M., Tröster, C., & Volberda, H. (2015). Entrepreneurial orientation and performance: Investigating local requirements for entrepreneurial decision-making. In *Cognition and strategy* (Vol. 32, pp. 211–239). Emerald Group Publishing Limited.

Van Praag, C. M., & Versloot, P. H. (2007). What is the value of entrepreneurship? A review of recent research. *Small Business Economics*, *29*(4), 351–382.

Van Wynsberghe, A. (2021). Sustainable AI: AI for sustainability and the sustainability of AI. *AI and Ethics*, *1*(3), 213–218.

Veale, M., Binns, R., & Edwards, L. (2018). Algorithms that remember: Model inversion attacks and Data Protection Law. *Philosophical Transactions. Series A, Mathematical, Physical, and Engineering Sciences*, *376*(2133), 20180083. DOI: 10.1098/rsta.2018.0083 PMID: 30322998

Veluru, C. S. (2024). Responsible Artificial Intelligence on Large Scale Data to Prevent Misuse, Unethical Challenges and Security Breaches. *Journal of Artificial Intelligence & Cloud Computing*. DOI: 10.47363/JAICC/2024

Vermesan, O., John, R., Pype, P., Daalderop, G., Kriegel, K., Mitic, G., & Waldhör, S. (2021). Automotive intelligence embedded in electric connected autonomous and shared vehicles technology for sustainable green mobility. *Frontiers in Future Transportation*, *2*, 688482.

Vincenzo, B., Annalisa, C., & Elisa, U. (2020). Network dynamics in business angel group investment decisions. *Journal of Corporate Finance*, *66*(101812), 101812. DOI: 10.1016/j.jcorpfin.2020.101812

Voigt, P., & Von dem Bussche, A. (2017). *The EU General Data Protection Regulation (GDPR): A practical guide*. Springer.

Von Krogh, G., Ben-Menahem, S. M., & Shrestha, Y. R. (2021). Artificial intelligence in strategizing: Prospects and challenges. *Future of Strategic Management*, 625-646.

Votto, A. M., Valecha, R., Najafirad, P., & Rao, H. R. (2021). Artificial intelligence in tactical human resource management: A systematic literature review. *International Journal of Information Management Data Insights*, *1*(2), 1–15.

Voulvoulis, N., Giakoumis, T., Hunt, C., Kioupi, V., Petrou, N., Souliotis, I., & Vaghela, C., & binti Wan Rosely, WIH. (2022). Systems Thinking as a Paradigm Shift for Sustainability Transformation. *Global Environmental Change*, *75*(102544), 102544. DOI: 10.1016/j.gloenvcha.2022.102544

Walker, J. (2024, June 4). *Understanding Different Types of Startup Funding | Rooled*. Rooled. https://rooled.com/resources/understanding-different-types-of-startup-funding/

Walsack, J. (2019, July 23). *How to Prepare Your Business to Raise Funding*. Https://Www.uschamber.com/Co. https://www.uschamber.com/co/run/business-financing/how-to-prepare-to-raise-funding

Walsh, N. (2023). *Business Bites: Writing a business case - ABDO*. ABDO. https://www.abdo.org.uk/news/business-bites-writing-a-business-case/

Wamba-Taguimdje, S. L., Wamba, S. F., Kamdjoug, J. R. K., & Wanko, C. E. T. (2020). Influence of artificial intelligence (AI) on firm performance: The business value of AI-based transformation projects. *Business Process Management Journal*, *26*(7), 1893–1924.

Wang, Y., & Witlox, F. (2025). Global trends in electric vehicle adoption and the impact of environmental awareness, user attributes, and barriers. *Energy Reports*, *13*, 1125–1137. DOI: 10.1016/j.egyr.2024.12.054

Wasim, J., Youssef, M. H., Christodoulou, I., & Reinhardt, R. (2023). The Path to Entrepreneurship: The Role of Social Networks in Driving Entrepreneurial Learning and Education. *Journal of Management Education*, *48*(3). Advance online publication. DOI: 10.1177/10525629231219235

West, J., & Bhattacharya, M. (2016). Intelligent financial fraud detection: A comprehensive review. *Computers & Security*, *57*, 47–66.

White, K., Hardisty, D. J., & Habib, R. (2019). The elusive green consumer. *Harvard Business Review*, *97*(4), 124–133.

Whittlestone, J., Nyrup, R., Alexandrova, A., Dihal, K., & Cave, S. (2019). *Ethical and societal implications of algorithms, data, and artificial intelligence: a roadmap for research*. Nuffield Foundation.

Wiklund, J., & Shepherd, D. (2005). Entrepreneurial orientation and small business performance: A configurational approach. *Journal of Business Venturing*, *20*(1), 71–91.

Williamson, M. (2021, September 26). *Clive Sinclair: Visionary who helped create the first home computers*. The Independent. https://www.independent.co.uk/news/obituaries/clive-sinclair-pc-computer-c5-obituary-death-b1926557.html

Wilson, H. J., & Daugherty, P. R. (2018). Collaborative intelligence: Humans and AI are joining forces. *Harvard Business Review*, *96*(4), 114–123.

Wittmer, D. P. (2019). Ethical decision-making. In *Handbook of administrative ethics* (pp. 481–507). Routledge.

WMO. (2024a). *State of the Climate 2024 update for COP 2029*. Wmo.int; WMO. https://library.wmo.int/viewer/69075/?offset=#page=4&viewer=picture&o=bookmarks&n=0&q=

WMO. (2024b, October). *WMO report highlights growing shortfalls and stress in global water resources*. World Meteorological Organization. https://wmo.int/news/media-centre/wmo-report-highlights-growing-shortfalls-and-stress-global-water-resources

World Economic Forum. (2023). *AI governance: The role of corporations in ethical AI deployment*. WEF Annual Report.

World Economic Forum. (2023, April 30). *The Future of Jobs Report 2023*. World Economic Forum. https://www.weforum.org/publications/the-future-of-jobs-report-2023/

WPAB. (2024, November 20). *Creating a Financial Management Plan for Your Grant Proposal - fundsforNGOs - Grants and Resources for Sustainability*. FundsforNGOs - Grants and Resources for Sustainability - Grants and Resources for Sustainability. https://www.fundsforngos.org/how-to-write-a-proposal/creating-a-financial-management-plan-for-your-grant-proposal/

Wuest, T., Weimer, D., Irgens, C., & Thoben, K. D. (2016). Machine learning in manufacturing. *Production & Manufacturing Research*, *4*(1), 23–45.

Wujarso, R. (2023). *Effect of digital transformation on company operational efficiency*. Asadel Publisher.

Wu, W. T., Li, Y. J., Feng, A. Z., Li, L., Huang, T., Xu, A. D., & Lyu, J. (2021). Data mining in clinical big data: The frequently used databases, steps, and methodological models. *Military Medical Research*, *8*, 1–12. PMID: 34380547

Yadav, N., & Mankavil Kovil Veettil, N. (2021). Developing a comprehensive business case for sustainability: an inductive study. *International Journal of Organizational Analysis, ahead-of-print*(ahead-of-print). https://doi.org/DOI: 10.1108/ijoa-04-2020-2146

Yarimoglu, E., & Binboga, G. (2019). Understanding sustainable consumption in an emerging country: The antecedents and consequences of the ecologically conscious consumer behavior model. *Business Strategy and the Environment*, *28*(4), 642–651.

Yasir, N., Babar, M., Mehmood, H. S., Xie, R., & Guo, G. (2023). The Environmental Values Play a Role in the Development of Green Entrepreneurship to Achieve Sustainable Entrepreneurial Intention. *Sustainability*, *15*(8), 6451. DOI: 10.3390/su15086451

Yeomans, M., Shah, A., Mullainathan, S., & Kleinberg, J. (2019). Making sense of recommendations. *Journal of Behavioral Decision Making*, *32*(4), 403–414.

Yigitcanlar, T., & Cugurullo, F. (2020). The sustainability of artificial intelligence: An urbanistic viewpoint from the lens of smart and sustainable cities. *Sustainability*, *12*(20), 8548.

Yousfi-Monod, M., Farzindar, A., & Lapalme, G. (2010). Supervised machine learning for summarizing legal documents. *Advances in Artificial Intelligence: 23rd Canadian Conference on Artificial Intelligence, Canadian AI 2010, Ottawa, Canada, May 31–June 2, 2010 Proceedings*, *23*, 51–62.

Zafarani, R. (2014). *Social Media Mining: An Introduction*. Cambridge University Press.

Zahra, S. A. (1991). Predictors and financial outcomes of corporate entrepreneurship: An exploratory study. *Journal of Business Venturing*, *6*(4), 259–285.

Zajko, M. (2021). Conservative AI and social inequality: Conceptualizing alternatives to bias through social theory. *AI & Society*, *36*(3), 1047–1056.

Zamfir Cristina Mihaela. (2018). Reprogramming Mind for Business Success. *Ovidius University Annals: Economic Sciences Series, 18*(2), 372–375. https://doaj.org/article/3e51bd939b1f4e5fbedbca7d1fedfa4a

Zao, S. (2024). Intrapreneurship Examples. https://www.studiozao.com/knowledge/intrapreneurship-examples

Zhang, Y. (2020). How Venture Capitalists Bet: Evidence from Two Randomized Controlled Trials. SSRN *Electronic Journal*. DOI: 10.2139/ssrn.3724424

Zhang, C., & Lu, Y. (2021). Study on artificial intelligence: The state of the art and future prospects. *Journal of Industrial Information Integration*, *23*, 1–9.

Zhao, H., & Seibert, S. E. (2006). The Big Five personality dimensions and entrepreneurial status: A meta-analytical review. *The Journal of Applied Psychology*, *91*(2), 259–271. DOI: 10.1037/0021-9010.91.2.259 PMID: 16551182

Zhao, Q. (2009). A survey on virtual reality. *Science in China Series F: Information Sciences*, *52*(3), 348–400.

Zhu, L., Mou, W., Lai, Y., Lin, J., & Luo, P. (2024). Language and cultural bias in AI: Comparing the performance of large language models developed in different countries on Traditional Chinese Medicine highlights the need for localized models. *Journal of Translational Medicine*, *22*(1). Advance online publication. DOI: 10.1186/s12967-024-05128-4 PMID: 38553705

Zou, X. (2022). *Perspectives and experiences of gender inclusion for STEM programs through an intersectional lens* (Doctoral dissertation, University of Oxford).

Zuboff, S. (2019). *The age of surveillance capitalism: The fight for a human future at the new frontier of power*. PublicAffairs.

Zuloaga-Rotta, L., Borja-Rosales, R., Rodríguez Mallma, M. J., Mauricio, D., & Maculan, N. (2024). Method to Forecast the Presidential Election Results Based on Simulation and Machine Learning. *Computation (Basel, Switzerland)*, *12*(3), 1–16.

About the Contributors

Muhammad Abu Naser holds extensive expertise as a proficient consultant, researcher, and course leader, accumulating more than two decades of teaching and research involvement. Additionally, he brings seven years of valuable commercial experience in the field of Information Technology. Dr.Naser demonstrates confidence in delivering presentations to diverse audiences, ranging from technical experts to those with less technical background. He is enthusiastic about embracing new intellectual challenges in his professional journey. Dr. Naser embarked on his academic journey at London Metropolitan University in 2003, starting as a consultant and later progressing to the position of a lecturer in 2005. His significant contributions resonate not only within London Met but also encompass prestigious institutions worldwide and the University of London. Prior to his entry into academia, Dr. Naser held managerial positions in renowned organisations such as Ford, Granada, Tesco, Command Software Systems, and Corona IT. Notably, he served as the Managing Director in a multinational organisation. As a business consultant, Dr. Naser played a pivotal role in revitalising a financially struggling company, steering it towards profitability through successful ventures and direct sales, both nationally and internationally. Dr. Naser has actively participated in numerous collaborative research projects on both national and international scales. His involvement underscores a commitment to advancing knowledge and contributing to the global research community. In addition, he has taken on leadership roles in organising and chairing several national and international research conferences. This demonstrates not only his dedication to academic discourse but also his ability to facilitate and contribute to scholarly discussions on a broad spectrum of topics. Dr Naser hold a pivotal position within London Met's Centre for Applied Research in Empowering Society (CARES), specifically contributing to the Education for Sustainable Development (ESD) Specialist Group and the Developing Economics group. These centers are committed to tackling real-world challenges, fostering innovation, and advancing knowledge in relevant fields. This year, he and his team successfully secured research funding from the Mayor of London and are actively working to address social and economic issues affecting the city's youth. Recently, he submitted a €1 million proposal for an international collaborative research project involving Switzerland, Poland, and Romania, where he served as a consultant. Currently, he and his team are preparing a near million research bid in collaboration between the UK and Brazil. Overseeing and presiding over global academic conferences across diverse locations, skilfully generating income and publications through effective management.

Jagbir Singh Kadyan is a post graduate in Commerce, Management, Economics & Social Work. Master of Commerce from Savitribai Phule Pune University & Tilak Maharashtra University Pune; Master of Management Science from Bharati Vidyapeeth Deemed University Pune; Master of Economics from Savitribai Phule Pune University; Master of Social Work from IGNOU- Indira Gandhi National Open University, New Delhi and has been awarded Ph.D. from Maharishi Dayanand University, Rohtak, Haryana, India. He is an "Accredited Management Teacher" by AIMA – All India Management Association, New Delhi, India & "Certified CSR Professional" by ICSI- Institute of Company Secretary of India, New Delhi, India. Published around 35 research papers, authored 04 books and contributed 10 chapters. Publication has been done in Peer reviewed, UGC Care, Scopus Indexed Journals and in Springer, Palgrave, IGI-Global publications & others. Delivered key note addresses, invited lectures, chaired technical sessions at national and international seminars, conferences and symposiums. With Google Research Citation of 77, h-index of 04 & i10-index of 02, he has been recipient of several best research paper awards. He is "Editorial Board Member" & "Reviewer" of various national, international and Scopus indexed journals, research guide for PhD students and has evaluated over 20 PhD thesis on Commerce & Business Management subjects for different Indian universities. He has been a "Principal Investigator" for two "Innovation Research Project" awarded by the Cluster Innovation Centre, University of Delhi and has been a "Principal Co-ordinator" for three projects funded by AICTE - All India Council of Technical Education, Govt. of India. He is a Life Member of - ICA- Indian Commerce Association, New Delhi, India; IAA – Indian Accounting Association, New Delhi, India; NIPM - National Institute of Personnel Management, Kolkata, India; ISTD - Indian Society for Training & Development, New Delhi, India and Member of - CEGR- Centre for Economic Growth and Research, New Delhi, India; AIMA - All India Management Association, New Delhi, India; SRRNet - Social Responsibility Research Network, UK and ISA- International Sociological Association, Madrid, Spain. He has previously worked for Swami Shraddhanand College & Shri Ram College of Commerce, University of Delhi and Presently he is Associate Professor, School of Management & Commerce, Manav Rachna

University, Faridabad, Haryana, India and Honorary Associate Director - Research with Centre for Socio-economic & Sustainability Research, New Delhi, India.

Liliane Cristina Segura has a PhD in Business Administration in the area of Finance from Universidade Presbiteriana Mackenzie, Master's in Business Administration in the area of Strategy from FEA-USP. Degree in Accounting Sciences from FEA-USP. Post-Doctorate in Business Administration at the University of Salamanca (Spain), Specialist at CSU - Fresno in Entrepreneurship Business Plan at California State University, Fresno, United States. Certified by IACAFM (International Association of Certified Accountants and Financial Managers) in IFRS. She is Coordinator of the Undergraduate Course in Accounting Sciences at Universidade Presbiteriana Mackenzie. She works as a research professor at Universidade Presbiteriana Mackenzie, in the Undergraduate, Masters and Doctoral courses (PPG-CFE). Professor of several MBAs and in-company courses. He actively participates in national and international projects with funding from Capes and international funding agencies. Managing partner of Open-book Assessoria Contábil e Financeira. Consultant and partner of the company L&L Segura in the financial and accounting area. He has extensive experience in the financial and accounting areas of retail companies. Lines of research: Corporate Governance, Corporate Social Responsibility, Corporate Finance and Corporate Accounting.

* * *

Toyin Coker is a Doctor of Education (EdD) Degree holder and a Lecturer in Business and Management with over 20 years of experience in teaching. Toyin Coker is dedicated to delivering insightful perspectives that connect theoretical concepts with real-world applications, aimed at equipping businesses with strategic tools crucial for navigating the complex nature of the modern business landscape. His current research focus is on digital transformation, AI, sustainable business and the challenges they pose.

Oindrilla Ghosh is a Research Scholar hailing from the School of Law at Christ (Deemed to be University) Bangalore, India, who focuses her research on the health of tribal communities. Her work includes total 20 publications on Neuroscience on Organizational Behavior at IGI Global and also Environmental Disasters that are indexed in SCOPUS and Web of Sciences conference proceedings. She completed her early education at Loreto Day School, Bowbazar, and achieved distinction in her undergraduate (B.A/LL.B) and postgraduate (LL.M) studies at Calcutta University. Having served as an Assistant Professor of Law at Kingston Law College, Barasat,

Kolkata, Ghosh has actively participated in numerous National Conferences, International Conferences, UN Global Summits, webinars, and seminars organized by prestigious academic institutions. Her expertise lies in health perspectives, environmental studies, human behavior, and related areas. Additionally, she has conducted various workshops and lectures in educational institutions, and is engaged with NGO's to help the needy.

Ishani Gupta is a third-year Bachelor of Business Administration (BBA) student at Christ University, Bengaluru, India. With a strong academic foundation in business strategy, digital marketing, and project management, she has gained hands-on experience through virtual internships at JPMorgan Chase, GE Aerospace, Accenture, and PepsiCo. Passionate about research and innovation, she aims to bridge business insights with practical solutions, contributing to the evolving landscape of management and strategy.

Shayak Hussain is a BBA (Honours) Candidate at Christ University, specializing in the intersection of Artificial Intelligence (AI) and Corporate Social Responsibility (CSR). Their research focuses on AI-driven sustainability strategies, ethical AI governance, and the role of technology in enhancing corporate transparency and stakeholder engagement. Shayak Hussain has an academic background in business administration, AI ethics, and sustainability management, with expertise in AI-powered CSR reporting, environmental monitoring, and AI-driven decision-making frameworks. Their research employs quantitative and qualitative methodologies, including machine learning models, sentiment analysis, and case study evaluations, to analyze AI's impact on corporate ethics, regulatory compliance, and sustainable business practices.

Binod Kumar is a graduate student known for his academic excellence, with his total 15 scholarly works indexed in Scopus database on Neuroscience in Organizational Behavior, Neuromarketing and AI Applications on Wildlife Conservation. Hailing from Ranchi, Jharkhand in India, Binod is currently pursuing a Master of Laws (LL.M) at the prestigious Radha Govind University. His passion for technology and innovation along with climate changes is evident through his high academic performance and numerous projects. Binod has a keen interest in artificial intelligence, machine learning, neuropsychology, climate changes and disaster management, fields in which he has undertaken several research projects. He is particularly fascinated by the potential of AI to solve real-world problems and is dedicated to learning and applying new techniques in these areas. He volunteers at local NGOs, teaching underprivileged children basic computer skills. With a strong foundation in law and a commitment to making a positive impact, Binod Kumar is poised to become a future leader in the legal industry.

Ramji Nagariya is working as an Assistant Professor in the School of Business and Management, CHRIST University, Bengaluru, India. He holds a Ph.D. in the area of sustainable service supply chain from the Department of Management Studies, Malaviya National Institute of Technology, Jaipur, India. He holds an M. Tech in Industrial Management from Indian Institute of Technology (BHU), Varanasi and a bachelor's degree in Aeronautical Engineering. His research papers are published in Production Planning & Control, International Journal of Logistics Management, Business Process Management Journal, Benchmarking: An International Journal, International Journal of Productivity & Performance Management, Management of Environmental Quality, Decision, and International Journal of Services and Operations Management. His research interest includes service supply chain, buyer-supplier relationship, and sustainability in supply chain.

V.R. Palanivelu, Professor in the Department of Management Studies, Periyar University, Salem, India with over 31 years' experience in teaching Management subjects. Inspire students to pursue academic and personal excellence. Organized and driven with innate ability to stay on task. Interested in learning and implementing innovative methods and technologies in teaching learning process. To be able to contribute to the growth of the Organization and to achieve greater heights of excellence on par with the brightest in the Organization by performing my duties to the best of my ability. As a dynamic leader, he has spearheaded numerous initiatives to enhance the department's academic excellence and industry collaboration. Dr. Palanivelu's contributions to research and pedagogy have earned him recognition in academic circles, making him a pivotal figure in shaping future management professionals.

Stephanie Sandland holds a Master's degree in Environment Policy and Society from the Open University and her PhD explored how local governments support SMEs in advancing environmental sustainability. With two decades of experience teaching environmental sustainability, entrepreneurship and corporate social responsibility, both in dedicated modules as well those focused on strategy and operations, Stephanie brings deep expertise in fostering sustainable practices across sectors. Passionate about sustainable futures, Stephanie combines academic insight with a commitment to practical solutions that enhance entrepreneurial success.

Jyothsna Thimmaiah B. is a dedicated academician and researcher with extensive experience in management studies. She is pursuing her doctoral research at the Department of Management Studies, Periyar University, Salem.

With an academic foundation that includes an MBA, a Postgraduate Diploma in Human Resource Management (PGDHRM), and an M.Phil., she brings a wealth of knowledge and expertise to her work. As an Associate Professor at Maharani Lakshmi Ammanni College for Women (Autonomous) in Bangalore, she actively contributes to teaching and mentoring in the management field. Her research interests are reflected in her scholarly pursuits, focusing on advancing knowledge in her discipline. ORCID iD: https://orcid.org/0000-0003-0325-464X.

Alina Vaduva brings 21 years of professional expertise spanning banking and finance, academia, European Union innovation programmes, and local government. She is a Senior Lecturer in Business Strategy and Sustainable Business at the University of East London, where she also leads the MBA Business Advice Centre, supporting future business leaders with strategic guidance. Dr. Vaduva is the Co-Chair of the Women's Network at UEL, championing gender equity and inclusion, and plays a pivotal role in shaping sustainability initiatives as the shadow lead for Net Zero local policy in her community. Her dedication to fostering innovation, sustainability, and impactful policy makes her a valued contributor.

Index

A

AI 1, 2, 3, 6, 7, 8, 9, 10, 11, 12, 13, 14, 15, 16, 17, 18, 19, 20, 21, 22, 23, 24, 25, 26, 28, 29, 30, 31, 32, 33, 34, 35, 36, 37, 39, 41, 42, 43, 44, 45, 46, 47, 48, 49, 50, 51, 52, 53, 54, 55, 56, 57, 58, 59, 60, 61, 62, 63, 64, 65, 66, 67, 68, 69, 70, 76, 77, 86, 87, 88, 89, 90, 91, 93, 94, 97, 98, 99, 101, 104, 105, 106, 107, 108, 109, 110, 111, 112, 121, 122, 123, 124, 125, 126, 128, 129, 130, 131, 132, 133, 134, 135, 136, 137, 138, 139, 140, 141, 144, 145, 174, 175, 176, 177, 178, 179, 180, 181, 182, 184, 185, 186, 187, 189, 191, 192, 193, 194, 195, 196, 197, 198, 199, 202, 203, 204, 206, 207, 208, 209, 210, 211, 212, 216, 217, 218, 219, 220, 221, 222, 223, 224, 225, 226, 227, 228, 229, 230, 231, 232, 233, 234, 235, 236, 237, 238, 239, 241, 242, 243, 244, 245, 246, 247, 248, 249, 250, 251, 252, 253, 254, 255, 257, 258, 259, 260, 261, 262, 263, 264, 266, 267

AI-Driven Strategies 239, 241, 249, 266

AI-Driven Sustainability 1, 12, 14, 15, 18, 66, 69, 136

AI-Driven Tools 44, 54, 123, 145, 174, 178, 179

AI Governance 43, 45, 55, 56, 57, 64, 65, 66, 67, 70, 135

Automation 3, 6, 7, 9, 14, 15, 22, 26, 28, 33, 34, 36, 41, 42, 43, 44, 48, 49, 53, 95, 96, 105, 109, 112, 123, 124, 130, 133, 136, 175, 196, 211, 222, 237, 242, 243, 244, 246, 247, 250, 251, 252, 262, 266

B

Bangalore 241, 242, 243, 245, 246, 249, 250, 254, 257, 260, 261, 262, 263, 266, 267

Bangladesh 20, 31, 32, 33, 35, 36, 37, 38, 39, 40

Business Ethics 235, 236

Business Strategy 4, 5, 25, 27, 29, 42, 69, 87, 92, 102, 106, 134, 187, 193, 204, 224, 250, 257

C

Carbon Footprint 16, 17, 18, 27, 29, 60, 67, 84, 125, 131, 159, 217, 247

Chatbots 7, 8, 33, 34, 43, 48, 57, 62, 66, 107, 193, 216, 237, 249

Circular Economy 5, 11, 16, 25, 26, 29, 62, 84, 103, 111, 130, 140, 146, 167, 190, 245, 251

Consumer Trust 50, 63, 66, 85, 103, 233

Corporate Social Responsibility 4, 28, 41, 42, 46, 49, 50, 53, 56, 60, 65, 70, 72, 73, 76, 77, 82, 83, 102, 103, 121, 122, 139, 213, 235, 239

Corporate Social Responsibility (CSR) 46

D

Decision-Making 6, 7, 9, 10, 12, 16, 22, 23, 26, 31, 41, 42, 43, 44, 45, 46, 47, 48, 49, 54, 55, 56, 57, 58, 60, 61, 63, 65, 75, 76, 82, 91, 93, 97, 102, 105, 107, 119, 123, 124, 130, 131, 132, 133, 144, 169, 178, 180, 182, 185, 186, 195, 207, 208, 209, 210, 211, 212, 216, 220, 221, 222, 223, 224, 225, 233, 235, 236, 238, 239, 241, 244, 246, 249, 251, 252, 254, 260, 261, 262

E

Entrepreneurial Mindset 143, 144, 153, 158, 176, 183, 202, 203, 204, 241, 267

Entrepreneurship 45, 71, 72, 73, 74, 75, 76, 78, 80, 81, 83, 86, 87, 88, 89, 90,

91, 92, 93, 94, 95, 96, 97, 98, 99, 101, 104, 105, 109, 135, 138, 139, 140, 141, 144, 145, 148, 154, 160, 171, 175, 179, 186, 187, 195, 198, 203, 205, 206, 207, 208, 209, 210, 211, 212, 213, 214, 215, 216, 224, 225, 226, 227, 230, 231, 232, 234, 235, 238, 239, 242, 243, 244, 247, 249, 251, 256, 257, 261, 262, 263, 264, 267
Environmental Impact 2, 5, 10, 12, 16, 19, 23, 29, 43, 47, 57, 59, 60, 61, 67, 68, 77, 84, 103, 105, 109, 125, 130, 132, 133, 146, 175, 181, 182, 188, 248
Ethical AI 9, 21, 29, 42, 45, 48, 56, 57, 61, 62, 64, 65, 66, 68, 69, 70, 105, 108, 109, 110, 111, 128, 130, 132, 133, 135, 136, 137, 138, 207, 209, 210, 212, 216, 219, 224, 225, 226, 227, 229, 232, 233, 234
Ethical Entrepreneurship 80, 207, 208, 210, 211, 212, 213, 214, 215, 216, 230, 231, 232, 239
Ethical Sourcing 54, 57, 62, 68, 71, 76, 78, 84, 248

G

Green Technologies 17, 19, 71

I

Innovation 1, 3, 5, 6, 7, 8, 9, 12, 13, 15, 16, 18, 19, 20, 23, 25, 26, 27, 31, 33, 39, 44, 45, 48, 49, 65, 68, 70, 72, 74, 79, 82, 83, 84, 86, 87, 88, 89, 90, 91, 92, 93, 94, 96, 97, 99, 101, 103, 104, 105, 106, 108, 109, 110, 111, 122, 123, 124, 125, 128, 131, 132, 133, 134, 135, 136, 137, 138, 140, 141, 143, 144, 145, 146, 147, 148, 151, 154, 155, 156, 157, 158, 167, 168, 170, 173, 174, 178, 179, 182, 183, 189, 191, 192, 194, 196, 198, 199, 200, 201, 202, 203, 204, 207, 208, 210, 212, 213, 214, 216, 219, 220, 224, 230, 232, 233, 234, 235, 237, 238, 239, 242, 243, 244, 246, 247, 248, 250, 251, 252, 253, 255, 256, 257, 258, 259, 260, 261, 262, 264, 266, 267

M

Machine Learning 2, 7, 8, 13, 17, 25, 33, 34, 38, 43, 48, 51, 53, 57, 58, 61, 66, 85, 88, 90, 91, 95, 98, 99, 130, 136, 139, 141, 142, 177, 178, 185, 225, 236, 243, 247, 266

P

Personality Traits 241, 242, 244, 245, 248, 252, 261, 262, 264, 267

R

Radical Innovation 143, 262
Renewable Energy 5, 10, 12, 17, 28, 30, 43, 62, 71, 74, 76, 79, 84, 103, 104, 120, 124, 174, 214, 228, 229
Resource Optimization 30, 76, 175, 242
Responsible Business 50, 72, 74, 207
Responsible Innovation 23, 104, 106, 134, 135, 136, 210, 234, 235, 250, 259, 260
Risk Mitigation 136, 167

S

Stakeholder Engagement 42, 45, 49, 50, 54, 58, 60, 62, 63, 65, 66, 69, 74, 82, 138
Sustainability 1, 2, 3, 4, 5, 6, 9, 10, 11, 12, 13, 14, 15, 16, 18, 19, 20, 21, 22, 23, 24, 25, 26, 27, 28, 29, 30, 31, 32, 41, 42, 43, 45, 46, 47, 49, 50, 51, 52, 53, 54, 55, 56, 57, 58, 59, 60, 61, 62, 64, 65, 66, 67, 68, 69, 70, 71, 72, 73, 74, 75, 76, 77, 78, 79, 81, 82, 83, 84, 85, 88, 92, 101, 102, 103, 104, 105, 109, 111, 112, 113, 118, 119, 120, 121, 122, 124, 125, 126, 129, 130, 131, 132, 133, 134, 135, 136, 138, 139, 140, 141, 143, 144, 145, 146, 147, 148, 156, 158, 160, 162, 164, 167, 174, 175, 176, 177, 182, 187, 188, 192, 193, 194, 197, 198, 199, 200,

201, 204, 205, 206, 207, 208, 209, 213, 214, 215, 216, 217, 218, 219, 227, 228, 229, 230, 231, 232, 233, 234, 235, 236, 239, 241, 242, 243, 244, 245, 246, 247, 248, 250, 251, 252, 253, 255, 257, 258, 259, 260, 261, 262, 263, 265, 266, 267
Sustainability Principles 1, 12, 13, 23, 207, 239, 241, 244, 245, 248, 250, 252, 259, 267
Sustainable Development Goal 27, 134, 266
Sustainable Growth 16, 101, 137, 241, 244, 249, 253, 263, 267
Systems Thinking 124, 143, 148, 149, 183, 186, 200, 205

T

Transparency 9, 12, 15, 19, 20, 29, 41, 42, 44, 45, 46, 47, 48, 49, 50, 54, 55, 56, 57, 58, 59, 60, 61, 62, 64, 65, 66, 67, 68, 69, 70, 76, 77, 78, 79, 80, 83, 84, 103, 105, 106, 107, 108, 109, 110, 120, 121, 128, 129, 131, 132, 133, 134, 136, 137, 138, 181, 182, 186, 208, 209, 211, 213, 216, 219, 220, 221, 222, 226, 229, 230, 231, 232, 233, 234, 235, 236, 238, 239, 248, 259, 262

W

Women Entrepreneurs 241, 242, 243, 244, 245, 246, 247, 248, 249, 250, 251, 252, 253, 254, 255, 257, 258, 259, 260, 261, 262, 263, 264, 267

www.ingramcontent.com/pod-product-compliance
Lightning Source LLC
LaVergne TN
LVHW080900300926
849162LV00003B/491